Making the patient-consumer

Manchester University Press

Making the patient-consumer
Patient organisations and health consumerism in Britain

Alex Mold

Manchester University Press

Copyright © Alex Mold 2015

The right of Alex Mold to be identified as the author of this work has been asserted by her in accordance with the Copyright, Designs and Patents Act 1988.

Published by Manchester University Press
Altrincham Street, Manchester M1 7JA

www.manchesteruniversitypress.co.uk

British Library Cataloguing-in-Publication Data
A catalogue record for this book is available from the British Library

Library of Congress Cataloging-in-Publication Data applied for

ISBN 978 0 7190 9531 3 hardback

First published 2015

The publisher has no responsibility for the persistence or accuracy of URLs for any external or third-party internet websites referred to in this book, and does not guarantee that any content on such websites is, or will remain, accurate or appropriate.

Edited and typeset
by Frances Hackeson Freelance Publishing Services, Brinscall, Lancs
Printed in Great Britain
by CPI Group (UK) Ltd, Croydon CR0 4YY

Contents

Acknowledgements		*page* vii
Abbreviations		ix
Introduction		1
1	Autonomy	18
2	Representation	42
3	Complaint	69
4	Rights	94
5	Information	117
6	Voice	142
7	Choice	169
Conclusion		192
Bibliography		209
Index		233

Acknowledgements

This book is based on research carried out as part of a Wellcome Trust University Award (grant no. 081454/Z/LS/HH) on the construction of the patient-consumer in Britain from 1960 to 1991. I am grateful to the Wellcome Trust for this grant and to the Faculty of Public Health and Policy at the London School of Hygiene & Tropical Medicine (LSHTM) who took on the funding of my position. The LSHTM is a fantastic place for a historian of medicine to be based, close to the 'coalface' of contemporary health policy and practice, but also surrounded by a group of historians and social scientists. Members of the Centre for History in Public Health, and especially Stuart Anderson, Martin Gorsky, Angela Grainger, Anne Hardy, Ingrid James, Susanne MacGregor, Gareth Millward, Jane Seymour, Chris Sirrs and Sue Taylor have all supported and enriched my work in innumerable ways. The Centre's Director, Virginia Berridge, has been and continues to be, a wonderful mentor, offering invaluable advice and guidance throughout this project and beyond.

Away from the LSHTM, discussions with Gayle Davis, Matthew Hilton, Beatrix Hoffman, Hilary Marland, David Reubi, Sally Sheard, Nancy Tomes, Elizabeth Toon and Duncan Wilson all helped my work develop. So too, did the numerous seminar and conference audiences who listened to me talk about my work over the years; particularly helpful were those at Imperial College, the universities of Cambridge, Warwick, Exeter, Birmingham, Manchester, Liverpool, Zurich and Glasgow. I feel extraordinarily lucky to be a part of a vibrant history of medicine community that spans the UK, Europe and North America, and the work of people within this community has fed into this book in all sorts of ways.

Historians, even those that study the contemporary period, remain reliant on libraries and archives. Archivists at the Wellcome Library, The National Archives, the Modern Records Centre at the University of Warwick, The Churchill Archives, Churchill College, Cambridge and Birmingham City

Archives all provided invaluable assistance. The libraries of the LSHTM and the London School of Economics, as well as Senate House Library, the Wellcome Library and the British Library gave me access to books and articles that were crucial to this project. I would also like to thank the many individuals that I interviewed and spoke to informally about the history of patient consumerism.

Some parts of this book have been published as articles in the *Historical Journal*, the *American Journal of Public Health*, the *Journal of Social Policy* and the *Bulletin of the History of Medicine*. I am grateful to the peer reviewers of these articles, and also of this book, for their insightful comments, and suggestions for improvements. Thanks also to Tony Mason at Manchester University Press who oversaw the publication of this book.

Last, but by no means least, I would like to thank my friends and family. During the research and writing of this book, I lost my grandmother Doreen Tanswell and my dear friend Francesca Carnevali. The dignity of both of these strong women taught me more about what it means to be a patient in the modern NHS than any book or article. My parents, Richard and Lindsay Mold, my grandmother Elsie, my sister Becky, my brother-in-law Tim, my mother in-law Lois, my nieces Annabelle and Eloise and my nephew Tom, have all helped to keep me sane and remind me that there is life away from academia. Most of all, I would like to thank Noelle, for her love, her patience, and her smile. It is to her that this book is dedicated.

Abbreviations

ACHCEW	Association of Community Health Councils of England and Wales
AHA	Area Health Authority
AIMS	Association for Improvement in Maternity Services
ATP	Association of Trained Patients
BCA	Birmingham City Archives
BHA	Birmingham Health Authority
BMA	British Medical Association
BPAS	British Pregnancy Advisory Service
CA	Consumers' Association
CCC	Churchill College Cambridge
CHC	Community Health Council
CMAC	Contemporary Medical Archives Centre
CoH	College of Health
DHSS	Department of Health and Social Security
EBCHC	East Birmingham Community Health Council
FPC	Family Practitioner Committee
GMC	General Medical Council
GMSC	General Medical Services Committee
ICAS	Independent Complaints Advisory Service
ICESCR	International Covenant on Economic, Social and Cultural Rights
ICS	Institute of Community Studies
IEA	Institute for Economic Affairs
IPPR	Institute for Public Policy Research
JCC	Joint Consultants Committee
MRC	Modern Records Centre
NAMH	National Association for Mental Health
NAWCH	National Association for the Welfare of Children in Hospital

NCC	National Consumer Council
NHI	National Health Insurance (Act)
OSC	Overview and Scrutiny Committee
PA	Patients Association
PALS	Patient Advice and Liaison Service
PCA	Parliamentary Commissioner for Administration
PEP	Political and Economic Planning
PFI	Private Finance Initiative
PPI	Public and Patient Involvement
RHA	Regional Health Authority
RHB	Regional Hospital Boards
RICA	Research Institute for Consumer Affairs
SBCHC	South Birmingham Community Health Council
TNA	The National Archives
UHBT	University Hospital Birmingham Trust
UNDHR	United Nations Universal Declaration of Human Rights
WBCHC	West Birmingham Community Health Council
WHO	World Health Organization

Introduction

Since the 1960s, patients in Britain have been made into consumers. Consumerist concepts have found a place in health policy and practice. Ideas like autonomy; collective and individual representation; the ability to make a complaint; rights; the provision of information; voice and choice are now central to the National Health Service (NHS) and the demands patients make of it. Over a few decades, the position of patients in Britain appears to have changed fundamentally. During the early 1960s, for example, it was not uncommon for patients to be told little about the condition that they were suffering from or its likely outcome. That such a situation would be (almost) inconceivable today points not only to changes in the doctor–patient relationship, but also to a wider shift in the way in which patients see themselves and are seen by others. This book aims to explore how and why such a shift took place, and why it was that these changes were framed by the concept of consumerism.

Patients operated as 'consumers' in the medical marketplace that pre-dated the establishment of the NHS, yet this activity was rarely described using the language of consumption.[1] Consumerism was also alien to the early NHS. The new system swept away pre-existing forms of patient representation and individual patient voices were rarely heard. It was not until the 1960s that consumerist thought began to be applied to the NHS. Patient groups, such as the Patients Association (established in 1962), and consumer bodies, such as the Consumers' Association (established in 1956), engaged with health consumerism as a way of giving the patient more say in his or her treatment and that of others. By the 1970s, the state began to see the value of greater consumer representation as a means to improve service efficiency, and a number of mechanisms, such as the establishment of the Community Health Councils (CHCs) in 1974, were introduced to speak for the patient-consumer. The notion of the patient as consumer shifted during the 1970s and 1980s, when patient organisations campaigned for the establishment of a series of patients' rights, such as the right to consent, the right to access medical records and the right to complain. The meaning of patient consumerism, however, was far from stable, and in the 1980s and 1990s the Conservative government put forward new ideas about what it meant to be a patient-consumer. Their conceptualisation of patient consumerism revolved around markets and choice, not rights and representation. During the 2000s, collective voice mechanisms for patient-consumers were weakened and fragmented as the state came to position itself as the primary authority on the patient-consumer. Such a situation allowed for the re-shaping of patient-consumer identity to prioritise individual choice rather than the wider collection of collective rights proposed by patient organisations since the 1960s.

Examining the activities of generic patient-consumer groups – that is groups that tried to represent all patients, no matter what disease they had or how they identified themselves – also allows for the exploration of deeper themes within British politics and society. The growth of patient-consumerism implied more fundamental changes in the relationship between the government and the governed, as ordinary citizens began to ask questions about the nature and quality of public services, such as health care. At the same time, more assertive patients appeared to challenge the power of health professionals, highlighting tensions between lay and expert forms of knowledge. Drawing on examples of patient organisations such as the Patients Association (PA), the National Association for the Welfare of Children in Hospital (NAWCH), the College of Health (CoH) and the CHCs, as well as consumers' groups like the Consumers' Association (CA) and the National Consumer Council (NCC), this book will interrogate the changing meaning of choice and consumption in post-war British health care. This is important, both as a means to evaluate the evolving nature of public service provision in post-industrial society, and as a way of explaining the central place of the patient within current health policy. From the White Paper *Patients First* in 1979, up to and including the Health and Social Care Act in 2012, the figure of the patient-consumer has grown in symbolic and practical significance. By exploring how and why such a shift took place, this book will provide insight into the dynamic nature of health care, politics and society in modern Britain.

To locate the making of the patient-consumer in context, this Introduction will first consider historical approaches to the separate figures of the patient and the consumer, and then examine how these two distinct entities were brought together in the early 1960s. The application of consumerism to health was (and to a great extent remains) contested. Key debates about the meaning of consumerism within health care, such as whether or not it is appropriate to talk about consumerism in the context of health, and the extent to which the patient-consumer can even be said to exist, will be examined. Finally, the content and key arguments of the book will be surveyed.

Making the patient-consumer: historical approaches

Although the figure of the patient-consumer first came into being in Britain during the 1960s, the process of creating this identity began many decades earlier. The 'making up' of people, the creation of subjects, objects and identities, has been a fruitful avenue of historical and theoretical enquiry for many decades. Following Michel Foucault, numerous scholars have demonstrated that particular kinds of subjects were formed by scientific knowledge, expertise and regulation.[2] As biomedicine proliferated, so too did 'made up people', from the autistic to the obese.[3] The 'patient' as one party within the medical encounter has inevitably always existed, but there is debate about how this figure was constructed. Before 1950, according to David Armstrong, the medical gaze focused on the lesion, rather than the patient. When the location of disease shifted away from the physical body to the social body, however, what patients had to say became significant: 'illness was being transformed from what was visible to what was heard'.[4] The renewed importance attached to the patient's view allowed for a change in patienthood during the latter half of the twentieth century, placing fresh emphasis on patients' rights and representation.[5] Yet for other analysts, particularly those concerned with the era before the dominance of biomedicine, the patient was always an active figure. Roy Porter suggested that the patient was not just the product of the medical gaze, but also an individual with a degree of autonomy and choice.[6] More recent studies of the patient's position in a variety of periods and settings have stressed that recipients of health care were far from being 'passive in the face of whatever was put before them'.[7] It should not, therefore, be assumed that individual agency disappeared with the development of biomedicine, but nor is it the case that patients were either autonomous individuals or powerless subjects.[8] Expert forms of knowledge could combine with lay understandings, and individuals were able to adapt categories to suit their own ends.

Such a practice was not confined to the biomedical world; it can also be observed in the making of the consumer. There has been much debate about when and where to locate the 'birth' of consumer society, and as Frank Trentmann has argued, it is perhaps more accurate to speak of two consumer revolutions: one in the eighteenth century that was about the proliferation of goods, luxury and sensibility; and one in the twentieth century that was centred on mass consumption, affluence and advertising.[9] Moreover, the consumer revolutions did not automatically turn people into consumers; what Trentmann calls 'political synapses' were necessary to configure the consumer. Political traditions and languages came into effect that allowed individuals to connect material experiences with a sense of belonging, interest and entitlement. For Trentmann, 'the consumer, like "class", "citizen" or "nation", is no natural or universal category, but the product of historical identity formations, in which actors through available traditions make sense of the relationships between material culture and collective identity'.[10] Furthermore, the making of the consumer involved more than one type of actor: as Matthew Hilton and Martin Daunton point out, the consumer interest was defined by an inter-play of political and business interests, varying kinds of expertise, and the activities of consumers themselves.[11]

What it meant to be a consumer also changed over time and place. In the early twentieth century, consumer identity was tied to the development of welfare politics and social citizenship, but by the middle of the century, the 'citizen consumer' and the 'rational consumer' came into being.[12] According to Hilton, 'consumerism' was more than a description of a commodified culture; it was the 'site upon which battles over new forms of citizenship and political expression have been fought'.[13] Many of these disputes surrounded the issue of who spoke for the consumer. Throughout the twentieth century, a series of different groups attempted to represent the consumer, including employers, workers, political parties, bureaucrats and consumers themselves. Yet it was not until the 1950s, with the establishment of the Consumers' Association (CA) in 1956, that a 'professional' consumers' organisation was created. Initially, the CA was concerned chiefly with the comparative testing of products, highlighting the 'best buy' for the discerning shopper. However, according to Hilton, this largely individualistic, materialistic image of the consumer co-existed alongside a much broader definition of the consumer and consumerism that included social and economic issues and questions of citizenship.[14] This was particularly the case when the CA was under the leadership of the sociologist Michael Young.[15] Young argued for a consumerism that 'moved beyond things' to areas such as public services.

The application of this form of consumerism to the health service was different to the consumerist behaviour that had existed prior to the mid-twentieth century. Before the NHS, patients had what Porter called the 'power of the purse', as they were able to pick and choose practitioners in the medical marketplace.[16] There were also some forms of collective representation for patients, especially within inter-war hospital contributory schemes. Yet, such mechanisms were not described in terms of consumption.[17] Medical economists had discussed the concept of health consumerism since at least the 1930s, but as Nancy Tomes has demonstrated, consumerism in health was revived and given new meaning by patient organisations in the USA during the 1960s. For such groups, consumerism was a way of 'liberating' themselves from the paternalism of the doctor–patient relationship.[18] Similarly, Rob Irvine suggests that the health consumer first materialised in the public discourse in Australia in the 1970s due to the efforts of the Australian Consumer Council and the Australian Federation of Consumer Organisations.[19] Irvine argues that patient groups mobilised around the notion of the 'consumer' rather than the 'patient' because the patient was embedded within a regime of professional power. That, 'In order to facilitate change in the status of patients and displace professionals from the centre of meaning and the "production" of health care, critics of the system argued that, for political reasons, it was necessary to redefine the patient as a "health consumer".'[20]

In the UK (as will be explored in more detail in Chapter 1) consumerism was also brought into the health discourse by consumer organisations during the 1960s. Although economists had shown some interest in the notion of consumerism in health in this period, it was groups like the Research Institute for Consumer Affairs (RICA) and Political and Economic Planning (PEP) that helped to bring the notion of the patient-consumer to wider attention.[21] The activities of consumer groups prompted the medical journal *The Lancet* to report on 'patients as consumers' in 1961 and again in 1962.[22]

Explanations as to how and why the patient-consumer emerged in Britain at this point are few and far between. Although there is a large body of historical work on consumerism in the UK, few authors have considered its application to public services like health care.[23] There are a number of accounts of the development of patient consumerism written by protagonists, such as the former CHC Secretary Christine Hogg, and self-styled 'patient activist', Charlotte Williamson. Such works provide much useful detail, but sometimes lack balance.[24] Historian Glen O'Hara began to tease out the complexities of consumerism in health care during the 1960s and 1970s, but to understand the changing meaning of consumerism within health it is necessary to go beyond 1979.[25] Broad (but brief) overviews of the development of consumerism in British health care provided by Graham Smith and John Pickstone both point to the 1960s as the decade in which the patient-consumer first began to emerge. Pickstone contended that a specifically 'consumerist' era within British health care began in this period as ambitions for health rose in tandem with individuals' demands as consumers in other spheres of life.[26] For Smith, patient consumerism was connected to a wider 'empowerment of the laity' that took place in the 1960s, as groups formed in order to challenge medical authority and paternalism more widely.[27]

Indeed, this period saw the emergence of a number of disease-specific patient organisations, some of which have been studied. Groups that were concerned with mental illness have attracted particular attention, as have those around disability, illegal drug use and AIDS.[28] Generic patient organisations, groups that attempted to represent all patients irrespective of the condition that they suffered from or the population group to which they belonged, have not been subjected to the same degree of analysis. Such organisations, however, were of central importance to giving voice to the concerns of patients from the 1960s onwards. Generic patient-consumer groups are worthy of study for five reasons. Firstly, there were some issues that affected all patients, no matter who they were or what illness they had. This period saw the development of universal principles – such as informed consent – that had an impact upon every patient, and the role played by patient-consumer organisations in dealing with such concerns was significant. Secondly, politicians and policy makers often spoke of patients as if they were all the same and all wanted similar things. Of course, this was not the case, but the manufacture of such a generic patient-consumer, and its implications, needs further analysis. Thirdly, considering the generic patient-consumer facilitates a move away from the politics of specific diseases and population groups. Such issues were important, but it can be hard to separate out concerns that were only of interest to one specific group of patients from wider problems applicable to a broader range of patients. Fourthly, taking the notion of the patient-consumer as the object of analysis allows us to look beyond health specific groups, like the PA and the CHCs, to consider how consumerism and its proponents expanded over the course of the last 50 years. Finally, centring on generic patient-consumer organisations helps to maintain a clear focus in a field that grew exponentially over time. By the 2000s, there were hundreds, if not thousands of disease-specific groups.[29] Some organisations were small, others were large, some focused on rare conditions and others on much wider disease categories. Studying all of these in a meaningful way would be almost impossible. By concentrating on generic patient organisations it is possible to explore the development of the patient-consumer in a coherent and focused manner.

The patient-consumer: a problematic identity

Although there has been little historical work on the development of patient consumerism in the UK, there is a considerable social science literature that has considered consumerism in health since it first came to academic attention in the early 1970s. Such work has tended to focus on three areas:

firstly, the meaning or meanings of consumerism in health; secondly, whether or not it is appropriate to talk about consumerism in the context of health; and finally, the extent to which the patient-consumer existed, and if so, whether or not it was possible to represent him/her. Professor of Social Work, Richard Hugman, identified two different types of consumerism: democratic consumerism and market consumerism. Democratic consumerism, he suggested, was concerned with the participation of service user groups in the social processes which defined health and welfare needs. In contrast, market consumerism was associated with freedom of choice through purchasing power.[30] These different types of consumerism were, to some extent, time specific. The leading proponent of democratic consumerism was the sociologist and social entrepreneur Michael Young. For Young, consumerism was about obtaining better representation for consumers to the state, and about the interests of marginalised groups as much as the affluent. During the period from the 1960s to the 1980s, through the organisations with which he was heavily involved, such as the CA, the NCC and the College of Health, Young put forward a form of consumerism that could be mapped onto citizenship and broader, collective goals.[31] From the 1990s onwards, however, market consumerism appeared to come to the fore. The introduction of competition within the health service and more choice for the consumer was designed to reform the NHS along market lines, with the intention of improving the quality of services and giving more autonomy to patient-consumers.[32]

Yet, these two different types of consumerism did not necessarily cancel each other out. As social scientists John Clarke, Janet E. Newman, Nick Smith, Elizabeth Vidler and Louise Westmarland have shown, market consumerism and democratic consumerism co-existed during the late 1990s and into the 2000s through the hybrid figure of the 'citizen-consumer'.[33] Ideas about citizenship and consumption could and did overlap. Martin Powell, Ian Greener, Isabelle Szmigin, Shane Doheny and Nick Mills suggest that concepts associated with citizenship, such as rights, participation and democracy, could be found within consumerist approaches to health care. There was not, they argued, a binary distinction between citizenship and consumption.[34] Sociologist Timothy Milewa asserted that the government's promotion of 'active citizenship' in health care during the late 1990s combined ideas central to consumerism and citizenship in order to secure a 'third way' between the state and the market.[35]

However it was defined, health consumerism, and particularly market consumerism, attracted a good deal of disapproval. Many critics questioned the appropriateness of applying consumerist ideology to health care. Richard Titmuss was one of the first theorists to raise concerns about consumerism in health during the 1960s. Titmuss asserted that medical care was not like other consumer goods or services. He argued that consumers may not realise that they need or desire medical care; that they could rarely know in advance how much it would cost; that they were unable to learn from experience or assess the value of the care provided; that medical care could not be returned or exchanged; and that it was difficult for consumers to change their minds during the course of medical care.[36] The sociologist Margaret Stacey also doubted the appropriateness of consumerism within health, contending that medicine was a service industry that did things to and not for people; that the patient was both work object and social actor.[37] Health economists Phil Shackley and Mandy Ryan pointed out that it was health status and not health care that was valued by patient-consumers, but this could not, in and of itself, be bought. Moreover, they suggested, patient-consumers were not always the best judges of their own interests, in part because they lacked sufficient knowledge.[38]

The knowledge–power imbalance between doctors and patients, and its ability to impinge upon consumer sovereignty was a key concern for many critics of health consumerism. According to Shackley and Ryan, patient-consumers were in possession of relatively little information about their condition or appropriate treatment when compared to the knowledge held by doctors. The patient-consumer had to rely on an agency relationship with his or her doctor: that the doctor would act on the patient's behalf and in their best interests.[39] As Deborah Lupton, Cam Donaldson and Peter Lloyd explained, the illness state placed the patient in the role of supplicant, reliant upon the doctor to make him or her well again.[40] The asymmetry of the doctor–patient knowledge–power relationship therefore made it difficult for patient-consumers to act as autonomous individuals.

For some critics, such problems brought into question the very notion of the patient-consumer. A plethora of labels have been used at different times and by various actors to describe the users of health services: consumer, customer, client, user, stakeholder, citizen and taxpayer have all been used in place of or in conjunction with, the term 'patient'. There were, according to Powell and colleagues, almost as many terms as there were people that used them.[41] The meaning of these different terms was uncertain; as sometimes labels were used interchangeably and at other times appeared to denote clear differences. For instance, for Secretary of Hackney CHC, Fedelma Winkler, seeing health service users as 'customers' clearly implied a 'supermarket model' of health care.[42] The extent to which such language was taken up by patients themselves can also be brought into question. Research by Clarke and Newman found that many individuals resisted the label 'consumer', preferring 'patient' instead.[43] Health care, an interview respondent asserted, was 'not like shopping'.[44]

If some critics saw the label patient-consumer or its supposed synonyms as too loaded, others found the term to be rather empty. Stacey, initially an enthusiast for health consumerism, later branded the patient-consumer a 'sociological misconception'. There was, she contended, 'no coherent shared ideology to support the role of the patient as actor, decision maker or partner in the health enterprise'.[45] Patients were a heterogeneous group that did not necessarily share common interests. According to health policy analyst Chris Ham there was a lack of 'patient consciousness'.[46] Patient-consumer identity could be fragmented by disease and condition type and by a range of other categories such as age, ethnicity, gender, religion and sexuality. Yet, at the same time, the period since the 1960s witnessed a significant growth in the number of patient organisations and groups, which would suggest that some patients did find common cause.

Indeed, the size and scale of the growth of patient organisations, especially since the 1980s, has led some commentators to posit the existence of a patient movement.[47] For some protagonists, like Williamson, this was an 'emancipation movement', campaigning for patient autonomy and challenging the power and supremacy of medical professionals. Although Williamson was emphatic that 'Emancipation movements are not consumer movements', other commentators saw patient organisations in such terms.[48] Rob Baggott, Judith Allsop and Kathryn Jones, in their study of patient groups in the early 2000s pointed to the development of a 'health consumer movement'. They suggested that the growth of formal alliance organisations (such as the PA and the Long-term Medical Conditions Alliance), coupled with the rise of condition-based groups established by service users themselves either to campaign for or to provide mutual support, denoted the emergence of a health consumer movement.[49] Other analysts, drawing explicitly on new social movement theory, suggest that there were different types of health movement, with some orientated primarily towards access, others towards helping particular constituencies, and yet others challenging science on aetiology, diagnosis, treatment and prevention.[50] What is missing from such accounts, however, is a sense of how such movements came to be. This book aims to fill the void, by providing an empirical analysis of why patient-consumer organisations were formed, what they understood patient consumerism to mean, what they wanted, what they achieved and how this changed over time.

Outline of the book

Based on the papers of key patient-consumer organisations, government records, published sources and oral history interviews, *Making the*

Patient-Consumer explores the role played by generic patient-consumer organisations in the development of patient consumerism from the 1960s to the present. Seven issues were central to the making of patient-consumer identity over the last 50 years: autonomy; representation; complaint; rights; information; voice and choice. Each theme will be dealt with in a separate chapter, but attention will also be paid to the ways in which these concerns overlapped. Moving forward in time from the 1960s to the 2010s, the book charts the evolution of patient consumerism as individual choice eventually won out over collective voice.

In the 1960s, one of the first areas in which patient consumerism began to manifest itself was around demands for greater patient autonomy. It was not uncommon in this period for patients to have scant knowledge about their condition and little say in its treatment. Hospital visiting hours were very restricted and parents were not permitted to stay overnight with their sick children. Chapter 1 examines the efforts of patient-consumer organisations such as the PA and NAWCH to challenge such practices. The PA demanded that patients be able to make decisions about their own care, especially if this was experimental. The organisation also wanted to establish a right for patients to consent to the presence of medical students during treatment and examinations. The NAWCH pushed for unrestricted visiting hours for the parents of children in hospital and for mothers to be able to stay with their offspring overnight. But the motivation behind such groups came not just as a response to specific scandals, but was also rooted in wider developments, such as the emergence of bioethics and the development of identity politics. The notion that individuals should have a right to decide what happened to their bodies was gaining traction in other fields too. By engaging with such ideas, and framing them in the context of consumption, patient organisations were able to press for changes to the ways in which the NHS dealt with patients.

Patient groups were not only concerned with the views of individual patient-consumers; they wanted to represent the needs of all patients. Chapter 2 analyses the development of patient representation during the late 1960s and early 1970s. In this period both Conservative and Labour governments expressed an interest in enhancing citizen representation within public services. There were various moves to improve opportunities for groups and individuals to make their voices heard, and increasingly these were framed around consumption. Such efforts spanned the gamut of public services, from housing to health care. As part of the re-organisation of the NHS in 1973, 207 Community Health Councils (CHCs) were created to be the 'voice of the consumer' within the health service. The establishment of the CHCs, and the ongoing activities of groups like the PA, raised questions about who could speak for the patient-consumer and to what extent they could be heard. The CHCs, like other patient-consumer organisations, were not necessarily representative of the communities that they served. Moreover, such groups sometimes struggled to make their voices heard, especially above those of health professionals and managers. Yet, many CHCs took their responsibility to represent the needs of the community seriously, and they made strenuous efforts to solicit the views of groups who were poorly served by the NHS, such as the elderly and the mentally ill.

The issue of patient complaints offered opportunities for individual and collective action on behalf of patients. Chapter 3 will consider a series of attempts to improve complaints mechanisms throughout the 1970s and 1980s. Patient organisations lobbied for the introduction of a coordinated hospital complaints system and for the establishment of the health service ombudsman. Although a formal right to complain about hospital treatment was eventually introduced in 1985, the process that led to the establishment of such a right reveals much about the limitations to the power of patient-consumer organisations. Sections of the medical profession were opposed to the strengthening of complaints procedures and doctors were able to use their superior position within the British health care system to frustrate efforts to enhance complaints mechanisms. It took many years for a coordinated hospital complaints procedure to be introduced, and even then the right to complain appeared as much by chance as by design. A key problem for patient organisations was that the basis of their efforts was unclear: were patients complaining as consumers or as citizens?

One way of resolving such an impasse was to appeal to the language of rights. Chapter 4 examines patient-consumer organisations' engagement with the notion of patients' rights. The idea that patients were in possession of certain rights within health care was not new, but during the 1970s and 1980s 'rights talk' became more common. Patient-consumer organisations produced numerous rights guides and charters listing the rights that they thought patients either had or should have had. Such documents were necessary because patients possessed few legal rights and by laying claim to things such as the right to a second opinion, patient-consumer groups hoped to broaden the range of patient entitlements. At the same time, groups like the PA lobbied (unsuccessfully) for the establishment of a patients' bill of rights. Their failure to introduce such a bill pointed to some of the problems with the language of rights. Patient-consumer organisations were unclear about what kind of rights they were campaigning for: were these consumers' rights, citizens' rights, human rights, or was there enough that was distinctive about patients' rights to make these a different kind of rights claim all together? Patient-consumer groups also appeared to be confused as to whether they should prioritise the collective rights of all patients, or the individual rights of the patient. Such lack of clarity meant that the rights agenda was open to co-option by other actors. The Conservative government's introduction of the *Patient's Charter* in 1991 was a pyrrhic victory for patient-consumer groups. On the one hand, it represented official adoption of the notion of patients' rights and gave these some (albeit limited) purchase. Yet on the other hand, the rights put forward in the *Patient's Charter* were constrained, and focused on the individual patient rather than all patients. The collective aspect of patients' rights had been stripped away by a government keen to begin remaking the patient-consumer into a new and more individualistic figure.

Rights, it was clear, could only take patient-consumers so far. More information for consumers was needed in order to bridge the knowledge–power gap between doctors and patients. Chapter 5 considers the efforts of patient-consumer groups around the provision of information to patients. Obtaining more information about the services offered by the NHS and the treatment of specific conditions had always been a key goal for patient groups, but by the 1980s and 1990s access to information was of greater importance. In part, this was because of the increasing marketisation of the NHS, and for patient-consumers to operate effectively within this system more information was required. One issue where patient organisations were particularly successful was in the provision of information about hospital waiting lists. The College of Health (established by Michael Young in 1983) published details of the waiting times for in-patient treatment at all hospitals in the UK, enabling patient-consumers to 'shop around' for the shortest wait time. But, efforts to improve access to information were not just aimed at bettering the lot of individuals; data was also used to point to wider deficiencies within the NHS. At the same time, other actors were generating alternative kinds of information that did not necessarily enhance the power of the patient directly. The auditing of services was intended to introduce greater levels of professional accountability, but it also placed emphasis on a fairly narrow range of outcomes that may have been of lesser importance to patients. The Conservative government and patient organisations were thus increasingly at odds over the nature and significance of patient information.

Tensions between patient-consumer groups and the government (whether Conservative or Labour) can also be observed over the development of patient voice mechanisms in the 1990s and 2000s. Chapter 6 explores the concept of patient 'voice'. Patient voice was in some ways similar to patient representation, but the new term signalled a change in ideas about, and methods for, listening to patients' views. In 2003, despite vigorous opposition, the CHCs were abolished and replaced with a succession of different bodies including the Patient Advice and Liaison Service (PALS), the Commission for Patient and Public Involvement (CPPIH), Patient Forums, Overview and Scrutiny Committees (OSCs), and the Independent Complaints Advisory

Service (ICAS). Other forms of soliciting patient opinion, such as citizens' juries and 'listening exercises', were also utilised. Such a plethora of bodies indicated an added emphasis on listening to patients' opinions, but many of these groups were rather short-lived, making it difficult for the patient voice to be heard. At the same time, such organisations also tended to focus on the views of the individual, rather than any notion of collective representation. The voice of the patient, rather than patients' voices appeared to be being prioritised.

Focusing on individual demands was a consequence of an increasingly marketised health service. Under the Labour government (1997–2010) a series of 'reforms' were introduced to make the NHS operate more like a market. Chief among these was the promotion of patient choice. Chapter 7 analyses the development of choice policy within the NHS and its implications for patients, patient-consumer organisations and wider society. Although choice had played a role in earlier discussions about the meaning of patient consumption, it came to the foreground in the late 1990s and 2000s. During this period a number of policies were introduced with the aim of giving patients more choice. Initiatives such as the Choose and Book scheme, which allowed patients to choose the hospital they wished to visit as well as the date and time of their appointment, were intended to satisfy patient demands for more choice and improve the efficiency of the health service. Yet, the choice agenda was not welcomed universally by patient-consumer organisations. Patient groups and other critics were quick to point out that choice had down-sides too; that satisfying one vocal individual's demands may have implications for other, less outspoken patients.

Indeed, as the Conclusion to this book will suggest, initiatives to introduce more choice were only able to achieve partial success within a collective system. Despite the ongoing marketisation of the NHS, the values and demands fought for by patient-consumer organisations, such as autonomy, representation complaint and rights, and have not gone away. Although patient-consumer groups themselves may play less of a role today than they did in the 1960s or 1970s, their legacy lives on.

Notes

1   Mark Jenner and Patrick Wallis (eds), *Medicine and the Market in England and Its Colonies, c.1450–c.1850* (Basingstoke: Palgrave 2007); Roy Porter, 'The patient's view: doing medical history from below', *Theory and Society*, 14:2 (1985), 175–198.
2   Foucault's most influential works in this context are Michel Foucault, *The History of Sexuality, Volume One: An Introduction* (Middlesex: Penguin, 1990) and *Discipline and Punish: The Birth of the Prison* (New York: Vintage, 1979). See also Nikolas Rose, *Governing the Soul: The Shaping of the Private Self* (London: Free Association

3   Ian Hacking, 'Making up people', *London Review of Books*, 28 (17 August 2006), 23–26.
4   David Armstrong, 'The patient's view', *Social Science and Medicine*, 18:9 (1984), 737–744, at p. 739.
5   *Ibid.*, p. 743.
6   Porter, 'The patient's view'.
7   Anne Borsay and Peter Shapely (eds), 'Introduction', in *Medicine, Charity and Mutual Aid: The Consumption of Health and Welfare in Britain c. 1550–1950* (Aldershot: Ashgate, 2007), p. 1.
8   Flurin Condrau, 'The patient's view meets the clinical gaze', *Social History of Medicine*, 20 (2007), 525–540.
9   Frank Trentmann, 'The modern genealogy of the consumer: meanings, identities and political synapses', in Frank Trentmann and John Brewer (eds), *Consuming Cultures, Global Perspectives: Historical Trajectories, Transnational Exchanges* (Oxford: Berg, 2006), 19–69, p. 50.
10 *Ibid.*, p. 50.
11 Matthew Hilton and Martin Daunton, 'Material politics: an introduction', in Martin Daunton and Matthew Hilton (eds), *The Politics of Consumption: Material Culture and Citizenship in Europe and America* (Oxford: Berg, 2001), 1–32, p. 4.
12 Trentmann, 'The modern genealogy', 43–48.
13 Matthew Hilton, *Consumerism in Twentieth Century Britain: The Search for a Historical Movement* (Cambridge: Cambridge University Press, 2003), p. 2.
14 *Ibid.*, pp. 80, 245–252.
15 Matthew Hilton, 'Michael Young and the consumer movement', *Contemporary British History*, 19:3 (2005), 311–319.
16 Porter, 'The patient's view', p. 189.
17 Martin Gorsky, 'Community involvement in hospital governance in Britain: evidence from before the National Health Service', *International Journal of Health Services*, 38:4 (2008), 751–771.
18 Nancy Tomes, 'Patients or health-care consumers? Why the history of contested terms matters', in Rosemary A. Stephens, Charles E. Rosenberg and Lawton R. Burns, *History and Health Policy in the United States: Putting the Past Back In* (New Brunswick: Rutgers University Press, 2006), 83–110, p. 92.
19 Rob Irvine, 'Fabricating "health consumers" in health care politics', in Sara Henderson and Alan Petersen, *Consuming Health: The Commodification of Health Care* (London: Routledge, 2002), 31–47, pp. 32–33.
20 *Ibid.*, p. 34.
21 For an economic view of consumerism in health in this period see D.S. Lees, *Health Through Choice: An Economic Study of the British National Health Service* (London: Institute of Economic Affairs, 1961). This text is discussed in more detail in Chapter 7. Political and Economic Planning (PEP), *Family Needs and the Social Services* (London: PEP, 1961); Research Institute for Consumer Affairs (RICA), *General Practice a Consumer Commentary* (London: RICA, 1963).
22 Anon., 'Patients as consumers: wants and needs', *The Lancet* (29 April 1961), 927–928; Anon., 'Patients as consumers', *The Lancet*, 957 (5 May 1962).

23 There is some discussion of the application of consumerism in Steven Fielding, *The Labour Governments 1964-1970 Volume 1: Labour and Cultural Change* (Manchester: Manchester University Press, 2003) and a more detailed consideration of consumerism in the context of public housing in Peter Shapely, 'Tenants arise! Consumerism, tenants and the challenge to council authority in Manchester, 1968-92', *Social History*, 31:1 (2006), 60–78.
24 Christine Hogg, *Patients, Power and Politics: From Patients to Citizens* (London: Sage, 1999); Christine Hogg, *Citizens, Consumers and the NHS: Capturing Voices* (Basingstoke: Palgrave, 2009); Charlotte Williamson, *Towards the Emancipation of Patients: Patients' Experiences and the Patient Movement* (Bristol: The Policy Press, 2010).
25 Glen O'Hara, 'The complexities of "consumerism": choice, collectivism and participation within Britain's National Health Service, c.1961-1979', *Social History of Medicine*, 26:2 (2013), 288–304.
26 John Pickstone, 'Production, community and consumption: the political economy of twentieth-century medicine', in Roger Cooter and John Pickstone (eds), *Medicine in the Twentieth Century* (Amsterdam: Harwood, 2000), 1–19.
27 Graham Smith, 'The rise of the "new consumerism" in health and medicine in Britain, c.1948–1989', in Jennifer Burr and Paula Nicholson (eds), *Researching Health Care Consumers* (Basingstoke: Palgrave Macmillan, 2005), 13–38, p. 15.
28 See, for example, Nick Crossley, 'Transforming the mental health field: the early history of the National Association for Mental Health', *Sociology of Health and Illness*, 20:4 (1998), 458–488; Nick Crossley and M. Crossley, 'Patient voices, social movements and habitus. How psychiatric survivors speak out', *Social Science and Medicine*, 52 (2001), 1477–1489; Anne Rogers and David Pilgrim, 'Pulling down churches: accounting for the British mental health users movement', *Sociology of Health and Illness*, 13:2 (1991), 129–148; Anne Borsay, *Disability and Social Policy in Britain Since 1750* (Basingstoke: Palgrave, 2004); Malcolm Nicholson, and G.W. Lowis, 'The early history of the Multiple Sclerosis Society of Great Britain and Northern Ireland: a socio-historical study of lay/practitioner interaction in the context of a medical charity', *Medical History*, 46 (2002) 141–174; Alex Mold and Virginia Berridge, *Voluntary Action and Illegal Drugs: Health and Society in Britain since the 1960s* (Basingstoke: Palgrave Macmillan, 2010); Virginia Berridge, 'AIDS and patient support groups', in Roger Cooter and John Pickstone, *Medicine in the Twentieth Century* (Amsterdam: Harwood, 2000), 687–701.
29 The College of Health estimated that there were c.1,200 patient groups in 1987. Michael Young Papers, Churchill College Cambridge (hereafter) CCC YUNG/6/10/4, College of Health: Background and Aims, no date [1987?]. At the time of writing in 2013, the website patient.co.uk listed 1,848 organisations. See www.patient.co.uk/selfhelp.asp, accessed 24 October 2013.
30 Richard Hugman, 'Consuming health and welfare', in Russell Keat, Nigel Whiteley and Nicholas Abercrombie (eds), *The Authority of the Consumer* (London: Routledge, 1994), 207–222.
31 See Hilton, *Consumerism in Twentieth Century Britain*, pp. 268–275.
32 For an advocate's view of such developments, see Julian Le Grand, *The Other Invisible Hand: Delivering Public Services Through Choice and Competition* (Princeton: Princeton University Press, 2007).

33 John Clarke, Janet E. Newman, Nick Smith, Elizabeth Vidler and Louise Westmarland, *Creating Citizen-Consumers: Changing Publics and Changing Public Services* (London: Sage, 2007); John Clarke, 'Unsettled connections: citizens, consumers and the reform of public services', *Journal of Consumer Culture*, 7:2 (2007), 159–178.
34 Martin Powell, Ian Greener, Isabelle Szmigin, Shane Doheny and Nick Mills, 'Broadening the focus of public service consumerism', *Public Management Review*, 12.3 (2010), 324–339.
35 Timothy Milewa, 'Local participatory democracy in Britain's health service: innovation of fragmentation of a universal citizenship?', *Social Policy and Administration*, 38:3 (2004), 240–252; Timothy Milewa, Justin Valentine and Michael Calan, 'Managerialism and active citizenship in Britain's reformed health service: power and community in an era of decentralisation', *Social Science and Medicine*, 47:4 (1998), 507–517.
36 Richard M. Titmuss, 'Choice and the welfare state', in Richard M. Titmuss, *Commitment to Welfare* (London: George Allen, 1968), 138–152, pp. 146–147.
37 Margaret Stacey, 'The health service consumer: a sociological misconception', *The Sociological Review Monograph*, 22 (1978), 194–200.
38 Phil Shackley and Mandy Ryan, 'What is the role of the consumer in health care?', *Journal of Social Policy*, 23:4 (1994), 517–541.
39 Ibid.
40 Deborah Lupton, Cam Donaldson, and Peter Lloyd, 'Caveat emptor or blissful ignorance? Patients and the consumerist ethos', *Social Science and Medicine*, 33:5 (1991), 559–568.
41 Powell, Greener, Szmigin, Doheny and Mills, 'Broadening the focus of public service consumerism', p. 326.
42 Fedelma Winkler, 'Consumerism in health care: beyond the supermarket model', *Policy and* Politics, 15:1 (1987), 1–8.
43 John Clarke and Janet Newman, 'What's in a name? New Labour's citizen-consumers and the remaking of public services', *Cultural Studies*, 21 (2007), 738–757.
44 John Clarke, '"It's not like shopping": citizens, consumers and the reform of public services', in Mark Bevir and Frank Trentmann (eds), *Governance, Consumers and Citizens: Agency and Resistance in Contemporary Politics* (Basingstoke: Palgrave, 2007), 97–118.
45 Stacey, 'The health service consumer', p. 198.
46 Chris Ham, 'Power, patients and pluralism', in Keith Barnard and Kenneth Lee, *Conflicts in the National Health Service* (London: Croom Helm, 1977), 99–120, p. 116.
47 Brian Wood, *Patient Power? The Politics of Patients' Associations in Britain and America* (Buckingham: Open University Press, 2000), p. 39.
48 Williamson, *Towards the Emancipation of Patients*, p. 2.
49 Rob Baggott, Judith Allsop and Kathryn Jones, *Speaking for Patients and Carers: Health Consumer Groups and the Policy Process* (Basingstoke: Palgrave, 2005), pp. 84–89.
50 See Phil Brown, Stephen Zavestoski, Sabrina McCormick, Brian Mayer, Rachel Morello-Frosch and Rebecca Gasior Altman, 'Embodied health movements: new approaches to social movements in health', *Sociology of Health and Illness*, 26:1

(2004), 50–80; and Phil Brown and Stephen Zavestoski, 'Social movements in health: an introduction', *Sociology of Health and Illness*, 26:6 (2004), 679–694.

1

Autonomy

In Britain during the early 1960s patients were rarely thought of as autonomous actors. Ann Cartwright, in her 1964 survey of human relations and hospital care, found that many British patients complained about a lack of information concerning their illness, its treatment and prognosis. One patient told researchers: 'I'd like to have known just what was wrong with me, which kidney it was and if I'd be completely cured. Also I wanted to know if I could have any children. They just jump down your throat if you ask them.'[1] From its foundation in 1948, the NHS provided universal access to health care that was free at the point of use, but the early health service was structured in such a way that there was no real mechanism for hearing the views of patients. Furthermore, a culture of paternalism existed within the medical profession perpetuating the view that 'doctor knows best' and patients should accept a largely passive role.

Yet there were signs from the early 1960s onwards that such views were beginning to be challenged. As the journalist Gerda Cohen remarked in 1964, 'patients are becoming impatient: of being treated like chipped flowerpots in for repair; of queues; of being kept in ignorance'.[2] At both the individual and collective level patients were demanding more say in their own treatment and in the management and development of health services. The patient, in both the hospital ward and in the corridors of power, could no longer be ignored. This chapter will explore the extent to which, by the end of the 1970s, the patient had been re-positioned as an autonomous entity within British health care. A range of factors contributed to changes in the role of patients. Emerging medical technologies and the growing power of the pharmaceutical industry helped to reconfigure patient's minds and bodies.[3] But there were also developments that led to patients being viewed as *political actors*, and it is these shifts that this chapter will seek to illuminate.

The changing political role of the patient can be explained in the light of two inter-related developments: firstly, the growing importance placed on individual patient autonomy; and secondly, the development of consumerism within health care. During the early 1960s, the notion that patients had the capacity to 'reflect and decide' on their treatment, a concept that was to become crucial to later formulations of bioethics, began to gather support.[4] Autonomy, that is the ability to make decisions about individual care and treatment, was being foregrounded by patient organisations such as the PA. At the same time, autonomy was also central to the idea that patients could be thought of as 'consumers' of health care. Interest in consumer 'rights' started to attract academic and political attention: even *The Lancet* commented in 1961 that 'Emphasising the "consumer point of view" can be very valuable'.[5]

To explore the ways in which patient organisations began to re-position the patient through emerging notions of health consumerism and patient autonomy in Britain, this chapter will focus on four areas. Firstly, it will consider the place of autonomy within concepts of bioethics and consumerism as they developed during the 1960s and 1970s. Secondly, the chapter will attempt to uncover what patients themselves thought of health care in this period. This is difficult to do, as the opinions of patients were not collected systematically at this time: indeed, seeking patients' views on the health service was a new development. In a sense then, this section is as much about views of the patient as it is about the patient's view, as other actors, including sociologists, whistle-blowers and consumer organisations came increasingly to speak for and about the patient. What these various groups seemed to be saying was that there was something wrong with aspects of the care and services being provided: that the patient should have more of a say in determining what happened to his or her own body, but also in the fate of services as a whole.

The extent to which this call for more autonomy and involvement was taken up by patients themselves can be assessed through the examination of two case studies, considered in the third and fourth sections of the chapter. The first case study is offered by the work of NAWCH and their attempts to get hospitals to permit the unrestricted visiting of children in hospital. NAWCH provide a particularly pertinent example because the organisation worked both with and against the medical profession. The group challenged current practices, but at the same time, they were always careful not to be seen as too radical. In this way NAWCH occupied a space between the research-focused and doctor-orientated medical charities of the 1940s and 1950s and the more patient-centred organisations that came into being in the 1960s and 1970s.[6] A rather different example to the work of NAWCH is suggested by the activities of the PA and their campaign to establish a right for patients to consent to participate in the teaching of medical students. The PA was more overtly hostile towards the medical profession, and more willing to challenge openly what they saw as bad practices. The PA's work encapsulates neatly the difficulties facing those who attempted to speak for patients in the 1960s and 1970s, as they struggled to reconcile the demands of the individual patient with the needs of all patients.

Although NAWCH and the PA took contrasting approaches to lobbying government and health professionals in order to achieve change, underpinning the work of both of these organisations was the notion that the patient, or his or her parent, should have some say in what happened to his or her body. By the beginning of the 1970s the patient had been repositioned as an autonomous actor, and while more emphasis was undoubtedly placed on individual sovereignty, patient groups did not entirely retreat from communal approaches. The patient-consumer conjured into being during the 1960s and 1970s was not a selfish, market-orientated figure: patient groups like NAWCH and the PA were interested in the fate of patients as well as the patient.

Autonomy, bioethics and consumerism

This apparently contradictory notion of the patient, as both individual and as part of a group, can be discerned in the new approaches to patienthood being discussed in the 1960s and 1970s. A critical change in the way that patients were viewed, and in the ways in which they came to view themselves, was linked to the emergence of bioethics. Beginning in the USA in the 1960s, but spreading rapidly around the world, 'bioethics' was characterised as being different to the medical ethics of the recent past, as it was primarily concerned with relationships between doctors and their patients, rather than between doctors and other doctors.[7] What became known as the 'four principles' of bioethics – non-malfeasance; beneficence; justice and autonomy – emphasised the patient's right to make decisions for him or herself, an approach that led to the establishment of a legal right to informed consent in the USA.[8] In the UK, the notion of informed consent also began to receive attention, particularly in the context of medical research conducted on humans. During the late 1960s and early 1970s, ethical codes regulating human medical experimentation were developed, and research ethics committees to govern the use of human subjects were established.[9] Ethical discussions also became more commonplace in British medical schools, and eventually became part of the medical curriculum.[10]

The wider ethics of human experimentation had, of course, been a matter of interest at the international and national level for some years. Following the Nuremberg Trials of Nazi concentration camp doctors, a series of international codes governing the use of humans in experiments were established.[11] The Nuremberg Code (1947) stressed the importance of the voluntary participation of the research subject, and the Helsinki Declaration (1964) asserted that researchers should 'seek the potential subject's freely-given informed consent, preferably in writing'.[12] Although these codes were symbolically very important, they had less immediate impact on clinical research than might be supposed. Patients were often used in medical trials in both the UK and the USA during this period without their knowledge or consent.[13] In an article, and later book, entitled 'Human Guinea Pigs', the British physician Maurice Pappworth exposed such practices to public scrutiny in the early 1960s. Pappworth detailed a series of experiments conducted on patients in NHS hospitals over the previous 20 years, some of which involved potentially dangerous procedures including cardiac catheterisation and liver biopsies.[14] Other British medical scandals during the early 1960s, such as the deformities caused by thalidomide, and around the treatment of long-stay patients, highlighted the fallibility of modern medicine.[15]

While some historians, like David Rothman, have stressed the importance of 'scandals' and 'whistle-blowers' such as Pappworth in the making of bioethics, for whistle-blowers to make much noise an audience was required who shared their sense that what was going on within medicine was wrong.[16] For the roots of this changing sensibility, we need to look to wider developments within politics and society. There is little scope here to explore such factors in any detail, but clearly the emergence of medical sociology and the broader attack on the authority of the professions was significant, as was the emergence of rights-based new social movements and the development of novel medical technologies, which raised troubling questions about the very boundaries of life and death.[17] These developments combined to form a more questioning attitude toward the medical profession and medical practice. The authority of doctors as the sole decision makers within medicine was being challenged: not just by ethicists or sociologists, but by patients too.

All of this is not to say, however, that the rise of bioethics was somehow inevitable. As Roger Cooter has pointed out, much of what we know about the history of bioethics was produced by bioethicists themselves, and tends to revolve around the 'bioethicists' tale'.[18] This self-perpetuated myth places bioethicists at the centre of the emergence of a new medical ethical sensibility in the 1970s, one in which bioethicists were required to expose bad practices and formulate codes of conduct based on sound ethical principles.[19] There were, of course, continuities between the 'new' bioethics and the 'old' medical ethics, and the approaches that bioethicists began to develop from the 1970s onwards were not universal truths, but historically contingent. Indeed, the rise of bioethics needs to be placed in the context of wider shifts in Anglo-American politics and society. Many of the new social movements of the 1960s and 1970s (such as those around women's rights and gay rights) placed great emphasis on autonomy and allowing individuals to speak and act for themselves.[20] But the rise of bioethics also paralleled the emergence of neo-liberal governments, with their attendant technologies of audit, accountability and market models.[21] Bioethics adopted many of these tools, something also seen in the growing tendency to describe patients as consumers.

By the early 1960s, as explored in the Introduction, the language of consumption was beginning to enter discussions about health services in Britain. Nancy Tomes has suggested that the term 'consumer' was first used in relation to health by American medical economists in the inter-war period, and taken up again by consumer groups in the USA during the 1960s and 1970s as way of counteracting the paternalism of the doctor–patient relationship.[22] In the UK, a sustained engagement with the notion of patients as consumers also seems to have started in the 1960s, and it came not so much from health economists, but principally from think tanks and consumer groups. One explicitly economic approach can be found in D.S. Lees's *Health Through Choice: an Economic Study of the British National Health Service* produced by the pro-market Institute for Economic Affairs (IEA) in 1961.[23] However, such publications were easily outnumbered by those that approached the issue from the consumers' point of view rather than drawing on economic theory to make their case. The consumer perspective was paramount in PEP's *Family Needs and the Social Services* (1961); RICA's *General Practice: A Consumer Commentary* (1963); and Ann Cartwright's *Human Relations and Hospital Care* (1964), which was based on research carried out at the Institute of Community Studies (ICS).[24] All of these groups had connections to the development of organised consumerism in Britain, particularly through the social entrepreneur Michael Young.[25] Moreover, the political affiliation of PEP, RICA and the ICS was to the left of centre, in contrast to the right of centre, pro-market IEA.[26] For organisations like PEP and RICA, consumerism was not about the application of market principles to the NHS; instead it was a continuation of the ideal of social citizenship upon which the health service had been founded.[27] Such a view emphasised the importance of universal access to care that was free at the point of use as part of the post-war bargain between state and citizen. For RICA, the 'adult "consumers" whom the National Health Service sustains as patients are also those who maintain it as citizens'.[28]

Once in use, the language of consumption in health proliferated rapidly: a literature search of British medical and social science journals reveals that one of the earliest references to the consumer appeared in a *Lancet* editorial published in 1961, entitled 'Patients as consumers: wants and needs'. This piece considered the findings of a survey of public services conducted by PEP, a key report that will be discussed in more detail later in this chapter.[29] A further editorial in the *Lancet* published one year later, pointed to the growing activity by consumer groups around health-related topics.[30] The connection of the term 'patient-consumer' with the work of consumer groups suggests that these organisations played a key part in introducing the language of consumption, and specifically the notion of the patient as consumer, to the discourse around health. Yet the appearance of the patient-consumer was not merely a semantic shift; but was instead representative of wider changes in relationships between doctors and patients, and between patients and health care providers and policy makers.

Consumer autonomy, the idea that the consumer was 'an individual faced with a plethora of choices and increasingly free to make the choices she or he desired', was part of the notion of consumerism that had been put forward by groups such as the Consumers' Association.[31] They believed that the objective, comparative assessment of branded goods would rectify imbalances within the marketplace and enable the consumer to become the true sovereign of the economy.[32] Given accurate information, the individual would be able to choose the goods and services that would best satisfy their needs. Within the context of public services, the notion of providing individuals with more choice was almost unheard of in the 1960s.[33] As will be discussed in Chapter 7, choice only began to play a major role in ideas about consumerism in health during the 1990s. In the 1960s, the concept of patient-consumer autonomy was not centred on choice so much as recognising that patients were individuals with discrete needs and views.

Views of the patient and the patients' view

The very idea that patients' opinions on public services were worth seeking was a novel one in this period. Although the survey as a methodological tool was nothing new, the period after the Second World War saw it being put to original and more diverse uses.[34] As John Welshman has shown, the birth cohort survey was crucial to the development of social science research in Britain.[35] Surveyors were, however, also turning their attention to finding out what the public thought on a variety of topics.[36] In 1957 PEP conducted one of the first surveys of public opinion about a range of public services including health, welfare, housing, social security and education. PEP set out to determine the extent to which public services established in the late 1940s 'fit present day needs and desires'. The survey, PEP contended, was 'primarily a study of the consumer point of view'.[37] What PEP found was that satisfaction with public services in general, and the NHS in particular, was high: 86 per cent of families reported being satisfied with the attention given to them by their GP, and 95 per cent said there was no inconvenient delay in getting into hospital to see a specialist.[38] Complaints were fairly few and far between: some complaint was made about their last visit to the General Practitioner (GP) by 12 per cent of mothers, and 13 per cent of individuals questioned had some complaint about their last hospitalisation or on some other occasion.[39] PEP concluded that the individuals surveyed thought that 'the services are good and [they] are more likely to feel grateful than critical'.[40]

Ann Cartwright also found a similar picture of generally high satisfaction in a series of surveys of patients' views on general practice and hospital care conducted on behalf of the ICS during the first half of the 1960s. Cartwright asked respondents if there were any qualities that they felt a GP should have, but that their GP lacked: 75 per cent could not think of anything. A fifth had some criticism; the remainder did not know.[41] She concluded, 'The general picture that emerges from the response to these questions is of satisfied and appreciative patients'.[42] But, Cartwright also sounded a note of caution: 'behind the satisfaction of most patients there lies an uncritical acceptance and lack of discrimination which is conducive to stagnation and apathy'.[43] Indeed, her study of patients in hospitals revealed some potentially troubling issues from the patients' point of view. Although 'The majority of patients were satisfied with the medical treatment they received in hospital and had nothing but praise for the nurses and the way they looked after them' a significant proportion identified problems communicating with doctors and other medical staff.[44] Three-fifths of patients reported some difficulty in getting information while they were in hospital, and 23 per cent said that they were unable to find out all they wanted to know about their condition.[45] Cartwright contended that

> Doctors tend to underestimate both patients' desire for information and their ability to understand explanations. They often seem to discourage patients from asking questions and they sometimes use patients' feelings of respect and deference to evade discussion ... If communications are to be improved, some doctors need to be more approachable people, less like inaccessible gods.[46]

Bettering communications was important, Cartwright suggested, not only for increasing patient satisfaction but also for improving the service as a whole. She asserted, 'In a National Health Service public opinion could and should be a potent weapon for incentive and improvement. If it is to be effective, it must be based on a knowledge of the facts, and the public needs to recognize that the interests of both patients and staff can be served by informed criticism and demands for improvements'.[47]

Indeed, the significance of patient satisfaction surveys like those carried out by Cartwright and PEP was not so much the content of their findings, but that they were conducted at all. As the PEP report remarked, up until that point most other enquiries into the NHS had 'been concerned with administrative or operational efficiency, and the users of services have mostly been regarded as passive objects. Very little has been heard from those whom the services are designed to serve. In a democratic community this seems a major omission'.[48] But the voices of groups and individuals using services were beginning to be heard by the early 1960s. An important mechanism for highlighting such concerns was through the activities of patient organisations. The early 1960s witnessed a dramatic upswing in the number of British voluntary organisations in general and around health-related issues in particular. In the health field, 66 new organisations came into being between 1960 and 1979, compared with the 14 established between 1940 and 1959.[49] The meaning of this development for the position of the patient within British health care is best explored by turning to the first of two case studies: the National Association for the Welfare of Children in Hospital and their campaign around hospital visiting.

The National Association for the Welfare of Children in Hospital (NAWCH)

Up until the late 1940s, it was widely believed that it was undesirable for children in British hospitals to be visited regularly by the parents. Many hospitals permitted parents to visit their children just once a month, or not at all. During the 1950s, however, research carried out at the Tavistock Clinic by the psychologist John Bowlby into 'separation anxiety' began to change the opinion of some health professionals and Ministry of Health officials.[50] A film made by Bowlby's assistant, James Robertson, entitled *A Two-Year Old Goes to Hospital*, demonstrated graphically the trauma that many children experienced on admission to hospital, and spurred the Ministry of Health into action. A committee of the Central Health Services Council was formed under the orthopaedic surgeon Sir Harry Platt to investigate the welfare of children in hospital. The Platt report, published in 1959, recommended that hospitals should allow the unrestricted visiting of children by their parents, and that overnight accommodation should be provided for mothers wishing to stay with their offspring.[51] Initially, the report received little attention, but when the British Broadcasting Corporation (BBC) showed excerpts of *A Two-Year Old Goes to Hospital* on television in 1961, and Robertson followed this up with a series of articles in the *Guardian* and *The Observer*, the issue began to gain traction.[52] Jane Thomas, a young mother living in Battersea, south London, got in contact with Robertson and asked what she should do if her own child was hospitalised. Robertson suggested forming an organisation, and so Thomas got together with a group of other women and established Mother Care for Children in Hospital.[53] The organisation, which became the National Association for the Welfare of Children in Hospital (NAWCH) in 1965, established branches rapidly across the country. By 1969 NAWCH had 50 branches and 3,000 members, and by 1974 they had a branch in almost every major city in the country.[54]

Initially, NAWCH had one core aim: and that was to get the Platt report's recommendations around unrestricted hospital visiting and overnight stays implemented.[55] Inspired by the work of Bowlby and Robertson, but also by their own research and experiences, NAWCH developed a series of different techniques for getting hospitals to relax visiting rules. The organisation carried out a survey of hospitals asking them about their visiting policies. NAWCH found that although many hospitals said that they allowed unrestricted visiting, the reality could be very different. One hospital stated that 'visiting is unrestricted. Although of course we don't allow it in the mornings.'[56] Another said 'It is the aim of the Board of Governors to have "unrestricted visiting" provided that parents understand this does not mean that they can be in the wards all the time.'[57] Ear, Nose and Throat wards were particularly notorious for their attitude toward the presence of visitors. Some parents were asked to sign a consent form before their child underwent surgery (usually for a tonsillectomy) stating that they agreed not to visit on the day of the operation.[58]

NAWCH drew attention to such practices through press releases summarising their survey findings. The issue was then taken up by newspapers and raised in a series of questions in Parliament.[59] By 1964, three-quarters of hospitals supposedly allowed unrestricted visiting for parents, but NAWCH sought to ensure that such policies were adhered to by presenting hospitals with leaflets to be given to parents indicating that they could visit whenever they liked.[60] NAWCH also gave hospitals foldaway beds to be used by mothers who wished to stay the night. Such a tactic, described by one early NAWCH member as being 'like Greeks bearing gifts', placed pressure on hospitals to liberalise visiting policies in a subtle but persistent way: indeed the organisation was always careful to be 'nice' to hospitals, refusing to name, for example, hospitals that opposed their efforts for fear of alienating them altogether.[61] Moreover, NAWCH had a powerful ally in the Ministry of Health, and later the Department of Health and Social Security (DHSS), who also wanted to ensure that the Platt report was implemented.⁶² The Health Minister, Kenneth Robinson, spoke at NAWCH's annual conference in 1966, and he met with the organisation in 1968 to discuss the problem of children in long-stay hospitals.⁶³

Despite opposition from some health professionals and hospital authorities, the discrete pressure exerted by NAWCH, together with ever more insistent memos produced by the Ministry of Health, resulted in the gradual liberalisation of visiting policies.⁶⁴ By the 1970s, most hospitals allowed unrestricted visiting, and NAWCH began to take on other work, including the provision of low-cost transport for parents of children in hospital, and the general welfare of sick children.⁶⁵ The organisation also became involved in a wider range of health consumer issues, particularly through a deliberate campaign to get their members onto the locally based CHCs from 1973 onwards.⁶⁶

On a practical level, NAWCH's work can be rooted in a specific view of the emotional needs of children that was becoming more widely accepted during the 1960s and 1970s. The notion that separating young children from their parents, and especially their mothers, could cause lasting psychological damage was beginning to find its way into mainstream opinion both inside and outside of the medical profession.⁶⁷ Yet, NAWCH's activities and attitudes reflected deeper trends too. Most obviously, NAWCH perpetuated the gendered assumption that it was primarily the mother's responsibility to stay with the sick child. As the organisation's initial name, Mother Care for Children in Hospital, made plain, it was women and mothers that they were appealing to, not men and fathers. This was perhaps unsurprising at a time when women were largely responsible for child-rearing, but some NAWCH members held fairly conservative views on bringing up children and the role of women. In 1973, a founder member of NAWCH, Peg Belson, gave a talk entitled 'Motherhood as career', bemoaning the fact that motherhood 'as a full-time occupation, as a career, is more and more being given a secondary role'.⁶⁸

NAWCH were clearly not a proto-second-wave feminist group, but that does not mean that their work was insignificant, or in its own quiet way, radical. NAWCH were part of a stream of pre-women's liberation activity in Britain that sought to challenge the consensus on many key topics. As Caitriona Beaumont has shown, even supposedly conservative women's groups, like the Mothers' Union and the Women's Institutes (WI), became involved in important social and political issues during the 1950s and 1960s, such as the campaign for equal pay and the extension of family planning services.⁶⁹ Like the WI and the Mothers' Union, NAWCH was primarily a middle-class organisation, and they did not always appear to understand the difficulties experienced by less affluent mothers with sick children. The group felt that some mothers needed to be persuaded to visit their children in hospital, and did not perhaps appreciate the fact that poorer mothers may have been unable to visit their children regularly because of employment, lack of resources, poor public transport, or other family commitments. Later on NAWCH did begin to address such issues when they launched an enquiry into public transport for parents visiting hospitals, recommending that fares be waived for the parents of sick children as a non-means tested benefit.[70]

Despite the obvious wider socio-political significance of their work, NAWCH were uncomfortable with being seen as the political actors that they undoubtedly were. In his address to the fourth NAWCH conference in 1966, the Health Minister Kenneth Robinson made the mistake of referring to NAWCH as a 'pressure group' at which, according to a NAWCH member, 'One felt people bristle' but 'they relaxed when he charmingly called them a "most responsible pressure group"'.[71] NAWCH were careful not to question clinical judgement, 'because we weren't in a position to do that', and they worked closely with friendly health professionals whenever possible.[72] Looking back, a NAWCH member was struck by how 'polite and feeble' they were, that they took pains not to appear to be aggressive, and that they looked to the more antagonistic PA as an example of what not to do.[73] Other NAWCH members were afraid of being seen as 'difficult': partly out of a fear that hospital staff would exact a reprisal on their children, but also because they resented the implication that by asking questions or making certain demands they were moving beyond their expected role. One NAWCH member recalled going to a meeting of the Sheffield Regional Hospital Board, and on being introduced to the other members was told 'Ah, you're a difficult woman'. But, she said, she was not being 'difficult', she was simply asking questions.[74]

NAWCH's work and attitudes were thus somewhat paradoxical. On the one hand, the organisation could appear to be timid and reluctant to challenge professional opinion and power openly. On the other, NAWCH's seemingly passive techniques undoubtedly helped the organisation to achieve its aims. Working with, rather than against, hospitals, health professionals and government officials was probably a wise tactic given the power imbalance between NAWCH and the other actors involved. NAWCH's cautiousness could be seen as being a function of their age, gender and social class, but there was also a degree of reluctance on the part of the organisation to associate themselves too closely with any particular cause beyond their own narrow interests. For example, NAWCH were slow to engage with the nascent consumer movement and its language. Peg Belson, one of NAWCH's founder members, remembered that

We were around at the beginning of the consumer movement if you like, but I don't recall that we were aware of any of that at all. It was a couple of years later that the famous journalist, Mary Stott, wrote about us in the *Guardian* as part of the consumer movement.[75]

NAWCH were also careful not to use the discourse of rights to make their case. Belson remarked, 'The information about parents' accommodation was never written in terms of rights. There were no patients' rights about it. It was all to do with "this is the pattern and if you ask ... ".[76] It was only later, during the late 1970s, that NAWCH engaged explicitly with the notion of rights, and then they were concerned primarily with the rights of the child, not the rights of the parent.[77] Yet NAWCH did want more say for parents, and in their own quiet way they revolutionised a particular field. They may not have framed their protest explicitly in terms of consumerism or patient autonomy, but NAWCH's work did represent a challenge to the conventional methods of hospital care and medical practice. By speaking up for what parents and their children wanted, NAWCH were taking an important stand not only in the field of paediatric medicine, but also in health care more generally. The presence of groups like NAWCH made it plain that the patients' voice could no longer be ignored completely.

The Patients Association (PA)

A somewhat different manifestation of the patients' voice can be found in the work of the PA. Helen Hodgson, a part-time teacher, established the PA in 1963. Hodgson was moved to set up the organisation by 'reports on thalidomide babies, wrong patient operations and tests on patients'.[78] Hodgson and her fellow committee members (who included two lawyers, an engineer, a local government official and a housewife) were deeply concerned about the issue of patient consent to participate in medical trials or experimental treatment.[79] Hodgson was appalled that 'Patients are not told if they are receiving new or orthodox treatment. I maintain that they *should* be told.'[80] The patient, she asserted, 'is entitled to know what treatment, if any, he is receiving.'[81] But Hodgson was not just concerned with more information for the individual; she wanted more say for patients collectively. She asserted that the PA aimed 'to give a voice to patients, because it believes that any group with a common interest has this right. It does not represent the interests of any one particular group of patients but of all patients.'[82]

The PA was formed partly in reaction to 'scandals' such as Pappworth's 'human guinea pig' revelations, and the ethical conduct of medical research provided a focus for many of their early activities.[83] Work by Jenny Hazelgrove and Adam Hedgecoe has shown that the association played an important role in getting research ethics committees established in hospitals where clinical research was being conducted.[84] With these committees came wider recognition of the patient's right to informed consent to participate in non-therapeutic, and to a lesser extent, therapeutic research too. But the PA's target was always wider than the narrow application of consent to the experimental setting. Hodgson asserted that

> Modern medicine creates new issues, moral, economic and practical. The patient should be able to share in both the responsibilities involved and the decisions to be taken. A patient should have no cause to think that he is helpless in the grip of a soulless machine or that he is little more than a clinical specimen or even a sitting duck for students.[85]

The PA was established to 'represent and further the interests of patients', to improve communication between doctors and patients, to campaign for a greater role for patients in decision-making and to provide a form of consumer protection for patients.[86] Underpinning this work was a belief in patient autonomy: in the patient's right to make decisions about the treatment of his or her body. As a result, the PA began quickly to widen the scenarios where they thought patient consent should be sought.

A key area of concern for the PA was how patients were used in medical education. Hodgson told the *Guardian* that 'the practice of using patients as teaching material without due regard for their dignity as sentient human beings symbolises the kind of contempt or disregard for human feelings which leads to more serious abuses'.[87] The association conducted a survey of practices in teaching hospitals in 1963/4, which found that only half of undergraduate teaching hospitals, and a third of postgraduate teaching hospitals, included any reference to their teaching activities in the literature supplied to patients.[88] Moreover, the PA felt that even when the possibility of patients being used in teaching was mentioned, this was often done in an unsatisfactory way. Patients, they argued, should give their explicit consent to the presence of students during clinical examinations or treatment, and crucially, care should not be conditional on the patient's willingness to participate in teaching.[89] Yet, many hospitals did just this: the PA found that half of London's teaching hospitals refused to treat patients who would not consent to the presence of students.[90] The case of Doris Scott, reported in the *Sunday Express* in July 1965, was far from unusual. Scott refused to remove her clothes in preparation for a gynaecological examination in front of a group of male medical students, prompting the consultant and the students to walk out.[91]

The establishment of the Royal Commission on Medical Education in 1965 presented an opportunity for the PA to challenge such practices. The association gave both written and oral evidence on the use of patients in teaching to the Commission, chaired by the Nobel Prize winning biochemist Lord Alexander Todd. The minutes of one of the commission's meetings noted that oral evidence from the PA should be sought not because they believed there was anything much to add to the association's written testimony, but for 'quasi-political reasons'. This suggested that the PA had become a something of an irritant: that their campaign of letter-writing to the commission and the Ministry of Health had paid off.[92] The PA told the commission that all patients admitted to teaching hospitals should be warned of the possibility of being used in medical education; that the treatment of patients should not be conditional on their willingness to participate in teaching; and that the consent of the patient should always be obtained.[93] Todd largely agreed with the PA, and the commission recommended in their final report that patients should be 'consulted' when being used in teaching and 'given a proper understanding of the situation and asked to cooperate'. The commission also asserted that 'no hospital whatever its status should confine its services to patients who undertake to contribute to medical education', a view shared by the Ministry of Health and the Scottish Home and Health Department.[94]

Although Todd's recommendations were in line broadly with the PA's view, getting hospitals to implement these changes was more problematic. Many of the practices highlighted by the association – such as hospitals' refusal to treat patients unwilling to participate in teaching – continued. The Department of Health did issue guidance to hospitals in 1973 stressing the importance of providing patients in teaching hospitals with an information leaflet, and urging hospitals to seek the explicit cooperation of patients in medical education. But Helen Hodgson's own experience at University College Hospital in 1975 suggested that consent was not always sought from patients when students were present, even at the most intimate of examinations.[95] Another Department of Health circular was issued in 1977, reiterating the importance of seeking the patient's consent during teaching, and this gradually became common practice. Indeed, by 1991, patient consent to the presence of students was included in the Conservative government's *Patient's Charter* as one of the 'rights' long held by patients.[96]

The reconstitution of patient consent in teaching as a 'right' in 1991 represented a complete turn-around by the DHSS. The language of rights was certainly present in earlier discussions about patient consent and the presence of students, but in the 1960s and 1970s it was being used by the PA, not by government officials or medical staff. For the PA, individual patient rights and autonomy were crucial. This can be seen in the way in which the PA viewed the doctor–patient relationship in general, and how this should operate in the context of teaching in particular. The PA saw 'the public demonstration and discussion of NHS patients before large classes, frequently without warning or consent' as an 'uncivilised relic of the charity days', as the result of 'outmoded attitudes to patients dating from a time when hospitals were a charity for the sick poor'.[97] The Association believed that doctors working in teaching hospitals still treated patients as if they were receiving free or low-cost treatment in exchange for offering their bodies in the service of medical education, a practice that should have been eradicated by the introduction of the NHS in 1948. NHS treatment was, of course, free to all at the point of use, but it also held deeper significance as part of a package of social rights conferred on citizens through the post-war welfare state. Following a brief stay in hospital shortly after the establishment of the NHS, the sociologist Margaret Stacey commented, 'I and others like me were fully aware that we had every right to be there, that we paid through our taxes according to our means and that what treatment we had depended on our condition alone: it wasn't charity: it was as of right'.[98] Rights to treatment were extended by patient groups like the PA and others to include the right to know what this treatment was, and whether or not this was experimental; a right to know what condition the patient was suffering from; a right to some say in the management of this condition, and so on.[99] The Patients Association wanted patients to gain control of their own bodies, and through this they were questioning the notion that doctors alone should decide what was best for patients.

The PA used the language of rights in the context of teaching in two ways. Firstly, they believed that not asking patients whether they minded being used in clinical teaching was an invasion of the patient's right to privacy. As Helen Hodgson remarked in the *Daily Express*, patients 'are not cranks or prudes. They simply want to be treated as humans – not as specimens. They want the right to preserve their human dignity and modesty'.[100] Secondly, the PA believed that the patient should also have a right to refuse to participate in teaching if they so wished.[101] To give these rights legal purchase, the PA began a campaign to create legislation on the issue. Their efforts, which are discussed in greater detail in Chapter 5, were largely unsuccessful, in part because health officials, senior physicians and hospitals were unconvinced by the language of patients' rights and individual autonomy. Such actors placed more emphasis on patients' duty to contribute towards clinical teaching and the advance of medicine. An information sheet given to out-patients at University College Hospital in 1972 stated that 'This is a Teaching Hospital … this may entail the presence of students during the consultation and the consultant may wish to talk to the students about your condition at the same time. Your co-operation is sought in carrying out this important part of the Hospital's duty to the community.'[102] Placing emphasis on the collective duty that patients had to society was an example of what Richard Titmuss described as the 'Gift Relationship'. Although Titmuss used the case of blood donation to illustrate his arguments about the collective nature of medicine and society – that the individual should freely give of him or herself in order to benefit the community – he stated that he could have used the 'giving role of the patient as "teaching material"' to make the same points. Titmuss noted that patients'

> willingness to be 'taught on' and to give of themselves, physically, and psychologically, is presumed. It is taken for granted that in the name of research, the advancement of medical science, society's need for doctors, the better training and more rapid progression of doctors professionally and financially, and ultimately, for the good of all patients irrespective of race, religion, colour or territory.[103]

For Titmuss, patients had a duty to take part in the teaching of medical students, not a right to refuse to do so.

Titmuss's work is an example of what David Reubi has called 'hameto-social rule', an approach to governing the use of human bodies in medical science which, he suggests, was being replaced by more the more individualistic view inherent within bioethics by end of the 1970s.[104] The Patients Association's campaign to establish a right to consent would seem to run counter to 'hameto-social rule', as it emphasised the right of the individual to privacy over the duty he or she had to participate in medical education in order to benefit the wider community, and thus offers an early preview of the bioethical understanding of the patient. More broadly, the PA's campaign could be seen as one of the first steps away from the kind of social democracy based on social rights and responsibilities envisaged by people like Titmuss, and toward the individualised, consumer-orientated vision of society often associated with neo-liberalism. Yet, the PA did not dismiss entirely the collective value of participating in teaching or of the need to think of patients as well as the patient. Hodgson remarked in an article sent to the Todd Commission in 1965 that

> Most patients readily accept students as apprentices ... They do not object to students learning to be doctors in a practical and natural way. They do object to being used for teaching without warning or consent, to being treated without respect or discretion as a kind of laboratory specimen.[105]

What the PA wanted was for patients to have a say in whether or not they were used in teaching, and to participate in decisions about their own medical treatment and the structure of the health service more broadly. Whether the demands of the individual patient were reconcilable with those of all patients was, however, an open question.

Conclusion

Indeed, tensions between the individual and collective view of the patient's role in teaching, and between patient's rights and patient's duties, were an ongoing issue for patients' organisations like the PA. These applied not just to the particular problem of consent and the presence of medical students, but to a range of other considerations too. Indeed, it could be suggested that balancing individual wants with collective needs became a key problem for all those involved in health services in the later decades of the twentieth century and into the twenty-first. Patient groups like NAWCH and the PA clearly had a part to play in re-positioning the patient as an autonomous individual. Campaigns around visiting children in hospital and the use of patients in teaching drew attention to autonomy, and the extent to which individuals were able to make decisions for themselves, or for their children. Although NAWCH were uncomfortable initially with being labelled as a 'consumer group', their particular brand of feminised (although not feminist), seemingly apolitical activism foregrounded a more assertive and questioning patient or parent. The PA was more at home with the consumerist label, but their work was also related to concerns about the ethics of modern medicine.

The re-positioning of the patient as an actor in his or her own right within British health care policy and practice can be seen in a number of developments that took place from the mid-1970s onwards. The establishment of the CHCs in England and Wales (Local Health Councils in Scotland) was, at least in part, recognition of this shift. Created in 1974 through the reorganisation of the NHS, 207 CHCs were established at the local level to be the 'voice of the consumer' within the health service.[106] The CHCs also recognised the importance of both individual rights and collective responsibilities, as they took on work that helped individuals, such as assisting patients wishing to make a complaint, but also of wider concern, such as the provision of maternity services or the quality of hospital food.[107] Patients' views, as well as the views of the patient, were being taken increasingly into account. By the end of the 1970s, the patient had been re-positioned as a distinct actor within British health politics and policy. Patients, individually and collectively, could no longer be ignored.

The extent to which patient groups like the PA and NAWCH can be credited with such a re-positioning of the patient is, of course, hard to quantify. Disentangling the impact of patient-consumer groups from the wider socio-political shifts that also helped to drive such changes forward is almost impossible: were patient groups and the issues they fought for the symptom or the cause? Perhaps they were both. The campaigns pursued by patient groups were indicative of broader changes around the place of the individual within society, changes also seen in the rise of bioethics and of consumerism. At the same time, patient organisations had an impact on the development of ethical practices and consumerism, through the issues they drew attention to, and through their own re-fashioning of the patient, not only with the 'capacity to reflect and decide', but also to choose and complain.[108] The consequences of the co-existence of the patient as both bioethical subject and as autonomous consumer, and the ways in which these related, but sometimes conflicting, identities might interact were not yet clear. The autonomous patient-consumer, as we shall see, also needed collective representation.

Notes

1 Ann Cartwright, *Human Relations and Hospital Care* (London: Routledge & Kegan Paul, 1964), p. 75.
2 Gerda L. Cohen, *What's Wrong With Hospitals?* (Harmondsworth: Penguin, 1964), p. 9.
3 See, for example, Ayesha Nathoo on heart transplants in *Hearts Exposed: Transplants and the Media in 1960s Britain* (Basingstoke: Palgrave, 2009). For a more recent take on the reconfiguration of the patient by the pharmaceutical industry in a global context see Adriana Petryna, *When Experiments Travel: Clinical Trials and the Global Search for Human Subjects* (Princeton, NJ: Princeton University Press, 2009).
4 David Reubi, 'Ethics governance, modernity and human beings' capacity to reflect and decide: a genealogy of medical research ethics in the UK and Singapore' (PhD diss., London School of Economics & Political Science, 2009), p. 69.
5 Anon., 'Patients as consumers: wants and needs', *The Lancet* (29 April 1961), 927–928, quotation on p. 928.
6 For an example of how the orientation of a particular organisation changed its focus during this period see Malcolm Nicholson and G.W. Lowis, 'The early history of the Multiple Sclerosis Society of Great Britain and Northern Ireland: a socio-historical study of lay/practitioner interaction in the context of a medical charity', *Medical History*, 46 (2002), 141–174.
7 Robert Martensen, 'The history of bioethics: an essay review', *Journal of the History of Medicine and Allied Sciences*, 56 (2001), 168–175; Renee C. Fox and Judith P. Swazey, *Observing Bioethics* (New York: Oxford University Press, 2008).
8 Tom L. Beauchamp and James P. Childress, *Principles of Biomedical Ethics* (5th edn. Oxford: Oxford University Press, 2001).

9   Adam Hedgecoe, '"A form of practical machinery": the origins of research ethics committees in the UK, 1967–72', *Medical History*, 53 (2009), 331–350; Jenny Hazelgrove, 'The old faith and the new science: the Nuremberg code and human experimentation ethics in Britain, 1946–73', *Social History of Medicine*, 15:1 (2002), 109–135; Paul Weindling, 'The origins of informed consent: the international scientific commission on medical war crimes, and the Nuremberg Code', *Bulletin of the History of Medicine*, 75 (2001), 37–71; Ulf Schmidt, 'Cold War at Porton Down: informed consent in Britain's biological and chemical warfare experiments', *Cambridge Quarterly of Healthcare Ethics*, 15 (2006), 366–380.
10 Michael Whong-Barr, 'Clinical ethics teaching in Britain: a history of the London Medical Group', *New Review of Bioethics*, 1:1 (2003), 73–84.
11 Paul Weindling, *Nazi Medicine and the Nuremberg Trials: From Medical War Crimes to Informed Consent* (Basingstoke: Palgrave Macmillan, 2004); Ulf Schmidt, *Justice at Nuremberg: Leo Alexander and the Nazi Doctors' Trial* (Basingstoke: Palgrave Macmillan, 2004); George Annas and Michael Grodin (eds), *The Nazi Doctors and the Nuremberg Code: Human Rights in Human Experimentation* (New York: Oxford University Press, 1995).
12 The Nuremberg Code can be viewed at www.hhs.gov/ohrp/archive/nurcode.html, accessed 14 October 2013. World Medical Association Declaration of Helsinki, *Ethical Principles for Research Involving Human Subjects* (Helsinki, 1964), www.wma.net/en/30publications/10policies/b3/17c.pdf, accessed 14 October 2013.
13 For the USA see David J. Rothman, *Strangers at the Bedside: A History of How Law and Bioethics Transformed Medical Decision Making* (New York: Basic Books, 1991). For the UK see Hazelgrove, 'The old faith and the new science' and Hedgecoe, '"A form of practical machinery"'.
14 Maurice Pappworth, 'Human guinea pigs: a warning', *Twentieth Century*, 171 (1962), 67–75; Maurice Pappworth, *Human Guinea Pigs: Experimentation on Man* (London: Routledge & Kegan Paul, 1967).
15 Gordon E. Appelbe, 'From arsenic to thalidomide: a brief history of medicine safety', in Stuart Anderson (ed.), *Making Medicines: A History of Pharmacy and Pharmaceuticals* (London: The Pharmaceutical Press, 2005), 243–260; Barbara Robb, *Sans Everything: A Case to Answer* (London: Nelson, 1967); Cmnd. 3687, *Findings and Recommendations Following Enquires Into Allegations Concerning the Care of Elderly Patients in Certain Hospitals* (London: HMSO, 1968); Cmnd. 3975, *Report of the Committee on Inquiry Into Allegations of Ill-Treatment of Patients and Other Irregularities at the Ely Hospital Cardiff* (London: HMSO, 1969); Cmnd. 4557, *Report of the Farleigh Hospital Inquiry* (London: HMSO, 1971); Cmnd. 4681, *Report of the Committee of Inquiry Into Whittingham Hospital* (London: HMSO, 1972).
16 Rothman, *Strangers at the Bedside*.
17 Harold Perkin, *The Rise of Professional Society: England Since 1880* (London: Routledge, 1990); Ivan Illich, *Limits to Medicine – Medical Nemesis: The Expropriation of Health* (London: Marion Boyars, 1976); Paul Byrne, *Social Movements in Britain* (London: Routledge, 1997); Stanley Joel Reiser, *Technological Medicine: The Changing World of Doctors and Patients* (Cambridge: Cambridge University Press, 2009).

18 Roger Cooter, 'The ethical body', in Roger Cooter and John Pickstone (eds), *Medicine in the Twentieth Century* (Amsterdam: Harwood Academic Publishers, 2000), 451–468.
19 Roger Cooter, 'The resistible rise of medical ethics', *Social History of Medicine*, 8:2 (1995), 257–270.
20 David J. Rothman, 'The origins and consequences of patient autonomy: a 25-year retrospective', *Health Care Analysis*, 9 (2001), 255–264.
21 Reubi, 'Ethics governance, modernity and human beings', p. 61; Duncan Wilson, 'Creating the "ethics industry": Mary Warnock, *in vitro* fertilization and the history of bioethics in Britain', *Biosocieties*, 6:2 (2011), 121–141.
22 Nancy Tomes, 'Patients or health-care consumers? Why the history of contested terms matters', in Rosemary A. Stephens, Charles E. Rosenberg and Lawton R. Burns, *History and Health Policy in the United States: Putting the Past Back In* (New Brunswick: Rutgers University Press, 2006).
23 D.S. Lees, *Health Through Choice: An Economic Study of the British National Health Service* (London: Institute of Economic Affairs, 1961).
24 Political and Economic Planning (PEP), *Family Needs and the Social Services* (London: PEP, 1961); Research Institute for Consumer Affairs (RICA), *General Practice a Consumer Commentary* (London: RICA, 1963); Cartwright, *Human Relations and Hospital Care*.
25 On the importance of Michael Young see Matthew Hilton, 'Michael Young and the consumer movement', *Contemporary British History*, 19:3 (2005), 311–319.
26 For more information on the history of PEP and the IEA see Andrew Denham and Mark Garnett, *British Think-Tanks and the Climate of Opinion* (London: UCL Press, 1998).
27 The classic exposition of social citizenship can be found in T.H. Marshall, 'Citizenship and Social Class', in T.H. Marshall and Tom Bottomore, *Citizenship and Social Class* (London: Pluto Press, 1992), 3–51.
28 RICA, *General Practice*, p. 4.
29 Anon., 'Patients as consumers: wants and needs', *The Lancet* (1961), 927–928.
30 Anon., 'Patients as consumers', *The Lancet* (1962), p. 957.
31 Kim Humphrey, *Shelf Life: Supermarkets and the Changing Cultures of Consumption* (Cambridge: Cambridge University Press, 1998), p. 22.
32 Matthew Hilton, *Consumerism in Twentieth Century Britain: The Search for a Historical Movement* (Cambridge: Cambridge University Press, 2003), p. 196.
33 A notable exception was Lees, *Health Through Choice*. For an analysis of this and the place of choice in British health care see Chapter 7, pp. 171–172.
34 Martin Bulmer, Kevin Bales and Kathryn Kish Sklar (eds), *The Social Survey in Historical Perspective, 1880–1940* (Cambridge: Cambridge University Press, 1991).
35 John Welshman, 'Time, money and social science: the British birth cohort surveys of 1946 and 1958', *Social History of Medicine*, 25.1 (2012), 175–192.
36 Sarah E. Igo, *The Averaged American: Surveys, Citizens and the Making of a Mass Public* (Cambridge, MA: Harvard University Press, 2007).
37 PEP, *Family Needs and the Social Services*, pp. 1–2.
38 *Ibid.*, pp. 100, 114.
39 *Ibid.*, pp. 113, 117.
40 *Ibid.*, p. 121.

41 Ann Cartwright, *Patients and Their Doctors: A Study of General Practice* (London: Routledge & Kegan Paul, 1967), p. 7.
42 *Ibid.*, p. 9.
43 *Ibid.*, p. 216.
44 Cartwright, *Human Relations and Hospital Care*, p. 10.
45 *Ibid.*, p. 74.
46 *Ibid.*, p. 100.
47 *Ibid.*, p. 205.
48 PEP, *Family Needs and the Social Services*, p. 188.
49 Bruce Wood, *Patient Power? The Politics of Patients' Associations in Britain and America* (Buckingham: Open University Press, 2000), figure quoted on p. 36.
50 Harry Hendrik, 'Children's emotional well-being and mental health in early post-Second World War Britain: the case of unrestricted hospital visiting', in Marijke Gijswit-Hofstra and Hilary Marland (eds), *Cultures of Child Health in Britain and the Netherlands in the Twentieth Century* (Amsterdam & New York: Rodopi, 2003), 213–242.
51 Central Health Services Council, *The Welfare of Children in Hospital: Report of a Committee of the Central Health Services Council* (London: HMSO, 1959).
52 James Robertson, 'The truth about settling in', the *Guardian*, 15 January 1961, p. 24; James Robertson, 'Maintaining the bond', the *Guardian*, 22 January 1961, p. 24; James Robertson, 'How parents can help now', *The Observer*, 29 January 1961, p. 33; James Robertson, 'Now over to the mothers', *The Observer*, 12 February 1961, p. 34.
53 Peg Belson, 'To get our agenda onto other people's agenda', in Helene Curtis and Mimi Sanderson, *The Unsung Sixties: Memoirs of Social Innovation*, pp. 357–370 (London: Whiting and Birch, 2004).
54 The National Archives (hereafter TNA), Kew, Ministry of Health papers (MH) 150/348, National Association for the Welfare of Children in Hospital, note prepared by Ministry of Health attached to memo from Mr Hewitt to AR Elliott, 25 February 1969.
55 Modern Records Centre (hereafter MRC), University of Warwick, MSS.21/1628/1, NAWCH Newsletter, 1970/71.
56 Notes taken by author at NAWCH Roundtable Meeting, Cambridge, 20 June 2009.
57 Quoted in Cohen, *What's Wrong With Hospitals?*, p. 43.
58 NAWCH Roundtable.
59 See, for example, 'Children (Admission of Mothers)', *House of Commons Debates*, 24 February 1964, vol. 690, cols 3–4; Anon., 'Mothers by the sickbed', the *Guardian*, 20 December 1964, p. 3; Jacky Gillott, 'Welcomed to the wards?', *The Observer*, 26 September 1965, p. 30.
60 Anon., 'Mothers and children in hospital', the *Guardian*, 25 February 1965; Belson, 'To get our agenda', p. 361.
61 NAWCH Roundtable.
62 The Department of Health and Social Security (DHSS) replaced the Ministry of Health in 1968.
63 TNA MH 150/348, National Association for the Welfare of Children in Hospital, note prepared by MH attached to memo from Mr Hewitt to A.R. Elliott, 25 February 1969.

64 MRC MSS.21/1628/5, National Health Service: Visiting Children in Hospital. HM(66) 18, 10 March 1966.
65 MRC MSS.21/1628/1: NAWCH Newsletter 1970/71; MRC MSS.21/1628/1/18, NAWCH Annual report, 1972/3.
66 MRC MSS.21/1628/1/18, NAWCH Annual report, 1972/3; MRC MSS.21/1628/19/1, NAWCH AGM, 1 April 1973; Belson, 'To get our agenda', p. 364.
67 Hendrik, 'Children's emotional well-being and mental health'.
68 MSS.21/1628/29 Paper given by Mrs Margaret Belson at the National Association for Maternal & Child Welfare Diamond Jubilee Conference, 27 June 1973: 'Motherhood as career'.
69 Caitriona Beaumont, 'Housewives, workers and citizens: voluntary women's organizations and the campaign for women's rights in England and Wales during the post-war period', in Nick Crowson, Matthew Hilton and James McKay (eds), *NGOs in Contemporary Britain: Non State Actors in Society and Politics Since 1945* (Basingstoke: Palgrave Macmillan, 2009), 59–75.
70 MRC MSS.21/1628/25: Letter from Mrs Barbara Browse, Vice-Chairman of NAWCH to the editor of *The Times*, 7 June 1973; MRC MSS.21/1628/38: Fares Enquiry II: A Position Statement on Fares Assistance, October 1973.
71 MRC MSS.378/APSW/P/10/27/7a, Fourth Annual Conference of the National Association for the Welfare of Children in Hospital, Report by K.S. Griffith, n.d. [1966].
72 Belson, 'To get our agenda', p. 361.
73 Personal communication with NAWCH member, June 2009.
74 NAWCH Roundtable.
75 Belson, 'To get our agenda', p. 360.
76 *Ibid.*, p. 363.
77 NAWCH Roundtable.
78 Contemporary Medical Archives Centre (hereafter CMAC) Wellcome Library, London, SA/PAT/H/1 Press Cuttings November 1962–November 1963, Letter to the *Sunday Times* from Helen Hodgson, 25 November 1962.
79 Members' occupations listed in Anon., 'Now a voice for patients', *The Times*, 17 June 1963, p. 15. See, for example, the debate sparked by Bradford Hill's article on medical ethics and controlled trials in the *British Medical Journal*, which Hodgson took part in, demanding a greater say for patients. Helen Hodgson, 'Medical ethics and controlled trials', letter to the *British Medical Journal*, 18 May 1963, pp. 1339–1340.
80 Hodgson quoted in Anon., 'Now a voice for patients', *The Times*, 17 June 1963, p. 15.
81 Helen Hodgson, 'Medical ethics and controlled trials'.
82 CMAC SA/PAT/H/2, 'The Patients Association'. Letter from Helen Hodgson in response to Carr's article, in *Hospital and Health Management*, May 1963.
83 CMAC PP/MHP/C/1/6–10, Letters from chairman of The Patients Association concerning founding of the association, newspaper clippings re the association, advice regarding people claiming they were experimented on and the publication of Human Guinea Pigs, 1963–67; CMAC SA/PAT/H/4, Letter from Hogdson to the *Guardian*, 'Pooh-poohing human guinea pigs', 24 May 1967.

84 Hazelgrove, 'The old faith and the new science' and Hedgecoe, '"A form of practical machinery"'.
85 CMAC SA/PAT/H/1, Letter from Helen Hodgson to *Medical News*, 23 December 1963.
86 CMAC SA/PAT/H/1, John Gale, 'Patients' association', *The Observer*, 3 February 1963; Anon., 'Now a voice for patients' p. 15; Anon., 'Patients association', *The Lancet*, 19 January 1963, p. 151.
87 CMAC SA/PAT/H/1, 'The patient's voice', Letter from Helen Hodgson to the *Guardian*, 12 February 1963.
88 CMAC SA/CME/B/156, Written evidence, Patients Association, Addendum, 1967, Press release: the Patients Association: survey of teaching hospital leaflets for patients with reference to teaching activities and visiting arrangements.
89 CMAC SA/CME/B/156, Written evidence, Patients Association, 1965; Letter from Mrs U. Miller, Secretary of the Patients Association to Lord Todd, 4 November 1965.
90 CMAC SA/CME/B/156, Helen Hodgson, 'The Relationship Between Patient, Doctor and Student in a Teaching Hospital', n.d. [1965].
91 CMAC SA/PAT/H/3, Anon., 'I won't strip, Doris tells a doctor', *The Sunday Express*, 11 July 1965.
92 TNA, ED/129/23, Extract from minutes of the fourth meeting of the Todd Commission, 22 December 1965.
93 CMAC SA/CME/B/156, Written evidence Patients Association, 1965; Letter from Mrs U. Miller, Secretary of the Patients Association to Lord Todd, 4 November 1965.
94 Cmnd. 359, *Royal Commission on Medical Education 1965–8: Report* (London: HMSO, 1965) 119; TNA, ED/129/23, Letter from Gregson to Hodges, 16 December 1965.
95 For details of Helen Hodgson's complaint against University College Hospital, see CMAC SA/PAT/E/1/3 Teaching Hospitals.
96 Department of Health, *Patient's Charter* (London: HMSO, 1991).
97 CMAC SA/PAT/H/3, Letter from Helen Hodgson to the *Guardian*, 'Getting more doctors more quickly', 12 February 1965; CMAC SA/PAT/H/2, 'How am I?' Letter from Helen Hodgson to *The Times*, 29 June 1964.
98 MRC Private Papers of Margaret Stacey, MSS.184 Box 2: The NHS Complaints Procedure, address by M. Stacey, 1999: The Public Law Project Complaints Forum March 25, 1999. The NHS Complaints Procedure Three Years On: Opening Address by Meg Stacey.
99 Rights are discussed in more detail in Chapter 5, but see also Alex Mold, 'Patients' rights and the National Health Service in Britain, 1960s–1980s', *American Journal of Public Health*, 102:11 (2012), 2030–2038.
100 CMAC SA/PAT/H/2, Colin Riach, 'Woman protests at being hospital "specimen"', *Daily Express*, 10 October 1963.
101 CMAC SA/CME/B/156, Written evidence Patients Association, 1965, Letter from Mrs U. Miller, Secretary of the Patients Association to Lord Todd, 4 November 1965; CMAC SA/CME/B/156, Written evidence Patients Association, Addendum, 1967; Letter from Helen Hodgson to Mr M.W. Hodges [secretary of the Todd Commission], 16 March 1967.

102 CMAC SA/PAT/E/1/3, University College Hospital: Notes for the Guidance of Out-Patients, April 1972.
103 Richard M. Titmuss, *The Gift Relationship: From Human Blood to Social Policy* (revised edn. New York: The New Press, 1997), pp. 280–281.
104 Reubi, 'Ethics governance, modernity and human beings'.
105 CMAC SA/CME/B/156, Written evidence of the Patients Association to the Todd Commission, 1965.
106 Health Minister Keith Joseph in the House of Commons, *House of Commons Debates*, 19 June 1973, vol. 858, col. 380.
107 Jack Hallas, *CHCs in Action: A Review* (London: Nuffield Hospitals Trust, 1976); Ruth Levitt, *The People's Voice in the NHS* (King Edwards Hospital Fund for London: London, 1980). The role of the CHCs is discussed in greater detail in Chapter 2.
108 Reubi, 'Ethics governance, modernity and human beings'.

2

Representation

Patient autonomy did not just concern more say for individuals. Collective representation of the interests of patient-consumers as a whole was an important issue during the late 1960s and early 1970s. At this time, the notion that the patient-consumer should be represented within health services gathered political and practical impetus. A critical development was the creation of the CHCs. Formed as part of the reorganisation of the NHS in 1973, 207 CHCs were established in England and Wales, with similar bodies in Scotland and Northern Ireland. Each CHC was intended to 'represent the interests in the health service of the public in its district'.[1] According to the Secretary of State for Social Services, Keith Joseph, the CHCs were to be 'intensely concerned with the public's views and needs', bodies that would operate as the 'main voice of the consumer'.[2]

What this voice should say, and the extent to which it was listened to, was, however, another matter. Although political commitment to the notion of patient-consumer representation appeared to be strong, the meaning and effectiveness of this type of representation was much less definite. This chapter will examine attempts to represent the patient-consumer during the 1970s, focusing particularly on the role played by the CHCs. It will suggest that a lack of clarity about what patient-consumer representation was, who was being represented, how this could best be achieved, and its ability to have any impact on health services, beset the CHCs from the outset. Uncertainty about the meaning and purpose of patient representation manifested itself in conflicting views about the CHCs' role and effectiveness that impinged upon their ability to represent patients' interests. Moreover, the CHCs had to contend with better established and more powerful interest groups within health care such as health professionals and health service administrators.

That is not to say that the CHCs had no or little impact. The councils were able to achieve many small-scale successes at the local level, such as improving patient transport services and bettering hospital food, achievements which should not be underestimated due to their importance to patients. CHCs were also able to draw attention to deeper, more structural problems within the NHS, such as the existence of health inequalities. Yet, their ability to effect change at a wider level was severely constrained. Although the CHCs were represented by a national organisation, the Association for the Community Health Councils of England and Wales (ACHCEW), they were primarily local bodies, with little capacity to reach beyond what Rudolf Klein and Janet Lewis called the 'small change of life and work within the NHS'.[3] Beginning with the origins of the CHCs, moving on to consider the meanings of representation, and then assessing the effectiveness of the councils, this chapter will demonstrate that having a voice and being heard were not the same thing.

Origins of the CHCs

The establishment of the CHCs as bodies to represent the patient-consumer in 1974 was the product of a series of inter-related developments stretching back into the previous decade and beyond. The creation of the CHCs needs to be understood in the context of wider moves to enhance citizen and consumer representation within public services and the nationalised industries. Consumers' Councils were formed in the late 1940s to represent the consumer in industries such as coal, gas, electricity and transport. Although the Consumers' Councils were seen as being largely ineffective, their existence did denote some recognition that there was such an entity as the consumer interest and that this needed to be taken into account by utility and public service providers.[4] The Consumers' Association, established in 1956, was by no means the first autonomous organisation purporting to represent the consumer, but its activities, as discussed in the Introduction and Chapter 1, helped to establish a particular understanding of consumerism and the consumer that went 'beyond things'. Government recognition of the consumer interest and the need for consumer representation was confirmed with the creation of the Consumer Council in 1963. As Hilton notes, the Consumer Council was interested primarily in consumers as individual shoppers, but for consumer activists such as Michael Young, there was more to the good life than material possessions.[5] The establishment of the NCC under Young's chairmanship in 1975 went beyond a simple replacement of the Consumer Council which had been disbanded in 1970. The NCC was an explicit attempt by the Labour government to facilitate the representation of consumers of public services. The NCC was intended to bring the rights and protection won by consumer in the private sector into the public sector. For the NCC, the consumer was also a citizen and vice-versa.[6]

Citizen-consumer representation was also taken up in other areas of government during the late 1960s and early 1970s. An early adopter of this approach was town and country planning. The 1968 Town and Country Planning Act, and the 1969 Skeffington Report, gave the public a much greater say in development within their local communities.[7] Other mechanisms to represent the interests of the ordinary citizen included the creation, in 1967, of the Parliamentary Commissioner for Administration (the Ombudsman) who dealt with complaints against government departments, although not health.[8] As will be discussed in Chapter 3, the health service got its own ombudsman in 1973. The notion of citizen 'participation' was becoming politically fashionable, particularly on the left, with participation featuring heavily in Labour party policy documents in the late 1960s and also in the party's 1970 election manifesto.[9] The 1970s, according to Klein and Lewis, were the 'era of participation'.[10]

A key driving factor behind such developments was a rapid growth in the number of pressure groups in Britain, and a sense that politics was moving away from the traditional machinery of political parties and parliamentary representation.[11] The appearance of new social movements surrounding issues such as peace, the environment, homosexuality and gender equality were expressions of a new kind of politics concerned with questions of identity and lifestyle rather than capital and labour.[12] Connected to these movements were a plethora of voluntary organisations and pressure groups, often claiming to speak for what the architect of the welfare state, William Beveridge, called the 'distressed minorities'.[13] In areas such as housing, poverty, drug use and sexuality, voluntary organisations were formed to campaign on behalf of groups and individuals.[14] Between 1961 and 1971 the number of registered charities rose from 1,182 to 76,648. This dramatic increase can be accounted for largely by the introduction of more efficient methods for registering charities, but it is estimated that around 10,500 of these were entirely new organisations.[15]

The presence of such bodies put pressure on central government to improve services but also to take the views of users of these into account. For organisations like RICA, patients were citizen-consumers who had a right to representation within the NHS: 'If taxpayers are to pay more for the GP service, it is reasonable to expect doctors to allow "consumers" more say in running it.' But, RICA suggested, existing methods of patient representation left a great deal to be desired. The NHS, they contended,

> is subject to democratic control, but the control is very remote, embodied in a complex of committees of which the public is scarcely aware. It almost reproduces, at the administrative level, the clinical relationship: the layman is not encouraged to tell the doctor what to do.[16]

Demands for a greater say for patients were further strengthened by a series of scandals in the 1960s that exposed deficiencies within the health service and also highlighted the weakness of existing methods of patient representation. As discussed in Chapter 1, the human guinea pigs revelations, and the outcry over restrictions placed on the visiting of children in hospital, had already prompted the establishment of organisations claiming to represent the patient like NAWCH and the PA. Additional problems with the attitude of some NHS staff towards patients, particularly the elderly and mentally ill, were exposed by reports into practices at Ely Hospital, Farleigh Hospital and Whittingham Hospital.[17] Scandals like these pointed to the weakness of complaints procedures, something discussed in more detail in Chapter 3, but also highlighted the fact that patients had little voice within the existing system.

Indeed, the mechanisms for patient representation within the NHS were extremely limited before the service was reorganised in 1973. Regional Hospital Boards (RHBs) did contain non-medical members, but, according to Martin Gorsky, these tended to be outnumbered by doctors and other local elites.[18] Members of the RHB were not answerable to their local community and so were not 'representatives', Klein suggested, in any meaningful sense.[19] Jean Robinson (who was chair of the PA between 1973 and 1975 and a member of the Oxford CHC) was invited to join the Oxford RHB in the late 1960s. It was, she said,

> a very, very odd experience for me. It was all very polite and you arrived and you had a ritual glass of sherry, you were welcomed and you were told what a friendly board this is and you went in and you had a pile of papers and the Board Meetings lasted about 40 minutes and you just approved everything. I thought we are spending huge amounts of public money and nobody asks any questions.

Robinson obtained the Board's annual statistics and began to query data and practices within Oxford's hospitals: 'Then I was taken on one side by the Chair Woman, Dame Isabel Graham-Bryce, the wife of a surgeon, who said … you are asking a lot of questions and our officials are very busy people.' Robinson was eventually invited to meet the Secretary of State for Health and Social Services, Richard Crossman, because, she said, he told her that 'they really hate you in Oxford and I [Crossman] was curious to see what you did'.[20] The Labour MP for Nuneaton, Leslie Huckfield, who had served on the Birmingham RHB, recounted a similarly negative experience. Huckfield resigned from the RHB because he 'thought the composition and actions of the board were totally unrepresentative of the horizons and aspirations of the ordinary working people'.[21]

At the same time, civil servants, health managers and doctors expressed doubts about the ability of organisations operating outside of the NHS, like the PA, to represent the interests of patients. Harold Carr, Group Secretary of the Lancaster Moor Hospital Management Committee took issue with the notion that patients were a distinct group who needed representation. He argued that 'The concept that the community can be divided into "the patient class" and "the others" is ill-conceived and away from reality'.[22] An article in *Medical News* suggested that 'more than average resentment against the profession [is] felt by many members of the Patients Association. Many have "chips on their shoulders"'.[23] Despite Hodgson's assertion that 'The only organisation which endeavours to represent *all* patients in *all* spheres is the Patients Association', officials at the Department of Health were sceptical about the PA's representational capacity.[24] Civil servants contended that

> they [the PA] have no real local network, the total membership has never risen above 2/3000 ... In other words it is nothing like the body its title and its few leading lights claim it to be, though it occasionally does some good as a ginger group.[25]

An official noted that the PA 'has not been regarded as sufficiently representative of consumers of health services to merit special recognition. They have been apt to take up issues on which they have inadequate information and pursue them to unreasonable lengths.'[26] Of course, the questions raised about the PA's ability to represent patient-consumers by doctors, administrators and officials could, in some ways, be seen as evidence of their effectiveness. As Janet Newman and John Clarke point out, officials tend to distrust user- or patient-controlled organisations, despite the fact that these can be capable of contributing positively to public debate.[27] Civil servants' scepticism about the PA could be seen as being the product of a desire to enhance patient representation in the NHS, but within limits acceptable to existing actors in the field, such as health professionals, administrators and officials.

An opportunity to strengthen patient representation inside the NHS arose during the various attempts to reorganise the service that occurred throughout the 1960s and early 1970s. Both Labour and the Conservatives accepted the need for a restructuring of the NHS, and particularly the removal of the tripartite system of hospitals, family practitioner services and local authority provided services.[28] In 1968, the Labour Minister of Health, Kenneth Robinson, put forward a Green Paper proposing changes to the administrative structure of the NHS. The Green Paper called for the establishment of area authorities who would have responsibility for providing services and area boards that would manage and allocate resources.[29] What was missing from the Green Paper, however, as the PA was quick to point out in a letter to the minister, was any form of patient representation.[30] The PA contended that 'There should be consumer representation at all levels' and the organisation proposed the establishment of a National Patients Consumer Council and Local Patients Consumer Groups.[31] Other organisations also criticised the Green Paper for the apparent absence of patient representation. The Disablement Income Group (DIG) asserted that 'At national, area and local level the consumer of the services planned (at such cost) must be the participant: he must feel he can contribute as well as receive.'[32] Even the rather anodyne Consumer Council suggested that 'that the Green Paper devotes insufficient attention to the participation of local interests in the running of the area boards'.[33]

The lack of patient representation within Robinson's Green Paper, together with a lukewarm reception from both health professionals and administrators, meant that work began almost immediately on another Green Paper under the new minister, Richard Crossman. In his Foreword to the second Green Paper on reorganisation, published in 1970, Crossman conceded that the lack of participation of local people 'would have made the day-to-day running of the health service too remote from the people it serves'. He accepted the argument that 'there must be more, not less, local participation'. To provide this, Crossman's paper proposed the establishment of District Committees 'on which people drawn from the local community and people working in the local health service can contribute to the work of running the district's services'.[34]

Crossman did not get a chance to develop his proposals as the general election of 1970 resulted in a change of government, meaning that the Conservative Health Minister, Keith Joseph, took up the issue of NHS reorganisation. Although Joseph was sceptical initially about community participation at the district level, his Consultative Document on NHS reorganisation, published in 1971, proposed the introduction of Community Health Councils.[35] The CHCs would 'ensure that in making plans and operating services, area authorities take full account of the views the public they serve'.[36] The Consultative Document, and the CHCs in particular, were criticised in both the House of Commons and the House of Lords. Three main concerns about the CHCs were expressed. Firstly, it was suggested that the proposed method of appointment to CHCs, nomination by the Area Health Authority (AHA), meant that the councils would lack independence. The Conservative Baroness Young questioned whether 'these people [will] be prepared to speak out against the system, if necessary?'[37] Secondly, MPs and Lords were unconvinced that the CHCs would be truly representative bodies. Labour MP for Huddersfield West, Kenneth Lomas, said 'It is not use talking about democracy unless one is prepared to practice it. Community health councils are to be appointed rather than elected by those to whom they are responsible. This is a bad principle'.[38] Finally, doubts were expressed about the power of the CHCs. The Labour peer Baroness Serota described the councils as 'toothless and vague and really lacking any real powers'.[39] Shirley Williams, Labour MP for Hitchen, called the CHCs 'the strangest bunch of administrative eunuchs that any Department has yet foisted upon the House – a kind of seraglio of the Secretary of State of utterly useless and emasculated bodies which have no powers'.[40]

Pressure to strengthen the role played by CHCs also came from patient-consumer organisations. Margaret Belson, leader of NAWCH, said that the organisation was supportive of the CHCs in principle, but felt 'the position of the Community Health Councils, excluded from decision making, "reacting to Management", dependent upon the AHA, to be a weak one'.[41] Similarly, Mary Appleby of the National Association for Mental Health (NAMH) commented that 'We do not believe that volunteers will come forward to serve unless a meaningful role is spelled out for them as members giving an opportunity to promote and pursue consumer interests at management level.'[42] Such representations, together with Michael Young's assertion that 'The growth of voluntary bodies and the spirit of participation in local affairs has been one of the great phenomena of the second half of this century. Government has not yet responded to this new mood in an organised way. It has now a chance of doing so which may not recur'[43] appears to have had an impact on Joseph. Although Young's proposal for the establishment of Neighbourhood Councils to represent consumers of national and local services did not come to fruition, Joseph told the Environment Secretary Peter Walker that 'For my part I intend to put a lot of emphasis on the contribution to the National Health Service that can be made by strong, locally formed, community health councils'.[44]

In order to strengthen the CHCs, and to respond to the various criticisms levelled at them, the DHSS altered the way in which appointments to the CHCs were to be made. Ministers and officials rejected the idea that the CHCs should be directly elected. Following a meeting with Joseph, one civil servant told another that

> the measures we are taking to secure participation in decision-making by doctors, nurses etc. are generally helpful, though they are not, strictly speaking, democracy in the sense of government by the elected representatives of the consumers.[45]

To justify such a decision, the DHSS pointed to the low turn-out for elections to Parish Councils, and the complication and cost of putting electoral machinery in place for the CHCs.[46] The Department did, however, want to counter the accusation that the CHCs would be the creature of management, so instead of being selected purely by the AHA, it was decided that local voluntary organisations should be represented on the CHCs. The Department toyed with the idea of creating a list of 'approved' organisations who could nominate CHC members, including groups like the PA, NAWCH, the Red Cross, Age Concern and the NAMH, but officials conceded that 'Unless it is a pretty long list it could well cause more trouble than satisfaction.'[47] Nonetheless, the principle of voluntary organisation representation on the CHCs was accepted, something which demonstrated clearly the significance of such groups in this field. It was eventually agreed that half of each CHC's members would be appointed by the local authority, one third by voluntary organisations and the rest by the Regional Health Authority (RHA), the body responsible for strategy and resource allocation in each region.[48]

Despite the DHSS's attempts to reform the proposed CHCs, reaction to these bodies in parliament and the press was not entirely positive. The CHCs were seen in one of two diametrically opposed ways. On the one hand, critics complained that the CHCs would be too powerful, and on the other that they were not powerful enough. Health professionals were concerned that the CHCs would interfere in clinical matters. A.M. Lamb, the Deputy Chief Nursing Officer, was worried about proposals that CHCs should assess the quality of health services in each district, and the Chief Medical Officer for Wales wanted to make sure that CHCs would not advise on clinical effectiveness.[49] Even Joseph himself 'was anxious that CHCs should not provide forums for mischief makers'.[50] Most critics of the proposed CHCs, however, felt that these bodies would be too weak. Labour MP George Thomas contended that though the CHCs were 'the supposed watchdogs for the consumers', they lacked any real independence. The CHCs, he asserted, were to 'start life with false teeth; they have no bite'.[51] The *Observer* called them 'paper tigers' and the *Guardian* 'very tame watchdogs'.[52]

Meanings of representation

The contradictory response to the establishment of the CHCs can be explained, at least in part, by confusion about what representation meant, who was being represented and what it was supposed to achieve. As Klein and Lewis remarked 'There are few more cloudy concepts than that of "consumer representation".'[53] Newman and Clarke suggest that the notion of representation is based on an essentialised form of identity, where representatives 'stand for' specific categories of people, be they young or old, black or white, male or female.[54] Representation was thus distinguishable from 'participation' and 'involvement', which were supposedly more active, resulting in direct engagement with decision and policy-making.[55] Observers and the CHCs themselves, when describing the activities of the CHCs, however, sometimes used these terms synonymously suggesting a perceived overlap between participation and representation.[56]

The legislation that created the CHCs did not define how these were supposed to 'represent the interests in the health service of the public in its district'.[57] Social policy expert Chris Ham outlined three ways in which bodies could be representative: firstly, they were freely elected; secondly they were typical of the wider community; and finally, they were able to act as agents for the people that they claimed to represent.[58] The DHSS had, of course, dismissed the idea that the CHCs be elected, but it was unclear whether the councils were intended to be literally representative of the communities they served, or act as their agents. Research by Klein and Lewis conducted during the early days of the CHCs suggested that the councils were not representative in the sense of including a proportional number of members from different communities or population groups. A national survey of CHC members in England and Wales indicated that these were a 'distorting mirror', offering an inaccurate reflection of the population.[59] Klein and Lewis found that the CHCs tended to be made up of middle-class, middle-aged people to the extent that 'If they represent anyone, it is the solidly established and settled citizen, well-entrenched in his or her own community'.[60]

Issues surrounding the representativeness of the CHCs were further exacerbated by a lack of clarity about who it was that was supposed to be being represented. CHCs were described variously as representing 'patients', 'consumers', the 'public' and the 'community', but these different actors were not necessarily the same, and nor did they all want the same things. Defining the nature of the 'community' the CHCs were supposed to be representing was very problematic. Mike Gerrard, Director of ACHCEW from 1977–83, said that there were 'constant imponderables': what was a district, or a community, or a patient, or a user, and how were these to be defined?[61] Technically, each CHC was responsible for representing the interests of people living in their health district (the smallest administrative unit within the reorganised NHS), although these varied in population size from 86,000 to 530,000, and in nature from densely populated inner-city boroughs, to sparsely peopled rural areas.[62]

Beyond these pre-imposed communities there were other, potentially conflicting, ways of defining community. Certain groups, such as the elderly, the mentally ill and ethnic minorities, formed 'communities of interest' which may have had more in common than people living within certain geographical boundaries.[63] Another potential meaning of 'community' derived from the notion of 'community medicine'. Again, this was an ill-defined concept, but broadly speaking community medicine was concerned with the population rather than the individual, and with prevention rather than cure. Following the reorganisation of the NHS, Medical Officers of Health (local public health doctors) became 'community physicians'.[64]

For the CHCs, the promotion of community medicine had two potential implications: firstly, that they should concern themselves with collective issues as much as individual troubles; and secondly, that they should be interested in the wider causes of health problems.

Theoretical distinctions between different types of community translated into real-world difficulties for the CHCs. Gerrard stated that the CHCs were 'never able to say with absolute certainty that they represented their districts in a personal way'.[65] As Ruth Levitt, editor of the newsletter *CHC News*, noted, 'An acknowledged problem for all CHCs is to know exactly who is the public that they are obliged to represent.'[66] CHCs, she suggested, had to

> discover who 'the public' was in any particular case, how it was going to be able to express a view, and how the community health council as an organisation was going to accommodate the views of its own members to the views that were being expressed to it by the public. Often, community health councils have found themselves not necessarily in agreement with some members of the public whose interests they represent.[67]

Many CHCs were conscious of their lack of representativeness in an absolute sense. West Birmingham CHC stated in their annual report for 1977–78 that 'CHCs are frequently accused of representing nobody but themselves'.[68] Klein and Lewis found that CHCs did not 'see themselves as spokesmen of the community but as guardians of the community's interests, and as such responsible for investigating and inspecting the provision of healthcare in the district'.[69]

Indeed, awareness about the questionable nature of the representation offered by CHCs operated as a spur to action for some councils. Christine Hogg, Secretary of Kensington and Chelsea CHC, and long-time analyst of CHC activities, said that

> You could use it [lack of representativeness] as a way of saying well you can't speak for yourself, you've actually got to find out what other people think, that's why we need to do outreach to the public, that's why you need to go round and talk to local groups and ask them their views, that is why we need to talk to the voluntary sector, that's why we need to co-opt members because you can't talk from your own personal experience of your GP, you've got to find out what other people think.[70]

A key activity for CHCs was asking local people for their views on health services in their district. For many CHCs, this was achieved by conducting public opinion surveys. West Birmingham CHC noted that although surveys could be 'very time-consuming, especially those undertaken by interview in order to probe deeply' these could 'give a CHC a valid feel of the community's views. It is much better to do this than to rely on pressure groups or individual complaints which, however valid in themselves, are fortunately rarely typical.'[71] Surveys were used by CHCs to identify gaps in services. Brent CHC, for example, conducted a survey in 1978 of abortion facilities in the district and found these to be inadequate. The CHC drew attention to their findings in their newsletter, and then pressed (successfully) for the establishment of a day care abortion clinic.[72] CHC surveys also monitored general levels of satisfaction with services. Kensington and Chelsea CHC found that patients were unhappy with GP services in the district, particularly with appointment systems, something the CHC worked with the Family Practitioner Committee to improve.[73] Methods other than the survey were also employed to solicit local views. West Birmingham CHC, for instance, set up a 'Panel of the Public' in 1979. This group was made up of 200–250 people from the district that were broadly representative of the district in terms of age, gender and area of residence. The panel was intended, the council said 'to provide the CHC with a representative group of people who are [a] microcosm of the population of the District in every way except that they know more about the Health Service than ordinary people'.[74]

As well as finding out what patients thought of services, the CHCs also attempted to represent groups and individuals who may otherwise have struggled to make their voices heard. Many CHCs acted upon the DHSS's suggestion that they take a special interest in services for groups like the mentally ill, the physically disabled, the elderly and ethnic minorities.[75] According to Klein and Lewis, voluntary organisations involved in such areas tended to be well represented on CHCs.[76] Attention to the needs of the vulnerable was also something reflected in the early activities of the CHCs. South Birmingham CHC, for example, set up working groups to examine issues such as the care of the elderly; maternity and child health; acute hospital services; the mentally ill; and the physically disabled.[77]

In order to speak for patients (whether these were in disadvantaged groups or not), the CHCs felt that they had to be known to their local communities. The councils spent a good deal of time and resources, especially in the early days, publicising themselves and their activities. CHCs produced newsletters, annual reports and other literature; they held fun days and had stalls at local events; they advertised their services in local media and even on the side of buses; and some had 'shop-front' facilities where they encouraged members of the public to drop in.[78] Despite these efforts, many CHCs complained about public ignorance and even apathy. In 1978, four years after the CHCs had been established, North Surrey CHC reported that

> One of the CHC's most difficult tasks is how to make the public aware of its existence. Although the Council's office is situated in a busy shopping parade, and the number of our callers, over a 1000 a year, is well above average, members

are fully aware that the majority of people in the locality have never heard of the CHC let alone the important role is has to play as an integral part of the National Health Service.[79]

Jack Hallas, in a review of the CHCs in action for the Nuffield Provincial Hospitals Trust noted that 'Very few councils can be said to have achieved a solid following of supporters amongst their district population.'[80] Writing in the national newsletter for CHCs, *CHC News* in 1975 Bernadette Fallon reported on a survey conducted in a 'large town' which had found that only 9 out of 94 people had heard of the CHC, and only 7 of these had any idea about what it did. Fallon commented 'However [*sic*] successful individual publicity exercises may be, though, the fundamental problem remains the same. Until they become ill, people are not interested in the health service.'[81] Irene Watson, Secretary of Hull CHC, echoed such a sentiment in *CHC News* a few months later. Watson suggested that 'the majority of the members of the public will remain fairly dormant as regards ideas for improving the health service until such time as they themselves are affected'.[82] The apparent lack of public interest in the CHCs again pointed to the fact that these were not literally representative of the public, but rather acting as their agents. Questions about the nature of representation offered by the CHCs did not go away, and had a considerable impact on the way that these organisations operated.

Effectiveness

The ability of the CHCs to represent the patient-consumer was shaped by the nature of the councils themselves, the role they were expected to play and the relationships that they formed with health professionals and administrators. CHCs were endowed with a limited number of rights and a wider set of responsibilities. CHCs had the right to obtain information from health authorities, to visit hospitals and other facilities, to attend AHA meetings (but not vote), to play some role in planning local services and to be consulted on hospital closures.[83] Such rights were accompanied by a long list of matters to which the CHC 'might wish to direct their attention', as suggested by the DHSS. These included issues such as: the effectiveness and planning of services; cooperation between health services and local authorities; standards of care and facilities; waiting periods for inpatients and outpatients; the quality of catering in institutions; and helping patients to make complaints.[84] Many CHCs interpreted these duties quite widely. A handbook for CHC members produced by the Nuffield Provincial Hospitals Trust stated that the councils 'must be concerned not only with what happens to 80-year-old Mary Smith when she goes into the geriatric unit, but also how large-scale resources are allocated'.[85] Levitt, in her 1980 study of the CHCs, found that most councils were active on three fronts: giving advice to people on how to access services or make a complaint; commenting on plans and dealing with proposals to close facilities; and improving public knowledge about disease prevention.[86]

Such activities were carried out by paid staff and also by CHC members who volunteered their time and energy. The local authority appointed half of CHC members; voluntary organisations nominated a third; and the rest were selected by the RHA. The CHCs were allowed to employ a Secretary (later called the Chief Officer) and occupy their own premises away from local health care facilities if they chose to do so. Although the DHSS had envisaged originally that an individual already working within the NHS bureaucracy would fill the role of Secretary, the position was openly advertised. Of 60 CHC Secretaries interviewed by Hallas just after the establishment of the councils less than half (27) had NHS experience, with the others coming from a range of backgrounds including voluntary organisations, local government and education.[87] Some of the Secretaries, such as Hogg, were young and dynamic, others perhaps less so. There were, Hogg suggested, 'quite a few bit jobs for like older men, you know like retired colonels'.[88] Similarly, the level of engagement of the other members of the CHC with its work varied considerably. The size of the CHC was not specified, but most contained between 20 and 30 members. Non-attendance of members at CHC meetings was an issue for councils. East Birmingham CHC cited the non-participation of some CHC members, especially the local authority representatives as one of the constraints hampering their work. In 1976/77 they recorded that local authority members attended 45.7 per cent of meetings, in comparison to the regional health authority appointees who came to 60 per cent of meetings and the voluntary organisation appointees who attended 85.7 per cent of sessions.[89]

Differences in the energy of the CHC secretary and membership was just one aspect of what amounted to considerable variability between CHCs both in terms of what they actually did, and what they thought they should be doing. Klein and Lewis found that CHC members understood their role in one of three ways. Firstly, the majority of members saw themselves as representing the views of the community to those running the health services. Secondly, there were members who believed themselves to be middlemen, operating between the consumers and the management. Finally, a few CHC members regarded themselves as representatives of the NHS to consumers.[90] Klein and Lewis's early research was refined by a later study of the CHCs, conducted by Carol Lupton and Graham Moon in 1989. Based on questionnaires sent to all CHCs in England and Wales, Lupton and Moon identified five types of CHC. 'Consumer advocates' worked actively for consumer rights, but within existing structures. 'District Health Authority (DHA) Partners' worked closely with the DHA in decision-making and were more likely than other types of CHC to actively 'sell' DHA plans to the consumer. 'Independent arbiters' saw their primary role as working between consumers and the DHA, and not taking the side of either. 'Independent challengers' were on the side of the consumer, and often tended to challenge the government and the DHA. Finally, the 'patient's friend' worked for the consumer on the individual level, rather than for consumers' rights in general. Distribution across the different types of CHC was relatively even: of the sample 14.6 per cent were 'consumer advocates'; 25.4 per cent 'District Health Authority partners'; 21.6 per cent 'independent arbiters'; 19.1 per cent 'independent challengers' and 19.1 per cent were the 'patient's friend'.[91]

Clearly, there were considerable differences between CHCs in how they saw their role and how they went about fulfilling this. Such variability was rooted in the rather vague guidance issued about what CHCs should do, something that was in turn underpinned by the difficulty of defining the meaning and purpose of representation within the NHS. The variability between the CHCs posed significant problems for the CHCs in practical as well as theoretical terms. The chief complaint made against the CHCs by their critics was their variability, indeed, it was one of the reasons put forward in support of their disestablishment in 2003, something discussed in further detail in Chapter 6. In defence of the CHCs, Hogg pointed out that all local services varied considerably, and so it was unsurprising that CHCs did too.[92] Gerrard admitted that the variability argument did contain a 'fatal grain of truth', but what was more important 'at the time was to establish a patient centred bridgehead at the gates of the NHS'.[93]

Gerrard's remark also hinted at a sense that the CHCs were required to defend the patient against an unspecified foe. CHCs were described repeatedly as 'watchdogs', and a handbook produced for CHC members in 1974 was entitled *Mounting the Health Guard*.[94] What, or who the CHCs were supposed to guard against was unclear. Hogg spoke of being motivated by anger at gaps in services and poor standards, but also about the way in which the NHS operated as 'a closed system, it was actually largely run for the benefit of the doctors'.[95] Such feelings generated the potential for conflict between CHCs and health professionals and managers. Once again, CHCs varied widely over time and location with respect to their relationship with other actors in the health field. Hogg found that

> if you had a reasonable relationship and you were talking reasonable sense, you had your district management team and at least some of them would be on your side and at least half the consultants would be on your side and half the consultants would like to see you dead.[96]

Gerrard reported that most of the early CHC secretaries found 'the management face of their AHA overbearing or cynical, and reluctant to provide any information which it felt might be used against it'.[97] Once again, such tensions were rooted in uncertainty about the nature and authority of the CHCs representative role. Chris Ham, in a study of the CHCs' role in NHS planning found that 68 per cent of CHCs had some form of dispute or misunderstanding with health authorities about the meaning of consultation. Furthermore, there were 'signs that administrators are becoming more skilful in using CHCs to achieve their own policy objectives, and there is a clear possibility that CHCs may be manipulated to bring about changes not of their own choosing'.[98]

If relationships with administrators could be tense, dealings with health professionals had the potential to be even more so. Although the British Medical Association (BMA) welcomed the establishment of the CHCs, which they saw as protecting the consumer against the power of management, doctors and other professionals were unequivocal that the councils should not stray into the clinical domain.[99] The case of abortion services and South Birmingham CHC illustrates the dynamic well. A survey carried out by the CHC 'revealed a very considerable gap' in the provision of abortion in the city.[100] Of the 667 terminations of pregnancy performed in South Birmingham Health District in 1975, only 41 (6 per cent) were carried out on the NHS, a sharp contrast to other cities in the England such as Manchester, where 64 per cent of abortions were conducted within the NHS, and Newcastle, where the NHS abortion rate was as high as 95 per cent.[101]

The low number of NHS abortions performed in Birmingham was explained by the fact that many doctors working in the city refused to carry out the procedure. Under the Abortion Act (1967) doctors were entitled to object to performing an abortion; they were under no obligation to carry out the procedure if a woman requested it. Indeed, the Abortion Act did not legislate for abortion on demand, but rather stipulated a series of situations where termination of pregnancy would not be a crime under the Offences Against the Person Act (1861). Two doctors had to agree that the continuation of the pregnancy was likely to result in damage to the woman's mental or physical health, or that of her existing children. Abortion was also permitted when there was a risk that the child would be born with serious physical abnormalities.[102] Doctors, therefore, had considerable individual and collective control over the provision of abortion.[103] Particularly significant, as Gayle Davis and Roger Davidson have shown, was the role played by senior doctors in each area. Such physicians could behave like 'Big White Chiefs', effectively dictating policy on termination, either for or against, within their jurisdiction.[104] In Birmingham, the senior obstetrician gynaecologist was Professor Hugh McLaren, a Roman Catholic and well-known opponent of abortion.[105] McLaren prevented any gynaecologist working under his control from performing a termination in all but a fraction of cases throughout the 1970s.[106] The vast majority of abortions in Birmingham were, therefore, either performed in private clinics or through voluntary agencies, such as the Birmingham (later British) Pregnancy Advisory Service (BPAS), a group set up in the city specifically to provide low-cost terminations for women.[107]

Abortion was a contentious issue for South Birmingham CHC (SBCHC), as members held contrasting personal views on the provision of termination. In May 1975, the CHC debated the matter in response to a bill put forward by MP James White which proposed a number of restrictions to abortion provision.[108] Angela Court, who was a member of the CHC through her work with the sexual health advice organisation, the Brook Advisory Centre, was vigorously opposed to any limitations being placed on existing provision, whereas Father B.N. O'Malley, from the Irish Development Association, was equally against the notion that a woman had a right to an abortion.[109] Nonetheless, the CHC agreed by a majority of twelve to six to submit a resolution to the Parliamentary Select Committee debating White's Bill stating that 'The NHS has a duty to provide this service and to ensure that all women have equal access to such a service, regardless of where they live within the United Kingdom.'[110] A similar statement was made by the CHC four years later when discussing the Corrie Bill, which also proposed limitations to the Abortion Act, including the restriction of abortion in private and voluntary sector facilities.[111] SBCHC passed (by nine votes to seven) the motion that:

> while being aware of differing personal views of members on the issue of termination of pregnancy, [SBCHC] considers that the CHC is a body charged with the responsibility of representing the interests and needs of the public, and notes that although the need for terminations is evidenced by the statistics, in South Birmingham women are deprived of NHS facilities for which provision should be made under the 1967 Abortion Act, and therefore rely heavily on the private sector.[112]

The majority of SBCHC members seemed to believe that whatever their personal views on abortion, the NHS had a duty to provide this service, a duty which was not being fulfilled in the Birmingham area. It would appear that the CHC was broadly in line with the views of the wider public on this topic. Although abortion provision was still a sensitive issue, from the late 1960s onwards the majority of people in Britain were in favour of termination of pregnancy in some circumstances, and a minority thought that abortion should be available on demand.[113] Taking on the issue of abortion provision was thus a legitimate area of activity for SBCHC as a body tasked with representing local people within the NHS. However, unlike some of the voluntary groups that lobbied for the expansion of abortion services, SBCHC did not advocate a woman's right to choose so much as her right to receive a specific service through the NHS.[114] This view was similar to that put forward by the Lane Committee, which investigated the working of the Abortion Act, and concluded in 1974 that the NHS had a responsibility to provide adequate services for women seeking terminations in every part of the country.[115] Naomi Pfeffer has argued that 'In effect, [Lane] Committee members associated citizenship with entitlement to free care from the NHS and with a right to therapeutic abortion.'[116] The Royal Commission on the NHS (the Merrison Commission) went even further in 1979. The Commission highlighted the significant regional variation in NHS abortion rates and called for an expansion of facilities, recommending that the health service provide 75 per cent of all abortions.[117] SBCHC thus seemed to be in line not only with what expert committees recommended, but also with a wider view of the patient-consumer put forward in this period which emphasised the right to receive a democratically agreed level of service.

Seeing abortion as an issue of service provision led SBCHC to lobby for the development of NHS abortion facilities in the area. The council attempted to put pressure on the AHA and the RHA to provide more terminations, and though they seem to have had some support from area health officials, they met with considerable resistance from medical professionals. In July 1976, the West Midlands Association of CHCs (a body made up of the CHCs for South, Central, North, East and West Birmingham) recommended to the RHA that NHS abortion services in the region be expanded. The RHA responded by forming a working party to examine the issue made up of health professionals with only one 'lay' member, and no representative from the CHCs.[118] SBCHC's Maternity and Child Welfare group condemned this move, and argued that 'a committee with a much wider representation should have been set up since the present deplorable situation in the Area regarding the availability of NHS abortions has stemmed from the attitudes of the medical professions'.[119] Yet local officials felt unable to challenge doctors' control of the abortion issue: the AHA told the Birmingham CHCs that 'The Authority is aware of the small proportion of legal abortions performed in NHS hospitals in both Birmingham and the West Midlands. Equally it must recognise the right of each clinician in contract with it to interpret current legislation and to practice accordingly.'[120]

In an attempt to remedy the situation, SBCHC lobbied for the appointment of a gynaecologist willing to perform NHS abortions.[121] The AHA working party on family planning services agreed with the CHC, also recommending that a new consultant with more liberal views on abortion be appointed in 1978.[122] Wider support for such a policy was also to be found in the Lane Committee's recommendation that when appointing a consultant gynaecologist in areas where statutory abortion provision was low, appointment bodies should discriminate against doctors who would not perform abortions.[123] Yet, despite the pressure exerted by SBCHC and the AHA, it remained difficult to obtain an NHS abortion in the region: in 1978 22 per cent of terminations in the West Midlands were carried out on the NHS, compared with 90 per cent in the Northern Region and 52 per cent nationally.[124] It was not until the 1980s (after McLaren had retired) that an expansion in NHS facilities in the city was seriously contemplated.[125]

Obviously, SBCHC failed in their attempts to widen NHS abortion provision in Birmingham. Given the extent to which the abortion issue was medicalised, and the way in which senior gynaecologists were able to control local policy on abortion provision, it is perhaps not surprising the CHC made little headway. The CHC had very limited powers: they could lobby the AHA and the DHA, they could talk to the press and highlight the inequality of service being provided, but it is difficult to see how they could have broken the stranglehold of the consultants. Even though they had the partial support of the AHA (who did start to pay for abortions to be provided by other agencies, like BPAS) SBCHC could not interfere with clinical autonomy on the abortion issue. Local authorities could ignore representations from the CHC and so too, most pertinently in this instance, could doctors. The case of SBCHC and abortion services in Birmingham demonstrates clearly that representing the interests of patients was not the same as actively participating in decisions about service delivery.

The CHCs were able to make more impact around less dramatic, but nonetheless important, improvements to provision at the local level. A flavour of the kinds of issues where CHCs were able to achieve a measure of success can be gained from their annual reports. One area of accomplishment surrounded getting hospitals to take into account the needs of ethnically diverse populations in their area. Both Brent CHC and Central Birmingham CHC reported success in obliging local hospitals to provide halal and vegetarian food for Asian patients. Brent CHC also set up a working group to translate menus into Gujarati and Urdu, and Central Birmingham CHC got a local hospital to employ a translator to assist patients who did not speak English.[126] Other improvements surrounded transport services: Central Birmingham CHC lobbied successfully for the construction of a bridge between the Queen Elizabeth Hospital and the train station and bus stops, as well as for new bus services to and from the hospital.[127]

Such victories, though they were undoubtedly important to patients, could be dismissed for being concerned with Klein and Lewis's 'small change' of hospital life, areas that did not threaten the power or authority of health professionals. Yet, there were other, more clinical, victories too. Brent CHC was successful in their campaign to establish a day care abortion centre, demonstrating that results were possible in this highly medicalised area.[128] Central Birmingham CHC were able to get a new health centre set up in the Balsall Heath area of the city and make improvements in arranging prescriptions for patients discharged from hospital.[129] West Birmingham CHC listed areas of success and failure in their 1978 annual report. On the positive side, they reported service improvements such as a reduction in waiting times for gynaecology appointments, the construction of new operating theatres and more ambulances. On the negative side, the CHC said that they were unable to reduce waiting lists for eye operations or increase the availability of short-stay accommodation.[130] CHCs also gave considerable support to individuals, particularly around the making of complaints, an issue discussed in more detail in Chapter 3.

On the management side, CHCs once again had mixed results. Although CHCs' statutory powers were limited, they did have the right to be consulted about hospital closures. The AHA were required to consult the CHC if they were planning on closing a local hospital, and if the CHC opposed the closure they could appeal to the Secretary of State. Between 1974 and 1977 106 hospital closures were proposed. The CHCs opposed nine of the closures, but the Secretary of State approved all of these.[131] CHC protests could evidently be ignored. However, according to Hogg, hospital closures did provide CHCs with leverage to achieve improvements in other areas. She said that 'closures were an enormous opportunity for negotiation to do something for community services and the Cinderella services'. By strategtically not opposing the closures of some units Kensington and Chelsea CHC was able to lobby for the establishment of other facilities, often catering for under-served populations, such as the homeless.[132]

The impact of the CHCs on wider issues, particularly those relating to structural factors, was, however, more questionable. The CHCs had limited capacity to achieve change at this level. Through their actions CHCs could hint at deeper problems, such as health inequalities, but they were unable to do much about these. In part, this was because of their local status and restricted remit. The establishment of ACHCEW in 1976, did, however, give the CHCs a national voice. Mike Gerrard, who was director of ACHCEW from 1977 to 1983, asserted that the organisation was a 'diplomatic initiative, on the one hand with government, the health service, the professions and the academic and voluntary organisations with whom we wished to establish working relations, and on the other, with CHCs'.[133] Through ACHCEW, and its publications such as *CHC News*, the CHCs were able to offer a collective critique of government health policies, something which, Hogg suggests, caused concern within Whitehall.[134] ACHCEW's activities, together with somewhat ambivalent support from the CHCs, some of which thought that, as local bodies, the CHCs should not play a role in national policy, meant that the organisation was threatened repeatedly with closure.[135]

Conclusion

By the end of the 1970s, the CHCs themselves appeared to be in danger. The Merrison Commission, which had been tasked with reviewing all aspects of the NHS, heard evidence from every CHC in the country and was largely complimentary about the councils. In 1979, the Commission stated that 'In our view CHCs have been an experiment which should be supported further ... They need to be involved in the formative stages of policy development.'[136] However, the change of government later that year also heralded a change in attitude towards the CHCs in particular and patient consumerism in general. The publication of the consultative paper, *Patients First* by the Conservative government in 1979 placed the future of the CHCs, and the whole notion of specific bodies for consumer representation within the health service, in doubt. The document recommended a 'restructuring' of AHAs so that members would be less 'remote' from local services. Such a move, the paper suggested, made the 'need for separate consumer representation in these circumstances less clear'. The Government welcomed 'views on whether community health councils should be retained'.[137] Predictably enough, opinion was divided. The National Association of Health Authorities supported the abolition of the CHCs, and though the BMA voted by a small margin to scrap the councils the General Medical Services Committee of the BMA thought that they should stay, as did several regional health authorities.[138] An editorial in *The Lancet* argued 'Rather than disband them [CHCs], now would seem a good moment to give them the commitment and support necessary to make the most of their potential.'[139]

The CHCs survived, albeit, according to Gerrard, in a 'neutered' form.[140] Yet, their existence appeared to be ever more anachronistic as the meaning of patient consumerism, and thus representation, began to change. The 1980s saw the Conservative government begin to reshape patient consumerism. What the Secretary of Hackney and City CHC, Fedelma Winkler, called the 'supermarket model', where patients were seen 'in the same way as supermarkets, and so health service managers talk about the "customer"', appeared to be moving centre-stage.[141] This market-style approach to patient consumerism focused more on the demands of the individual patient-consumer rather than the collective needs of patient-consumers. Group representation was thus less important as individuals were thought to be best able to determine their own requirements. By the early 1980s, the 'era of representation' seemed to have come to an end.

The end of the era of representation did not, however, mark the end of CHCs, which continued until 2003. But, doubts about the need for the CHCs raised in *Patients First*, and in many subsequent documents and discussions, also generated questions about what this experiment had achieved. The meaning and purpose of patient-consumer representation as manifested within the CHCs was always uncertain, and it was, therefore, difficult to ascertain what the role of CHCs was and how successful they were in fulfilling it. The CHCs had a limited capacity to effect change, as their activities were constrained by more powerful groups in the field (such as health professionals and managers) and they were further hamstrung by their own restricted remit. Despite these constraints, the CHCs did have some successes, particularly around improvements to daily life for patients in the NHS.

Moreover, the true significance of the CHCs lay not so much in a balance sheet of success or failure, but in the fact that they existed at all. The establishment and maintenance of dedicated bodies to represent the patient-consumer within the NHS was indicative of recognition that patients could no longer be ignored. The patient voice had been added to the cacophony of noises within the health care arena. Being heard was not, as this chapter has demonstrated, the same as being listened to, and in order to bring about change more powerful mechanisms were clearly required. Other tools, such as the ability to complain and the language of rights, were needed to prise open a closed system.

Notes

1 Department of Health and Social Security, *Community Health Councils: HRC (74)4*, January 1974.
2 *House of Commons Debates*, 19 June 1973, vol. 858, col. 380.
3 Rudolf Klein and Janet Lewis, *The Politics of Consumer Representation: A Study of Community Health Councils* (London: Centre for Studies in Social Policy, 1976), pp. 139–140.
4 Matthew Hilton, *Consumerism in Twentieth Century Britain: The Search for a Historical Movement* (Cambridge: Cambridge University Press, 2003), pp. 145–149.
5 *Ibid.*, pp. 228–241; Lawrence Black, 'Which?craft in post-war Britain: the Consumers' Association and the politics of affluence', *Albion*, 36:1 (2004), 52–82.
6 See, for example, National Consumer Council (NCC), *The Fourth Right of Citizenship: A Review of Local Advice Services* (NCC: London, 1977); National Consumer Council, *The Consumer and the State: Getting Value for Public Money* (NCC: London, 1979).

7   Steven Fielding, *The Labour Governments 1964–1970 Volume 1: Labour and Cultural Change* (Manchester: Manchester University Press, 2003).
8   Glen O'Hara, 'Parties, people and parliament: Britain's "ombudsman" and the politics of the 1960s', *Journal of British Studies*, 50:3 (2011), 690–714.
9   Fielding, *The Labour Governments*, pp. 191–196; Labour Party Manifesto 1970, www.labour-party.org.uk/manifestos/1970/1970-labour-manifesto.shtml, accessed 2 August 2012.
10 Klein and Lewis, *The Politics of Consumer Representation*, p. 13.
11 Lawrence Black, *Redefining British Politics: Culture, Consumerism and Participation, 1954–70* (Basingstoke: Palgrave Macmillan, 2010); Geoff Eley, *Forging Democracy: The History of the Left in Europe, 1850–2000* (Oxford: Oxford University Press, 2002).
12 Jurgen Habermas, 'New social movements', *Telos*, 49 (1981), 33–37; Nick Crossley, *Making Sense of Social Movements* (Buckingham: Open University Press, 2002); Paul Byrne, *Social Movements in Britain* (London: Routledge, 1997).
13 Beveridge quoted in Geoffrey Finlayson, *Citizen, State and Social Welfare in Britain 1830–1990* (Oxford: Oxford University Press, 1994), p. 328.
14 For examples, see Helene Curtis and Mimi Sanderson (eds), *The Unsung Sixties: Memoirs of Social Innovation* (London: Whiting and Birch, 2008); Nick Crowson, Matthew Hilton and James McKay (eds), *NGOs in Contemporary Britain: Non-state Actors in Society and Politics Since 1945* (Basingstoke: Palgrave Macmillan, 2009); and Alex Mold and Virginia Berridge, *Voluntary Action and Illegal Drugs: Health and Society in Britain since the 1960s* (Basingstoke: Palgrave Macmillan, 2010).
15 Nigel Johnson, 'The changing role of the voluntary sector in Britain from 1945 to the present day', in Stein Kunhle and Per Selle (eds), *Government and Voluntary Organisations* (Aldershot: Ashgate, 1992), 87–107, p. 89.
16 RICA, *General Practice: A Consumer Commentary* (London: RICA, 1963), pp. 24–25.
17 See, for example, Barbara Robb, *Sans Everything: A Case to Answer* (London: Nelson, 1967); Cmnd. 3687, *Findings and Recommendations Following Enquires Into Allegations Concerning the Care of Elderly Patients in Certain Hospitals*; Cmnd. 3975, *Report of the Committee on Inquiry Into Allegations of Ill-Treatment of Patients and Other Irregularities at the Ely Hospital Cardiff*; Cmnd. 4557, *Report of the Farleigh Hospital Inquiry*; Cmnd. 4681, *Report of the Committee of Inquiry Into Whittingham Hospital*.
18 Martin Gorsky, 'Memorandum submitted to the Health Select Committee inquiry into Public and Patient Involvement in the NHS, January 2007', www.historyandpolicy.org/docs/gorsky_memo.pdf, accessed 2 August 2012.
19 Rudolf Klein, 'Control, participation and the British National Health Service', *Milbank Quarterly*, 57:1 (1979), 70–94, p. 73.
20 Interview between Alex Mold and Jean Robinson, 17 March 2009.
21 *House of Commons Debates*, 27 March 1973, vol. 853, cols 1101–232, col. 1204.
22 Harold Carr, 'The Patients Association: is it needed?', *Hospital and Health Management*, April 1963, 287–288.
23 Anon., 'Hospitals "the laughing stock of Europe"', *Medical News*, 14 May 1965.
24 Letter from Helen Hodgson to the *Observer*, 7 March 1965, 'Guinea pig patients'.
25 TNA MH 166/148, M.W. Perry to Mr de Peyer, 31 August 1972.

26 TNA MH 166/157, Briefing note for meeting between DHSS and PA [n.d., 1975].
27 Janet Newman and John Clarke, *Publics, Politics and Power: Remaking the Public in Public Services* (London: Sage, 2009), pp. 142–143.
28 See Charles Webster, *The Health Services Since the War Volume II: Government and Health Care, The National Health Service 1958–1979* (London: The Stationery Office, 1996), pp. 321–373, 451–479.
29 Ministry of Health, *National Health Service: The Administrative Structure of the Medical and Related Service in England and Wales* (London: HMSO, 1968).
30 TNA MH 166/55, Letter from Helen Hodgson to Richard Crossman, 4 December 1968.
31 CMAC SA/PAT/A/1/2 Minutes of the Meeting of the Committee of the PA, 7 October 1968. See also TNA MH 166/55, The Patients Association. Green Paper on the National Health Service, 4 December 1968.
32 TNA MH 166/55, Disablement Income Group on the Green Paper, November 1968.
33 TNA MH 166/56, Comments on the Green Paper – National Health Service: The Administrative Structure of the Medical and Related Service in England and Wales, 3 January 1969 by the Consumer Council.
34 Department of Health and Social Security, *The Future Structure of the National Health Service* (London: HMSO, 1970), pp. v–vi.
35 See Webster, *Health Services Since the War vol. II*, pp. 460–461.
36 Department of Health and Social Security, *National Health Service Reorganisation: Consultative Document* (London: DHSS, 1971), p. 10.
37 *House of Lords Debates*, 29 November 1971, vol. 326, cols 6–134, col. 113.
38 *House of Commons Debates*, 1 July 1971, vol. 820, cols 591–657, col. 624.
39 *House of Lords Debates*, 29 November 1971, vol. 326, cols 6–134, col. 21.
40 *House of Commons Debates*, 1 July 1971, vol. 820, cols 591–657, col. 598–599.
41 TNA MH 166/146, Margaret Belson, Chairman of NAWCH, Comments upon the consultative document on the NHS reorganisation, 17 August 1971.
42 TNA MH 166/146, Letter from Miss Mary Appleby, NAMH to Sir Keith Joseph, 28 July 1971.
43 TNA MH 166/146, Neighbourhood Councils Needed to Represent the Consumers of National and Local Services, by Michael Young, Leslie Farrer-Brown and John Baker, of the Association for Neighbourhood Councils, n.d. but attached to a letter from Young to Joseph, 16 August 1971.
44 TNA MH 166/146, Draft letter to Mr Peter Walker, n.d. [October 1971?].
45 TNA MH 166/148, Mr Dodds to Mr Cashman, 'Democracy in the reorganised NHS', 6 September 1972.
46 TNA MH 166/148, T.F. Crawley to Mr de Peyer, 20 September 1972; Mr de Peyer to Mr Cashman, 22 September 1972.
47 TNA MH 166/148, M.W. Perry to Miss Thorne, 24 August 1972.
48 NHS Reorganisation Act, 1973.
49 TNA MH 166/151, A.M. Lamb, Deputy Chief Nursing Officer to Mr Foster, 17 May 1973; TNA MH 166/151, Letter from R.A. Owen, Welsh Office to P.V. Foster, 1 June 1973.
50 TNA MH 166/148, Minutes of meeting on Community Health Councils, 13 November 1972.

51 *House of Commons Debates,* vol. 858, 19 June 1973, col. 405.
52 Christine Doyle, 'Blow to "patient power"', *The Observer,* 6 August 1972, p. 3; quote from the *Guardian* in Webster, *The Health Services Since the War Volume II,* p. 511.
53 Klein and Lewis, *The Politics of Consumer Representation,* p. 8.
54 Newman and Clarke, *Publics, Politics and Power,* pp. 140–141.
55 Suzanne Wait and Ellen Nolte, 'Public involvement policies in health: exploring their conceptual basis', *Health Economics and Law,* 1 (2006), 149–162.
56 See, for example, Chris Ham, 'Community health participation in the NHS planning system', *Social Policy and Administration,* 14:3 (1980), 221–231; Malcolm Johnson, 'Patients: receivers or participants?', in Keith Barnard and Kenneth Lee (eds), *Conflicts in the National Health Service* (London: Croom Helm, 1977), 72–98.
57 NHS Reorganisation Act, 1973.
58 Chris Ham, 'Power, patients and pluralism', in Keith Barnard and Kenneth Lee, *Conflicts in the National Health Service* (London: Croom Helm, 1977), 99–120, p. 101.
59 Klein and Lewis, *Politics of Consumer Representation,* p. 29.
60 *Ibid.,* p. 30.
61 Mike Gerrard, *A Stifled Voice: Community Health Councils in England 1974–2003* (Brighton: Pen Press, 2006), p. 39.
62 Klein, 'Control, participation and the British National Health Service', p. 81.
63 J.S. MacKeith, 'Community participation in health care', *The Hospital and Health Services Review* (December 1974), 425–428.
64 See Jane Lewis, *What Price Community Medicine? The Philosophy, Practice and Politics of Public Health Since 1919* (Brighton: Wheatsheaf Books, 1986).
65 Gerrard, *A Stifled Voice,* p. 39.
66 Ruth Levitt, 'Community Health Councils: Evidence for the Royal Commission on the National Health Service', in Christine Farrell and Ruth Levitt, *Consumers, Community Health Councils and the NHS* (London: Kings Fund, 1980), 25–41, p. 31.
67 Ruth Levitt, *The People's Voice in the NHS* (London: King Edwards Hospital Fund for London, 1980), p. 42.
68 West Birmingham Community Health Council, *Annual report of West Birmingham CHC, 1977–78* (Birmingham: WBCHC, 1978), p. 56.
69 Klein and Lewis, *Politics of Consumer Representation,* p. 122.
70 Interview between Alex Mold and Christine Hogg, 5 February 2009.
71 WBCHC, *Annual report of West Birmingham CHC, 1977–78,* p. 6.
72 ACHCEW CD ROM, *Brent Health: A News Sheet from Brent Community Health Council,* Autumn 1978; *Brent Health: A News Sheet from Brent Community Health Council,* Winter/Spring 1979.
73 ACHCEW CD ROM, *CHC Newsletter, Kensington, Chelsea & Westminster Community Health Council,* Spring 1978.
74 West Birmingham Community Health Council, *Annual Report of West Birmingham CHC, 1979–80* (Birmingham: WBCHC, 1980), p. 21.
75 DHSS, *Community Health Councils: HRC(74)4, Appendix 5.*
76 Klein and Lewis, *Politics of Consumer Representation,* pp. 38–40.

77 Birmingham City Archives (hereafter BCA) MS 2588/1/2, South Birmingham CHC Minutes, 1975: Minutes of the meeting of 29 January 1975.
78 ACHCEW, *The Golden Age of Patient Involvement in the NHS*, CD ROM, vol. 3, Public Activities folder.
79 ACHCEW CD ROM, 'Organise an exhibition and stay sane' letter from North Surrey CHC to ACHCEW, 21 December 1978.
80 Jack Hallas, *CHCs in Action: A Review* (London: Nuffield Hospitals Trust, 1976), p. 41.
81 ACHCEW CD ROM, Bernadette Fallon, 'Publicity', *CHC News*, vol. 1, May 1975, 29–31, p. 31.
82 ACHCEW CD ROM, Irene Watson, 'How do you make contact with the public?', *CHC News*, vol. 4, November 1975, pp. 9–11.
83 *The National Health Service (Community Health Councils) Regulations 1973*, Statutory Instrument No. 2217, 1973; DHSS, *Community Health Councils: HRC(74)4*.
84 DHSS, *Community Health Councils: HRC(74)4, Appendix 5*.
85 Jack Hallas and Bernadette Fallon, *Mounting the Health Guard: A Handbook for Community Health Council Members* (Oxford: Nuffield Provincial Hospitals Trust, 1974), p. 14.
86 Levitt, *The People's Voice in the NHS*, pp. 28–29.
87 Hallas, *CHCs in Action*, p. 14.
88 Interview with Christine Hogg.
89 East Birmingham CHC, *East Birmingham Community Health Council, Second Annual Report, 1976/77* (Birmingham: EBCHC, 1977) pp. 3, 10.
90 Klein and Lewis, *Politics of Consumer Representation*, p. 85.
91 Sarah Buckland, Carol Lupton and Graham Moon, *An Evaluation of the Role and Impact of Community Health Councils* (Portsmouth: Social Service Research and Information Unit, 1994), pp. 1–2.
92 Interview with Christine Hogg.
93 Gerrard, *A Stifled Voice*, pp. 21–22.
94 Hallas and Fallon, *Mounting the Health Guard*.
95 Interview with Christine Hogg.
96 *Ibid.*
97 Gerrard, *A Stifled Voice*, p. 78.
98 Ham, 'Community participation in the NHS', p. 228.
99 Anon., 'British Medical Association Annual Representative Meeting, Leicester 1971', *British Medical Journal Supplement*, 3472 (1971), 85–114, p. 105.
100 South Birmingham Community Health Council, *South Birmingham CHC First Annual Report, 1975* (Birmingham: SBCHC, 1975), p. 5.
101 BCA, MS 1226/15, British Pregnancy Advisory Service, *Birmingham Women Seeking the Assistance of BPAS with Regard to Pregnancy During the Period November 1974-March 1975: A Report to the Birmingham Area Health Authority (Teaching) Working Party of Family Planning*, 15 April 1975; David Spilsbury, *Trumpet Voluntary: An Informal History of Central and South Birmingham Community Health Councils 1974-2003* (South Birmingham CHC, 2003), p. 75.
102 Abortion Act (1967).

103 On medical power and abortion, see Sally Sheldon, *Beyond Control: Medical Power and Abortion Law* (London: Pluto Press, 1997).
104 Gayle Davis and Roger Davidson, '"Big White Chief", "Pontius Pilate" and the "Plumber": the impact of the 1967 Abortion Act on the Scottish Medical Community, c.1967–1980', *Social History of Medicine*, 18:2 (2005), 283–306.
105 Gayle Davis, '"A fifth freedom" or "hideous atheistic expediency"? The medical community and abortion law reform in Scotland, c. 1960–1975', *Medical History*, 50 (2006), 29–48, p. 34; Madeline Simms, 'Abortion law and medical freedom', *British Journal of Criminology*, 14:2 (1974), 118–131, p. 128.
106 H.C. McLaren, 'Attitudes to abortion', letter to the *British Medical Journal*, 11 May 1974, p. 329; BCA, MS1226/15 National Abortion Campaign [n.d., 1975/6?]; Martin Cole, 'Calthorpe Clinic Medical Seminar: 40 Years of Legal Abortion', speech given at University of Birmingham, 26 November 2007, www.calthorpe-clinic.co.uk/keynote_speech.pdf, accessed 2 December 2009; 'Abortion: a painful lesson from Britain', *Time*, 7 March 1969.
107 Audrey Leatherhead, *The Fight For Family Planning* (Basingstoke: Macmillan, 1980) p. 174; Naomi Pfeffer, 'Fertility counts: from equity to outcome', in Steve Sturdy (ed.), *Medicine, Health and the Public Sphere in Britain 1600–2000* (London: Routledge, 2002), 260–278, p. 268.
108 On White's Bill see John Keown, *Abortion, Doctors and the Law: Some Aspects of the Legal Regulation of Abortion in England, 1803–1982* (Cambridge: Cambridge University Press, 1988), pp. 141–142.
109 BCA MS 2588/1/2, SBCHC Minutes 1975: Minutes of the meeting of 28 May 1975.
110 *Ibid.*
111 Keown, *Abortion, Doctors and the Law*, pp. 152–158.
112 BCA MS 2588/1/4, SBCHC Minutes 1978/9: Minutes of the meeting of 24 July 1979.
113 Leatherhead, *The Fight For Family Planning*, p. 175.
114 See, for example, the work of the Birmingham branch of the National Abortion Campaign as described in an undated leaflet in BCA, MS1226/15, Maternity and Child Welfare Working Group Papers, 1974–1980.
115 Cmnd. 5579, *Report of the Committee on the Working of the Abortion Act* (London: HMSO, 1974). On the Lane Committee see Ashley Wivel, 'Abortion policy and politics on the Lane Committee of Enquiry, 1971–74', *Social History of Medicine*, 11:1 (1998), 109–135.
116 Pfeffer, 'Fertility counts', p. 268.
117 Royal Commission on the National Health Service, *Report of the Royal Commission on the National Health Service* (London: HMSO, 1979), pp. 286–287.
118 BCA MS 2588/1/3, Report of the Maternity and Child Welfare Working Group, 15 October 1976; BCA MS 2588/1/3, Minutes of the SBCHC Meeting, 14 December 1976.
119 BCA MS 1226/15, South Birmingham CHC: NHS Abortion Facilities, September 1976.
120 BCA MS 2588/1/3, Birmingham Area Health Authority (Teaching): Commentary on the First Annual Reports of the Five Birmingham CHCs, 25 October 1976.
121 BCA MS 2588/1/3, Minutes of the SBCHC meeting, 26 April 1977.

122 BCA MS 1226/16, South Birmingham Health District: Annual Report of the Working Party on Family Planning Services, n.d. [1977].
123 Wivel, 'Abortion policy and the Lane Committee', p. 120.
124 Royal Commission on the National Health Service, *Report*, pp. 286, 429.
125 Anon., 'Better abortion service planned', *Birmingham Post*, 26 February 1980, p. 7; Spilsbury, *Trumpet Voluntary*, p. 91.
126 ACHCEW CD ROM, vol. 3, Public Activities folder, Brent CHC, *Brent Health*, Winter/Spring 1979; Birmingham Central Library, Central Birmingham CHC, *Report* 1 June 1979–31 May 1980.
127 ACHCEW CD ROM, vol. 3, Public Activities folder, Central Birmingham CHC, *Report* 1978.
128 ACHCEW CD ROM, vol. 3, Public Activities folder, Brent CHC, *Brent Health*, Winter/Spring 1979.
129 ACHCEW CD ROM, vol. 3, Public Activities folder, Central Birmingham CHC, *Report* 1978.
130 ACHCEW CD ROM, vol. 3, Public Activities folder, West Birmingham CHC, *Annual Report*, 1978.
131 Ham, 'Community health participation in the NHS planning system', p. 225.
132 Interview with Christine Hogg.
133 Gerrard, *A Stifled Voice*, p. 64.
134 Hogg, *Citizens, Consumers and the NHS*, p. 32.
135 Gerrard, *A Stifled Voice*, pp. 115–127, 142–146.
136 Cmnd 7615, *Royal Commission on the National Health Service* (London: HMSO, 1979), p. 150.
137 DHSS, *Patients First* (London: HMSO, 1979), p. 14.
138 Anon., 'Community Health Councils: a chance to take stock', *The Lancet*, 19 July 1980, 130–131.
139 *Ibid.*, p. 131.
140 Gerrard, *A Stifled Voice*, p. 123.
141 Fedelma Winkler, 'Consumerism in health care: beyond the supermarket model', *Policy and Politics*, 15:1 (1987), 1–8, p. 1.

3

Complaint

Complaining about health care is nothing new. Some patients always have, and probably always will, feel displeased with aspects of their medical treatment and want to make this dissatisfaction known. However, the re-imagining of the patient as a consumer altered the meaning and importance ascribed to the act of complaining. Complaint was fundamental to the notion of consumerism put forward by consumer organisations such as the Consumers' Association in the latter half of the twentieth century. Enhancing the consumer's ability to complain about faulty or otherwise unsatisfactory goods and services was a key area of activity for consumer groups. The right to complain was also enshrined within the International Organisation of Consumer's Unions bill of consumer rights through the right to be heard and the right to redress.[1] The 'making of a complaint', according to medical law expert Linda Mulcahy, 'provides an example of consumer activism'.[2]

If patients were to be seen as consumers, then it was perhaps inevitable that their capacity to complain should come under renewed scrutiny. There were, however, additional reasons why complaining within the medical sphere garnered attention in Britain from the late 1960s onwards. Demands for enhanced patient autonomy and representation led naturally to calls for stronger mechanisms of complaint. The attack on medical paternalism put forward by patient organisations, women's groups and theorists, coupled with a series of scandals about specific treatments (such as thalidomide) and more general systems of care (such as at Ely Hospital) opened up a space where questioning medical authority and seeking redress for perceived wrongs was possible.

This chapter will examine the development of patient complaints in the 1970s and early 1980s. It will focus on three areas. The first concerns the activities of patient-consumer organisations around complaining. Groups such as the Patients Association and the CHCs played an important role in informing patients about complaints procedures and assisting them in making complaints, as well as using patient complaints as a tool to point to wider failings within the health service. Patient-consumer organisations also lobbied for the reform of complaints procedures, the second area of focus of this chapter. Complaints mechanisms in hospitals and family practitioner services were re-examined and reinforced, partly as a result of consumer group pressure. Finally, the capacity of the patient to complain was further strengthened by the introduction of the Health Service Commissioner, or the Ombudsman, in 1973. The creation of an independent authority to which complainants could appeal had long been a goal for patient-consumer organisations, and groups such as the PA hailed the establishment of the Ombudsman as one of their key achievements.[3]

While it was certainly true that a patient wishing to make a complaint in 1985, or even 1975, was in a better position than he or she had been in 1965, the activities of patient-consumer organisations around complaining and the process by which measures such as the introduction of the Ombudsman came into force point to a set of deeper problems. Firstly, the development of mechanisms like a coordinated hospital complaints system and the appointment of the Ombudsman were extraordinarily protracted. It took more than 12 years to reform the hospital complaints procedure and nine years for the Ombudsman to take office. Moreover, the medical profession opposed the introduction of such measures at almost every turn, and the instruments that were introduced were weaker than they might have been. This highlights the dominance of medical power despite the rise of the patient-consumer. Secondly, the tensions around the complaints process between the medical profession, patient-consumer groups and other advocates for change, points to a deeper contest about the meaning, nature and purpose of complaint. For doctors, patient complaints were a threat to their ability to practise as they saw fit and posed a fundamental challenge to their power and authority. Yet, for patient-consumer organisations, complaint was both a vital consumer right and an opportunity to improve services for individuals and the wider population. Complaint, this chapter will suggest, was an area of disputed territory that brought patient-consumers into direct conflict with the medical profession.

Complaining about medicine

To complain, according to the *Oxford English Dictionary*, is to 'give expression to sorrow or suffering', which may pass into 'that of grievance or blame'. Complaining may involve making 'a formal statement of grievance to or before a competent authority; to lodge a complaint, to bring a charge'.[4] Complaint, as the philosopher Julian Baggini points out, is, therefore, doubly transitive: you complain to someone as well as about something. In this way, he suggests, a complaint is 'a directed expression or refusal to accept that things are not as they ought to be'.⁵ According to the psychologist Robin Kowalski, people complain in order to express their dissatisfaction, but also to prompt others to address their grievances.⁶ Complaining is thus more than moaning; Baggini argues that complaint 'has a noble history': that the 'belief that people have a right to complain and should not suffer injustice in silence is implicit in all movements for social change'.⁷ Complaint can bind people together, increasing solidarity amongst group members who have a common experience.⁸ In the context of medicine, complaint has a further set of meanings attached to it. A patient may 'complain' of pain or discomfort, and a patient's condition may be described as their 'complaint'. Although such terminology is used less commonly today, the dual meaning of complaint as a condition and complaint as a form of protest hints at some of the complexities that surround complaining within and about medicine.

Patients have long objected to aspects of their care. The expansion of the medical profession in the eighteenth century brought doctors into contact with patients in ever-greater numbers. Dorothy and Roy Porter contend that patients were apt to complain about the attitude of doctors towards them, their lateness, their ineptitude and absence of humanity. Patients also complained about the over-administration of remedies, which was strongly linked to over-charging.⁹ Coordinated systems that dealt with patient complaints, as opposed to individuals complaining about their treatment, are, however, a more recent invention. Before the NHS, contributor representatives within pre-war voluntary hospital governing bodies were able to put forward patient complaints. Common complaints, notes Martin Gorsky, revolved around waiting lists, visiting times, poor treatment by individual doctors and the quality of accommodation.¹⁰ Beyond appealing to the contributor representative, there were, however, few options available to individual patients wishing to complain. Patients were able to complain about a specific doctor's conduct to the General Medical Council (GMC), but the GMC was not primarily a machine to handle patients' complaints, but rather a regulatory body for doctors.¹¹ Patients could sue a doctor for malpractice or negligence, but this was not a remedy available to many due to the high costs involved. Complaint mechanisms within the early NHS were ad hoc and often varied from hospital to hospital. There was no statutory procedure for making complaints about treatment in hospital (as will be explored in greater detail later in this chapter) until 1985.

Despite such obstacles, by the 1960s there were indications that patients were becoming more willing to complain. Patient satisfaction with the NHS appeared to be high in this period: in 1961 PEP reported that 86 per cent of patients surveyed were satisfied with their GP and 'the majority of mothers had no complaint about the kind of service which their family had received'. Yet, the same survey also found that some complaint about her last visit to the GP was made by 12 per cent of mothers and in 'a quarter of families, one member had been dissatisfied enough to think of changing to another doctor, although only half in this group had actually done so'.[12] Although the majority of patients were reluctant to take formal action, complaining was on the increase. The total number of written complaints investigated by hospital authorities in England and Wales rose from 7,984 in 1967, to 9,614 in 1971. This represented a slight rise from 1.59 complaints per 1,000 discharges in 1967 to 1.75 complaints per 1,000 discharges in 1971.[13] Moreover, written complaints were likely to represent just a fraction of the total number of complaints made. Research in Scotland found that 25 per cent of patients interviewed in hospital claimed to have made some sort of suggestion about 'desired improvements', and a study commissioned by the Davies Committee on complaints found that 4 per cent of patients interviewed after discharge from hospital said that they had either spoken or written to someone in authority about an 'unsatisfactory aspect' of their stay.[14] The fact that few of these criticisms translated into formal complaints says rather more about hospital complaints procedures than unwillingness on the part of patients to complain.

The issue of complaining in medicine was also brought to the fore in the late 1960s and early 1970s by a series of scandals that highlighted the inadequacy of existing means of complaint. The Department of Health had long been aware of poor conditions in long-stay hospitals, which cared for the elderly, mentally ill or disabled, but a succession of reports published in the late 1960s and early 1970s also demonstrated problems with complaining.[15] The publication of *Sans Everything: A Case to Answer* by Barbara Robb and the organisation Aid for the Elderly in Government Institutions (AEGIS) presented a number of case studies of mistreatment of the elderly in NHS hospitals but also pointed to the unsatisfactory state of complaints procedures.[16] In 1969, a Council of Tribunals report into the allegations made by Robb echoed her criticism of complaints procedures and called for 'radical revision' of the complaints investigation machinery.[17] The need for reform of complaints procedures was further underscored by the report on the Ely Hospital scandal which was also released in 1969. Two years earlier, the *News of the World* had printed allegations made by a nurse at Ely Hospital in Cardiff (a psychiatric institution) pointing to the mistreatment of patients, but also the suppression of complaints made by staff and patients' relatives and the victimisation of staff who did complain. The Ely report determined that the nurse's allegations were well-founded, and that a culture had been created at the hospital in which 'members of the nursing staff had been persuaded that it was useless, if not positively hazardous, to complain of matters which disturbed them'.[18] The report recommended that existing complaints procedures be reconsidered, and called for the establishment of an inspectorate for long-stay hospitals.[19] The Ely scandal was quickly followed by another, this time in a hospital for the 'mentally handicapped', in Dorset. Once again, the subsequent report into conditions at the Farleigh Hospital (published in 1971) found that complaints were poorly handled, and the reports authors asserted that the existing system for dealing with complaints within the NHS was inadequate.[20] A year later, yet another enquiry, this time into the situation at Whittingham psychiatric hospital in Lancashire, found that complaints by staff were suppressed and that there was a failure to investigate other complaints. The report recommended that procedures for dealing with complaints from staff and patients be improved.[21]

Taken together, these reports demonstrated powerfully that existing complaints procedures were in need of radical overhaul. Although many of the scandals centred on the difficulties experienced by staff wishing to speak out about conditions, they also shone a light on the whole issue of complaints, whether these were made by staff, patients or their relatives. The problem, it seemed, was not just confined to long-stay hospitals. Even *The Lancet* pointed out in 1963 that patient dissatisfaction was important, and that 'when complaints are well founded, the patient does not always know what to do about it'.[22]

Patient-consumer organisations and complaining

Patient-consumer organisations, like the PA, were set up (at least in part), to improve the situation around patient complaints. Helping patients to complain, informing people of the correct procedures and dealing with specific complaints, as well as campaigning for improvements in complaints mechanisms, was a key area of activity for such groups. A specific complaint – about the use of patients in NHS hospitals in research without their knowledge or consent – was the motivation behind the creation of the PA, as discussed in Chapter 1. But the Association rapidly found itself dealing with a broad range of issues relating to complaints. In its first 18 months of existence, the PA received 525 complaints from patients.[23] The PA did not take up individual complaints, but they did advise people on whether they were likely to have a case and how to negotiate the various levels of complaints procedure. A similar function was performed by the CHCs; indeed one of their statutory roles was to act as the 'patient's friend' and assist patients in making complaints. Although all CHCs received complaints, the volume of complaints that they dealt with varied widely from council to council and changed over time. For its first three months of existence, one CHC reported receiving 22 complaints, while others reported 'minimal' complaints in their early years.[24] Yet, by the 1980s, South Birmingham CHC reported that complaints work took up about a quarter of the council's time, and a study of CHCs by a firm of management consultants in the 1990s found that councils spent 50 per cent of their time dealing with complaints.[25]

Although complaints work was time consuming, complaints were a useful source of information for patient-consumer organisations about the state of the NHS. Some attempt was made to analyse the complaints received by groups like the PA and the CHCs in order to point to wider failings in NHS care. In 1964, the PA reported that of the complaints they had received, 21 per cent were about negligence, but over a third concerned what Hodgson termed 'attitude to patients', including bad organisation, lack of communication, 'inhumanity' and discourtesy.[26] The PA tried to conduct a more formal analysis of complaints in the mid-1970s with the help of the CA, but this project never got off the ground.[27] As Glen O'Hara points out, in the 1960s and 1970s there was a lack of information about complaints and their handling. Little work had been done on categorising different types of complaint or using these to determine broader patterns.[28] One CHC examined the complaints that it had received in its first year of activity and found that these could be placed in three categories. The first was 'grumbles, comments and suggestions'; these required no specific action. The second was 'expressions of distress and dissatisfaction'; these were usually dealt with informally. Finally, there were 'protests, grievances or accusations'; these were more formal complaints that required referral to the relevant authority.[29]

Analysing complaints, even in this rather crude way, demonstrated to patient-consumer organisations the significance and value of complaints at both an individual and collective level. In their handbook for CHCs, Jack Hallas and Bernadette Fallon argued that helping patients with complaints was 'one of the most important aspects of community health council work'. Aiding individuals who were less able to make their dissatisfaction known, what they termed 'submerged groups', was particularly vital. In this way, Hallas and Fallon suggested, CHCs could act as an 'early warning system', bringing the AHA's attention to potential causes for dissatisfaction.[30] Even minor 'grumbles' had their use. West Birmingham Community Health Council noted in their 1976/77 report that 'many of the incidents about which the public grumble are not such as would follow a formal complaint', but 'Discontent is not overcome by disqualifying attempts to express it, and the extent of even invalid criticism should be a matter of concern to the health service.'[31] Patient-consumer groups were well aware that formal complaints told only part of the story. Elizabeth Stanton, writing in the NCC's magazine, the *Clapham Omnibus*, stated that 'Most patients are grateful for any good done to them by the National Health Service, and are reluctant to complain formally if things go wrong'. But, she noted, 'consumer activists have realised for some years that this "gratitude barrier" is unhealthy not only for patients and their families but also for the medical profession and the NHS itself'.[32]

Complaints, patient-consumer groups suggested, operated as indicators of the quality of services being provided. Jean Robinson of the PA urged the CHCs to use complaints to 'make rational assessments of the quality of care'.[33] According to the editor of *CHC News*, Ruth Levitt, complaints were rarely isolated incidents; it was possible to generalise from specific misfortune and so advocate for wider change.[34] This was a view later echoed by the Royal Commission on the NHS, which established that there was a 'need to develop an effective role for CHCs, not simply as an aid to complainants, but on the much wider front of influencing health service provision to meet the needs of patients'.[35]

By the mid-1970s, it was evident that patient-consumer organisations had two key roles with respect to complaints. The first consisted of assisting patients in making complaints and offering practical support and guidance on complaints procedures. The second was about using complaints in a broader sense as a means to highlight deficiencies in the NHS and campaign for improvements. To perform both of these roles more effectively, patient-consumer groups recognised that the existing complaints mechanisms needed to be improved.

The reform of hospital complaints procedures, 1971–85

During the early years of the NHS, there was no formal process for handling complaints about treatment in hospital. Each hospital dealt with complaints in its own way, with hospital boards, management committees and boards of governors taking varied approaches to the handling of complaints. In 1966, the Ministry of Health issued a circular offering official guidance on the establishment of hospital complaints procedures, but much was still left to local discretion, and so there was widespread variation.[36] Indeed, the PA contended that in their experience few hospitals had taken any notice of the Ministry of Health circular.[37] Hospitals certainly differed significantly in the kind of information that they provided to patients about complaint. A survey of 144 hospitals found that 29 (20 per cent) did not issue any kind of leaflet to patients on admission to hospital; 23 per cent issued a booklet but offered no guidance on making suggestions or complaints; 31 per cent provided a booklet that mentioned 'suggestions or comments' only;

26 per cent gave out a booklet that mentioned 'criticisms or complaints' specifically.[38]

There were other problems with hospital complaints procedures in addition to local variation. There was no system for dealing with complaints made by staff on behalf of patients, as had already been highlighted by the Ely, Farleigh and Whittingham inquires.[39] Doctors handled complaints about other doctors, there was little or no external oversight and the complaint procedures themselves were not binding.[40] To deal with some of these issues, patient-consumer groups wanted to see the complaints mechanisms strengthened. The Patients Association proposed that an appeals process be put in place to deal with dissatisfied complainants.[41] NAWCH too were anxious that complaints procedures be improved, but they attempted to put a more positive spin on the issue of complaints. They suggested that 'Some of the reluctance to discuss complaints in hospital could be overcome if it were explained to staff as not a function of *criticism* but of *consumer relations*, so that the hospital could be seen as getting useful pointers to future development from suggestions and complaints [original emphasis].'[42]

Such an approach found favour with the Davies Committee, which was established in 1971 to examine hospital complaints procedures. The committee, chaired by Sir Michael Davies, a senior lawyer and later High Court judge, was made up of individuals from a diverse array of professional backgrounds, including Mary Appleby, director of the mental health charity MIND and the sociologist Margaret Stacey. What was particularly significant about the committee's membership was that doctors and other health professionals were in a minority: of the 17 committee members just three were doctors. This mixed membership suggested a real willingness to investigate the complaints issue not only from the point of view of the doctor, but also from the perspective of the patient. This can be seen in the way in which the Davies Committee conducted their investigation. They did hear from the various professional bodies and royal colleges, but in addition the committee sought the views of a number of patient groups, including the PA and NAWCH. The opinions of these organisations were also reflected in the committee's final report.

Indeed, the Davies Committee was keen to place their findings within the context of growing consumerism. The report commented, 'This is an age in which the legitimate interests of the consumer, who in the hospital service is the patient, are rightly receiving increased protection in many fields … We see no reason why these general principles should not apply to the hospital service.'[43] Such a consumerist approach influenced the way in which the committee regarded complaints. 'Complaint', the committee argued, 'need not and ought not ever to be regarded as a dirty word.'[44] The effect of what they termed 'softer' alternatives such as 'comments', 'suggestions' or 'views on improvements' used in hospital literature, 'may well be to stifle legitimate complaints. A complaint is one way in which a patient can speak to the hospital, and it is a mechanism through which management is able to test and improve itself.'[45] Moreover, the Davies committee contended, 'Few [patients] have any serious grievances. But those who do have the legitimate right – no less – to have their dissatisfaction fully and fairly investigated.'[46]

In order to fulfil this right, the Davies Committee proposed a number of changes to the hospital complaints system. They called for the introduction of a uniform code of practice for dealing with complaints. Although the Committee recommended that the initial investigation of complaints should take place at the local level, they also suggested that a system be put in place for external review and that an ombudsman be introduced for unsuccessful complainants to appeal to. Davies also proposed that the CHCs play a greater role in helping with complaints. The report recognised that there was a distinction between clinical and non-clinical complaints, asserting that clinical judgement may vary between doctors. For this reason, the committee recommended that the doctor concerned should first deal with clinical complaints. The issue of clinical complaints was a vexed one, and was of particular importance in the debate over the establishment of the Ombudsman, but it was also a divisive issue for the Davies Committee. According to Mulcahy, Stacey and another member of the committee considered submitting a minority report because of the level of compromise reached with the medical profession, but were dissuaded by Davies himself and the suggestion that the Ombudsman might consider such issues.[47] As the report concluded, 'The public will expect *all* complaints to be fully and fairly investigated'.[48]

Any hope that the Davies report would meet with swift action, was, however, quickly dashed. Despite the concessions made to professional self-regulation regarding clinical complaints, the report was not well received among the medical community. The joint Medico-Legal Subcommittee of the Central Committee for Hospital Medical Services of the BMA and the Joint Consultants Committee (JCC, the body which represented senior doctors from the BMA and the Royal Colleges) argued that the report implied that 'every encouragement be given to all citizens … to make a suggestion or complaint, not only when it is reasonable, but on any occasion, however trivial'. The effect of this atmosphere of complaining, they contended, would be 'to damage the service profoundly and to the detriment rather than to the advantage of the community in which it exists to serve'.[49] The Council of the BMA and the JCC told Sir Henry Yellowlees (the Chief Medical Officer) that 'no part of the proposals put forward by the Davies Committee can be considered as acceptable to the medical profession until the considered view of the Association has been submitted'.[50] Despite the fact that the BMA had given evidence to the Davies Committee, doctors were obviously unhappy with its findings.

In contrast, patient groups were broadly supportive. For example, the PA 'welcome[d] the constructive nature of the report and its sympathetic approach to the anxieties and preoccupations of patients'.[51] But the reception of the Davies report illustrated the relative lack of power of patient groups when compared to professional groups. As Charles Webster noted, support for the Davies report 'derived from the relatively powerless consumer groups, whereas within the NHS it possessed few friends and many powerful enemies'.[52] The report, according to the sociologist Margaret Stacey, was met with 'thundering silence' and long delay.[53] A draft code on hospital complaints procedure was produced in 1976, but this simply reproduced the JCC's own suggestions for handling complaints and avoided the issue of how to deal with clinical complaints.[54] Furthermore, as the PA pointed out,

> The code will be ineffective unless its existence is taken as a fact of their professional life by health service staff at all levels and its philosophy and content are soaked into their consciousness. This requirement will not be met unless the members of health authorities, lay and professional alike, recognise, and make it clear that they recognise, the importance of proper complaints procedure and its observance by staff.[55]

An independent review of hospital complaints procedures was carried out by the House of Commons Select Committee on the Parliamentary Commissioner for Administration (the Ombudsman) in 1977. The Select Committee found that the complaints process was complicated and slow, and contained many 'disquieting' elements, particularly in relation to the investigation of clinical complaints. Many complainants, they suggested, were left dissatisfied.[56] Another consultation document on hospital complaints mechanisms was sent out in 1978, and in 1981 a Department of Health circular was issued to all hospitals, but the complaints procedure was still a draft and not compulsory. It was not until 1985 and the passing of the Hospital Complaints Procedure Act (12 years after Davies reported) that hospitals were required to have any sort of complaints procedure in place.

Moreover, even the creation of this piece of legislation was due to serendipity as much as design. In January 1984, Conservative MP for Newbury, Michael McNair-Wilson, was taken seriously ill with kidney failure.[57] Following months of hospitalisation, and a number of medical mishaps, McNair-Wilson published a 'Patient's Charter' which he hoped would redress the power imbalance between doctors and patients 'by laying down certain basic patients rights which will apply to every person'.[58] Though he was unfortunate to have been so unwell, McNair-Wilson was lucky enough to have his name drawn in the members' ballot in 1985, allowing him the opportunity to put forward a piece of legislation. Most MPs, when given this chance to get their name on the statute books, opted to put forward a technical piece of legislation that the government wished to see passed, but was not significant enough to be included in the main legislative programme.[59] Lots of important legislation has been passed through private members' bills, particularly on social and moral issues, like the Abortion Act in 1967, but most of these bills resulted from pressure group lobbying. However, this does not appear to have been the case with the Hospital Complaints Procedure Act: patient-consumer groups had no direct involvement in the creation of the Act. Instead, McNair-Wilson acted alone. According to Mulcahy, who interviewed McNair-Wilson before he died in 1993, the MP had wanted to use his bill to get his entire charter made into legislation, but the Secretary of State for Health told him that he would only get government backing if he selected just one clause from the charter to form a bill.[60] McNair-Wilson chose the introduction of a complaints procedure; this was duly translated into legislation, and passed unopposed in February 1985.[61] The Hospital Complaints Procedure Act required health authorities in England and Wales and health boards in Scotland to establish a complaints procedure and draw this to the attention of patients.[62] The Department of Health drafted further guidelines on complaints procedure, and this was finally issued to all hospitals in 1988.[63]

The introduction of the Hospital Complaints Procedure Act might seem like a rather small victory given the amount of time that had passed since Davies recommended the establishment of a coordinated complaints procedure and the pressure exerted by patient-consumer groups and others. Though patient groups played some role in getting complaints onto the agenda and in shaping the findings of the Davies Committee, the reaction of the medical profession to the report, and the fact that they were able to delay the implementation of a coordinated complaints procedure for many years, raises significant issues about the relative power of patient-consumer groups.

Complaints about family practitioner services, 1970s

A similar pattern of professional opposition and obstruction can also be observed in attempts to revise complaints procedures within the family practitioner services. Complaints about GPs and other NHS contractors (such as optometrists and dentists) were dealt with by a separate system, but it was no more effective or coordinated than that for hospital complaints. Since 1911, Family Practitioner Committees (FPCs) were empowered to examine breaches in terms of service by GPs, but not other kinds of grievances. Those wishing to make a complaint had to put their case to the Committee in person, a process that, as Christine Hogg observed, was 'daunting' and put the complainant in the position of prosecution rather than witness.[64] Appealing to the FPC was the only recourse patients had regarding complaints about GPs, unless they had a case which could be put before the GMC or a court.

The Department of Health instigated a review of family practitioner services' complaints procedures in 1974, but decided to wait until after the government had responded to the Davies report before issuing any guidance. In 1976, various technical changes were proposed, involving aspects such as the size of the committee hearing the case, the extension of the time limit within which a complaint could be made from six to eight weeks, and the legal representation of the patient at hearings.[65] The PA was critical of the proposals, arguing that the investigating committee should be independent of the FPC. The association also envisaged a much wider role for the complaints investigation mechanism. The PA suggested that 'consideration should be given to the establishment of a roving inspectorate at the service of FPCs as well as the GMC which would visit NHS practice premises and take a general view of the way they are run'. The Association believed that the introduction of such an inspectorate 'could be not only a contracting party and a complaints body, but also make a positive contribution to the standards of family practitioner services in its area'.[66] Criticism of the DHSS's proposals came from other quarters too. The journalist Jill Turner, writing in the periodical *New Society*, pointed out that although the committees that heard complaints against GPs were made up of a mixture of medical and non-medical members the 'lay' members had to accept the clinical judgement of medical members. This, she asserted 'makes a nonsense of the hearing, especially when the lay members turn out to be doctors' wives and the medical members local friends of the defendant'.[67]

Doctors, in contrast, were largely opposed to the DHSS's proposed reforms. The General Medical Services Committee of the BMA was concerned that the changes did not do enough to protect doctors from patients who made 'unreasonable demands'. They were also incensed by a suggestion that notices be placed in doctors' surgeries explaining the complaints procedure.[68] The DHSS re-examined their proposals, and made another attempt to reform FPS complaints procedures in 1978.[69] Once again, GPs opposed many of the suggested measures vigorously. The General Medical Services Committee issued a statement which said that GPs were 'seriously affronted by the proposals'.[70] Chief among their concerns was the proposal that complainants and their legal advisors be given access to the patient's medical records. GPs were also resistant towards a further extension of the time limit for complaints to be lodged from eight weeks to six months.[71]

The DHSS later decided not to make any substantial changes to the FPS complaints mechanism. An official told the PA in 1979 that the Minister was 'not convinced that the existing, long-standing procedure is so much in need of amendment that it demands, and at a time of great difficulty for the National Health Service, the expenditure of what will undoubtedly amount to a considerable proportion of the time of senior officers of the Department'.[72] Cost may well have been a factor; yet it is hard to avoid the conclusion that the profession's reaction to the proposed changes forced the DHSS to put the reform of GP complaints procedures to one side. As will be discussed in Chapter 5, access to medical records was to prove a major sticking point, and the procedure for dealing with complaints about GPs went largely unaltered until 1996. Once again, the medical professionals seemed to hold greater sway over the complaints system than the patient-consumer groups.

The introduction of the Health Service Commissioner (Ombudsman), 1967–73

A slightly different picture of professional versus consumer power around complaints can be seen in the process surrounding the introduction of the Health Service Commissioner (the Ombudsman). The appointment of an independent official to investigate complaints against public bodies and government departments on behalf of citizens was a Scandinavian model imported to the UK and other countries from the 1960s onwards.[73] In England, the creation of the Parliamentary Commissioner for Administration, more commonly called the Ombudsman, came about in part because of perceived injustice suffered by citizens at the hands of the state. The Crichel Down affair, which involved the compulsory purchase of land during the Second World War and the failure to return the land to its owners after the war, was often cited as case of individual rights being ignored.[74] Yet, as O'Hara points out, the introduction of the ombudsman was also rooted in a consumerist view of public services, and was intended to protect individual rights at the same time as offering a mechanism (in the style of Albert Hirschman's famous model) for 'voice' and 'loyalty' rather than 'exit'.[75] The ombudsman can thus be seen as one of a series of mechanisms designed to enhance citizen-consumer representation, like those discussed in Chapter 2. The office of the Parliamentary Commissioner for Administration (PCA) or the Ombudsman was established in 1967, and the PCA was empowered to investigate complaints made by a member of the public to their MP when an individual claimed to have suffered injustice as a result of 'maladministration' by a government department or body.[76]

Complaints about the NHS, however, were specifically excluded from the Ombudsman's remit. Ostensibly, this was because the Ministry of Health was not directly responsible for the Family Practitioner Services or services provided by local authorities and it was thought unfair to subject staff in hospitals to a system that independent contractors, like GPs, were free of.[77]

Despite the Ministry's opposition, there was pressure to bring health within the remit of the PCA even before he took office. Patient-consumer organisations, such as the PA, had long been in favour of the establishment of an ombudsman. The PA wrote to the Ministry of Health in 1965 calling for the appointment of a 'special ombudsman for health'.[78] Support for the extension of the PCA's powers came from other quarters too. At the second reading of the Parliamentary Commissioner Bill in the House of Lords in 1967, the Bill was criticised for its exclusion of the health service. Baroness Elliot of Harwood argued that 'the administration of the National Health Service, is something which the Ombudsman might very profitably be allowed to inquire into, for quite often it is most inadequate. Indeed, in the priority of candidates for the Ombudsman's protection, I would put the National Health Service very high in the list.'[79] In 1968, the second report of the Select Committee on the PCA and the Council of Tribunals Annual Report both called for the establishment of a health ombudsman.[80]

Within the Ministry of Health, there were signs that the notion of a dedicated health ombudsman was gaining support. Initially, officials were divided on the issue. One civil servant noted in 1967 that she was 'not convinced that a separate Health Commissioner is required or is desirable'.[81] Other officials worried about 'what sort of person the Commissioner would be. Is it intended that he should be a doctor, a lawyer, an administrator or what?'[82] It was the proposed restructuring of the health service that finally convinced the Ministry that the introduction of a health ombudsman could no longer be avoided. Plans to bring services currently administered by local authorities under central control removed one of the key objections to the ombudsman, but there was also a sense that as 'services are no longer subject to democratic control, there may well be strong public pressure for some independent handling of complaints'.[83] The 1968 Green Paper on the restructuring of the NHS duly suggested that health could be brought within the remit of the PCA, or an alternative dedicated Health Commissioner be established.[84]

Such proposals were welcomed by patient-consumer organisations. DIG, the Consumer Council and the Maternity and Infant Care Association were all in favour of the establishment of a Health Commissioner, as were some Regional Hospital Boards.[85] The PA also supported the idea, but wanted to see the remit of the PCA extended to cover health.[86] Spurred on by the Ely report, the DHSS (the Ministry of Health became the DHSS in

1968) recognised that 'there is a widespread feeling, not confined to the less reasonable organisations, that investigation by officers often leaves the complaint unsatisfied but he does not know how to take a complaint further'.[87] In 1969, an internal working group recommended the establishment of a Health Commissioner, and the DHSS began to solicit views on the issue from interested parties.[88]

From the outset, officials were aware that obtaining the support of the medical profession was likely to be challenging. In a letter to a counterpart at the Council of Tribunals under-secretary J.P. Dodds remarked drily that 'I think it is pretty clear that the enthusiasm of the profession for a Health Commissioner will be considerably less than that of the Government'.[89] The deputy Chief Medical Officer, Dr R.M. Shaw, approached Dr D.C. Cameron, Chairman of the General Medical Services Committee of the BMA, asking for his personal view on the issue. Cameron thought that GPs would likely be opposed to the suggestion that the Ombudsman consider complaints that related to clinical judgement. He was also concerned that any proposals should 'provide protection and redress both for independent contractors and professional staff of the health service from exposure to the unreasonable demands and abuse of the Service by that minority of unreasonable "consumers" which undoubtedly exists'.[90] The BMA discussed the introduction of an ombudsman at its annual meeting in May 1970, and passed a resolution stating that 'The meeting is not convinced that the health commissioner is justified and cannot accept the proposals unless or until stronger arguments are forthcoming.'[91] An amendment by a representative from Tyneside added that the 'The complaints and disciplinary machinery of the NHS is greatly loaded against the doctor and in view of this must be urgently reviewed.'[92] The JCC told the DHSS that they were 'not convinced that a case for the appointment of a Health Commissioner has been made out. Mechanism [sic] for the investigation of complaints already exists, and the JCC feels that a good deal of experience and "case law" must, after 20 years' experience of the National Health Service, exist within the Department of Health.'[93] Not all sections of the medical profession, however, were so vehemently opposed to the suggested introduction of an ombudsman. An editorial in *The Lancet* argued that 'There is need, between the hospital at one end and the courts and Parliament at the other, for an independent system of scrutinising complaints.' The piece supported the introduction of a health ombudsman, stating that 'The profession's proper insistence that its dealings with patients are confidential should not lead it to claim a protected private position in a public service. For once, cannot the profession shake itself free from its occupational obscurantism?'[94]

Perhaps unsurprisingly, patient-consumer groups were also keen on the introduction of an ombudsman for health care.[95] In response to the DHSS's request for their views, organisations put forward a range of arguments in support of the ombudsman. NAWCH asserted that 'This Association has for some years felt that a "Health Ombudsman" was urgently needed, and we hope that an appointment will be made as soon as possible, without waiting for the re-organisation of the National Health Service.' The association also expressed the view that 'as well as providing a corrective to the inflexible attitude of some hospitals, the existence of the Health Commissioner would prevent attempts to suppress complaints, which are occasionally encountered'.[96] The NAMH welcomed the proposed ombudsman, and issued a plea that 'if justice is to be seen to be done by complainants the independence of the process of investigation from the administration of the Health Service is of paramount importance'.[97] The Consumer Council also believed that an ombudsman would introduce greater fairness to the complaints system, noting that 'a National Health Commissioner would ensure that patients not only get a fair deal but would also encourage the providers of health services to listen to complaints sympathetically and promptly'.[98] The National Association of Leagues of Hospital Friends believed that the ombudsman could have a wider role in ensuring equality across the NHS, arguing that the 'first purpose of a Health Commissioner should be to watch the interests of those who cannot watch their own: most patients must be in this category'. Moreover, the association contended that 'In a National Health Service, the patient can be considered to have a positive right to grumble and complain if he or she feels the need: they are the customers in the shop and shareholders in the business.'[99]

In contrast, many members of the medical profession were strongly opposed to any notion that the patient had a 'right' to complain. By July 1970, DHSS officials were convinced of the need to establish an ombudsman, but were well aware that that 'although the consumer interests would welcome such a proposal there would be opposition from some medical interests and early consultation would be necessary'.[100] A long process of consultation took place, so long that the PA organised a petition to press the Health Secretary, Keith Joseph, to appoint the Health Commissioner at 'the earliest possible moment'.[101] The DHSS were almost ready to announce the establishment of the ombudsman in June 1971, but representatives of the medical profession de-railed the proposals following a meeting between Joseph, officials, the BMA and the JCC. The BMA and JCC's chief objection to the ombudsman was the suggestion that he or she should have limited power to review the exercise of clinical judgement: 'They felt that it would be quite wrong for a "lay" official to stand in judgement over doctors carrying out their professional duties'.[102] The profession's representatives were also concerned that 'the addition of a health commissioner to the battery of procedures for investigating the actions of doctors … would mark out the profession still more clearly as peculiarly vulnerable to complaint and punitive action'. The BMA and JCC argued that

> The profession had a real fear that an ombudsman procedure would inevitably put into the citizen's mind that he had a right to complain and should exercise the right without hesitation. The result might be that doctors would become unduly cautious and enterprising in their work, so as to avoid the danger of stimulating complaints.[103]

As with the hospital complaints procedure, many doctors appeared to be opposed to any notion that the patient had a 'right' to complain.

Once again, however, it would seem that the BMA and JCC did not speak for all of the profession on the broader issue of whether or not to create an ombudsman. Contrasting editorials appeared in *The Lancet* and the *British Medical Journal*. *The Lancet* pointed out that consumer groups and nursing bodies were in favour of the Health Commissioner, whereas the medical organisations were opposed, leading the author to suggest that 'Where such a strong conflict of interests exists, the case for an independent health commissioner seems clear enough.'[104] The *British Medical Journal* was opposed to the ombudsman, asserting that 'If a patient or his relatives believe that he has suffered because of a doctor's error of clinical judgement, there is a remedy available in the courts, which will apply long-established principles of the law of negligence.'[105]

In the end, something of a compromise was reached: the ombudsman was finally introduced as part of the NHS Reorganisation Act in 1973, but he or she was prevented from considering clinical complaints. Although health officials felt it would be difficult to exclude clinical matters from the ombudsman's remit, 'the investigation of actions taken by a doctor in the course of diagnosis, treatment or clinical care of an individual patients, which in the commissioner's opinion, were taken in the exercise of clinical judgement' were excluded from the ombudsman's brief.[106] The Department also decided that the role of Health Service Commissioner (the health ombudsman) should be given to the PCA (the existing ombudsman), in a 'two-hat' arrangement.[107] The PCA, Sir Alan Marre, had been pressing to add health to his brief for some years, but he was unhappy about the exclusion of clinical complaints. At a meeting with officials he said that 'The Department's proposals would limit the powers of the health commissioner still further and in such a way as to raise doubts among the general public as to the Government's seriousness in establishing the post.' In defence of their proposals, civil servants argued that 'There would no doubt always be criticism of the scope both of the PCA's and health commissioner's powers, but the public in general would prefer a commissioner with limited powers, to having no commissioner at all.'[108]

The benefit to patients of the Health Service Commissioner was foregrounded by Joseph in his announcement to the House of Commons about the post in February 1972. He asserted that the ombudsman would 'reinforce the rights of those who use the Health Service, without detracting from the responsibilities of the Health Service authorities or reflecting on the value of the work done by the staff of the service'.[109] The ombudsman would be empowered to investigate cases 'where it is claimed that an individual person has suffered injustice or hardship through maladministration, or through a failure to provide necessary treatment and care' but was unable to deal with deal with clinical complaints, or the actions of GPs or other independent contractors, as they were not employed by the health service.[110] The introduction of the ombudsman was welcomed in both the House of Commons and the House of Lords, although some parliamentarians questioned the exclusion of clinical complaints. Labour MP Maurice Miller (who was also a GP) suggested that 'there will be considerable weakening of the authority of the commissioner if he does not have the ability or the right to investigate clinical complaints'.[111] Joseph replied that he thought Miller likely to 'find himself in a very small minority among the professions in taking the line he has taken. The House must remember that clinical judgments are already open to challenge by hospital authorities, the General Medical Council and the courts, and complainants already have recourse to them.'[112]

The Ombudsman, known officially as Health Service Commissioner for England and Wales (there was a separate ombudsman for Scotland), took office in 1973 following the introduction of the NHS Reorganisation Act. The Ombudsman was empowered to investigate 'failures in a service' provided by the NHS, but not clinical complaints or those relating to services provided by independent contractors, like GPs.[113] Such exclusions remained a bone of contention. In 1977, the Select Committee on the Parliamentary Commissioner for Administration recommended that the ombudsman deal with clinical complaints.[114] A year later, the Merrison Commission also called for the expansion of the Health Commissioner's brief to include clinical matters.[115] In response, the BMA and JCC issued proposals on how to handle clinical complaints, a move an editorial in the *Guardian* described as 'a desperate attempt by the leaders of the medical profession to counter the determination of Parliament and the ministers at the Department of Health to place matters of clinical judgement under the scrutiny of the Ombudsman'.[116] In March 1980, Labour MP Jack Ashley (a key supporter of disabled people) presented a bill to the House of Commons designed to empower the Health Service Commissioner to hear complaints of a clinical nature. The aim of his Bill, Ashley said, was 'to prevent the medical establishment from gagging an aggrieved patient by murmuring the incantation "clinical judgment". Ashley asserted that 'When people suffer damage or disaster they have a right to know what when wrong and why it went wrong. They have a right to seek the truth. That right is curtailed by the present system.'[117] The lawyer and ethicist Ian Kennedy, in his 1980 Reith Lectures, also asserted that the Ombudsman should be empowered to consider clinical matters.[118] Despite Ashley and Kennedy's efforts, and those of others, clinical complaints and the actions of GPs stayed outside the remit of the ombudsman until 1996. As Webster remarked, 'In response to demands from the vested interests, the functions of the Health Service Commissioner were constricted to a minimum. The Health Service Commissioner was therefore dispatched to the position of long stop on a very large playing field.'[119]

Conclusion

The establishment of the ombudsman, like the introduction of the hospital complaints procedure, represented a partial victory for patient-consumer groups and others wishing to strengthen the capacity of the patient to complain. By the mid-1970s, and certainly by the mid-1980s, a number of mechanisms were in place that made complaining easier. Clear procedures, support and protection for complainants and recourse to an independent authority if he or she remained unsatisfied, were all measures that strengthened the position of the patient-consumer wishing to make a complaint. There was also some evidence to suggest that patient-consumer organisations' conception of the wider value of complaints was finding a degree of purchase. The Merrison report, for example, asserted that complaints 'should be seen as a positive contribution to making the NHS more efficient'.[120]

Yet, despite such measures, complaining about medical care remained difficult and contentious. The Hospital Complaints Procedure Act required hospitals to have a complaints process in place, and guidance to hospitals was issued on this in 1988, but much variation remained. In 1993, a report by the Audit Commission on complaining pointed to persistent difficulties, such as the reluctance of hospitals to inform patients about complaints. The Commission found that 45 per cent of wards did not display any information on how to complain.[121] Complaints about treatment by GPs continued to be particularly problematic, due, in part, to the flawed complaint mechanisms within the FPS and the fact that complainants had no recourse to the ombudsman. Moreover, as Jean Robinson of the PA noted, only a minority of patients (predominantly those who were middle-class and articulate) could be expected to be able to make use of the complaints system, a situation that perpetuated existing inequalities.[122] Many patients remained wary of making a complaint for fear of staff reprisals. Complaints and complaints procedures were, and continue to be, a fraught issue.

The persistence of such difficulties, and the relative weakness of the complaint mechanisms that were introduced during the 1970s and 1980s, can be explained by the strength of opposition mustered by the medical profession. Although the profession did not always speak with one voice on the complaints issue, it was clear that the majority of doctors viewed complaints as an attack on their expertise, authority and position. The profession was especially opposed to the notion that patients had a right to complain, yet it was clear that for patient-consumer groups complaint was just one of a growing number of things to which patients felt entitled. Increasingly, patient-consumer groups employed the language of rights as a tool for strengthening their demands. But, as the next chapter makes clear, rights talk, like complaint, could only go so far.

Notes

1. Matthew Hilton, 'The duties of citizens, the rights of consumers', *Consumer Policy Review*, 15:1 (2005), 6–12; Matthew Hilton, *Prosperity for All: Consumer Activism in an Era of Globalization* (Ithaca and London: Cornell University Press, 2009), pp. 186–187.
2. Linda Mulcahy, *Disputing Doctors: The Socio-Legal Dynamics of Complaints About Medical Care* (Maidenhead: Open University Press, 2003), p. 1.
3. TNA LCO 20/840, Patients Association Leaflet, n.d. [early 1970s].
4. Definitions taken from the Oxford English Dictionary online, www.oed.com/, accessed 17 April 2012.
5. Julian Baggini, *Complaint: From Minor Moans to Principled Protests* (London: Profile, 2008), p. 2.
6. Robin M. Kowalski, 'Complaints and complaining: functions, antecedents and consequences', *Psychological Bulletin*, 119:2 (1996), 179–196, p. 192.
7. Baggini, *Complaint*, pp. 3, 18.
8. Charles F. Hanna, 'Complaint as a form of association', *Qualitative Sociology*, 4:4 (1981), 298–311.
9. Dorothy Porter and Roy Porter, *Patients Progress: Doctors and Doctoring in Eighteenth Century England* (Stanford, CA: Stanford University Press, 1989), pp. 58–63.
10. Martin Gorsky, 'Community involvement in hospital governance in Britain: evidence from before the National Health Service', *International Journal of Health Studies*, 38:4 (2008), 751–771, p. 763.
11. Margaret Stacey, *Regulating British Medicine: The General Medical Council* (Chichester: John Wiley and Sons, 1992), p. 56.
12. PEP, *Family Needs and the Social Services* (London: PEP, 1961), pp. 100–113.
13. Stacey, *Regulating British Medicine*, p. 17.

14 Department of Health and Social Security, *Report of the Committee on Hospital Complaints Procedure* (London: HMSO, 1973), p. 7.
15 Charles Webster, *The Health Services Since the War, vol. II: Government and Health Care, The National Health Service 1958–1979* (London: The Stationery Office, 1996), p. 227.
16 Barbara Robb, *Sans Everything: A Case to Answer* (London: Nelson, 1967).
17 Council on Tribunals, *The Annual Report of the Council on Tribunals 1968* (London: HMSO, 1969), p. 10.
18 Cmnd. 3975, *Report of the Committee of Inquiry into Allegations of Ill-Treatment of Patients and Other Irregularities at the Ely Hospital, Cardiff* (London: HMSO, 1969), p. 73.
19 *Ibid.*, p. 132.
20 Cmnd. 4557, *Report of the Farleigh Hospital Committee of Inquiry* (Londno: HMSO, 1971), p. 23.
21 Cmnd. 4861, *Report of the Committee of Inquiry into Whittingham Hospital* (London: HMSO, 1972), p. 42.
22 Anon., 'Patients Association', *The Lancet* (19 January 1963), p. 151.
23 Anon., '525 complaints on the NHS: need for change of staff attitude', *Guardian*, 4 September 1964, p. 5.
24 ACHCEW, *The Golden Age of Paient Involvement in the NHS*, CD ROM, vol. 2, *CHC News* (January 1976), p. 8.
25 Anon., 'Joining the queue for good health', March 1987. Press Release on South Birmingham CHC Annual Report, inserted into 1984–86 Annual Report; Mike Gerrard, *A Stifled Voice: Community Health Councils in England 1974–2003* (Brighton: Pen Press, 2006), p. 174.
26 CMAC SA/PAT/H/3, Anon., 'Patients complain', *New Society*, 10 September 1964; Letter from Helen Hodgson to the *Sunday Telegraph*, 7 February 1965.
27 CMAC SA/PAT/D/13/1, Patient Complaints – Patients Association Complaints Analysis Project 1976–83.
28 Glen O'Hara, 'The complexities of "consumerism": choice, collection and participation within Britain's National Health Service, c. 1961–1979', *Social History of Medicine*, 26:2 (2013), 288–304, p. 297.
29 ACHCEW CD ROM, Vol 2, *CHC News* (January 1976), p. 8.
30 Jack Hallas and Bernadette Fallon, *Mounting the Health Guard: A Handbook for Community Health Council Members* (Oxford: Nuffield Provincial Hospitals Trust, 1974), p. 31.
31 West Birmingham Community Health Council, *Annual Report*, June 1976–May 1977, p. 22.
32 CMAC SA/PAT/A/1/6, Elizabeth Stanton, 'Patients' rights and responsibilities', *The Clapham Omnibus*, 11 (Winter 1981).
33 ACHCEW CD ROM, Vol 2, *CHC News* (May 1976), p. 1.
34 Levitt quoted in Gerrard, *A Stifled Voice*, p. 229.
35 Royal Commission on the NHS, *Report of the Royal Commission on the National Health Service* (London: HMSO, 1979), p. 155.
36 HM (66) 15. Reproduced in DHSS, *Report of the Committee on Hospital Complaints Procedure*.

37 TNA MH 159/263, Summary of Patients Association' response to questionnaire sent to interested bodies about complaints procedure, n.d. [1971].
38 DHSS, *Report of the Committee on Hospital Complaints Procedure*, pp. 12–13.
39 *Ibid.*, p. 8.
40 Mulcahy, *Disputing Doctors*, pp. 31–32.
41 TNA MH 159/263, Summary of Patients Association's response to questionnaire sent to interested bodies about complaints procedure, n.d. [1971].
42 TNA MH 159/263, Summary of Association for the Welfare of Children in Hospital's response to questionnaire sent to interested bodies about complaints procedure, n.d. [1971?]
43 DHSS, *Report of the Committee on Hospital Complaints*, p. 3.
44 *Ibid.*, p. 3
45 *Ibid.*, p. 14.
46 *Ibid.*, p. 4.
47 Mulcahy, *Disputing Doctors*, p. 37.
48 DHSS, *Report of the Committee on Hospital Complaints*, p. 31.
49 TNA MH 159/281, Hospital Complaints Procedure: The Report of the Davies Committee – Report of the Joint Medico-Legal Subcommittee to the CCHMS and JCC, n.d. [April 1974?].
50 TNA MH 159/281, Elston Grey-Turner, Deputy Secretary of the BMA to Dr H. Yellowlees (CMO) 25 April 1974.
51 TNA MH 159/281, The Patients Association: Comment on Report of the Committee on Hospitals Complaints Procedure, March 1974.
52 Webster, *The Health Services Since the War vol. II*, p. 640.
53 MRC MSS.184 Box 2: The NHS Complaints Procedure Three Years On: Opening Address by Meg Stacey.
54 Mulcahy, *Disputing Doctors*, p. 39.
55 CMAC SA/PAT/E/1/1, Patients Association's comments on Draft Health Services Complaints Procedure, 16 August 1976.
56 Select Committee on the Parliamentary Commissioner for Administration, *Independent Review of the Hospital Complaints Service* (London: House of Commons, 1977), pp. 9–10.
57 See *House of Commons Debates*, 22 February 1985, vol. 73, cols 1370–1386.
58 McNair-Wilson's charter was published by ACHCEW. See ACHCEW Health News Briefing, 19 November 1984, *The Patient's Charter*. ACHCEW CD ROM, vol. 2.
59 David Marsh and Melvyn Read, *Private Members' Bills* (Cambridge: Cambridge University Press, 1988), p. 42.
60 Mulcahy, *Disputing Doctors*, p. 41.
61 See *House of Commons Debates*, 22 February 1985, vol. 73, cols 1370–1386.
62 Hospital Complaints Procedure Act, 1985.
63 Mulcahy, *Disputing Doctors*, p. 41.
64 Christine Hogg, 'Health', in Nicholas Deakin and Anthony Wright (eds), *Consuming Public Services* (London: Routledge, 1990), 155–182, p. 163.
65 CMAC SA/PAT/D/13/2, Family Practitioner Service: Review of Complaints Investigation Procedures, DHSS, 1976.
66 CMAC SA/PAT/D/13/2, Complaints Investigation Procedures – Family Practitioner Services, 21 October 1976 by Elizabeth Ackroyd.

67 Jill Turner, 'Painful Complaints', *New Society*, 26 October 1978, p. 10.
68 Anon., 'From the GMS Committee: review of complaints procedure', *British Medical Journal* (5 March 1977), 662–664.
69 CMAC SA/PAT/D/13/2, Family Practitioner Service: Review of Service Committee Procedure, DHSS, 1978.
70 General Medical Services Committee statement on DHSS proposals, *British Medical Journal* (2 December 1978), p. 1583.
71 Anon., 'From the GMS Committee – changes in complaints procedures opposed', *British Medical Journal* (2 December 1978), p. 1583.
72 CMAC SA/PAT/D/13/2, Letter from M.G. Hyde, DHSS to Mrs W. Acheson, PA, 14 August 1979.
73 Roy Gregory and Philip Giddings, 'The ombudsman institution: growth and development', in Roy Gregory and Philip Giddings (eds), *Righting Wrongs: The Ombudsman in Six Continents* (Amsterdam: IOS Press, 2000), 1–20.
74 Mary Seneviratne, *Ombudsmen: Public Services and Administrative Justice* (London: Reed Elsvier, 2002), pp. 31–33; Roy Gregory and Philip Giddings, *The Ombudsman, The Citizen and Parliament: A History of the Office of the Parliamentary Commissioner for Administration and Health Service Commissioners* (London: Politicos, 2002).
75 Glen O'Hara, 'Parties, people and parliament: Britain's "ombudsman" and the politics of the 1960s', *Journal of British Studies*, 50:3 (2011), 690–714, p. 693.
76 Parliamentary Commissioner Act, 1967.
77 O'Hara, 'Parties, people and parliament', p. 707.
78 CMAC SA/PAT/1/1/1, Minutes of the Meeting of the Committee of the PA, 13 December 1965.
79 *House of Lords Debates*, 8 February 1967, vol. 279, Parliamentary Commissioner Bill, cols 1384–468, col. 1418.
80 House of Commons, *Second Report of the Select Committee on the Parliamentary Commissioner for Administration, 1967–68* (London: HMSO, 1968), p. xiv; Council on Tribunals, *The Annual Report of the Council on Tribunals 1968*, p. 13.
81 TNA MH 166/24, Catherine Dennis to Mr Dodds, 15 September 1967.
82 TNA MH 166/24, J.E. Pater to Mr Dodds, 11 September 1967.
83 TNA MH 166/24, Administrative Structure: Proposal for a Health Commissioner(s), n.d. [December 1967].
84 Ministry of Health, *National Health Service: The Administrative Structure of the Medical and Related Services in England and Wales* (London: HMSO, 1968), p. 24.
85 TNA MH 166/24, Comments of Associations etc. on the paragraphs of the Green Paper that suggest Health Commissioners, T.E. Nodder, 22 January 1969.
86 *Ibid.*; CMAC SA/PAT/A/1/2, Minutes of the Meeting of the Committee of the PA, 7 October 1968.
87 TNA MH 166/25, Post Ely Policy Working Party: Procedure for Investigating Complaints and Proposals for a Health Commissioner. Note by the Department, n.d. [1969].
88 TNA MH 166/25, Working Group on Complaints: Health Commissioner, n.d. [July 1969].
89 TNA MH 166/28, Letter from J.P. Dodds to A. Macdonald, Council on Tribunals, 13 January 1970.

90 TNA MH 166/27, Letter from Dr D.C. Cameron, Chairman of the General Medical Services Committee, BMA, to Dr R.M. Shaw, Deputy CMO, 2 December 1969.
91 TNA MH 166/29, British Medical Association: Resolutions of the Special Representative Meeting of 6/7th May 1970 on the 2nd Green Paper on the Future Structures of the National Health Service in England.
92 Quoted in TNA MH 166/28, Summary of comments on Departmental Paper of February 1970.
93 TNA MH 166/29, Joint Consultants Committee: Comments on proposal to appoint a Health Commissioner, 4 May 1970.
94 Anon., 'Complaints in hospital', *The Lancet*, 11 April 1970, p. 759.
95 The organisations approached for their view by the Ministry of Health were: the Consumer Council, the PA, the National Association for Mental Health, the National Society for Mentally Handicapped Children, the National Citizen's Advice Bureaux Council, the Spastics Society, NAWCH, AEGIS and the National Association of Leagues of Hospital Friends. TNA MH 166/28, Summary of comments on Departmental Paper of February 1970.
96 TNA MH 166/29, Comments of NAWCH on proposals for a health commissioner in the re-organised National Health Service, May 1970.
97 TNA MH 166/29, Letter from Mary Appleby, General Secretary of NAMH to J.P. Cashman, DHSS, 15 May 1970.
98 TNA MH 166/29, Press release from the Consumer Council, 7 May 1970.
99 TNA MH 166/29, Proposals for a Health Commissioner in the Reorganised National Health Service, Comments by the National Association of Leagues of Hospital Friends, May 1970.
100 TNA MH 166/30, Minutes of Meeting on Complaints Procedure; Health Commissioner and NHS Reorganisation, Between Secretary of State and DHSS officials, 29 July 1970.
101 TNA MH 166/30, Letter from Hodgson to Keith Joseph, 2 September 1970.
102 TNA MH 166/34, Health Commissioner: Meeting with representatives of the Medical Profession, 2 July 1971.
103 TNA MH 166/34, Note of Secretary of State's Meeting on 15 June 1971 with BMA and JCC to discuss proposals for a Health Commissioner.
104 Anon., 'The case for a health commissioner', *The Lancet*, 14 August 1971, p. 365.
105 Anon., 'Clinical judgement', *British Medical Journal*, 14 August 1971, p. 389.
106 TNA MH 166/34, Health Commissioner, Annex A, n.d. [September 1971].
107 TNA MH 166/35, J.P. Dodds to Mr Mottershead, 18 October 1971.
108 TNA MH 166/34, Note of Meeting with PCA and Dept, 30 September 1971.
109 *House of Commons Debates*, 22 February 1972, vol. 831, cols 1104–1114, Health Service Commissioner, col. 1104.
110 *Ibid.*, col. 1105.
111 *Ibid.*, col. 1111.
112 *Ibid.*, col. 1112.
113 NHS Reorganisation Act, 1973.
114 House of Commons, *First Report From the Select Committee on the Parliamentary Commissioner for Administration, 1977–78, Independent Review of Hospital Complaints in the National Health Service* (London: House of Commons, 1978), pp. xiii–xvi.

115 Royal Commission on the National Health Service, *Report*, p. 154.
116 CMAC SA/PAT/D/13/4, Editorial, 'A medical obstruction', the *Guardian*, 6 January 1981.
117 *House of Commons Debates*, 12 March 1980, vol. 980, cols 1336–1340, Health Service Commissioner (Powers), col. 1336.
118 Ian Kennedy, *The Unmasking of Medicine* (London: George Allen Unwin, 1981), p. 127.
119 Webster, *The Health Services Since the War vol. II*, p. 412.
120 Royal Commission on the NHS, *Report*, p. 150.
121 Audit Commission, *What Seems to be the Matter: Communication Between Hospitals and Patients* (London: Audit Commission, 1993), p. 43.
122 Robinson quoted in Jill Turner, 'Painful Complaints', *New Society*, 26 October 1978, p. 10.

4

Rights

The idea that patients were in possession of rights in relation to health has long permeated discussions about medicine and health in Britain, but during the 1970s and 1980s, 'rights talk' became more prominent. Patient-consumer organisations began to formulate many of their demands, such as access to information or the ability to complain, as 'rights'. A plethora of rights guides and charters were produced from the late 1970s onwards, designed to inform the patient of his or her rights, including things such as access to treatment on the NHS, to informed consent, and to a second opinion. Some degree of success was achieved, so that by the 1990s, patients held three rights established in law: the right to access medical records, the right to consent and the right to complain. The campaigns to establish each of these rights are explored in other chapters: the aim of this chapter is to explore the broader meaning and application of rights talk in connection with health from the 1970s to the early 1990s.

Even the most cursory examination of the rights discourse demonstrates that a legal conception of rights was not the only way of viewing patients' rights, and legalistic notions of rights have often been criticised for being too narrow in their focus.[1] Other conceptualisations of rights in the context of health were also on offer: human rights, consumers' rights and citizens' rights all appeared to overlap and intersect with ideas about rights to and within health care. For patient-consumer groups this presented both an opportunity and a threat. On the one hand, the multiple possible definitions and underpinnings to rights discourses allowed patient organisations considerable latitude when using the language of rights to lay claim to a range of objectives. But on the other, uncertainty about who was laying claim to what and on what basis left rights discourse open to co-option by other actors. By the late 1980s, ownership of patients' rights had transferred from patient-consumer organisations to the government, something symbolised by the establishment of the Department of Health's *Patient's Charter* in

1991. Such a development was indicative of a wider shift. Up until the end of the 1980s, the lead architect in constructing the patient-consumer had been patient organisations. But, as the Conservative government under Margaret Thatcher became interested in the market as the most effective and efficient way of delivering public services, citizens became reconfigured as consumers, a development which moved emphasis away from the duty of the state to provide universal coverage, and towards the rights of individuals to make choices about the services that they used. The supposed consensus around universal entitlements to welfare was eroded by the concept of individualistic rights to, and choice of, services. In a number of spheres, including housing, utilities and health, publicly owned services were either privatised or re-designed, often along market principles.[2] The patient-consumer that was to operate within such an environment was different to that which had been imagined by patient organisations. By the 1990s, a new kind of patient-consumer began to emerge, one that was concerned not so much with collective issues such as representation and group rights, but with individual matters such as choice.

This chapter will explore how and why such a shift took place through an examination of the changing use and application of patients' rights. It will begin by considering the various ways in which the language of rights was used in the context of health. The numerous methods of conceptualising rights in health spoke to their rhetorical power as a device for groups and individuals wishing to lay claim to treatment and services, but also serves to illustrate a key weakness with rights discourse in health: uncertainty about what kind of rights were being employed and by what kind of group or individual. Were these citizens' rights, consumers' rights or human rights? Or was there enough that was distinctive about rights claims in health to make patients' rights another category altogether? Patient-consumer organisations certainly thought so. The second section of this chapter considers attempts to introduce a Rights of Patients Bill in the early 1970s. The bill, sponsored by the Patients Association, did not pass in to law, but attempts to formulate demands around privacy as 'rights' and 'consumer protection' were indicative of a wider turn towards the language of rights to bolster patient-consumer demands. The employment of rights talk was much in evidence within the numerous patients' rights guides and charters produced by patient-consumer organisations throughout the 1970s and 1980s. Analysis of these documents suggests that patient-consumer groups were using rights language to broaden the range of things to which they felt patients were entitled. At the same time, many of these charters were unclear about the precise nature of patients' entitlements and whether patients on an individual level, or patients on a communal basis, should exercise these. A more collective understanding of patients' rights was exhibited by organisations such as the Community Rights Project, which aimed to enhance democracy and accountability within the NHS during the mid-1980s through the language of rights. The establishment of *The Patient's Charter* in 1991, however, undermined such collective conceptualisations of rights. Addressed to the individual patient rather than all patients, *The Patient's Charter* was indicative not only of an individualised approach to patients' rights, but of a wider shift in the conceptualisation of the patient as consumer and who could speak for this figure. The ownership and meaning of patients' rights was thus a bell-wether for bigger changes in ideas about the patient as consumer.

Rights and health in Britain

Three distinct, but overlapping, visions of health rights were articulated in Britain during the second half of the twentieth century: health as a human right, as a citizen's right, and as a consumer's right. The notion that health was a fundamental human right – that it was a right that individuals possess simply by being born – is almost as old as the notion of human rights itself. Most commentators place the 'invention' of human rights in the eighteenth century, and though the right to health was not amongst the initial rights established by the French National Assembly, it was added to the list of the state's obligations to its citizens by the Constituent Assembly in 1791.[3] From the close of the eighteenth century until the end of the Second World War, human rights disappeared from Western political discourses.[4] Rights remained fundamental to politics, but the nature of the rights being demanded changed. In the nineteenth century, the focus was on the rights of the citizen rather than the rights of man, and attention was directed towards a set of political rights, such as the right to vote. By the early twentieth century, as enfranchisement gradually became universal, citizens' calls for rights were increasingly social in nature. The establishment of welfare states in European nations went some way towards satisfying such demands, as housing, education and health care came to be seen as social rights.[5]

Universal human rights, as opposed to the rights citizens demanded of states, returned to global political prominence after 1945. The reappearance of human rights has sometimes been explained as being a consequence of the exposure of Nazi wartime atrocities, or as a result of the heroic actions of key figures such as Eleanor Roosevelt.[6] But, as Mark Mazower points out, attempts to establish a new doctrine of human rights succeeded only because nation states were prepared to accept this as part of a broader conception of liberal political thought which maintained that the individual required protection from the state.[7]

The post-war turn to human rights manifested itself in a number of ways. Perhaps the most iconic was the United Nations Universal Declaration of Human Rights (UNDHR) of 1948. Comprised of 30 articles, the UNDHR proclaimed the existence of a series of civil, political, economic, social and cultural rights, including 'the right to a standard of living adequate for health and well being of himself and his family, including food, clothing, housing and medical care'.[8] In 1946, the right to 'the enjoyment of the highest attainable standard of physical and mental health' was enshrined within the charter establishing the World Health Organization (WHO).[9] The International Covenant on Economic, Social and Cultural Rights (ICESCR), which was ratified in 1966 and came into effect for member countries ten years later, provided legal bite to such declarations.[10]

During this period another set of health rights were established around the use of human beings in medical research. As discussed in Chapter 1, a series of international codes governing medical experimentation were created following the Nuremberg Trials.[11] These were framed using the language of human rights. But by the 1970s, the language of human rights was being used by non-governmental organisations and other actors to make different kinds of demands at the national and international level.[12] In health, action coalesced initially around the concept of primary health care, which aimed to provide health services at the community level.[13] Primary health care was the focus of the Alma-Ata conference in 1978, and the resulting declaration proclaimed that health 'is a fundamental human right'.[14] Human rights language was used throughout the 1970s and early 1980s to advance the development of primary health care and also in attempts to address the social determinants of health, as well as in specific health campaigns, such as those against breast milk substitutes and the dumping of pharmaceutical drugs on markets in developing countries.[15] Health as a human rights issue was propelled further onto the global agenda in the late 1980s and early 1990s in the wake of HIV/AIDS.[16] The work of the American physician, Jonathan Mann, has often been seen as being central to the conceptualisation of HIV/AIDS within a human rights framework.[17] Mann's research on AIDS in Africa convinced him that the epidemic had social and economic causes as well as infectious ones. Mann developed the WHO's first Global Strategy on AIDS based on human rights principles, emphasising non-discrimination against people with AIDS and equitable access to health care.[18] Human rights principles were put forward as a tool for the analysis of AIDS and as means to address the many problems it posed.[19]

Although the notion of health as a human right was significant at the transnational level, in the UK the notion of rights in health took a rather different trajectory over this period. Instead of being concerned primarily with human rights, the rights discourse in Britain seemed to focus more on the rights of citizens. This could be partly explained by long-running discussions about individual rights within health in the UK. In the medical marketplace that pre-dated the NHS patients had contractual and common-law rights relating to health care, as with other goods and services.[20] Even within charitable provision, subscribers to hospital contributory schemes were entitled to some say in the way in which the institution was managed through representatives on hospital management committees.[21] Entitlement also lay at the heart of the gradual development of state-sponsored health care in Britain up to and including the establishment of the NHS. The National Health Insurance Act (NHI), 1911, introduced compulsory health insurance for manual workers. In return for their financial contribution, members received benefit when sick and access to medical care without additional payment.

The NHI has often been seen as harbinger of the NHS, but the precise form that Britain's health system should take was the subject of much debate throughout the 1930s and 1940s.[22] The service that emerged was based not on insurance contributions and individual entitlement, but on the universal principle: all citizens were eligible for care regardless of whether or not they had paid directly towards the funding of the service. Such a collective system implied a more collective view of rights with respect to health. While the National Health Service Act (1946) was framed around the *duty* of the Minister of Health to provide a comprehensive service not the *right* of the patient to receive this, the message that reached the public emphasised universal entitlement.[23] A leaflet distributed to all homes in 1948 asserted that the new service would 'provide you with all medical, dental and nursing care. Everyone – rich or poor, man, woman or child – can use it or any part of it.'[24] Underpinning such promises was the notion of social rights. For the sociologist T.H. Marshall, social rights permitted the citizen access to a minimum supply of essential social goods and services (such as medical attention, shelter and education), to be provided by the state.[25] The NHS, and the other achievements of the 'classic' era of the British welfare state (1945 to 1975), appeared to offer a kind of social citizenship based on collective rights.[26]

Interwoven with ideas about the health rights of citizens was another set of expectations: the rights individuals could demand as consumers. The relationship between citizenship and consumption has been the subject of much research in recent years, and the activities of citizen-consumers can be detected as far back as the nineteenth century and beyond.[27] But, by the middle of the twentieth century, citizen and consumer identities were becoming welded together more tightly. The establishment of the CA in 1956 was a significant point in the development of the organised consumer movement in Britain, introducing comparative testing and consumer activism based on rational principles. The activities of the CA and other consumer groups helped to shift consumerism 'beyond things', encompassing public goods and services as well as private ones.[28] By the 1960s and 1970s, this approach had found purchase inside government. Organisations like the NCC were created in 1975 to represent the consumer within public services. State-provided amenities from housing to health care were being discussed in increasingly consumerist terms.[29] The creation of the CHCs in 1973 was in line with the general trend towards the improvement of citizen-consumer representation, and mapped onto the demands for individual autonomy discussed in Chapter 1.

The demand for autonomy made by the PA echoed the kinds of rights claims made by the new social movements of this period. As the feminist historian Shelia Rowbotham commented 'Rights were not abstract or about politics alone, they were active and about sex as well as economics.'[30] This wider conception of rights was crucial for dealing with the problems of 'quality of life, equality, individual self-realization, participation and human rights,' representative, for Jurgen Habermas, of a 'new' form of politics.[31] The rights claims of the 1960s and 1970s were thus a different kind of rights claim to that of the past, rooted not in transactional contracts and the market place, or in the social contract between state and citizen, but in the politics of everyday life. For patient-consumer organisations, rights discourse became a way in which individual and collective demands could be articulated.

The Rights of Patients Bill, 1972–74

In the late 1960s, the PA, as discussed in Chapter 1, attempted to get legislation introduced that would have given patients a legal right to refuse to have students present during treatment or examinations. As the decade wore on, however, the PA's efforts broadened out from the single issue of the right to refuse to the presence of students to encompass other issues and other rights. In 1968, Labour MP Joyce Butler tried to add a clause to the Health Services and Public Health Bill on the treatment of patients in teaching hospitals.[32] A year later, the PA attempted to get Brian Walden to introduce a clause in his private members bill (which was concerned with privacy) on patient privacy and teaching.[33] Both of these efforts involved adding amendments to existing bills, but in the early 1970s, the PA and Butler endeavoured to establish a specific piece of legislation that framed the right to object to the presence of students. Butler first introduced her bill in January 1972, and though the legislation was concerned solely with 'the rights of patients to privacy when receiving hospital treatment under the National Health Service, and in regard to medical experiments on human beings', she set this right within a broader context.[34] Butler remarked that 'Although the principle of the patient's right to unconditional treatment in any hospital is now well established, only a few hospitals completely respect that right in practice.' Moreover, the Bill, she said, 'enters a comparatively new area of consumer protection'.[35] The right to refuse to consent to the presence of students was thus being linked to the broader right to unconditional treatment and framed as something that could protect the interests of patient-consumers.

Butler's Bill, described by the *New Scientist* as a 'mild enough Bill of Rights' met with objections from the BMA, who feared that it would undermine medical education.[36] The Bill was given insufficient time in the House, so it failed. Moreover, health ministers 'accepted, as did their predecessors, that this is not a suitable subject for legislation' and officials believed that 'The Bill itself is a very slipshod piece of drafting'.[37] DHSS papers suggest, however, that there were more fundamental reasons why the Rights of Patients Bill was opposed than due to poor drafting. Officials actively discouraged the use of the language of rights when devising a memorandum on the cooperation of patients in the teaching of medical students. Early drafts of the memo had included reference to the patient's 'right to refuse' to being used in teaching, but officials were unsure if any existing legislation actually gave patients a legal right to refuse.[38] Moreover, the JCC of the British Medical Association and the Royal College of Physicians were not keen on developing patients' rights in this area. Commenting on a draft of the memorandum on the use of patients in teaching, the JCC remarked that 'it rather under-stressed the importance of clinical teaching while over-stressing patients' rights in this matter.'[39] Although the JCC accepted the need for a circular on teaching, they argued that 'Medical science is advancing very rapidly these days and it is in the public interest that our doctors and medical students should be given every opportunity to keep abreast of the latest developments'. Teaching, the Committee contended, 'now takes place in practically every hospital and all patients have an opportunity to make a contribution to this important work'.[40]

Undeterred, Butler tried again in 1974, once more framing her Bill as one of 'consumer protection as it affects the health service'.[41] This bill was also unsuccessful, but its fate, and the fact that it was even introduced at all, was of significance. The failure of the Rights of Patients Bill could be read as another example of medical opposition to the activities of patient-consumer organisations, as seen in Chapter 3 on complaint, but it also illustrated an increasing willingness to phrase patient demands as 'rights' and create a firm basis to these. As demonstrated by the debate the Bill provoked within the DHSS, there was also considerable doubt about the nature and status of patients' rights within the NHS.

Patients' rights guides and charters, 1970s–1980s

To overcome such uncertainty, and broaden the range of patient-consumer entitlements, patient-consumer organisations began to formulate rights guides and charters to both educate patients about their rather limited, existing rights and lay claim to new ones. An early example of this was the PA's somewhat tentatively titled *Can I Insist?*, published in 1974. The pamphlet noted that 'there are many situations where patients are unsure of their rights as consumers in the National Health Service'. *Can I Insist?* was intended to 'give people the confidence of knowing where they stand.'[42] Set out as a series of questions and answers, apparently based on real queries that the PA had received, the booklet covered areas such as how to access health services, how to get information, how to visit patients in hospital and how to obtain additional services such as a second opinion.[43] The document illustrated the fact that patients had few rights: only the 'right to a National Health Service GP' and the 'right to refuse treatment' were clearly expressed as such. The notion that patients had other rights, such as to a second opinion or to see a particular consultant, was quashed definitively: 'Have I a right to see the consultant? No. The patient has no "right" to see a consultant or any particular doctor.'[44] This, together with the hesitant tone of the questions asked 'Can I … ', 'I think … ', 'I asked … ' points to considerable doubt about the status and nature of patients' rights. Yet, there were signs in *Can I Insist?* that the PA was beginning to see the potential power of the language of rights. In answer to the question 'Hasn't the patient got the right to know what's wrong with him?' the guide replied 'The doctor sometimes withholds information because he thinks this is in the patient's interest … However, we believe the patient has a moral right to know what's wrong if he really wants to.'[45] Through *Can I Insist?* the PA were starting to lay claim to additional entitlements for patient-consumers.

A similar sense of ambiguity mixed with new demands can be found in the various rights guides produced by other patient-consumer organisations. In 1980, the Consumers' Association published the *Which? Guide to Your Rights*, a book that covered rights across a range of services, not just health care. The guide specified that patients were entitled to NHS care and to be registered with a GP, but expressed uncertainty about the nature of such rights. There was, it stated, 'no comprehensive list of rights which you can consult, nor is there any specific area of law that deals with them. Your rights are scattered among hundreds, perhaps thousands, of Acts of

Parliament and secondary pieces of legislation ... Sometimes your rights are not written down at all. They may exist because of custom and tradition, or merely because there is nothing saying that they are absent.'[46]

Other groups expressed confusion about patients' rights, or rather the lack of these, too. Patients' rights and responsibilities were discussed at the 1979 NCC Consumer Congress, and as a result the NCC began to draw up a guide to patients' rights.[47] The difficulty was, as Elizabeth Stanton remarked in the NCC's journal, the *Clapham Omnibus*, that 'Patients' rights are not stated as such in law, but stem from doctors' duties in common law and the responsibilities placed on doctors by their contract and their professional code. Little is explicitly stated: much has to be inferred from doctors' duty to exercise professional expertise and discretion'.[48] Nonetheless, the NCC started work on a guide to patients' rights centred on the key consumer principles of access, information, choice, representation, complaint and redress.[49] The NCC's *Patients' Rights* was published in 1983, and like the *Which?* guide it expressed confusion about patients' rights. The NCC document stated that 'It is difficult to say precisely what health care patients are entitled to expect of the National Health Service (NHS). There are clues, but most of them are open to different interpretations, and circumstances greatly affect cases.'[50] *Patients' Rights* offered information and advice on accessing services, on choice and consent, on the treatment of children, and on representation and complaint. The guide also considered patients' responsibilities, one of the few of such documents to do so. The main purpose of *Patients' Rights*, however, was to inform patients about their rights in order that they would get the most from the service. Michael Shanks, Chairman of the NCC stated that 'The National Consumer Council believes that patients will get the best from the health service only when they know what is reasonable to expect of it, what their rights and responsibilities are and when they have the confidence and skill to exercise them.' Shanks went on to assert that the average family paid £18 per week towards the NHS, but 'too many of us behave as if we are being given charity – there is a tendency towards passive acceptance of health services. This is not the way for patients to get the highest quality of service.'[51] There were echoes here of the argument made by RICA in the 1960s: that as taxpayers patients had a right to a say in their own treatment and the wider development and management of health services.

A rival document to the NCC's guide, also published in 1983, was produced jointly by the Patients Association and the Consumers' Association. Their *A Guide to the National Health Service* covered similar ground to the NCC's *Patients' Rights* in terms of how to access services, how to complain, give consent and so on. The PA/CA guide also placed emphasis on knowledge about rights as a way to improve services for individuals and more broadly.

In her Foreword to the guide, Katharine Whitehorn, Vice-President of the PA, commented that 'if we knew what our rights were; if we knew how to complain, and to whom; if we knew what could be expected of our doctors and nurses and what should not be expected of them; then, I believe, a good deal of trouble would be controllable'.[52] Where the PA/CA guide differed from that produced by the NCC was in its suggestion that the text offered patients information in order to enable them to 'play the system as it now is'.[53]

Such an instrumentalist approach was less apparent in the *Patients' Charter* produced by ACHCEW in 1986. A resolution was passed at ACHCEW's 1985 AGM to produce a patients' charter which would 'act as guidelines to improve communications between patients and healthcare professionals'. Drawing explicitly on the WHO's founding principle that 'The enjoyment of the highest attainable standard of health is one of the fundamental rights of every human being', ACHCEW contended that this 'cannot be achieved unless there is communication between healthcare professionals and patients. Both have a role and viewpoint; and there is a need for each to respect the other.'[54] ACHCEW's *Patients' Charter: Guidelines for Good Practice* was published in 1986. The charter listed 17 rights, three of which (the right to health services appropriate to needs; to be treated with reasonable skill, care and consideration; and confidentiality of all records) ACHCEW stated were already legal rights. The remaining 14 rights included things such as the right to information about health services and individual care, the right to privacy, the right to complain and the right to a second opinion. These were aspirations rather than definite rights. *The Patients' Charter* was thus a list of demands as much as an inventory of existing entitlements. Indeed, ACHCEW intended their charter to have a campaigning function. In a document exploring the meaning of charters and the purpose of patients' rights, ACHCEW suggested that their charter 'be used for campaigns, pointing to changes which the Association for Community Health Councils in England and Wales (ACHCEW) and other consumer groups would like to see happen'.[55]

The charters produced by patient-consumer groups during the 1980s were put to a variety of uses. Charters and rights guides informed patients of existing rights and laid claim to new ones; they offered practical advice on how to access services, but also acted as a catalyst for change. Yet, the very proliferation of charters and rights guides points to a deeper level of uncertainty about rights talk. That so many organisations felt it necessary to produce rights guides suggests that they lacked confidence in their claim to such rights. An additional level of confusion surrounded the audience for such documents: were these directed at the individual patient or all patients? This can be seen in the titles of the documents. Some of the guides were addressed to the individual such as 'Can *I* Insist', and the 'Which Guide to *Your* Rights'. Others seem to concern all patients: '*Patients*' Rights', '*Patients*' Charter'. The placing of the apostrophe would appear to be significant here: after the 's' in 'patients' meaning rights belonging to patients plural, not the patient singular. Such nuances are not just a matter of grammatical pedantry, but point to a deeper level of ambiguity about whether patients' rights should be thought of and applied on an individual or a collective level.

The Community Rights Project, 1983–85

A concrete attempt to use the language of rights in effecting change for the wider community was made in the mid-1980s by the Community Rights Project (CRP). This small, London-based organisation began life in 1983 as the Local Government and Health Project.[56] It was staffed by Beverly Beech, who had worked at the Association for Improvement in Maternity Services (AIMS); Ron Bailey, who had worked at Shelter, and Madeline Holliday, a health campaigner and later Director of the Stroke Association in Scotland. Funding for the CRP came from the London Boroughs Grants Scheme administered by the Greater London Council (GLC). Such funding was in line with the GLC's support for a number of different voluntary organisations to campaign for the rights of minority groups and for improvements to services.[57] Connected to this broader goal, the CRP took up casework advising people on their rights with respect to health care and how to use the language of rights to make wider changes. The organisation wanted to help 'people to not only know their rights, but [also] to improve them'.[58] The CRP produced a number of publications offering advice on rights in specific areas, such as maternity services. They believed that 'everyone, irrespective of sex, race, colour, age, disability has the right to the health care and treatment they need and the right to health'. Such a goal could only be achieved, the CRP suggested, 'through substantial improvements in the nature, quality, and organisation of health services; and through more comprehensive and effective public health measures'.[59]

To achieve their objectives the CRP aimed to 'campaign for a health service that is more effectively controlled by the communities it serves'. This may, the organisation argued, 'necessitate some form of elected representation and will require improved rights of consultation, participation and access to information'.[60] Working with representatives from the National Childbirth Trust, Women and Medical Practice, and Greenwich and Brent CHCs, the CRP established a campaign group to press for the 'democratisation' of the NHS.[61] The group argued that 'The NHS is democratic in only a very narrow and constitutional sense through Parliament. Central government is too remote to deal with such a huge service in a way that is responsive and flexible to local needs.' They were critical of the growing influence of 'commercial interests' on the NHS, including pharmaceutical companies and the rise of general management. The CRP wanted to press for either elected Health Authorities, or the integration of health into local government, something that

> would be better than the present undemocratic system, but this does not necessarily ensure accountability and *participation*. The need for an informed and motivated electorate is vital if democracy is to work. Improved and clearly defined rights of access to information are essential for an informed public [original emphasis].[62]

To put such ambitions into action, the CRP worked with the GLC on a draft Bill concerned with the development of 'greater democracy and accountability within the NHS'.[63] Although the GLC had the power to put forward a bill in Parliament for the benefit of people in Greater London, plans for legislation were abandoned in favour of a Charter for a Democratic Health Service.[64] The reason for such a change of tactics is unclear, but the intention behind the Charter was much the same as the draft bill. It was designed 'to encourage wide public support for the principles of a democratic health service' and 'to encourage discussion of alternative ways of achieving a democratic health service'.[65] The Charter for a Democratic Health Service set out specific demands about the need for democracy and accountability as well as the integration of health services in a wider, collective context. The Charter demanded action to address health inequalities; the adoption of a preventative approach to health care; the taking into account of the health implications of social and economic policies; and efforts to make health services responsive to local needs.[66] The Charter also called for greater democratic representation and participation at the local level, as well as more accountability of staff to users and communities.

Despite its powerful claims, the Charter for a Democratic Health Service and the CRP appear to have had little definite impact. The Charter does not seem to have attracted much interest, and the CRP fizzled out when the GLC was dissolved in 1986. That does not mean, however, that their efforts were unimportant. The significance of the CRP lay in the fact that they offered an understanding of what rights discourse could do for patients on a collective level. Patients' rights were being connected to democracy, participation, representation, disease prevention and addressing health inequalities, not just improving services for the individual. Yet, such an approach was in stark contrast to that being developed by the Conservative government.

The Patient's Charter, 1991–94

The notion of a patient's charter had not always found favour within the corridors of power. In 1981, the Health Minister Dr Gerard Vaughn told an audience at the Conservative Medical Society that 'The term "Patients Charter" is irrelevant when a "Charter" is merely a headline under which these [CHC's campaigns] and other ideas can be conveniently grouped.'[67] Yet, by the early 1990s, charters were the government's 'big idea'.[68] Beginning with charters for council house tenants, and moving out to local government, and then to the national level with the introduction of the *Citizen's Charter* in 1991, the development of such 'charterism' has been explained in terms of wider changes within the public sector.[69] Charters to protect the rights of the individual were necessary in the more marketised public services that began to develop from the late 1980s onwards. As Kieron Walsh noted, 'The state was no longer to be a monolithic set of large organisations providing services directly to the public, but a body that played an "enabling" role, ensuring that proper services were provided on a market basis, and acting as a protector of citizen rights in the market for public services.'[70] In health, the prime example of this development was the introduction of the internal market in 1990. The reforms that followed the publication of the White Paper *Working for Patients* in 1989 separated health care purchasers from providers with the aim of creating an internal market within the NHS.[71] Instead of generating profits, financial incentives would encourage the more efficient use of public funds.[72] Such a market exchange model focused attention on principles such as quality, choice, competition, information, standards and value – principles that were encapsulated within *The Citizen's Charter*.[73]

A specific charter for the NHS, *The Patient's Charter*, was also introduced in 1991.[74] The process by which the charter was developed is unclear, and though patient-consumer organisations did meet with Stephen Dorrell, the health minister, plans for the charter were already well advanced.[75] Indeed, Hogg suggested that *The Patient's Charter* was introduced with great speed and little consultation with staff, managers or users. She argues that the charter was imposed on the health service by Downing Street without the agreement of some health ministers.[76]

Whatever the precise origins of the charter, it was obvious that it was a document located firmly within a broader programme for change. Writing in the Foreword to *The Patient's Charter* William Waldegrave, Secretary of State for Health, asserted that the rights and standards documented in the charter were 'a central part of the Government's programme to improve and modernise the delivery of service to the public whilst continuing to reaffirm the fundamental principles of the NHS'.[77] The charter set out seven 'well-established' rights: to receive health care on the basis of clinical need, regardless of ability to pay; to be registered with a GP; to receive emergency medical care at any time; to be referred to a consultant, when a GP thought it necessary; to be given a clear explanation of any treatment proposed, including risks and any alternatives; to have access to your health records; and to choose whether or not to take part in medical research or student training.[78] The Patient's Charter also listed three 'new' rights which would come into effect in April 1992: to be given detailed information on local health services, including quality standards and maximum waiting times; to be guaranteed admission for treatment by a specific date no later than two years from being placed on a waiting list; to have any complaint about NHS services investigated and to receive a full and prompt written reply from the chief executive or general manager.[79] In addition, the charter also put forward nine 'National charter standards' involving aspects of care such as respect for privacy, information for relatives and friends, and waiting times. These were, the Charter explained, 'not legal rights but major and specific standards which the government looks to the NHS to achieve'.[80]

Despite that fact that in many ways *The Patient's Charter* emulated patient-consumer groups' earlier efforts to promote patients' rights, the charter met with a less than enthusiastic response from such bodies. Some organisations welcomed the charter; the CA reportedly said that it was 'a golden opportunity to put patients first'.[81] Other groups saw it as at least better than nothing, but in the main patient-consumer organisations were critical of the *Patient's Charter*.[82] Their criticisms fell under three headings: firstly, the content and scope of the charter; secondly, problems with enforcement and implementation; and finally, questions about the impact and resourcing of the charter. The CoH and the PA were among the first groups to raise problems with the content and scope of *The Patient's Charter*. Jointly, the organisations produced their own list of rights and standards which went further than *The Patient's Charter* in both breadth and depth. The CoH and the PA itemised what they called twelve basic standards of health care, six underlying principles, and three practical proposals. These involved some of the same rights and standards as were listed in the *Patient's Charter*, such as confidentiality of medical records and the delivery of high quality services, but also went much further in laying claim to more collective goals. These included 'EQUITY between individuals or groups of patients so that no-one is made to feel like a second class citizen' and 'REPRESENTATION not tokenism. The views of patients and their representatives should play an integral part in setting, monitoring and improving standards of health care.'[83] This more collective approach contrasted with the individualistic focus of *The Patient's Charter*. Linda Lamont, director of the PA, noted that the charter 'could be interpreted as an attempt to specify the rights of the patient as an individual who speaks for her or himself' but also that 'Any rights to NHS care are dependent on the exigencies of the budget or competing claims of other groups of patients who also believe they have rights.'[84] For patient organisations like the PA, individual rights needed to be balanced with collective ones.

ACHCEW were also critical of the individualistic focus of *The Patient's Charter*. The association branded the charter 'thin' in content and identified gaps in the document that undermined patients' 'rights to equal access to health care, quality of care and treatment and real choice'.[85] As a result, ACHCEW put together their own much more comprehensive list of patients' rights. Entitled *The Patients' Agenda: What the Patient's Charter Leaves out – the Rights you don't yet Have in the NHS*, the document laid claim to a wide range of entitlements. Grouped under headings such as access to care and treatment, choice and information, and advocacy and support, *The Patients' Agenda* asserted the need for more specific rights, such as the right to a second opinion, but was also keen to place these in a more collective context. ACHCEW argued that *The Patient's Charter* 'could do far more to address important issues at the heart of the health service – equality of access to health care, the scope for patient participation on the basis of informed choice and the quality of care and treatment'.[86]

A second set of problems with *The Patient's Charter* identified by patient-consumer organisations revolved around enforcement and implementation. Michael Young told the *Guardian* that *The Patient's Charter* was 'a great disappointment. Talk about patients' rights will get us nowhere without the means to make the rights effective.'[87] As ACHCEW also pointed out, the charter lacked any legal standing and there was no way of enforcing the rights and standards it contained.[88] To resolve such issues, both ACHCEW and the PA suggested that some sort of agency be established to ensure that rights and standards were implemented. ACHCEW wanted an independent Health Rights Commission with statutory powers to enforce all Charter rights and standards, and evaluate how well the NHS was fulfilling the commitments in the charter. The Health Rights Commission, ACHCEW suggested, would be especially good at assessing performance on 'soft standards' such as respect for patients' dignity.[89] The PA proposed the creation of a Health Consumer Standards Board with the responsibility to 'consult with patients/consumers in order to set and monitor the standard of health care which people are entitled to expect'.[90]

Patient-consumer organisations also pointed out that to enforce the charter and for it to have any impact, additional resources would be required. As the PA and the CoH noted, the charter would only be of use if it also translated into better services.[91] For this to happen, ACHCEW asserted that more money would be needed.[92] The effectiveness of the charter would also lie in the extent to which patients were aware of it, and here again patient-consumer organisations pointed to difficulties. Although each household was supposed to receive a copy of *The Patient's Charter*, this costly enterprise did not translate into widespread recognition of the charter.[93] A series of surveys indicated that relatively few patients knew about the charter. An ICM survey published in August 1993 found that just over 40 per cent of respondents had heard of *The Patient's Charter*. Another survey conducted by the NCC and MORI a couple of months later suggested that 64 per cent of respondents had heard of the charter, but only 24 per cent recalled seeing one and only 19 per cent remembered reading it. Plus, there were differences between respondents according to socio-economic status: 79 per cent of middle-class respondents had heard of the charter compared to 53 per cent of working-class respondents.[94] Such a finding appeared to confirm the suggestion made by Barbara Stocking, the Director of the health think-tank the Kings Fund, that *The Patient's Charter* was 'something of a middle class charter: standards for waiting times and so on are important only if you already have reasonable access to health care. For a substantial number of people from ethnic minorities or with disabilities or who are homeless the charter may seem irrelevant.'[95]

Indeed, as many critics from academia and beyond pointed out, *The Patient's Charter* did not bestow the patient-consumer with substantial new powers. Klein suggested that although the charter appeared to shift influence from producers to consumers, 'there was nothing that the consumer could do directly: there were no decisions, informed or otherwise, to make – except, possibly, to opt out of the NHS and go private'.[96] The only individuals who did gain more power, according to social scientists Michael Calnan and Jonathan Gabe, were the managers.[97] The sociologist Iain Crinson concurred, arguing that the rights and standards set out in the Charter were 'essentially symbolic' and used as a means for indirectly re-imposing central control, in the name of the consumer, on local health care purchasers and providers.[98]

A more fundamental problem with *The Patient's Charter* for many critics was its apparent melding of citizenship with consumption. Writing in the *British Medical Journal*, Diane Plaming from the Kings Fund and Tony Delamothe, the journal's deputy editor, contended that 'The extolling of choice, competition, and commitment to service suggests that the government equates citizens' rights with consumers' rights. To conflate the two, however, is to miss much of the point of citizenship'. 'True citizens', they said, 'do more than consume.'[99] Calnan and Gabe were critical of the fact that *The Patient's Charter* 'presented the users of health care as individual consumers rather than as citizens with a collective voice, but in practice such users have not found themselves more empowered'.[100] For John Clarke and his colleagues, the problem with *The Patient's Charter* was that the rights it introduced were 'the *process* rights of consumers' rather than 'the *substantive* rights of citizens'.[101] Hilton suggested that through *The Citizen's Charter* and its spin-offs, like *The Patient's Charter*, 'Consumers were imagined solely as individuals and never as collectives of interested parties, and their role in "shopping" was equated with citizenship, thereby excluding many of the agendas that have inspired and fuelled consumer and citizen groups.'[102]

Conclusion

The real significance of *The Patient's Charter*, then, would seem to lie not in a shift of power from producers to consumers, or in the establishment of a concrete set of patient's rights, but in its re-imagining of the patient-consumer. The patient-consumer envisaged by *The Patient's Charter* was not part of a collective, or concerned with representation and group rights, but an individual interested in information, choice and quality services for themselves. Such a focus on the individual represented a rejection of the more collective aspects of patient consumerism put forward by patient groups throughout the 1970s and 1980s. Borrowing the language of rights from patient groups, the Conservative government set about creating an individualised patient-consumer designed to operate within increasingly marketised public services. Patient groups began to lose control of the figure that they had created.

For patient groups, this was a double defeat. First, as will be discussed in more detail in Chapter 6, the part played by patient organisations in representing patients diminished as alternative, government-sponsored forms of soliciting individual patient's opinions (such as satisfaction surveys and citizens' juries) came to the fore. Speaking for the patient-consumer became a task for government, an irony which suggests that Thatcherism was not so concerned with 'rolling back the state' as reinventing new roles for it. Second, the broader view put forward by patient organisations concerning citizens' collective entitlements was undermined. The marketisation of the NHS that began under Thatcher, but continued under Major, Blair and Brown, added greater weight to individual choice at the expense of collective voice. Given Thatcher's commitment to the individual as an agent of change, and her infamous distaste for society, the failure of patient groups to convince her government of a collective view of the patient-consumer was understandable. Although patient organisations had the ear of policy makers, the contradictory logic of some of their arguments, particularly around the meaning and application of patients' rights, resulted in a message that lacked clarity. This allowed the government the freedom to pick and choose from the ideas put forward by patient groups. Patient-consumer organisations also failed to gain much political purchase: they were never able to mobilise large-scale popular support, and they were forced to occupy a subordinate position, when compared to the medical profession, within the health policy community.

Yet, the Thatcher government's focus on the individual patient was not the inevitable consequence of reconfiguring patients as consumers. The work of patient groups demonstrated that health consumerism could draw attention to the needs of the many, as well as the demands of the few. Consumerism was about pursuing basic needs as well as luxuries, as could be seen in the expansion of the global consumer movement which concerned itself with wider issues during this period, such as those surrounding poverty, the environment and access to pharmaceutical drugs.[103] Combining consumers' rights to information and choice with the social rights of citizenship could have afforded the individual a greater say without undermining the security of collective entitlement. Indeed, the collective vision of patient organisations, with their emphasis on the needs of the wider population, never entirely disappeared from the horizon. Even within the Thatcher government there was a reluctance to devolve too much responsibility to individual consumers. It was doctors and managers, rather than patients, who were empowered to make choices within the internal market, allowing for some balance between the demands of the individual and the needs of the community.

All of this would suggest that the patient-consumer was a malleable figure, bearing the marks of more than one sculptor. That by the 1990s, the government had become the lead artist is perhaps no surprise, but an alternative artwork can be discerned beneath the outline. It is this ghost image that continues to haunt attempts to make the patient-consumer today, as patients and patient groups remake this identity to suit their own ends. New tools, such as access to information, were required for patient-consumer groups to go on shaping the patient-consumer in their own fashion.

Notes

1 Thomas Pogge, *World Poverty and Human Rights* (Cambridge: Polity Press, 2008).
2 Peter Shapely, 'Tenants arise! Consumerism, tenants and the challenge to council authority in Manchester, 1968–92', *Social History*, 31 (2006), 60–78; Alison Young, *The Politics of Regulation: Privatized Utilities in Britain* (Basingstoke: Palgrave, 2001).
3 Lynn Hunt, *Inventing Human Rights: A History* (New York: W.W. Norton & Co., 2007); Micheline R. Ishay, *The History of Human Rights: From Ancient Times to*

the Globalization Era (Berkeley, CA: University of California Press, 2004); Dorothy Porter, *Health Civilization and the State: A History of Public Health From Ancient to Modern Times* (London: Routledge, 1999), p. 57.

4   Stefan-Ludwig Hoffmann, 'Introduction: genealogies of human rights', in Stefan-Ludwig Hoffmann (ed.), *Human Rights in the Twentieth Century* (Cambridge: Cambridge University Press, 2011), 1–26.

5   T.H. Marshall, 'Citizenship and Social Class', in T.H. Marshall and Tom Bottomore, *Citizenship and Social Class* (London: Pluto Press, 1992), 3–51.

6   M.A Glendon, *A World Made New: Eleanor Roosevelt and the Universal Declaration of Human Rights* (New York: Random House, 2001).

7   Mark Mazower, 'The Strange Triumph of Human Rights, 1933–1950', *The Historical Journal*, 47 (2004), 379–398.

8   United Nations, 'The Universal Declaration of Human Rights' (1948), www.un.org/en/documents/udhr/index.shtml.

9   World Health Organization, 'Constitution of the World Health Organization', (1946), www.who.int/governance/eb/who_constitution_en.pdf.

10 United Nations (1966) 'International Covenant on Economic, Social and Cultural Rights', www2.ohchr.org/english/law/cescr.htm.

11 Paul Weindling, *Nazi Medicine and the Nuremberg Trials: From Medical War Crimes to Informed Consent* (Basingstoke: Palgrave Macmillan, 2004); Ulf Schmidt, *Justice at Nuremberg: Leo Alexander and the Nazi Doctors' Trial* (Basingstoke: Palgrave Macmillan, 2004); George Annas and Michael Grodin (eds), *The Nazi Doctors and the Nuremberg Code: Human Rights in Human Experimentation* (New York: Oxford University Press, 1995).

12 Samuel Moyn, *The Last Utopia: Human Rights in History* (Cambridge; MA: Harvard University Press, 2010). On the development of rights language in health see also David Reubi and Alex Mold, 'Introduction – global assemblages of virtue and vitality: genealogies and anthropologies of rights and health', in Alex Mold and David Reubi (eds), *Assembling Health Rights in Global Context: Genealogies and Anthropologies* (London: Routledge, 2013), 1–19.

13 Theodore Brown, Marcos Cueto and Elizabeth Fee, 'The World Health Organization and the transition from "international" to "global" public health', *American Journal of Public Health*, 96: (2006), 62–72.

14 Declaration of Alma Ata (1978), www.who.int/publications/almaata_declaration_en.pdf.

15 Marcos Cueto, 'The origins of primary health care and selective primary health care', *American Journal of Public Health*, 94 (2004), 1864–1874; Alec Irwin and E. Scali, 'Action on the social determinants of health: a historical perspective', *Global Public Health*, 2 (2007), 235–256; Matthew Hilton, *Prosperity for All: Consumer Activism in an Era of Globalization* (Ithaca, NY and London: Cornell University Press, 2009), pp. 144–147.

16 Jonathan Wolff, *The Human Right to Health* (New York: W.W. Norton & Co., 2012), pp. 39–91.

17 Elizabeth Fee and Manon Parry, 'Jonathan Mann, HIV/AIDS and Human Rights', *Journal of Public Health* Policy, 29 (2008), 54–71.

18 Sofia Gruskin, Edward Mills and Daniel Tarantola, 'History, principles and practice of health and human rights', *The Lancet*, 370 (2007), 449–455.

19 Daniel Tarantola, 'A perspective on the history of health and human rights: from the Cold War to the Gold War', *Journal of Public Health and Policy*, 29 (2008), 42–53.
20 See, for example, Catherine Crawford, 'Patients' rights and the law of contract in eighteenth century England', *Social History of Medicine*, 13:3 (2000), 381–410.
21 Martin Gorsky, 'Memorandum submitted to the Health Select Committee inquiry into Public and Patient Involvement in the NHS, January 2007', www.historyandpolicy.org/docs/gorsky_memo.pdf, accessed 2 August 2012; Martin Gorsky, 'Community involvement in hospital governance in Britain: evidence from before the National Health Service', *International Journal of Health Services*, 38:4 (2008), 751–771.
22 Charles Webster, *The Health Services Since the War, Volume I* (London: HMSO, 1988), 10–129.
23 NHS Act, 1946.
24 *The New National Health Service*, 1948. Quoted in Charles Webster, *The National Health Service: A Political History* (Oxford: Oxford University Press, 2002), p. 24.
25 Marshall, 'Citizenship and Social Class', 3–51.
26 On the 'classic' welfare state see Rodney Lowe, *The Welfare State in Britain since 1945* (Basingstoke: Palgrave Macmillan, 2005).
27 See, for example, Frank Trentmann, 'Citizenship and consumption', *Journal of Consumer Culture*, 7:2 (2007), 147–158; Matthew Hilton and Martin Daunton, 'Material politics: an introduction', in Martin Daunton and Matthew Hilton (eds), *The Politics of Consumption: Material Culture and Citizenship in Europe and America* (Oxford: Berg, 2001), 1–32; Frank Trentmann and Vanessa Taylor, 'From users to consumers: water politics in nineteenth-century London', in Frank Trentmann (ed.), *The Making of the Consumer: Knowledge, Power and Identity in the Modern World* (Oxford: Berg, 2005), 53–79.
28 Matthew Hilton, *Consumerism in Twentieth Century Britain: The Search for a Historical Movement* (Cambridge: Cambridge University Press, 2003); Lawrence Black, *Redefining British Politics: Culture, Consumerism and Participation, 1954-70* (Basingstoke: Palgrave Macmillan, 2010).
29 On consumerism and housing, see Shapely, 'Tenants arise!', pp. 60–78. Examples of the application of consumerism to health include: D.S. Lees, *Health Through Choice: An Economic Study of the British National Health Service* (London: Institute of Economic Affairs, 1961); Political and Economic Planning, *Family Needs and the Social Services* (London: PEP, 1961); Research Institute for Consumer Affairs, *General Practice: A Consumer Commentary* (London: RICA, 1963).
30 Shelia Rowbotham, 'Introduction', in Helene Curtis and Mimi Sanderson, *The Unsung Sixties: Memoirs of Social Innovation* (London: Whiting & Birch, 2004), ix–xii, p. xi.
31 Jurgen Habermas, 'New social movements', *Telos*, 49 (1981), 33–37.
32 *House of Commons Debates*, 1 April 1968, Treatment of Patients at Teaching and University Hospitals, vol. 762, cols 59–79.
33 CMAC SA/PAT/A/1/2, Minutes of the Meeting of the Committee of the PA, 16 December 1969.
34 *House of Commons Debates*, 26 January 1972, vol. 829, col. 1404, Rights of Patients.
35 *Ibid.*

36 Donald Gould, 'A groundling's notebook', *New Scientist*, 10 February 1972, p. 342.
37 TNA MH 160/885, A.F. Taggart to Dr Ford re. Rights of Patients Bill, 29 February 1972.
38 TNA MH 160/1185 F.D.K. Williams to Mr Chambers, re. clinical teaching, 16 October 1969 and Chambers to Mr Clark, 17 October 1969, handwritten note on bottom of above.
39 TNA MH 160/1185 Letter from Dr H. Yellowlees [Deputy Chief Medical Officer] to Sir John Richardson [JCC Chair], 15 March 1972.
40 TNA MH 160/1185 Extract of aide-memoire from Dr Grey-Turner to Dr H. Yellowlees regarding meeting with JCC on 28 July [1970].
41 *House of Commons Debates*, 22 January 1974, vol. 867, cols 1483–1486, Rights of Patients Bill.
42 Patients Association, *Can I Insist?* (London: Patients Association, 1974), p. 1.
43 CMAC SA/PAT/D/39 Miscellaneous queries on the NHS mainly concerning patients' rights, September 1969.
44 Patients Association, *Can I Insist?*, p. 6.
45 *Ibid.*, p. 6.
46 Consumers' Association, *The Which? Guide to Your Rights* (Consumers Association: London, 1980), p. 9.
47 Private papers of Michael Young, CCC YUNG 6/47/1, *The Clapham Omnibus: From the Supporters Desk of the National Consumer Council*, 5 (Winter 1979), p. 4.
48 CMAC SA/PAT/A/1/6, Elizabeth Stanton, 'Patients' rights and responsibilities', *The Clapham Omnibus*, 11 (Winter 1981).
49 *Ibid.*
50 National Consumer Council, *Patients' Rights: A Guide for NHS Patients and Doctors* (London: HMSO, 1983), p. 5.
51 *Ibid.*, p. 3.
52 Consumers' Association/Patients Association, *A Guide to the National Health Service* (London: Consumers' Association, 1983), p. 7.
53 *Ibid.*, p. 9.
54 CMAC SA/PAT/D/13/3, Letter from Tony Smythe (Secretary of ACHCEW) to organisations and individuals serving the health community, 17 January 1986.
55 CMAC SA/PAT/D/13/3, ACHCEW, Patient's Charter, January 1986.
56 CMAC SA/PAT/C/30, Redress the Balance, leaflet by the Local Government and Health Rights Project, n.d. [1983?]
57 See, for example, Greater London Council, *Changing the World: A London Charter for Gay and Lesbian Rights* (London: GLC, 1985).
58 CMAC SA/PAT/C/30, Redress the Balance, leaflet by the Local Government and Health Rights Project, nd. [1983?]
59 Beverly Lawrence Beech, *Who's Having Your Baby? A Health Rights Handbook for Maternity Care* (London: Camden Press, 1987), p. 125.
60 CMAC SA/PAT/C/30, London Health Democratisation Campaign: Campaign Update, October 1984.
61 CMAC SA/PAT/C/30, Londoners' Rights Bill – Democratisation NHS. Minutes of meeting, 30 November 1983.
62 CMAC SA/PAT/C/30, London Health Democratisation Campaign: Consultation Paper, March 1984.

63 CMAC SA/PAT/C/30, London Health Democratisation Campaign: History, Status, Aims, n.d. [1984].
64 CMAC SA/PAT/C/30, Letter to the PA from Madeleine Halliday, 14 November 1983.
65 CMAC SA/PAT/C/30, Charter for a Democratic Health Service, n.d. [1985].
66 CMAC SA/PAT/C/30, Charter for a Democratic Health Service, draft for comment by LDHC, 29 November 1984.
67 CMAC SA/PAT/D/39, News Service: Statement by Dr Gerard Vaughan, Minister for Health, speaking to the Conservative medical Society, Blackpool, 13 October 1981. 'Do we need a patients charter?'
68 David Taylor, 'A big idea for the nineties? The rise of the citizens' charters', *Critical Social Policy*, 33 (1992), 87–94.
69 Kieron Walsh, 'Citizens, charters and contracts', in Russell Keat, Nigel Whitely and Nicholas Abercrombie (eds), *The Authority of the Consumer* (London: Routledge, 1994), 189–206.
70 *Ibid.*, p. 190.
71 Cm. 555, *Working for Patients* (London: HMSO, 1989).
72 On the introduction of *Working for Patients* and the establishment of the internal market see Rudolf Klein, *The New Politics of the NHS: From Creation to Reinvention* (Oxford: Radcliffe Publishing, 2006), pp. 142–167; Webster, *The National Health Service: A Political History*, pp. 187–205.
73 Cm. 1599, *The Citizen's Charter: Raising the Standard* (London: HMSO, 1991).
74 Department of Health, *Patient's Charter* (London: HMSO, 1991).
75 I have been unable to find any government papers in the National Archives relating to *The Patient's Charter*. On the meeting between Dorrell and the patient consumer groups see CMAC SA/PAT/F/1/17 Linda Lamont, 'Director's Diary: Get it in Writing', *Patient Voice*, 54, Autumn 1991; *House of Commons Debates*, Patient's Charter, 25 July 1991, vol. 195, col. 906W.
76 Hogg, *Citizens, Consumers and the NHS*, p. 82.
77 Department of Health, *Patient's Charter*, p. 4.
78 *Ibid.*, pp. 8–9.
79 *Ibid.*, pp. 10–11.
80 *Ibid.*, pp. 6, 12–15.
81 *House of Commons Debates*, 5 November 1991, vol. 198, cols 316–318, col. 316.
82 National Consumer Council, *The Citizens' Charter: Getting it Right for the Consumer* (London: NCC, 1991); ACHCEW, *Health News Briefing: The Patient's Charter – The Patient's Perspective* (London: ACHCEW, 1994).
83 CMAC SA/PAT/K/2/1/17, The Patient's Charter: Response by the College of Health and Patients Association, 12 Basic Standards of Health Care, September 1991.
84 CMAC SA/PAT/K/2/1/17, Fax Containing a draft opinion piece by Linda Lamont for NAHAT Health Briefing, 30 October 1991.
85 ACHCEW CD Rom, vol. 3, ACHCEW, *Health News Briefing: The Patient's Charter – The Patient's Perspective* (London: ACHCEW, 1994); ACHCEW, 'Article for Agenda', n.d. [1995].
86 ACHCEW, *The Patients' Agenda: What the Patient's Charter Leaves Out – the Rights you don't yet have in the NHS* (London: ACHCEW, 1996), p. 1.

87 CCC YUNG/6/10/7, Young's Comments on the Patients Charter to David Brindle and Malcolm Dean at the *Guardian*, n.d. [1991].
88 ACHCEW, *Health News Briefing*; ACHCEW, 'Article for Agenda'.
89 ACHCEW, *The Patients' Agenda*, p. 16.
90 CMAC SA/PAT/K/2/1/17, The Patients Association's practical proposals to implement the principles of the Charter, 1991.
91 CMAC SA/PAT/K/2/1/17, The Patient's Charter: Response by the College of Health and Patients Association.
92 ACHCEW, *Health News Briefing: The Patient's Charter – The Patient's Perspective*.
93 It cost over £2 million to publicise and distribute the charter to every household. *House of Commons Debates*, 5 November 1991, vol. 198, cols 316–318, col. 317.
94 Surveys quoted in *Ibid.*, p. 14.
95 Barbara Stocking, 'Patient's charter: new rights issue', *British Medical Journal*, 303 (9 November 1991), 1148–1149.
96 Klein, *The New Politics of the NHS*, p. 169.
97 Michael Calnan and Jonathan Gabe, 'From consumerism to partnership? Britain's National Health Service at the turn of the century', *International Journal of Health Services*, 31:1 (2001), 119–131.
98 Iain Crinson, 'Putting patients first: the continuity of the consumerist discourse in health policy from the radical right to New Labour', *Critical Social Policy*, 18:2 (1998), 227–239.
99 Diane Plaming and Tony Delamothe, 'The citizen's charter and the NHS: true citizens do more than consume', *British Medical Journal*, 303 (27 July 1991), 203–204.
100 Calan and Gabe, 'From consumerism to partnership', p. 127.
101 John Clarke, Janet Newman, Janet E Newman, Nick Smith, Elizabeth Vidler, Louise Westmarland, *Creating Citizen-Consumers: Changing Publics and Changing Public Services* (London: Sage, 2007), p. 32.
102 Hilton, *Consumerism in Twentieth Century Britain*, p. 266.
103 Hilton, *Prosperity for all*.

5

Information

Facilitating access to information and producing new kinds of data was central to the work of patient consumer groups from their establishment in the 1960s to the present. The efforts of patient-consumer groups around autonomy, representation, complaint and rights all required the generation and reproduction of information for patients, but during the late 1980s and early 1990s, information became a key site of activity for patient-consumer organisations and the government. At stake was not just a debate about the kinds of information available to patient-consumers, but rather the very nature of patient consumerism. During this period, the identity of the patient-consumer as well as who was most responsible for fashioning this figure began to change. There was a move away from the collective understandings of the patient-consumer put forward by patient-consumer groups and towards a more individualised notion of patient consumerism developed by the Conservative government. As a result, information was coming to be directed at improving things for the individual patient-consumer rather than patient-consumers as a whole.

This chapter will explore such a shift through an analysis of the different kinds of information generated by patient-consumer groups and the uses to which they were put. While all parties agreed that information was essential to patient consumerism, there was less agreement about what kinds of information should be produced and how this should be used. The first section of this chapter will consider the purpose and meaning of information for patient-consumer organisations during the late 1980s and early 1990s. Focusing particularly (although not exclusively) on the CoH, established by the consumer activist Michael Young in 1983, it demonstrates that information was intended to empower patients, to promote good health and also to enhance patient choice. The second section of this chapter goes on to look at the activities of patient-consumer organisations both in terms of facilitating access to existing sources of information and in generating new kinds of information. What this chapter will suggest is that through their information-related activities, patient-consumer organisations were aiming to do more than create a 'super-patient' akin to the 'super-shopper': they wanted to promote collective as well as individual empowerment by helping patient-consumers as a whole to become better informed.

The final section of this chapter considers the long-running campaign by patient-consumer groups and others to introduce legislation that would allow patients to see their medical records. For patient-consumer groups access to this kind of information was a basic patient right, but they faced opposition from doctors who felt that the ability to see such records was potentially damaging to patients and to the profession more widely. At the same time, patient-consumer organisations were also concerned about the potential breaches to confidentiality posed by the development of information technology and computerisation which increased the number of people who had access to sensitive patient data. Legislation, in the form of the Data Protection Act, 1984, the Access to Personal Files Act, 1987, and the Access to Health Records Act, 1990, was created, but as with other legislative changes introduced apparently to the benefit of the patient-consumer, progress was slow and problems remained even after the law had been changed. Moreover, the introduction of such legislation was representative of a deeper shift, as the rights and demands of individual patient-consumers came to the fore. Such rights were of greater importance in the more marketised NHS that was being developed from the late 1980s onwards. The role and purpose of information for patients became more narrowly conceived, so that information was put to use to help individuals make better choices, rather than being directed towards collective empowerment.

Information, consumerism and the patient-consumer

Information was a crucial concept for organised consumerism. From the 1950s onwards, one of the key aims of the consumer movement was to improve access to information for consumers and to provide new material that would allow consumers to be better informed about goods and services. This kind of approach was embodied in the CA and its commitment to rational testing and the comparative analysis of products. The critical appraisal of goods by the CA in the pages of its magazine, *Which?*, as Matthew Hilton has noted, was central to the development of a kind of 'super-shopper', an efficient, rational, scientific and discriminating individual able to decide what to consume on the basis of objective information.[1] Yet, it would be a mistake, he argues, to see this purely as 'a selfish desire to obtain value for money'. Members of groups like the CA, Hilton suggests, were committed to a belief that 'independent information, provided to individual consumers through objective criteria, could solve many of the problems and inequities of the marketplace and lead the nation to an egalitarian participation in the affluent society'.[2]

Indeed, 'information' could mean many things. As Nancy Tomes points out, information was often portrayed in the health care field as neutral and value-free, when in reality it was anything but. She argues that 'The "godword" of information has come to have many different, sometimes contradictory meanings: as a neutral set of data, an economic driver of choice, a "right" of the modern consumer, and a sophisticated means of business competition.'[3] Tomes's analysis of the role of information in the activities of patient groups in the US from the 1960s onwards points to information as a tool for both individual and collective empowerment. Patient organisations believed that 'more democratic decision making required better information about health care providers, treatment and institutions'.[4] Their efforts to create 'shoppers' guides' to hospitals and medical services during the 1970s were, Tomes suggests, 'a tool of political advocacy, championed by critics of the health care "establishment"'.[5] Such guides helped individuals, but also contributed towards collective empowerment.

This kind of public-interest focused consumerism and its fascination with information, in the USA exemplified by Ralph Nader's Public Citizen and its health-related spin-offs, such as the Health Research Group, can also be found in the UK.[6] Nader inspired Charles Medawar, a researcher with the CA who went to work with Public Citizen for a year in the 1970s. On his return, Medawar founded the Public Interest Research Centre, a group that published its findings through a non-profit company called Social Audit.[7] Social Audit believed its role was 'to ask timely questions about the organisations whose decisions and actions shape our lives'. The organisation argued that 'The issues differ, but the conclusions are always the same: there is not enough accountability in the major centres of power. There is too much secrecy in government, and in the other organisations that direct and manage our lives.' To combat this, Social Audit produced reports on issues such as health and safety at work, accountability in the London Electricity Board and the promotion of British food and drug products in the developing world.[8] Social Audit were interested particularly in the safety and efficacy of drugs, an issue discussed in greater detail later in this chapter.

Health matters did not escape the attention of Britain's own Ralph Nader figure, Michael Young. Organisations that Young had helped establish, such as the CA, RICA and the NCC, had long been interested in health care, but in 1983 he founded a dedicated health consumer group, the College of

Health (CoH). Young was motivated partly by his own experiences following hospitalisation for treatment of bowel cancer. Young's doctor, Ian McColl, Professor of Surgery at Guys Hospital in London, met with patients towards the end of their stay and asked them about their experiences and whether or not anything could be improved.[9] Young worked with McColl and other doctors and consumer activists to form an organisation called initially the Association of Trained Patients (ATP).[10] The reason for its establishment lay in the belief that 'that too many patients, and their relatives, are ignorant about the health service and the best ways of communicating with doctors and other members of other medical professions'. The ATP was required 'in order to put some dynamism into the task of creating a more even-handed relationship between lay people and professionals, with less fear in it and more mutual respect'.[11] Young was able to gain support for the organisation, although few people liked the name, and after trying 'College of Patients' for a while, they eventually settled on the 'College of Health'.[12] The allusion to the medical Royal Colleges was intentional, being designed to put doctors and patients 'on a more equal basis than at the moment, with less fear and more confidence on the part of patients'.[13]

The College of Health was established formally in November 1983, and by the end of its first year in existence, had 10,000 members.[14] The College's principal objective was to 'encourage people to have a greater sense of responsibility for their own health and to become active partners in health care'. To this end, it had four aims, and information was crucial to each. The first revolved around prevention. The CoH was 'concerned not just with how to persuade people individually to adopt healthier lifestyles, but also with the influence on health of the environment and society in which we live'. The second involved what the College called 'self-care'. This was based on a recognition that 'the vast majority of illness is regularly dealt with by individuals rather than by doctors and other health professionals'. The third aim was to encourage people to make effective use of the health service. The goal, they suggested, was 'to give people the information they need to approach the health services as active partners in health care not as passive patients'. Finally, the CoH also sought to direct patient-consumers 'to sources of help which complement what is available from the NHS'.[15]

For the CoH, information seemed to have fulfilled three distinct but overlapping roles: patient empowerment, health promotion, and patient choice. Using knowledge to enhance patient power was central to the CoH's mission. In the first issue of their journal, *Self Health,* Young asserted that

> The reason for establishing the College of Health ... lies in the present imbalance between medical professionals and their patients. The former have power, the latter do not. This is not just due to the emotional dependence which many sick people cannot avoid. It is also due to the large gap between the knowledge and

information of the two parties. Information (as always) is power. The best way of putting professionals and patients on more level terms is therefore to endow patients with more of it.[16]

The CoH thought that the provision of information would lead to a more equal relationship between doctors and patients. In 1986, the Director of the College, Marianne Rigge told a conference of health managers that 'We believe that a spirit of partnership is essential. We want to encourage people to approach their doctors as active participants, not as passive patients.'[17] Other patient-consumer organisations held similar views. Katharine Whitehorn, chair of the PA, suggested in her Foreword to the joint PA/CA *Guide to the NHS*, that 'Doctors occasionally act as if patients getting hold of The Knowledge would threaten them almost as much as an apprentice getting hold of the sorcerer's spell book; but I think it's the other way round. Informed patients can actually be a huge help to the medical profession.'[18]

Indeed, both the CoH and PA argued that a more informed patient was also likely to be a healthier patient. The provision of information had a key role to play in health education, health promotion and disease prevention. Robert Gann and Sally Knight, in their *Consumers' Guide to Health Information* published on behalf of the CoH suggested that 'Over the last decade there has been a growing realisation that information is one of the keys to improvements in health … Further improvements will come about through people becoming partners in their own health care.'[19] According to Rigge, 'The first aim of my organisation, the College of Health, is to help people to keep themselves healthy.'[20]

But, for the CoH, and other patient-consumer organisations, health promotion and patient empowerment also overlapped with patient choice. Rigge told an audience at King's College Hospital Medical School that

> we aim to help people become active partners in health care instead of being passive patients. And if I were asked what single ingredient is necessary to effect that transformation the answer would be information. Without information there can be no real choice and I hope that the days are long gone when patients were not expected to exercise choice but rather follow the doctor's orders blindly in the knowledge that, of course, the doctor knew best.[21]

Similarly, Gann and Knight asserted that 'Active participants in health care must be able to make their own choices.'[22] The language of choice, however, frequently intersected with the discourse of rights. The NCC contended that 'Choice and information are the life-blood from which other consumer rights flow.'[23] Michael Shanks, chair of the NCC, wanted 'consumers to be enabled to stand on their own feet and exercise their rights as individuals. In order to do this, they need to be able to exercise choice in an informed way.'[24] Other groups expressed comparable views. In 1991, the newly established

Consumer Health Information Consortium organised a conference entitled 'Promoting choice: consumer health information in the 1990s'. Despite the apparent focus on choice, few speakers dealt with choice per se, and instead concerned themselves with patient-consumer empowerment and rights. Ed MacAlister-Smith, Chief Officer of Bath CHC expressed the view that 'I think people have *a right to know*, people have a right to information. It is a right, not something people ought to have to fight and argue for [original emphasis].'[25] The kinds of choices imagined by patient-consumer organisations were thus as much about having a say, about not being a passive patient, as they were about individual preference.

Patient-consumer groups and information access and generation

In order to achieve their goals in patient empowerment, health promotion and patient choice, patient-consumer organisations facilitated access to existing sources of information and generated new kinds of data. Some of this was in the form of the rights guides and charters discussed in Chapter 4, but other kinds of information about access to services was also collated and published by groups like the CoH. For instance, the College produced a guide for patients going in to hospital on what to expect as well as the patient's rights, or lack of, in this area.[26] Patient groups also provided practical advice for dealing with specific illnesses and maintaining good health. The CA published an extensive range of guides to common conditions such as heart disease, cancer, stress, allergies, backache and mental illness which explained the nature of each disease, its causes, treatment, prognosis and prevention.[27] Health-related topics also appeared in the pages of *Which?* Articles offered advice to subscribers with specific conditions, such as the September 1983 feature 'Baldness in men – is there an answer?' as well as guidance on healthy living, such as the potential dangers of consuming alcohol.[28] Health education and health promotion were also key features of *Self Health* (later *Which? Way to Health*) which considered, amongst other issues, the merits of wholemeal bread, cycling and yoga.[29] The audience for such material was not inconsiderable: by 1993 *Which?* had 690,000 subscribers and *Which? Way to Health*, 65,000.[30]

In addition, other, non-print based, sources of information were provided by patient-consumer groups. In 1984, the CoH set up a telephone helpline, Healthline. This was a free service, providing callers with access to a collection of over 200 pre-recorded tapes on a wide selection of topics including heartburn, nervous breakdown and the menopause. The switchboard received more than 7,000 calls in its first five months, and by 1986 was taking an average of 1,000 calls a month.[31] The rationale behind

Healthline was rooted in the CoH's commitment to health education and disease prevention. In a report on the advice service, Young remarked that 'For health, information is of the essence. It is essential for prevention and it is essential for treatment.'[32] The helpline, according to Rigge, was designed for situations where patients felt that '"I can't bother the doctor." ... it would give you proper factual information about how to look after yourself or your child or your elderly parent or whatever in minor illness.'[33] Healthline was also particularly valuable in providing information on conditions that callers may have felt uncomfortable discussing with their doctors, such as HIV/AIDS. Indeed, this was a contention supported by the DHSS, which gave the CoH a grant in 1985 to support their AIDS telephone information service.[34] Healthline was such a good idea, that it soon faced competition from commercial services like HealthCall.[35] Partly as a result, Healthline was forced to shut down in 1989, when the service became too expensive to maintain. The principle of a free, telephone health information and advice line was, however, taken up by the government with the creation of NHS Direct in 1998.[36] Indeed, the College's tapes were used in an early trial of NHS Direct in the North West Thames Region.[37]

Healthline, and the various guides produced by the CA and other groups, clearly played an important role in providing patients with information about medical conditions and how to seek help for their treatment. Another key area of activity was around the safety and efficacy of drugs. This topic had long been an interest of the CA, as seen in their *Drugs and Therapeutics Bulletin*, first published in 1963. The *Drugs and Therapeutics Bulletin* published reviews of drugs and their uses, aiming to provide a 'rational' assessment of their value. The publication was directed at doctors and pharmacists, but the CA and its spin-offs were also interested in communicating such information to a wider audience. Drug safety was a particular concern of Medawar and Social Audit. In 1984, the organisation published an A–Z list of commonly prescribed drugs and their side effects aimed at educating patient-consumers about such products. The intention was that readers could use the book to assess 'whether or not you have been prescribed a medicine that experts think is less effective or less safe than you would feel entitled to expect' as well as 'whether or not you might usefully have been told more about a prescribed medicine than you were in fact told' and 'whether or not your doctor prescribes medicines scientifically and economically, and whether or not this is what you want'.[38] But the guide, entitled *The Wrong Kind of Medicine*, also presented an attack on the pharmaceutical industry, drug regulation and unthinking prescribing by doctors. The book contended that 'because most people have been taught virtually nothing about the medicines they use, they know very little, and therefore do not seem worth teaching. Poorly informed medicine users encourage uncritical and excessive drug use.'[39] By becoming better educated about drugs and their effects, readers would become better patient-consumers.

To further strengthen the position of the patient-consumer, patient groups went beyond providing information that drew on existing sources and began to create new kinds of knowledge about health and the health service. For the groups most closely tied to the consumer movement, like the CA and the CoH, this meant subjecting goods and services to comparative testing. Throughout the 1980s and 1990s, *Which?* reported the results of comparative analysis of health-related services such as opticians, private medical insurance and allergy testing, and products including denture cleaners and fixatives, painkillers and condoms.[40] Results of the condom test were simultaneously published in *Self Health* in September 1987, at the height of concern about the transmission of HIV/AIDS, and revealed that several brands of condoms contained small holes.[41]

Patient-consumer group activity was not just limited to assessing the value of medical products: they also turned their attention to the services being provided by the NHS. The CA, the CoH, and many of the CHCs, surveyed patients' views of services and attempted to identify where services were failing, establish how these could be improved and consider how inequalities in service provision could be addressed. The survey was a key tool for the CHCs in particular; some of whose surveys identified a need for new facilities.[42] A study conducted by Central Birmingham CHC in 1979, for example, pointed to the need for an interpreter at several city hospitals to enable staff to communicate with some Asian patients.[43] Surveys could also expose failings in existing services: Tameside CHC reviewed local psychiatric facilities and concluded that although the shift towards outpatient provision was justified, better cooperation between services and more resources was required.[44] Furthermore, CHC surveys highlighted the significance of wider issues in health care provision. South Gwent CHC, for instance, conducted a survey in 1984 that examined the effect of socio-economic conditions on the health of people living in a housing estate on the outskirts of Newport.[45]

Finding out what patients thought of services became more common during the 1980s, particularly following the 1983 Griffiths enquiry into management in the NHS and the introduction of general management to the health service. One of the chief responsibilities of newly installed managers was to assess consumers' views of services and to adjust services accordingly.[46] The most common way of achieving these aims was through patient satisfaction surveys.[47] For groups like the CoH, however, patient satisfaction surveys did not go far enough. Critical of what it regarded as a 'tick box' approach to determining levels of patient satisfaction, the College developed what it saw as a more comprehensive approach, called 'consumer audit', towards the end of the 1980s.[48] Paralleling the increasingly common medical or clinical audit, a process by which clinicians examined each other's work and practices, and also the activities of Social Audit, consumer audit involved in-depth interviews with patients and staff at all levels.[49] The CoH asserted that 'The whole purpose of consumer audit is to make the processes of health care more responsive to the rightful expectations of the user.'[50] Funded initially by the Nuffield Provincial Hospital Trust and the King's Fund, the College was contracted by numerous hospitals to audit services, suggesting that NHS managers also saw the value of the CoH's approach.[51]

Managers were less welcoming, however, of another type of information gleaned by the CoH: data on the length of hospital waiting lists. Based on returns made by District Health Authorities to the DHSS, the CoH published its first *Guide to Hospital Waiting Lists* in 1984.[52] The *Guide* found that there were more than 700,000 people waiting for admission to hospital. Moreover, the DHSS's objective that urgent cases should wait no longer than a month for admission, and non-urgent cases no more than a year, was not being met. In 1984, 30,000 urgent cases had been waiting longer than a month, and 205,000 non-urgent cases had waited for longer than a year.[53] Subsequent guides also highlighted the fact that there was considerable regional variation in waiting times, and that patients could get treated faster if they 'shopped around'. The 1987 *Guide* stated that 'We hope that by publishing this Guide we can help patients and their GPs make effective use of the NHS by seeking treatment in another health district if they find an excessively long waiting list.'[54] But the College did not just want to help individual patients to get treated faster; they wanted to use regional variation in waiting times to make a broader point about inequality within the NHS. The 1989 *Guide* asserted that 'From the start … our concern has been that people should be treated with greater equity. As things are it still seems to be almost a matter of geographical accident whether patients find themselves on a long waiting list or a short one.' 'Fairness', the *Guide* continued, 'is the basic principle of the NHS. It could and should be extended.'[55]

The CoH's interest in issues of equity suggested that it saw the patient-consumer both as an individual and as part of a wider community of health service users. The College of Health and other groups, especially the CA, cultivated a view of the patient-consumer as a rational, informed, health-conscious individual. Information was a way of empowering patients and transforming the doctor–patient relationship. Moreover, this figure was not just a 'super-patient', but also a self-governing subject of the new public health, concerned with maintaining a 'healthy' lifestyle.[56] At the same time, groups like the CoH believed that information should do more than create healthy super-patients: information was a way of putting pressure on the government and health service managers to improve the quality and equality of services. This was a broader view of the role of information and also of the nature of the patient-consumer than that being proposed by the Thatcher government. The tools developed by patient groups to collect and disseminate information, such as patient surveys and advice lines, were taken on by the government, but put to rather different uses. The information gathered empowered managers, not patients, to make decisions. Few attempts were made to pass more information on to patients themselves; rather, it was left to managers to act as 'proxy consumers', making choices on behalf of patients. By contrast, patient groups wanted consumers themselves to use information to make better choices about their own care, but at the same time information was also vital to their aim to improve care for all. Information helped to produce patient-consumers, as well as the patient-consumer.

Confidentiality and medical records

Despite the centrality of information to the work of patient-consumer organisations, some groups and individuals were aware that improving access to information was not, in itself, likely to produce significant change. As Gann remarked, 'we shouldn't get too carried away with information as the answer to all our problems ... People also need rights, access to records, they need effective complaints mechanisms, real consultation, they need opportunities for participation and opportunities for representation.'[57] For information to be of value, it had to be paired with additional mechanisms such as legislative change. Improving patients' access to their medical records, as well as safeguarding their confidentiality in the context of computerisation and rapidly changing information technology, became a key battleground for patient-consumer groups in the 1980s and 1990s. The campaign for patients' rights to view their medical records was partly about individual empowerment, but it also represented an assault on medical paternalism and the secret state. Attempts to open up patients' records need to be seen in the context of wider changes in the relationship between the state and the people over access to information.

During the 1970s, official secrecy and the power of the state to restrict access to the records it held on individual citizens came under threat. In part, as historian David Vincent points out, this was because the nature of the state was itself in flux. As the state became less monolithic, blanket secrecy no longer made sense: 'Deference to the right of the state to determine what it allowed into the public domain was in sharp decline, as was confidence in the ability of a range of government, professional, and commercial bodies to make responsible use of new technologies of storage and transmission.'[58] The development of the personal computer and improvements in information technology meant that electronic records were slowly replacing paper files. This prompted a number of concerns. Firstly, existing mechanisms were designed to deal with paper records, not electronic ones, leading to fears about systems failure.[59] Secondly, individuals and groups such as the National Council for Civil Liberties (NCCL) were worried that computerisation would increase state intrusion and decrease confidentiality.[60]

To address such concerns, attempts were made to arrive at an agreed definition of 'privacy'. In May 1970, the Younger Committee was established in order to 'consider whether legislation is needed to give further protection to the individual citizen and to commercial and industrial interests against intrusion into privacy by private persons and organisations'.[61] Privacy, or more accurately, confidentiality, had, of course, long been central to medical ethics. As the 1988 BMA guide to medical ethics noted, 'The principle of confidentiality is basic to the practice of medicine and fundamental to the doctor/patient relationship.'[62] The Younger committee suggested that computerised data banks posed a potential threat to doctor–patient confidentiality as medical records became available to a wider range of people.[63] The BMA were concerned about 'lay' or 'non-medical' people including social workers, researchers and administrators, who were not subject to the same rules and traditions regarding confidentiality, gaining access to medical records. Richard Pryer, a consultant surgeon at the Royal Bucks and Stoke Mandeville Hospital typified such fears. Pryer told the *Sunday Telegraph* that a project trialling a computerised records system at his hospital 'causes a fundamental change to the doctor-patient relationship. It introduces into that relationship an anonymous body, not directly concerned with the clinical treatment of the patient, without the patient's consent being obtained.'[64] The Committee took on board such concerns, recommending that access to medical records for epidemiological and other kinds of research needed to be provided in such a way that it did not endanger individual privacy.[65]

Despite the fact that the Younger Committee concluded that 'the public are not much exercised about invasion of privacy in the practice of medicine', the issue failed to disappear.[66] Groups like the PA and the NCCL were keen to establish procedures on patient record confidentiality in the wake of the Younger report. The PA wrote to the DHSS in 1973 asking if there were 'guidelines covering conditions of access to this information, and methods of preserving the patient's anonymity where his history is to be used for general statistical purposes?'[67] The NCCL were also concerned about the confidentiality of medical records, preparing a memorandum on the subject in 1979.[68] Part of the problem stemmed from the fact that, according to Vincent, the Younger committee had been unable to provide a comprehensive definition of privacy that would satisfy judges or parliament.[69] Doctors were no more contented. An editorial in the *British Medical Journal* in 1976 asserted that 'Clinicians must not be seen to stand aside from the debate about computers and individual privacy' but also that 'many doctors would object strenuously to a system whereby a patient had – as of right – access to this information'.[70] Indeed, by the later 1970s, concerns around patient privacy started to be replaced by a debate about patients' access to records.

The Lindrop Committee on data protection, which was established in 1976, examined such issues within a wider brief to advise on the introduction of legislation to protect personal data held on a computer. The Committee determined that 'the function of data protection law should be different from that of a law on privacy: rather than establishing rights, it should provide a framework for finding a balance between the interests of the individual, the data user and the community at large'.[71] The notion of individual rights was thus less important than a broader understanding of the potential collective value of such information. When taking evidence, Lindrop heard from a range of interested groups, including the PA. The association told the committee that 'We do not believe that widespread computerisation of medical records would present a serious new threat to the confidentiality of medical records' and that 'Computer records should be subject to the same restrictions on access and the same safeguards for privacy as apply to manual records'. With respect to patient access to records, the PA asserted that 'We do not recommend – as we should in the case of most other kinds of personal information – that the patient should have the absolute right of access to his medical notes, computerised or not, although we believe that too often quite unnecessarily and unjustifiably this is refused by a doctor.'[72] The Lindrop Committee concurred, recommending that 'we do not think that patients should, as yet, always be able to have access to every part of their medical records'.[73]

Access to medical records

Indeed, in the late 1970s, the legal situation surrounding patient access to medical records was somewhat ambiguous. It was not even entirely clear who owned medical records. The DHSS had told the Lindrop Committee that it believed that the Secretary of State owned all NHS records, but such an assumption had not been tested in court.[74] As Derek Pheby from Wessex Regional Health Authority pointed out, without a solid understanding of to whom medical records belonged, rights of access were equally uncertain.[75]

Some limited rights of access for patients appeared to be provided following a medical litigation case that reached the House of Lords. In 1978, after hearing an appeal in the case of McIvor vs. Southern Health and Social Services Board (Northern Ireland) the Lords determined that in cases of litigation a patient's medical adviser, and by extension the patient him or herself, could have access to the relevant medical records. This ruling, did not, however, give patients an automatic right to access their records: these were only to be released following a successful application to the High Court.[76]

By the 1980s, pressure to open up medical records began to increase. Access to records in allied fields, such as social work, had already been improved. In 1980, social workers agreed to allow clients to access their records, a decision based on the recognition that individuals were active citizens who could make their own decisions about their care and treatment. This became official policy in 1983, when a DHSS circular was released stipulating that social workers should give clients access to their records.[77] Further impetus to open up records came from the European Community, as a directive issued by the Council of Europe in 1981 (to which the UK was a signatory) required nations to introduce laws to protect personal data.[78] In the wake of this directive, the Data Protection Act was introduced in 1984, which gave individuals access to personal data about themselves held in electronic or computerised form. Medical records were encompassed within the act, but could be exempted if a doctor thought that access might harm the patient. Paper records remained outside the remit of the act.[79]

At the same time, patient-consumer organisations and others were pressing for greater patient access to medical records. By 1981, the PA appeared to have changed their position from being against total freedom of access (as they had told the Lindrop Committee in 1976) to arguing that the patient should have 'a prima facie right of access to his medical records'.[80] The PA rejected the argument that unrestricted patient access to records would do more harm than good, contending that 'we do not consider that to deny people access to their medical records, protects their interests. Indeed, the contrary may be the case, as we know from the people who contact us on the subject'.[81] Preventing patients from accessing their records deliberately, the association suggested, 'sours rather than sweetens the doctor-patient relationship to the detriment of both parties'.[82] Other groups held similar views. The NCC passed a resolution at its 1983 Congress that legislation should be passed in order to provide 'greater rights in principle for data subjects to inspect and correct medical and social service records. The general right of data subjects to inspect and correct records of any kind should only be limited if it would prejudice the detection of a serious crime'.[83] The CA concurred, stating in the pages of *Which?* that the 'Consumers Association, among other organisations, strongly advocates that people should be able to see most kinds of information, medical and other, kept about them not only on computer but in manual files.'[84] Access to paper files and not just computerised ones was important, because, as the PA pointed out, 90 per cent of medical records in 1983 were paper-based.[85]

Patient-consumer groups put forward a number of arguments to support their demands for greater patient access to medical records. Organisations believed that opening up records would improve doctor–patient relationships. Following ACHCEW's resolution at its 1980 AGM to press for 'The right of every adult patient to have access to his or her own medical notes if they wish to', Central Birmingham CHC set out their case for open records. They asserted that 'Patients frequently express a desire to know more about themselves ... There is a great need to improve communication between doctors and patients.' If, the CHC suggested, 'patients were granted the right of access to their own medical notes (while the notes still remained the property of the Secretary of State) this, simply as a principle, would help to lessen the "gap" between doctor and patient, and would encourage the patient to be more involved in his own treatment'. The CHC concluded that that the right to access records 'is the biggest single factor that would help to improve relations between doctors and patients'.[86]

Other organisations, like the NCC, agreed. Ruth Cohen, senior research officer at the NCC suggested that records were more than a piece of paper or electronic file; rather they encapsulated the relationship between doctor and patient. 'What right', she argued, 'has a doctor or any other practitioner to expect respect from a person from who s/he is withholding information?'[87] Preventing patients from accessing information about themselves, Cohen asserted, caused distress, whereas allowing individuals to see their records could be part of therapy and treatment. Moreover, Cohen was keen to place patients' access to records within the context of a broader right to information. In an extended version of her argument published by the NCCL, and covering access to records in education, housing, social work and financial services as well as medical records, she asserted that files should be opened 'Because they are about us.' 'Access to information', Cohen suggested, 'is access to power. In the case of personal records it is access to power over our own lives.'[88] Such power, she argued, would counter the 'strong element of paternalism running through our bureaucracy'.[89] Young and the CoH agreed. The College maintained that denying patients access was rooted in 'paternalism on the part of doctors' which was 'no longer acceptable and it makes a mockery of informed consent'.[90] Secrecy, Cohen claimed, 'is sold to us as being for our own good ... We are being protected from ourselves.' But, such secrecy prevented data subjects from 'knowing a great deal of information that could help us to know what is happening'.[91]

For their part, doctors were aware that they needed to address the issues of both confidentiality and access to records. As Pheby noted, there was a feeling that if the medical profession did not deal with such matters, it 'could well find changes which may be unacceptable imposed on it from outside'.[92] In 1983, the BMA established the Inter-professional Working Group on Access to Personal Health Information. The group supported 'the right of patients and clients to have access to all information which is held about them on their behalf'. However, the working group were opposed to the idea of 'an *absolute* requirement to afford unrestricted access [original emphasis]' because this 'could inhibit health professionals from providing sensitive information or opinions: to the inevitable detriment of patient care'. The working group believed that unrestricted access to patient records may cause harm to the individual, and concluded that 'an acceptable mechanism must therefore be devised for the exercise of a proper discretion by the responsible clinician or other health professional'.[93] In response to the working group's findings and the introduction of the Data Protection Act, the DHSS opined that 'While there is an apparent move towards greater openness in the relationship between health professionals and patients and the freer exchange of information, we accept that it may not be appropriate to allow a general and unrestricted right of access to all personal health data.' The Department believed that 'Much of what is in them [medical records] will be highly technical and will mean very little to the lay person, they might be capable of misinterpretation. Wrong conclusions might be drawn from which unnecessary distress could result.' Officials suggested, therefore, that though access should be allowed in the majority of cases, responsibility for deciding whether or not this should be granted lay with doctors.[94]

Patient-consumer groups did not echo the paternalistic assessment put forward by doctors and civil servants. The NCC stated that 'It is our view that subjects should have the same access to their personal health data as to any other personal data in accordance with the general provisions of the [Data Protection] Act'. The Council believed that there should be just one exception: if access to the records would cause 'actual harm to the mental health of a patient with a record of mental or psychiatric illness'.[95] The PA wanted parity of access to paper records as well as electronic ones, especially as the majority of files remained in paper form.[96]

Patient-consumer organisations were supported in their work around access to medical records by a broader movement towards freedom of information and more open government. Groups like the NCCL had long strived towards greater openness and less secrecy from those in authority, and in 1984 a specific pressure group, the Campaign for the Freedom of Information (CFI), was established. Led by Maurice Frankel, who had worked previously for Social Audit, the CFI wanted to extend the limited rights of access to computerised medical records provided under the Data Protection Act. The Campaign declared that

> in most cases the health professionals responsible can deal with the situation *without* withholding the information, and should be encouraged to do so. Indeed, we think the alternatives to withholding information are often likely to be of positive therapeutic value and will also enhance relations between individual and professional where restriction of access would have the opposite effect [original emphasis].[97]

The CFI also wanted to expand patients' rights of access to include paper as well electronic records. In July 1984, they succeeded in getting Chris Smith, Labour MP for Islington and Finsbury, to introduce a private members' bill which would give individuals the right to see paper records about themselves including educational records, social service files and medical records. Smith framed his bill as an assault on the 'patronising and arrogant assumption that the professional knows best and that individuals cannot be trusted with recorded information about themselves'. Smith contended that not only were there practical benefits to allowing individuals access to their own data, he suggested that at 'an overriding moral issue' was at stake. 'Surely', he reasoned, 'a citizen should have a right to know what is being written and recorded about him by those employed by the community to provide services or exercise authority.'[98] Smith's bill failed, but the CFI were undeterred, and they tried again in October 1985, this time with a bill put forward by Archy Kirkwood, Liberal Democrat MP for Roxburgh and Berwickshire. Like Smith, Kirkwood was also keen to point to the wider ramifications of such legislation. He told the House of Commons that

> We need access as of right to information recorded about ourselves, and we need the right to ensure that such information is both fair and correct. The legislation to create those rights will do more to enhance the quality of our democracy and redress the balance between the administrative arm of government and the individual than almost any other Bill that could be introduced by a Back-Bench Member.[99]

Kirkwood's bill also fell, because there was insufficient time to hear it before the end of the Parliamentary session, but the main stumbling block to change came from within the medical profession.

Opinion amongst doctors on access to records varied widely. As the BMA's guide to medical ethics noted in 1988, 'The profession is much divided on this issue.'[100] A study of consultants' and patients' views of access to medical records found that 81 per cent of patients believed that they should be able to see their records if they wanted to, whereas less than half of the consultants interviewed thought that patients should be able to see their records.[101] In 1986, a dispute erupted within the BMA's General Medical Services Committee (GMSC) and on the pages of the *British Medical Journal* between doctors over access to records. At its January meeting, the GMSC agreed that patients should have 'modified' access to their records, in effect allowing patients to see their notes but with some restrictions.[102] In March, the *British Medical Journal* published two contrasting editorials; one making the case for patient access to medical records, the other against. David Metcalfe, Professor of General Practice at the University of Manchester, argued that 'the patient has a right to know what the doctor knows (or at any rate choose to write) about him. After all, it is his body and his health.' Metcalfe reiterated many of the arguments made by patient-consumer organisations that opening up records would improve doctor–patient relations and encourage patients to take greater responsibility for their own health.[103] In contrast, Alexander P. Ross, a consultant surgeon at the Royal Hampshire County Hospital in Winchester, stated that while he was 'not passionately against patients seeing their records, and I do recognize that people have some sort of right to see any records kept about them, but I cannot see that patients will benefit from full access – and doctors will surely lose'. Professional self-interest was not the only argument marshalled against patient access by Ross, he also indicated that 'The proponents of full disclosure of medical records have in mind, I suspect, middle aged, middle income, middle class patients who subscribe to *Which?* But what about children, mentally handicapped patients, and those who are profoundly disturbed or demented?' Completely open access, Ross suggested, would not benefit all patients.[104] Such arguments appear to have convinced doctors to vote against increased access to patient records, and at their June conference the GMSC overturned their earlier decision to allow restricted access.[105] Though opinions clearly differed, the profession's position was that medical records should be exempted from data access requirements.

Such a view held sway in the corridors of power: medical records were excluded from the Access to Personal Files Act in 1987. The act permitted data subjects' access to their paper records in areas such as local government, social work and housing, but medical records were exempted.[106] The Act was based on the bill drafted by Kirkwood, and the CFI, together with other groups including ACHCEW, the PA and the CoH, attempted to get an amendment added permitting access to medical records.[107] Their efforts, however, met with little success, and instead the BMA was instructed by the DHSS to devise a voluntary code on patient access.[108] This did little to satisfy the act's detractors: Frankel immediately branded the code, when it was published in 1989, as 'toothless'. The voluntary code proposed that patients be allowed to see their records only to learn about their health, not for a specific purpose, such as to make a complaint. Moreover, they would not be given access to the file itself, but rather to information about a single, specified visit to the doctor.[109]

Dissatisfied with such a response, the CFI and its supporters worked with Kirkwood to put forward another private members' bill, this time focused specifically on access to health records. When presenting his bill to the House in May 1989, Kirkwood noted that 'A voluntary code of practice is a very poor alternative to legislation because it cannot be enforced. It allows doctors who do not like the idea of patients seeing what is said about them – and there are many – to opt out altogether.' Furthermore, there were inconsistencies within the existing legislation. Patients had access already to computerised files under the Data Protection Act, and the Medical Reports Act of 1987 allowed individuals to see medical records sent to their employers and insurance companies. Kirkwood thought that 'A statutory right of access would exist for a patient who wanted to be 100 per cent in the picture, who wanted to know all the details and to understand them, rather than to rely unquestioningly on medical advice.'[110] In response to Kirkwood's bill, the Parliamentary Undersecretary of State for Health, Roger Freeman, stated that although the government was supportive of 'a policy of openness', they believed that it was a complex issue, that patients needed protection, and the voluntary code should be tried first.[111]

A second attempt to introduce legislation on access to medical records was made two years later. Another private members' bill, this time led by Doug Henderson, Labour MP for Newcastle upon Tyne, with support from Kirkwood and others, came to the House in February 1990. Once more, the bill's backers stressed the citizen's right to access to information about him or herself as well as the potential improvement to doctor–patient relations that would result from open access. Freeman, again speaking on the behalf of the Government, appeared to accept Henderson's arguments, as he accepted that the voluntary code had failed and there was, therefore, a need for legislation. Despite such support, the bill was talked out. In what Frankel called a 'dirty tricks' campaign, and the *Guardian* commentator Hugo Young, branded a 'conspiracy', the bill was 'sabotaged', apparently by the Home Office. The CFI and Young both suggested that the Access to Health Records Bill was opposed by the Home Office for fear that it set a precedent which would allow individuals to access other kinds of sensitive records including those produced by the police, prisons and immigration service.[112]

Despite the opposition of the Home Office, pressure mounted to open up medical records. Patients, it seemed, wanted greater access to their notes.

A survey conducted by the CA found that 91 per cent of patients were in favour of access to medical records, and the patient stories collected by the CFI made a powerful case for greater openness.[113] One patient reported learning that she had cerebral palsy from her notes, a diagnosis that had been kept from her for years. Another patient found that she had had an ectopic pregnancy and not been informed. Yet others found that their notes were wildly inaccurate: in one case a statistician had been mistakenly labelled as a bareback horse rider in a circus.[114] Opposition to patient access to records could no longer be justified, and in July 1990 the Access to Health Records Act was passed, giving patients access to paper records about themselves.[115]

While patient-consumer organisations welcomed such legislation, they also highlighted a number of deficiencies in the act. The PA noted that although the Access to Health Records Act gave patients the right to see their records, doctors could still prevent this if they believed that it would cause the patient physical or mental harm. Furthermore, there was no complaints procedure for patients who felt that they were being denied their right of access, and the act was not retrospective, so records created before November 1991 were inaccessible. The Association concluded that 'this Act is a step in the right direction; but a small one – there is a long way to go before patients will truly be able to say that they have the free and easy access to their health records that they deserve'.[116] ACHCEW also criticised the Act for not being retrospective, and their survey of members demonstrated that there were a number of other difficulties with the legislation in practice. Who had access to what was not always clear, especially when a patient had died. There was a lack of clarity about what a 'record' included, with the results of tests and diagnostic procedures not always provided, especially when a complaint was being made. Obstacles to access also existed. ACHCEW reported that there was a widespread perception that a doctor's approval was required to grant access, and the two-stage process whereby patients needed to write a letter to obtain a form to request access and then write again to actually gain access was laborious, time-consuming and off-putting to patients. Even once patients had obtained their records, ACHCEW stated that individuals sometimes struggled to understand these and found it very difficult to correct inaccuracies. The solution, according to ACHCEW, was to allow patients to hold their own records, something that would 'be in keeping with the promotion of personal responsibility for health and individual rights within the NHS'.[117] Access to medical records was thus more than just access to information: it was a tool for patient empowerment.

Conclusion

The Access to Health Records Act could be seen as another example of a piece of legislation that was, in many ways, a victory for patient-consumer groups. Combined with patient organisations' efforts to facilitate access to both new and existing sources of information, by the early 1990s patients had access to more and different kinds of data then ever before. It is difficult to quantify exactly how much of a role such organisations played in bringing access to patient records to the statute books, but their activities were certainly one of a number of influences including wider changes around secrecy and freedom of information, European Community legislation on data access, and concerns about information technology and computerisation. Together, these factors combined to press initially reluctant policy makers and the medical profession to open up medical records to patient scrutiny. Like the introduction of the Hospital Complaints Procedures Act, the Data Protection Act and the Access to Health Records Act appeared to increase the number of concrete patient's rights. Indeed, this was how such powers were presented in the Department of Health's *Patient's Charter*, which indicated that patients had a legal right to see their records.[118]

But, beneath such apparent empowerment, other dynamics were at work. As discussed in Chapter 4, the legitimacy and power of patients' rights was deeply suspect. The extent to which the sum total of patient's rights and their ability to effect change had been improved was questionable. At the same time, the very function of information for patients appeared to be undergoing change. Access to information, and the kinds of data being produced, was increasingly directed at improving the position of the individual patient, not patients as a whole. As the final statement of the ACHCEW report on the Access to Health Records Act made clear, obtaining information was the responsibility of the self-governing, autonomous patient. Individuals were to be required to access information in order to improve their own health and to make better health choices. Such a view fitted with macro shifts in health policy and the health service apparently directed at listening to the voice of the patient singular and enhancing individual choice rather than more collective goals. Nowhere are such changes more apparent than in the changes to patient representation in the late 1990s and 2000s. As the next chapter will suggest, the patient's voice came to drown out patients' voices.

Notes

1 Matthew Hilton, 'The fable of the sheep, or private virtues, public vices: the consumer revolution of the twentieth century', *Past and Present*, 176 (2002), 222–256, p. 238.

2   Matthew Hilton, *Consumerism in Twentieth Century Britain: The Search for a Historical Movement* (Cambridge: Cambridge University Press, 2003), p. 217.
3   Nancy Tomes, 'The "Information Rx"', in David J. Rothman and David Blumenthal (eds), *Medical Professionalism in the Information Age* (New Brunswick, NJ: Rutgers University Press, 2010), 40–65, p. 64.
4   *Ibid.*, p. 48.
5   *Ibid.*, p. 51.
6   Matthew Hilton, *Prosperity for All: Consumer Activism in an Era of Globalization* (Ithaca, NY and London: Cornell University Press, 2009), pp. 160–168; Beatrix Hoffman, *Health Care for Some: Rights and Rationing in the United States since 1930* (Chicago: University of Chicago Press, 2012), pp. 160–161.
7   Hilton, *Consumerism in Twentieth Century Britain*, pp. 275–276.
8   Charles Medawar/Social Audit, *The Wrong Kind of Medicine?* (Consumers' Association: London, 1984), p. 6.
9   Interview between Alex Mold and Marianne Rigge, 10 March 2010; Asa Briggs, *Michael Young: Social Entrepreneur* (Basingstoke: Palgrave, 2001), p. 293.
10 CCC YUNG 6/10/1, Letter from Young to Professor Ian McColl, Department of Surgery Guys Hospital, 31 December 1982.
11 CCC YUNG 6/10/1, Draft from the Mutual Aid Centre – Association of Trained Patients (ATP): A Body Designed to Increase Trust between Doctor and Patient, 1 January 1983.
12 CCC YUNG 6/10/1, Letter from Young to Bowyer, 3 February 1983; CCC YUNG 6/10/1, Letter from Young to Dr J.C. Hasler, Sonning Common Health Centre, 21 February 1983.
13 CCC YUNG 6/10/1, Letter from Young to Maurice Ash, Dartington Hall Trust, 25 February 1983.
14 CCC YUNG/6/10/10, College of Health First Annual Report, 1984.
15 *Ibid.*
16 CCC YUNG 6/10/13, Michael Young, 'The four purposes and the six methods', *Self Health: The Journal of the College of Health*, 1 (November 1983), p. 3.
17 CCC YUNG 6/10/2, Speech to Institute of Health Services Management Trent Branch Conference Personalising the Service, 7 February 1986.
18 Consumers' Association/Patients Association, *A Guide to the National Health Service* (London: Consumers' Association, 1983), p. 8.
19 CCC YUNG/6/10/10, Robert Gann and Sally Knight, *College of Health Consumers' Guide to Health Information* (London: College of Health, 1986), p. 1.
20 CCC YUNG 6/10/2, Speech to Institute of Health Services Management Trent Branch Conference Personalising the Service, 7 February 1986.
21 CCC YUNG/6/10/3, 'Information and choice for patients', talk at King's College Hospital Medical School, 9 September 1986 [by Marianne Rigge].
22 CCC YUNG/6/10/10, Gann and Knight, *College of Health Consumers' Guide to Health Information*, p. 3.
23 NCC, *Annual Report and Accounts, 1981/82* (London: NCC, 1982), p. 2.
24 NCC, *Annual Report and Accounts, 1983/84* (London: NCC, 1984), p. 8.
25 Ed McAlister-Smith, 'The CHC role in informing and empowering consumers', in Bob Gann and Gill Needham (eds), *Promoting Choice: Consumer Health*

Information in the 1990s (Winchester: Consumer Health Information Consortium, 1992), 19–28, p. 19.
26 CCC YUNG/6/10/10, *The College of Health Guide to Going Into Hospital*, 1985.
27 Consumers' Association (CA), *Avoiding Heart Trouble* (London: CA, 1980); Consumers' Association, *Understanding Stress* (London: CA, 1988); Consumers' Association, *Understanding Allergies* (London: CA, 1986); Consumers' Association, *Understanding Cancer* (London: CA, 1986); Consumers' Association, *Understanding Back Trouble* (London: CA, 1991).
28 Anon., 'Baldness in men: is there an answer?' *Which?*, November 1983; 'Drink', *Which?*, October 1984, 445–449.
29 *Self Health*, November 1983; *Self Health*, January 1984; *Self Health*, March 1985.
30 *Which?*, January 1993, p. 2.
31 Marianne Rigge, '"Healthline": a new service from the College of Health', *Health Libraries Review*, 3 (1986), 1–10; CCC YUNG 6/10/2, Speech to Institute of Health Services Management Trent Branch Conference Personalising the Service, 7 February 1986.
32 CCC YUNG 6/27/2, Healthline and Health Information Trust, Report from 1987, by Young.
33 Author interview with Marianne Rigge.
34 CCC YUNG/6/10/7, Very Preliminary paper on the College of Health, by Anthea Williams, 23 May 1991. See also Virginia Berridge, *AIDS in the UK: The Making of Policy, 1981–1994* (Oxford: Oxford University Press, 1996), pp. 89, 124.
35 CCC YUNG/6/10/3, Note of a meeting of the Vice Presidents of the College of Health, 5 February 1987.
36 www.nhsdirect.nhs.uk/About/WhatIsNHSDirect/History, accessed 7 June 2013.
37 CCC YUNG 6/27/3, A Future for Healthline? By Stephen Davies, 7 September 1989.
38 Medawar, *Wrong Kind of Medicine*, p. 11.
39 Ibid., p. 14.
40 *Which?*, March 1983; *Which?*, June 1984; *Which?*, January 1987; *Which?*, January 1983; *Which?*, February 1986; *Which?*, September 1987.
41 *Self* Health, 16 (September 1987); Author interview with Rigge.
42 ACHCEW, CD Rom, vol. 2, ACHCEW, *The Consumers View: A Review of CHCs Surveys on Outpatient Departments* (London: ACHCEW, 1984).
43 Central Birmingham CHC, *Annual Report*, 1 June 1979–31 May 1980.
44 ACHCEW CD Rom, vol. 2, *Community Health News*, Feb/March 1985, p. 10.
45 ACHCEW CD Rom, vol. 2, *Community Health News*, November 1984, p. 13.
46 Steven Harrison, *National Health Service Management in the 1980s: Policymaking on the Hoof?* (Aldershot: Avebury, 1994); Martin Gorsky (ed.), *The Griffiths NHS Management Enquiry: Its Origins, Nature and Impact* (London, 2010).
47 C. Batchelor, D.J. Owens, M. Read and M. Bloor, 'Patient satisfaction surveys: methodology, management and consumer evaluation', *International Journal of Health Care and Quality Assistance*, 7 (1994), 22–30.
48 CCC YUNG/6/10/11, College of Health Information Leaflet, n.d. [1990s?]; Marianne Rigge, 'Involving patients in clinical audit', *Quality in Healthcare*, 3 (1994) supplement, 2–5.
49 Medawar, *The Wrong Kind of Medicine*?

50   CCC YUNG/6/10/7, 'The patient speaks: good practice in consumer relations in the health service' by M. Young and the staff of the College of Health, March 1991.
51   Author interview with Marianne Rigge.
52   *Ibid.*
53   CCC YUNG/6/10/10, College of Health First Annual Report, 1984.
54   CCC YUNG/6/10/12, College of Health, *College of Health Guide to Hospital Waiting Lists, 1987*, p. 3.
55   CCC YUNG/6/10/12, College of Health, *Guide to Hospital Waiting Lists, 1989*, pp. 1–2.
56   Alan Petersen and Deborah Lupton, *The New Public Health: Health and Self in the Age of Risk* (London: Sage, 1996); Ian Shaw and Alan Aldridge, 'Consumerism, health and social order', *Social Policy and Society*, 2 (2003), 35–43.
57   Bob Gann, 'The Growth of Consumer Health Information in the UK', pp. 7–8, in Gann and Needham, *Promoting Choice*, p. 8.
58   David Vincent, *The Culture of Secrecy: Britain 1832–1998* (Oxford: Oxford University Press, 1998), p. 252.
59   *Ibid.*, p. 255.
60   Patricia Hewitt (ed.), *Computers, Records and the Right to Privacy* (London: NCCL, 1979).
61   Cmnd. 5012, *Report of the Committee on Privacy* (London: HMSO, 1972), p. 1.
62   British Medical Association, *Philosophy and Practice of Medical Ethics* (London: BMA, 1988), p. 19.
63   Cmnd. 5012, *Report of the Committee on Privacy*, pp. 109–110.
64   CMAC SA/PAT/D/16/1, David Woodhead, 'Doctors fear computer spy in hospitals', *Sunday Telegraph*, 24 June 1973.
65   Cmnd. 5012, *Report of the Committee on Privacy*, p. 110.
66   *Ibid.*, p. 114.
67   CMAC SA/PAT/D/16/1, Letter from Miss Kate Patrick, Secretary of the PA to Mr MJ Hewitt, DHSS, 8 August 1973.
68   CMAC SA/PAT/D/16/3 Pt 1 Letter from Patricia Hewitt, NCCL to Moira Tanner [?] PA, 29 December 1978.
69   Vincent, *Culture of Secrecy*, p. 272.
70   Anon., 'Computers and privacy', *British Medical Journal* (24 January 1976), pp. 178–179.
71   Cmnd. 7341, *Report of the Committee on Data Protection* (London: HMSO, 1978), p. xix.
72   TNA HO 261/265, The Data Protection Committee: Medical Records. Note by the Patients Association, 19 December 1976.
73   Cmnd. 7341, *Report of the Committee on Data Protection*, p. xxiv.
74   *Ibid.*, p. 69.
75   Derek Pheby, 'Changing practice on confidentiality: a cause for concern', *Journal of Medical Ethics*, 8 (1982), 12–24, p. 15.
76   'Confidentiality of medical records', letter from Dr E. Gray-Taylor [Secretary of the BMA] *British Medical Journal* (29 July 1978), p. 352.
77   Vincent, *Culture of Secrecy*, pp. 273–274.

78 Council of Europe, *Convention for the Protection of Individuals with regard to Automatic Processing of Personal Data*, Strasbourg, 1981, http://conventions.coe.int/Treaty/en/Treaties/Html/108.htm, accessed 26 June 2013.
79 Data Protection Act, 1984.
80 CMAC SA/PAT/D/16/1, Letter from Elizabeth Ackroyd to Miss Ginnie Bruce, CA, 31 January 1980.
81 CMAC SA/PAT/D/16/2: pt 1, Letter from WE Acheson, Executive Secretary PA to Home Office, 27 May 1982.
82 CMAC SA/PAT/D/16/2: pt 2, Secrets File no. 3: medical records, 10 February 1984.
83 CMAC SA/PAT/D/16/2: pt 1,Consumer Congress 83: Resolutions from Workshops.
84 'Patient's orders', *Which?*, 30 (February 1987), 60–63, p. 61.
85 CMAC SA/PAT/D/16/2: pt 1, Letter from Elizabeth Ackroyd to Mrs D. Layzell, 13 April 1983.
86 CMAC SA/PAT/D/16/3 Pt 1, Central Birmingham CHC, *The Case for: 'The right of every adult patient to have access to his or her own medical notes if they wish to'*, n.d. [1980?].
87 Ruth Cohen, 'Whose file is it anyway? Discussion paper', *Journal of the Royal Society of Medicine*, 78 (February 1985), 126–128, p. 126.
88 Ruth Cohen, *Whose File is it Anyway?* (London: NCCL, 1982), pp. 9, 11.
89 Cohen, 'Whose file is it anyway?', p. 128.
90 CCC YUNG/6/10/13, 'College of Health: Letter from the Director', *Self Health*, 12 (September 1986), p. 10.
91 Cohen, *Whose File is it Anyway?*, pp. 72–73.
92 Pheby, 'Changing practice on confidentiality', p. 17.
93 CMAC SA/PAT/D/16/2: pt 1, BMA Inter-professional Working Group on Access to Personal Health Information: Data Protection Bill – Statement on Subject Access to Personal Health Information, May 1983.
94 CMAC SA/PAT/K/2/1/11, Data Protection Act: Subject Access to Personal Health Information – A Consultation Paper, 1985.
95 CMAC SA/PAT/K/2/1/11, Data Protection Act: Subject Access to Personal Health Information. Response of the National Consumer Council, February 1986.
96 CMAC SA/PAT/K/2/1/11, The Patients Association: Confidentiality of Personal Health Information. Comments on DA (85)25, 25 February 1985.
97 CMAC SA/PAT/K/2/1/11, Letter from Maurice Frankel, Campaign for Freedom of Information to Mr K.G. Carpenter, DHSS, 3 March 1986.
98 *House of Commons Debates*, 10 July 1984, vol. 63, cols 887–889.
99 *House of Commons Debates*, 29 October 1985, vol. 84, cols 851–853.
100 BMA, *Philosophy and Practice of Medical Ethics*, p. 26.
101 N. Britten, J. Bartholomew, R. Morris and L. Zander, 'Consultants' and patients' views about patient access to their general practice records', *Journal of the Royal Society of Medicine*, 84 (May 1991), 284–287.
102 Anon., 'From the GMSC: Modified access to health records by patients approved', *British Medical Journal*, 292 (25 January 1986), p. 283.
103 David Metcalfe, 'Whose data are they anyway?', *British Medical Journal*, 292 (1 March 1986), 577–578.
104 Alexander P. Ross, 'The case against showing patients their records', *British Medical Journal*, 292 (1 March 1986), p. 578.

105 Anon., 'From the LMC conference: GMSC decision on medical records overturned', *British Medical Journal*, 292 (21 June 1986), p. 1688.
106 Access to Personal Files Act, 1987.
107 Anon., 'Access to personal files – new short Bill gets government backing', *Secrets: Newspaper of the Campaign for Freedom of Information*, 12 (April 1987), pp. 1–2.
108 Anon., 'Kirkwood's bill – much amended – passed by Commons on election eve' *Secrets: Newspaper of the Campaign for Freedom of Information*, 13 (October 1987), p. 2; Anon., 'BMA annual report of council: medical ethics, *British Medical Journal*, 30–32, p. 31.
109 CMAC SA/PAT/F/1/16, Maurice Frankel, 'The right to know is ours at last', *Patient Voice*, 50 (Autumn 1990), pp. 5–6.
110 *House of Commons Debates*, 26 May 1989, vol. 153, cols 1277–1284, col. 1277.
111 *House of Commons Debates*, 26 May 1989, vol. 153, cols 1277–1284, col. 1279.
112 Hugo Young, 'An open and shut-up case of conspiracy', the *Guardian*, 8 March 1990, p. 19; Anon., 'Campaign overcomes bid to sabotage Bill for access to medical records', *Secrets: Newspaper of the Campaign for Freedom of Information*, 19 (April 1990), p. 1; CMAC SA/PAT/F/1/16, Maurice Frankel, 'The right to know is ours at last' *Patient Voice*, 50 (Autumn 1990), pp. 5–6.
113 *House of Commons Debates*, 26 May 1989, vol. 153, cols 1277–1284, col. 1230.
114 Campaign for the Freedom of Information, 'It's our right to know: personal accounts of people who have seen or needed to see their own health records', 1990, www.cfoi.org.uk/mymedrecds.html, accessed 28 June 2013.
115 Access to Health Records Act, 1990.
116 CMAC SA/PAT/K/2/1/11 The Patients Association – Policy Paper: Access to Health Records, LJW, February 1992.
117 ACHCEW CD Rom, vol. 3, ACHCEW, *Access to Health Records Act 1990: The Concerns of Community Councils* (ACHCEW: London, 1994), p. 11.
118 Department of Health, *Patient's Charter* (London: HMSO, 1991), p. 9.

6

Voice

During the late 1990s and 2000s, the notion of patient 'voice' acquired increased attention from the government and health policy makers. Voice, alongside choice, was one of the key principles underpinning the reform of the NHS under the Labour government (1997–2010). In some ways, 'voice' could be seen as allied to notions of patient representation and participation that had been present within the British health care system since at least the 1970s, as discussed in Chapter 2. However, voice as it was conceptualised in the 1990s and 2000s, was something different to pre-existing ideas about patient representation. Firstly, patient voice was ascribed greater importance than it had been in the past, as can be seen in the number of policy documents produced throughout the period.[1] Secondly, the mechanisms for putting forward the patient voice were overhauled. In 2003, the CHCs were abolished and replaced with a plethora of other bodies including the Patient Advice and Liaison Service (PALS), the Commission for Patient and Public Involvement (CPPIH), Patient Forums, Overview and Scrutiny Committees (OSCs), and the Independent Complaints Advisory Service (ICAS). In addition, other forms of soliciting patient opinion, such as citizens' juries and listening exercises were also utilised.

Such a proliferation in the number of bodies claiming to speak for the patient-consumer demonstrated the growing importance of the patient voice within the NHS. Yet, at the same time, importance in policy terms did not necessarily equate to more power for patient-consumers. The presence of these numerous organisations led to concerns about fragmentation of patient representation, especially as many of the new organisations turned out to be somewhat short-lived. Patient Forums and the CPPIH were scrapped in 2008, to be replaced with Local Involvement Networks (LINks), which were themselves abolished in 2013 in favour of Local Healthwatch and Healthwatch England. In part, this constant revolution can be explained by the ongoing reform of the NHS in England (the situation in Scotland, Wales and Northern Ireland was somewhat different) but it was also underpinned by a deeper level of uncertainty and about the meaning and purpose/s of patient voice. Did patients speak with one voice, or many? Whose voice should be listened to and whose voices were often ignored?

This chapter will explain the rise of 'voice', explore its multiple meanings and the implications that this had for organisations claiming to speak for the patient-consumer. It will examine the weakening of existing mechanisms of collective representation in the NHS in the form of the CHCs by first looking at a local case-study and then going on to consider the demise of the CHCs at a national level. The abolition of the CHCs in 2003 was indicative of a change in ideas not only about who was best placed to speak for patient-consumers, but also in the kinds of things that they were expected to say. More attention was to be paid to the voice of the individual patient rather than patients' voices as a whole. Such a view fitted with the broader reform of the NHS that was directed towards a more marketised model with a tendency to see patients as individuals rather than as a group. Examining the 'alphabet soup' of organisations that replaced the CHCs suggests that despite growing attention, collective mechanisms for representing the patient-consumer were weakened. Individual voice began to be equated with greater individual choice, leaving less space for collective patient representation.

Explaining the rise of voice

As discussed in Chapter 2, patient representation within the NHS was nothing new, but in the 1990s and 2000s a novel language centred on the term 'voice' began to come in to use, signifying a different approach to patient involvement. The notion of patient voice first seemed to appear in the early 1990s, with the NHS Executive's attempt to involve local people in purchasing decisions within the NHS.[2] It was under the New Labour government, however, that 'voice' came to the forefront. A Department of Health discussion document, published in 2001, asserted that the government's vision was 'to move away from an outdated [sic] system of patients being on the outside, towards a new model where the voices of patients, their carers and the public are heard through every level of service, acting as a powerful lever for change and improvement'.[3] Patients and the public, according to Parliamentary Undersecretary for Health, David Lammy, 'rightly expect to be involved and consulted in all aspects of their lives – they are more likely to ask questions and less in awe of experts. There are more people wanting to "have a say" in decision-making and public authorities are more open to scrutiny and challenge.'[4] In 2006, Minister of

State for Health Services, Rosie Winterton, echoed such a sentiment when she stated that 'We want people to become active partners in their healthcare and wish to create a system where people are no longer passive recipients of NHS and social care services'.[5]

Alongside such collective aspirations for patient voice, were also more individualised conceptualisations. The then Secretary of State for Health, Alan Milburn, told the Fabian Society in 2001 that 'People grow up today in a consumer society. Services – whether they are private or public – succeed [or] fail according to their ability [to] respond [to] modern expectations'.[6] In 2009, another policy document, *Putting People at the Heart of Care* stated that 'As modern consumers, we demand services that understand and respond to our individual needs. In the minds of most people, the NHS should be no different.'[7]

This apparent mixture of collective and more individual ambitions for voice led many commentators to separate these into two strands: 'democratic' and 'consumerist'. A democratic understanding of voice, according to social scientists Suzanne Wait and Ellen Nolte, regarded the public as citizens and taxpayers with rights to use public services and duties to contribute/participate in society.[8] Rosemary Rowe and Michael Shepherd concurred, seeing the democratic model of public participation as both valuing participation in and of itself and also as a method to achieve democratic renewal. In contrast, the consumerist model, they suggested, emphasised individual rights to information, choice, access and redress.[9] Waite and Nolte also pointed to the importance of rights of individuals within the consumerist approach to voice, and the way in which this tended to see public involvement as a correction to market failure.[10] Such a separation of consumerist and democratic tendencies is useful, as it points to the different values and uses to which voice was being put, but as John Clarke and his colleagues have noted, democratic and consumerist approaches could also overlap. They suggest that the 'citizen-consumer' was at the heart of recent public service reform, a process that began under the Conservative government in the 1990s and continued under New Labour. The 'strange figure' of the citizen-consumer combined terms and values usually associated with citizenship, such as the state, public and collective, with those connected to consumption, such as the market, private and the individual.[11]

The development of the hybrid figure of the citizen-consumer can be seen as a product of a combination of both democratic and consumerist impulses. One of the most often cited reasons by commentators and politicians for improving patient voice was to address a supposed 'democratic deficit' within the NHS. In 1995, the Institute for Public Policy Research (IPPR), a centre-left think-tank, published a report entitled *Voices Off*, which identified a lack of democracy at local level in health care services. The IPPR argued that 'As a publicly funded organisation, providing services for the public, in the public interest, the NHS is widely acknowledged to owe accountability to the public.'[12] However, the creation of the internal market in the early 1990s, and the resulting purchaser/provider split had devolved and dispersed power within the NHS. Local health authorities, the report pointed out, were not directly accountable to patients and the public, meaning that the only democratic accountability within the NHS was through the health minister. Moreover, *Voices Off* suggested that the new emphasis on rationing and value for money increased the need to involve the public in such decisions. To rectify this democratic deficit, the report recommended strengthening the CHCs by providing them with more powers and resources and also experimenting with new methods of public involvement such as citizens' juries and 'electronic democracy', which involved making use of new information technology.[13]

The Labour government accepted the existence of a democratic deficit within the NHS and put forward measures intended to address this. In 2000, in the *NHS Plan* (an important document setting out the programme for reform of the health service) improving democracy within the NHS was a key objective. The *Plan* stated that 'Patients and citizens have had too little influence at every level of the NHS' and 'It is time to modernise, deepen and broaden the way that patient views are represented within the NHS.'[14] At the same time, the *NHS Plan* and other key policy documents suggested that improving patient voice would have value over and above addressing the democratic deficit. In 1999, a Department of Health report, *Patient and Public Involvement in the New NHS*, asserted that

> The NHS needs to work with its local communities not just because it is the right thing to do but because effective partnership will help deliver results in the form of: better quality and more responsive services; better outcomes of care and better health for the population; reductions in health inequalities; greater local ownership of health services; and a better understanding of who and how local services need to change and develop.[15]

Thus, improving patient and public involvement in the NHS was also seen as a way of improving services. A discussion document produced by the Department of Health in 2001 contended that 'We are determined to increase public involvement as much as public investment; to reform the way we engage the public as much as to reforming the way we deliver public services'.[16] Such sentiments were given a legislative grounding through the Health and Social Care Act, 2001 which made it a duty for every organisation providing health care services to involve and consult service users about the planning and provision of these and proposals for change.[17]

Moves to enhance public accountability and improve services through greater patient involvement were also being pushed forward by developments outside of the New Labour government. As had been the case in the 1960s and 1970s, public scandal over standards of NHS care seemed to reveal a gap between the service and the people it served. In 1998, an inquiry was launched into the deaths of 29 babies that had undergone heart surgery at the Bristol Royal Infirmary in the late 1980s and early 1990s. The inquiry, led by the lawyer and ethicist Ian Kennedy, exposed what it called an 'old boys' culture' amongst the surgeons: patients were left in the dark about treatment; there was secrecy about doctors' performance; and a lax approach to clinical safety. One of the ways of rectifying this, the report argued, was to enhance patient and public involvement. The Kennedy report recommended that 'The priority for involving the public should be that their interests are embedded into all organisations and institutions concerned with quality of performance in the NHS: in other words, the public should be "on the inside", rather than represented by some organisation "on the outside".[18] The report went on to establish a number of principles that it argued should inform policy on public involvement, including the embedding of patient and public involvement within all structures of the NHS. The government accepted these principles, reiterating them in its 2001 discussion document on involving patients and the public in health care.[19]

In addition to public outcry over the Bristol Royal Infirmary, there were other external forces pushing for greater patient and public involvement. There is some evidence to suggest that the number and type of patient-consumer organisations and other health groups began to change from the 1990s onwards. Organisations in the health field became more numerous. In the early 2000s, Brian Salter found that there were 2,500 organisations listed in the College of Health database.[20] In his study of 'patients associations' political scientist Brian Wood found that of 54 per cent of patient groups were founded after 1980, leading him to posit the existence of a 'patients movement' from this period.[21] Similarly, in their research on health consumer groups Rob Baggott and his colleagues noted that two-thirds of groups were established after 1981. Furthermore, they also pointed to a change in the type of organisations established: these were more likely to be groups founded *by* patients with a particular condition rather than an organisation created by others *for* sufferers. This led Baggott, Allsop and Jones to suggest that by the 1990s a health consumer movement was in existence.[22]

Of course, as this book has demonstrated, there had long been a number of organisations claiming to speak for the patient as consumer. In the 1990s and 2000s, though, there was a tendency to see such groups through the lens of social movement theory. Phil Brown and Stephen Zavestoski defined health social movements as 'collective challenges to medical policy, public health policy and politics, belief systems, research and practice which include an array of formal and informal organisations, supporters, networks of cooperation and media'.[23] They identified three different types of health social movement: health access movements, which sought equitable access to and provision of health services; embodied health movements; which addressed disease, disability or illness experience by challenging science on aetiology, diagnosis, treatment and prevention; and constituency-based movements which addressed inequalities based on race, ethnicity, gender, class, sexuality.[24] Brown and his colleagues suggested that though there had been health social movements in the past, a greater awareness of health issues in the 1990s and 2000s, connected with the success of allied social movements such as the women's movement and the environmental movement, facilitated the development of a distinctive health social movement.[25]

Empirical evidence for the existence of a new and more challenging type of patient organisation can be found by looking at some of the disease-specific groups that were established from the late 1980s onwards. The successes of organisations established by and for sufferers of AIDS are well known, but other groups such as those in the mental health field and illegal drug use could also be seen in this light.[26] Groups of and for the sufferers of specific diseases appeared to be making some inroads into the formation of health policy and practice, although, as Salter pointed out, patient organisations still remained in a subordinate position when compared to health professionals and the state.[27] What is more, the fate of generic patient-consumer groups, groups which attempted to represent all patients irrespective of the disease they suffered from or the population group to which they belonged, was less assured. The College of Health closed down in 2003 due to cash flow problems.[28] The Patients Association is still going at the time of writing (2014) and has continued to make regular contributions to debates about health care and health policy. Consumer groups like Which? (formerly the Consumers' Association) and the National Consumer Council (now Consumer Focus) maintain an interest in health issues, but, as will be discussed in greater detail below, the role that such organisations played in speaking for the patient as consumer appears to have reduced as a plethora of government-backed agencies have taken on this responsibility.

The creation of such bodies could be seen as a response to a more challenging health consumer movement, but there was also a perception that individual patient-consumers were becoming more demanding. For instance, a 2009 document setting out the NHS's 'vision for public and patient experience and engagement' contended that 'As modern consumers, we demand services that understand and respond to our individual needs.

In the minds of most people, the NHS should be no different.'[29] Giving patients more say in individual treatment decisions and in how services were planned, delivered and evaluated was seen as a logical response to the greater levels of consumer sovereignty people felt that they experienced in other areas of their lives.

Other arguments, and other views of the patient-consumer, were also marshalled in favour of greater patient involvement. Drawing on developments within public health, which stressed individual behaviour (such as smoking, over-eating and lack of exercise) as a leading cause of ill health, there was a move to get patients to become more 'fully engaged' with their own health and with health services.[30] Individuals were seen as 'co-producers' of health, expected to take responsibility for their health by making healthier lifestyle choices.[31] Connected to this was also an acknowledgement that patients' knowledge and experience of their condition could be of value in improving their own care and that of others. In 2001, the Expert Patient Initiative was launched, with the aim of creating a 'cadre of expert patients – people who have the confidence, skills, information and knowledge to play a central role in the management of life with chronic diseases and to minimise the impact of disease on their lives'.[32] Underpinning such developments was a view of the patient-consumer allied to what Nikolas Rose and Carlos Novas called 'biological citizenship', where the individual patient was no longer expected to be passive and compliant, but rather to engage in their own treatment and with the 'biosocial' groups that coalesced around their specific disease.[33]

Yet, other commentators took a less benign view of attempts to involve patient-consumers more fully in health care. Alan Shaw and Ian Aldridge argued that personal responsibility and risk prevention were being promoted in place of universal access to health care services. They asserted that 'we, as social citizens, are expected to be self-regulators of our actions and bodies. As part of this process collective rights to welfare are being replaced by individual obligations.'[34] Other critiques came from those who examined how patient involvement worked on the ground. Stephen Harrison and Maggie Mort carried out a study of public and user involvement during the late 1990s. They found that managers utilised involvement as a 'technology of legitimation', whereby users' views were drawn upon to buttress doctors' and managers' decisions. At the same time, Harrison and Mort noted that managers were able to ignore user involvement when it suited them.[35] Timothy Milewa, Justin Valentine and Michael Calan also highlighted the relative power of managers when compared to patients. Milewa and his colleagues assessed the changes in the health service during the late 1990s and concluded that despite increased attention towards 'active citizenship' and greater public involvement, this did not translate into significant changes in ideology or practice. Local populations, they suggested, still played a largely 'passive' role with respect to the determining the nature and priorities of health care.[36] Similarly, Rowe and Shepherd found that schemes designed to encourage greater public involvement were bounded by the principles of New Public Management, which tended to see participation as a form of organisational learning rather than it being about greater say for patients.[37] Despite the increased policy presence of patient voice there were clearly difficulties in translating this into action.

New voices?

To explore some of these difficulties in more depth, this section will consider patient and public involvement around the building of a new hospital in South Birmingham during the late 1990s and early 2000s. The sidelining of pre-existing methods of public participation in the form of the CHC, and the promotion of alternative techniques to gauge patient opinion in its place highlighted a desire on the part of local and national government to hear 'new voices', a development which raises further questions about the strength and meaning of public involvement in this period.

Throughout the 1970s and 1980s capital investment in hospital facilities in Birmingham and across the country had been low.[38] By the end of the 1990s, it was estimated that the maintenance backlog at Selly Oak Hospital and the Queen Elizabeth Hospital, both run by the University Hospital Birmingham Trust (UHBT), ran to £98 million.[39] In 1997, UHBT formed a series of working groups comprised of staff from both hospitals to examine what could be done to improve patient care and develop the future shape of services. A preference for more collaboration was expressed: services were split across two hospitals just over a mile apart, and staff felt that there were many benefits of working more closely together, possibly on a single site.[40]

To decide how to proceed, the Trust began a 'non-monetary option appraisal exercise', evaluating a series of shortlisted options that included doing nothing, re-developing the existing hospitals and building a new hospital at one of a number of different sites. South Birmingham CHC (SBCHC) was invited to take part in the option appraisal exercise, but after some debate, they declined to do so. The CHC decided not to take part because they thought that not enough information had been provided about each option; the assessment criteria were inadequate; and most significantly of all, they felt that the appraisal process did not take into account how the various options were to be funded.[41] One member of the CHC, Shirley Hoole, commented that 'the CHC should have been involved at an earlier stage to put the patient's perspective. She [Hoole] did not see how the CHC could assess the options in a non-financial way since PFI [Private Finance Initiative] would affect six out of the ten benefit criteria.'[42] SBCHC were concerned about the implications of building a new hospital since this would be financed under the PFI scheme. The Private Finance Initiative was introduced under the Conservative government in 1992, but was adopted by Labour in 1997. Under PFI, new hospitals would be built, financed and owned by the private sector, and then leased to the NHS for a fixed period.[43] Such schemes, according to the chair of SBCHC, Ursula Pearce, were 'bad value for money and not in the interests of patient care'.[44]

Following the appraisal exercise, in September 1997, UHBT announced that their preferred option was to build a new hospital in South Birmingham. As no central government funding was available for such projects, it was expected that any new hospital would have to be built under the PFI. To find out what people in the area thought of the proposed hospital, SBCHC conducted a survey of local residents. The council distributed 130,000 leaflets setting out UHBT's plan to build a hospital on a new site and also SBCHC's own 'alternative option' of gradual improvement of facilities at Selly Oak and the Queen Elizabeth Hospitals. The leaflet listed a number of factors for and against each proposal, and invited readers to indicate which option they preferred.[45] The survey garnered 3,373 replies, 3,159 (94 per cent) of which supported SBCHC's alternative option, 178 (5 per cent) supported the new hospital and 36 (1 per cent) expressed no preference.[46] Some respondents also used the survey to make further comments, and many of these centred on the use of PFI to build the new hospital. According to the CHC, respondents 'were against the idea of using private money in health care, thought that profits would come before patient care and some respondents saw PFI as a "backdoor" attempt to dismantle the health service'.[47]

SBCHC's survey pointed to a current of local feeling that was strongly against the building of a new hospital and not in favour of PFI, but the trust's managers questioned the extent to which this was an accurate representation of public opinion. Dr Shirley McIver and Professor Peter Spurgeon of the University of Birmingham's Health Service Management Centre were commissioned by UHBT to review the CHC's survey and 'determine whether the CHC have presented a fair and representative picture of the case for and against the new hospital.'[48] McIver and Spurgeon pointed out that though SBCHC had intended that every household in South Birmingham receive a copy of their leaflet, there had been problems with distribution. If approximately 90,000 copies of the leaflet had been distributed, and the CHC had received 3,373 replies, the survey had generated a response rate of around 4 per cent. Survey response rates of less than 60 per cent, the researchers argued, were not usually considered representative.[49] Moreover,

McIver and Spurgeon found significant problems with the leaflet itself. They asserted that 'the summary information provided to the public in the survey leaflet distributed by the CHC was incomplete, inaccurate and potentially misleading'.[50] A particular area of concern surrounded the connection made in the leaflet between the trust's proposal to build a new hospital and PFI. McIver and Spurgeon noted that 'it was misleading of the CHC to link the new hospital with the PFI because there is no local flexibility over whether or not this course of action should be taken'.[51] SBCHC, the researchers contended, had 'entangled two separate issues. Whether or not a new hospital is needed must be decided first. The source and nature of funding for any new hospital is a separate decision which may follow.'[52] Although a decision as to whether or not to build a new hospital could be made locally, the decision about how this should be funded would be made centrally in line with national government policy. McIver and Spurgeon conceded that the level of concern expressed in the SBCHC survey about the new hospital and PFI should not be completely disregarded, as 'It is unlikely that the CHC would have been able to stimulate concerns where none existed' but 'it is not known to what extent these respondents reflect the anxieties of larger numbers of the population'.[53]

There is some evidence to suggest that SBCHC's hostility towards the use of PFI in building the new hospital had wider resonance: the views of the general public on PFI were at best ambivalent. An opinion poll conducted in 2002 found that 63 per cent of people wanted a review of PFI projects before any more contracts were awarded; 19 per cent of people interviewed said PFI projects were good and more should be created; and 9 per cent said they were bad and should be stopped.[54] But, by basing their campaign against the new hospital on PFI, the CHC were easily dismissed as being ideologically opposed to PFI, and therefore not in a position to make reasoned arguments against the new hospital. Moreover, as local officials stressed repeatedly in their dealings with the CHC, it was not within their power to determine how any new hospital would be funded. John Charlton, chair of UHBT, told the *Health Services Journal* that 'I have discussions with those that do not agree with PFI and it is like sitting down to play Monopoly and saying that we should be playing to the rules of Scrabble. If someone tells you that this is the game, then you have to maximise the benefit in that context.'[55]

The fact that no one locally, not the CHC, the University Hospital Trust, or the health authority, were able to decide how any new hospital would be funded points to a dissonance between the supposed devolution of power from central to local government. A series of initiatives under the Conservative and Labour governments, beginning with the introduction of the internal market in 1990, had theoretically transferred decision-making power to the local level, but some areas of policy, such as financing health care, remained under central control. This had the effect of limiting the capacity for local involvement in some decisions: in the case of the new hospital for South Birmingham, people in the city were being asked whether or not they would like a new hospital, but were not permitted to decide how this would be funded. Limitations had been placed on local participation no matter how effective or representative this was.

Despite such restrictions, the Birmingham Health Authority (BHA) employed a range of methods to garner public opinion on the new hospital. In 1998, the BHA set up an 'Independent Advisory Panel', a 'citizens' jury', to examine the issue. The convening of a citizens' jury was itself indicative of changes in the way in which health authorities consulted with the public over decisions about local services. Citizens' juries were first trialled in the health sector in 1996, as an attempt to introduce more 'deliberative democracy' into the NHS.[56] Deliberative democracy, defined as 'decision making by discussion by free and equal citizens', was intended to address the supposed 'democratic deficit' within the NHS by increasing public participation in health care decisions.[57] But, as Susan Pickard has pointed out, deliberative methods such as citizens' juries were beset with similar problems to those experienced by CHCs: concerns were expressed about the accountability, authority, representativeness and legitimacy of citizens' juries. Pickard also identified difficulties that were specific to citizens' juries. Their temporary nature meant that citizens' juries were unable to provide ongoing representation, and they often lacked authority, as their decisions were not final or binding. Pickard concluded that citizens' juries 'may be properly described as consultation rather than participation'.[58] Moreover, although the model for citizens' juries drew on theories of deliberative democracy, their obvious parallels with focus groups and other research methods borrowed from the commercial sector pointed towards a more marketised approach to public involvement. Focus groups generated what Javier Lezaun has called 'tradable opinions' which may not reflect consumer preferences.[59] Furthermore, participating in such deliberative consultations has been shown to change the opinions of those taking part. Lezaun and Soneryd studied two different forms of public consultation about genetically modified (GM) food, and found that the individuals who took part in the focus groups altered their views on GM food as a result of their participation in the group discussions. These changed views, which were more favourable to the desired outcome, were later used to offset the negative views put forward in an open public consultation exercise.[60] David Price, in his examination of citizens' juries in the health sector came to a similar view. He argued that 'citizens' jury deliberations do not involve a rational enquiry into the justification and selection of values. Juries function as mechanisms for democratising the selection of values only in the very limited sense that they expose small groups to exercises in attitude change.'[61]

Given the apparent malleability of deliberative methods like citizens' juries, perhaps it was no surprise that in the case of Birmingham's new hospital, the citizens' jury recommended that a new hospital should be built, and asserted that it was 'inescapable' that this would be constructed under the PFI. SBCHC criticised the Independent Advisory Panel and its findings, arguing that the body lacked independence as its members were 'handpicked' by BHA, some of whom had links to the chairman of the health authority.[62] Following on from the citizens' jury, BHA also carried out other forms of public consultation. In the spring of 1999, they published a consultation document on the development of hospital services in the city. The report set out four options. The first three options were put forward by the University Hospital Birmingham Trust and comprised: firstly, doing the minimum repairs necessary to both hospitals; secondly, the 'plaza option', which involved building a new hospital close to the existing Queen Elizabeth Hospital; and thirdly the 'central option' which proposed the construction of a new hospital on a brownfield site between the two existing hospitals. The trust asserted that 'Having considered all the evidence it is clear that our existing buildings cannot adequately provide for the requirements of society and the rapidly changing world of medicine. We conclude that single site working under either the Plaza or Central options is the way forward.'[63] The fourth option was put forward by SBCHC. The CHC suggested that both the Queen Elizabeth and Selly Oak Hospitals be improved gradually, and an ambulatory care centre be built close to Selly Oak Hospital. SBCHC argued that their option would allow for a 'flexible evolution of services sensitive to changing patterns of care and needs' and, most importantly in their opinion, would avoid 'the financial and other severe drawbacks of PFI which would be involved in the UHB Trust's Preferred Option'.[64]

All four options were put to the public in the consultation document, and in September 1999 the Health Authority published the results. A total of 1,776 responses had been received, representing the views of at least 4,351 people (some letters had multiple signatories). Of these, 87 per cent said that they preferred the single site option, 2 per cent supported the do minimum option, 2 per cent supported the CHC's option, and 9 per cent wanted none of the options.[65] These results seemed to indicate a significant level of support for a new hospital amongst the general public, but the validity of these findings was brought into question by SBCHC. David Spilsbury, a SBCHC member and later Chair of the council, contended that many of the responses came not from the general public, but from trust staff and other NHS employees. He alleged that medical students at the University of Birmingham had been asked to sign identical letters supporting the new hospital when collecting their exam results. When one student asked to take the letter away as he intended to protest, he was told he could not have a copy.[66] The Health Authority did receive 269 identical letters from medical students, and 190 identical letters from trust staff. How many of the remaining responses came from the general public was not recorded.[67]

Finding out what the general public in Birmingham really thought about the new hospital was clearly difficult to assess with any degree of accuracy. Letters to local newspapers were both for and against the plan, but the new facility was widely supported by other important stakeholders in the area. The city council, most local MPs and MEPs, the regional newspapers, seven other local CHCs and, most critically, medical and support staff of both UHBT hospitals, were in favour of the new hospital.[68] With this backing, Birmingham Health Authority announced that it was supporting the Trust's plan to build a new hospital at the Plaza site.[69] SBCHC continued to oppose the decision, and lodged a formal objection with the Secretary of State, Alan Milburn. Ursula Pearce, Chair of SBCHC, told Milburn that 'Irrespective of the method of funding, the above [UHBT] proposals would lead to such a down sizing of acute beds, staff and facilities as to render the new hospital incapable of meeting either the current or future need for hospital care.'[70] A few months later, in February 2000, Yvette Cooper (a junior minister in the Department of Health) wrote to the CHC to tell them that she was upholding BHA's decision to build a new hospital in South Birmingham. Cooper stated that 'I am satisfied that, in the interest of addressing both the current difficulties of providing clinical care in poor accommodation and the inefficiencies associated with the services split between two sites, the centralisation of acute hospital services onto a single site represents the best solution.'[71] Although SBCHC continued to oppose the new hospital, construction went ahead and the Queen Elizabeth Hospital opened to patients in June 2010.

This case study points to two broader shifts in patient representation during the late 1990s and early 2000s. Firstly, the ability of local patient representation to feed in to policy making on the ground was restricted by a national policy (the introduction of PFI) over which they had no control. Indeed, patient and public input into the decision to introduce PFI at the national level was non-existent. This indicated that there were limits to the kinds of policy areas where public and patient involvement was deemed appropriate. Secondly, new methods of soliciting public opinion and involving the public at the local level were being made use of. This had the effect of sidelining the CHC and the opposition that they offered, but also highlighted a deeper move away from collective representation such as the CHCs and towards more deliberative approaches like citizens' juries and public consultations. Such methods were presented as being able to access untapped opinion – the 'silent majority' in contrast to the 'usual suspects' – but as Lezaun and Soneryd point out, the opinions of the 'silent majority' were valued precisely because they were movable, making it easier for consultation exercises to produce the desired result.[72] The days of the CHCs, and the form of patient voice that they offered, appeared to be numbered.

The demise of the CHCs

The CHCs had come under threat in the past. The 1979 White Paper, *Patients First*, proposed getting rid of CHCs and their position within the various subsequent reconfigurations of the health service was often unclear.[73] The introduction of general management in the mid-1980s encouraged the development of more direct methods of assessing patients' views such as public opinion surveys.[74] The CHCs sat outside the purchaser/provider split created by the establishment of the internal market in 1990, offering a form of patient-consumer representation that seemed at odds with the more individualised, marketised approach.[75] Mike Gerrard, Director of ACHCEW from 1977–83, remarked that from the government's perspective:

> CHCs were an oddity. They didn't do anything productive and they weren't saleable, which made them seem like a liability. But they were to do with the public, and the public were consumers, and entitled to choice, and quality services at competitive prices; and in cost terms they were not extortionate. By a simple rule of thumb, they were rather ambivalent, and probably unnecessary. And they were, at times, awkward. A legitimate target for abolition, therefore, in the view of several government ministers.[76]

The position of the CHCs was also undermined by a new focus on performance management.[77] The variability and inconsistency between CHCs came in for repeated criticism. In 1989, a Department of Health circular stated that 'CHCs are not uniformly effective; many are mediocre; and in some the legitimate activity of critical comment on the district's or FPC's health care provision shades into direct political action against the policies of the government of the day.'[78] Research by Sarah Buckland, Carol Lupton and Graham Moon identified 'considerable diversity between CHCs in both the work that they do and the approach that they take.'[79] For their part, the CHCs did attempt to address some of the issues around variability. In 1996, ACHCEW produced a performance evaluation framework setting out the functions of CHCs and the standards that they were expected to reach.[80]

At the same time as concerns were being raised about the CHCs, other methods of hearing patient and public voices were coming in to play. As discussed earlier in this chapter, deliberative methods, like citizens' juries, were trialled. So too was mass public consultation. In 2000, 12 million leaflets asking the public for their views on the NHS were made available at hospitals, GP's surgeries, pharmacies and even supermarkets. A website was set up to allow people to voice their opinions online, and public meetings were held in London and Leeds.[81] Voluntary organisations working in the health field, and particularly disease-specific groups, were also invited into discussions with key policy makers.[82]

At the same time, the position of the CHCs came under further attack following a report commissioned by the NHS Executive that once again pointed to variability and inconsistency amongst the CHCs, and also questioned their democratic legitimacy. As the *Guardian*'s Patrick Butler pointed out, there was a feeling amongst CHCs 'that change – if not abolition – is now firmly on the agenda'.[83] In 1999, the CHCs defended their position by forming an All Party Parliamentary Group on the CHCs. The group attracted 240 MPs, many of whom had themselves been members of a CHC in the past.[84] ACHCEW also established a commission, chaired by the journalist Will Hutton, to examine public interest and accountability within the NHS. The commission recommended that the CHCs be strengthened through additional funding and an 'enhanced statutory role as patient watchdogs and advocates'.[85]

Despite such rearguard action, the abolition of the CHCs was announced in 2000 with the publication of the *NHS Plan*. They were to be replaced with Patient Forums in every NHS Trust board 'to provide direct input from patients into how local NHS services are run' and by the PALS, which would support complainants.[86] The abolition of the CHCs met with strong opposition from the CHCs themselves, and from politicians from all parties in both the House of Commons and the House of Lords, perhaps because so many parliamentarians had worked with or for CHCs in the past.[87] The first criticism raised was that there had been no consultation about the disestablishment of the CHCs. Early drafts of the NHS plan circulated to interested parties did not contain any reference to the abolition of the councils.[88] Questions were asked in both the House of Lords and the House of Commons about the consultation process prior to the publication of the *NHS Plan*, but as Labour MP John Cryer noted 'it would seem that there has been little or no consultation of [with] the councils themselves' about their abolition.[89] An early day motion, sponsored by ACHCEW, and put forward by Conservative MP Peter Bottomley, challenged 'the Prime Minister and the Secretary of State for Health to give simple frank answers to the questions as to when they decided to abolish community health councils and how they consulted in advance of taking their decision.'[90] After the abolition had been announced, a six-week consultation exercise comprising of five national seminars on 'patient empowerment' took place, but according to ACHCEW these were open to invited participants only, and there was no scope to reopen the debate on the existence of the CHCs.[91] This did not, ACHCEW noted, meet the Cabinet Office's own guidelines on public consultation exercises and went against the Kennedy report's recommendation that consultation be more than presenting the public with a fait accompli.[92] It seemed ironic that though the *NHS Plan* was intended to create 'a health service designed around the patient', allowing patients to 'have a real say in the NHS', there was little public or patient consultation about the mechanisms through which this was to be achieved.[93]

Beyond the lack of consultation, various concerns were raised about the new arrangements. Perhaps the most often cited was the fear of fragmentation of patient representation and the resulting diminution of patient voice. Conservative peer Baroness Cumberlege stated that 'In the NHS plan, the Government have fragmented the previous powers and responsibilities of the CHCs so effectively that they have made the system impotent.'[94] Paul Truswell, Labour MP for Pudsey, argued that as a result of the new measures 'services will be fragmented among a range of providers and that the patient's voice element will be dissipated rather than coordinated'.[95] ACHCEW pointed out that fragmentation was likely to result in other problems. In a guest editorial for the *British Journal of Community Nursing*, Angeline Burke, senior policy officer for ACHCEW, remarked that 'fragmenting CHCs work in this way will mean that problems with local health provision or persistent medical blunders may never come to light'.[96] A document produced by ACHCEW outlining their criticisms of the new arrangements asserted that the breaking up of the 'monitoring function, currently performed by CHCs, means that it will not be possible for a single body to monitor the whole of a patient's experience'.[97]

Connected to anxieties about fragmentation were also worries about the lack of independence of the new arrangements. Labour peer Lord Harris (a former Director of ACHCEW) asserted that as the PALS would be based within hospitals, 'they will neither be independent of the service nor, perhaps even more importantly, will they be perceived as independent by the people who will need to use it'.[98] The Conservative Earl Howe concurred, stating that 'I do not believe that if PALS are employed by the trusts and situated on hospital premises patients will view them as truly independent. Advocates worthy of the name must be free of any conflicts of interest, either real or perceived.'[99] This was important, according to ACHCEW, because 'if patients and the public are to be meaningfully empowered, the new systems for complaints, patient representation and involvement will need to be independent of the management structures of the trusts, the NHS and the Department of Health'.[100] In addition, the intention to have local authorities provide oversight raised potential conflicts of interest as a result of the growing integration of health and social services.[101] The lack of clear statutory powers for the PALS and the Forums also worried peers and ACHCEW. As Earl Howe pointed out, 'CHCs have the right to be consulted, the right to require information from health authorities, the right to inspect and report on hospital facilities and others, and the right to refer contested plans to the Secretary of State for Health. Those rights are valuable levers.'[102]

Other limitations of the new arrangements, according to their critics, included their focus on hospitals and not primary care; potential tension between advocacy and support roles; the lack of clarity about how the new structures would be resourced and the absence of a national body to provide representation at the top level.[103] Supporters in the House of Commons and the House of Lords argued that, properly reformed, the CHCs could provide adequate opportunities for public involvement.[104] ACHCEW agreed. Donna Covey, Chair of ACHCEW told the *Guardian* that 'Renamed, reconstituted and given a higher public profile, CHCs could be transformed into new bodies that could rise from the ashes of the national plan's ill thought out proposals to deliver real patient power.'[105]

There was a sense, though, that this was unlikely to happen because the government wanted to abolish the CHCs for other motives. Lord Harris told the House of Lords that 'everyone will believe … that CHCs are being abolished because they are challenging, because they are an effective irritant and because they make people think'.[106] Conservative MP Dr Liam Fox remarked in the Commons that 'CHCs are being scrapped because the Labour Government dislike criticism from any quarter—especially from independent bodies.'[107] It was the case that some CHCs and ACHCEW had been vigorous in their opposition to aspects of the government's health policy, especially PFI. As Hogg suggested, 'Ministers found they were funding an organisation to attack them, which did not make sense.'[108] She also noted that while there were many rumours circulating about the 'real' reason for the abolition of the CHCs, their demise was more cock-up than conspiracy.[109]

Indeed, the government did have its own reasons for getting rid of the CHCs. Junior Health Minister, Gisela Stuart, told the Commons that 'Despite the significant changes in the NHS, CHCs have not changed'.[110] The Secretary of State, Alan Milburn, was reported as having remarked to a television interviewer that 'CHCs are "dinosaurs without relevance in the modern health service"'.[111] Stuart and others pointed to the 'patchy' performance of the CHCs, and the difficulties that they experienced in juggling their different roles.[112] The failings of the CHCs were also framed in terms of a lack of democracy. Milburn told the Commons the CHCs were 'insufficiently independent and lack the democratic legitimacy needed in today's NHS'. Milburn went on to say that 'We want more protections for the patient, more powers for the public, more democracy in the NHS'.[113] The new arrangements, it was argued, would rectify the democratic deficit and, according to the government's spokesman on health in the House of Lords, Lord Hunt, 'provide a much stronger voice for the public and patients than at present'.[114]

The framing of the abolition of the CHCs as a move designed to increase democratic accountability and strengthen the patient's voice within the NHS was indicative of two apparently contradictory tendencies. On the one hand, the introduction of a range of new mechanisms, and the profile of this as a policy issue suggested a commitment to patient voice on an unprecedented scale. On the other hand, the removal of existing mechanisms for patient and public involvement voice took place without consultation and in a manner that alienated many of the policy's natural supporters. There were, as will be discussed in the final section, considerable problems with the new mechanisms, not least their fragmentation and lack of independence, which raised questions about the government's willingness to listen to patients' voices plural rather than the singular patient voice.

Alphabet soup

The spirited defence of the CHCs by the CHCs and others did lead to some alterations to the government's plans for reforming patient involvement, even if the fate of the councils themselves remained unchanged. A national body to oversee the work of the Patient Forums and provide patient involvement at the national level, initially called 'Voice: The Commission for Patient and Public Involvement', and later shortened to the 'Commission for Patient and Public Involvement' (CPPIH), was established.[115] The Patient Forums were given more powers and made financially independent of the trusts in which they were based.[116] An Independent Complaints Advocacy Service (ICAS) was created to provide support for complainants. The Patient Advocacy and Liaison Service was changed to the Patient Advisory and Liaison Service (PALS) with the intention of offering help and advice to patients on-site at every NHS hospital.[117] In addition, Overview and Scrutiny Committees (OSCs) were introduced to scrutinise local authority provision of health and social services.[118]

The new arrangements came into effect in 2003, and almost immediately ran into difficulties. The Patient Forums experienced problems recruiting members, especially as there was an apparent desire to avoid the 'usual suspects', meaning people who had worked for the CHC or had prior experience of patient and public involvement activity.[119] There were differences of opinion between the Department of the Health and CPPIH over the organisation's role, with the Commission wanting to focus on public health and democratisation, and the Department seeing CPPIH's function more as to enhance user involvement and advise the NHS on how to improve this. There were also internal differences of opinion between the Commission's Chief Executive, Steve Lowden, and its Chair, Sharon Grant.[120] According to Baggott, CPPIH's focus on internal issues meant that it failed to build either grass-roots or elite support, leaving the Commission vulnerable when a review of arm's-length bodies examined its role.[121] In 2004, the arm's-length review recommended that CCPIH be scrapped. In 2006, an expert panel commissioned to review patient and public involvement concluded that the CPPIH and the Forums represented 'an over-prescriptive, centralised model', and the Commission came in for substantial criticism by the House of Commons Health Select Committee when it examined patient and public involvement that same year.[122] Witnesses told the committee that the support offered by CPPIH to the Patient Forums had been poor, and training opportunities and communication had also been lacking.[123] In defence of CPPIH, Grant asserted that 'only months after it became operational it [CCPIH] was informed that after a review of "arm's length bodies" it would be quickly abolished. This change in Government strategy – rather than failures by the organisation – was followed by five Government postponements of the actual closure date'.[124] The Commission, she felt, had achieved 'a great deal' in what she told the Health Select Committee were 'difficult circumstances'.[125]

The proposed scrapping of the CPPIH also left the Patient Forums looking vulnerable. Initially, the forums were supposed to outlive the CPPIH, but their abolition was also announced in 2006. Witnesses told the Health Select Committee that the Department of Health 'decided that it had to abolish CPPIH because of its manifest failings and subsequently abolished PPIfs [Public and Patient Involvement Forums] as well, almost as an afterthought'.[126] The Department did provide a list of reasons as to why it believed the forums had to go. They told the Select Committee that the forums were not representative of their communities; that the current system was poor value for money and too bureaucratic; it did not take into account the increasing diversity of providers; there needed to be greater emphasis on commissioning and primary care; and representative mechanisms should also include social care.[127] The expert review of patient and public involvement to a great extent concurred, raising concerns about the value for money offered by the forums and their difficulty in representing patients within a system that involved a plurality of providers, new systems of commissioning and payment by results.[128] In their response to this review, the government conceded that 'The nature of health and social care delivery is changing radically. We did not predict this level of change when the thinking behind PPI [Public and Patient Involvement] forums was formulated'. A new approach to patient and public involvement was required that would be 'more inclusive than the current system and to do this it must be flexible enough to enable people to participate in different ways'.[129]

The Patient Forums and the CCPIH were scrapped in 2008 and replaced with Local Involvement Networks (LINks). LINks were tasked with 'promoting, and supporting, the involvement of people in the commissioning, provision and scrutiny of local care services' and 'obtaining the views of people about their needs for, and the experiences of, local care services'.[130] Once again, questions were raised about the effectiveness of the new mechanisms for patient and public involvement, such as the lack of accountability of the LINks and their relatively limited powers and resources.[131] Moreover, there was no organisation to take over from CCPIH, so patients and the public were not represented at the national level. Despite the Health Select Committee's recommendation that the LINks be given 'a sufficient period to establish themselves before any further changes are made' and that 'Abolishing established structures and creating new and untested institutions has not proved successful in recent years', the Conservative–Liberal Democrat coalition government scrapped them in 2012.[132] Following the extensive changes made to the structure of the NHS in England after the Health and Social Care Act, 2012, in 2013 LINks were replaced with Local Healthwatch at the local level and a new national body, Healthwatch England, was also created. Local Healthwatches had similar functions to the LINks, but were focused more overtly on being a 'consumer champion' and 'supporting individuals to access information, which, in turn, will help them to make informed choices about their health and the care and treatment options available to them'.[133]

Conclusion

The existence of such an alphabet soup of acronyms and short-lived organisations hints at a set of deeper problems with patient voice. It is striking that the 'failings' of the CHCs, CPPIH, Patient Forums, and LINks all seem remarkably similar. Time and again, concerns were raised about the ability of such bodies to represent patients, about their variability, about how to make them accountable but at the same time independent, and how to integrate patient and public involvement within the existing health system. Such issues, as the Health Select Committee recognised, highlighted the difficulties of achieving representation and the fact that there would always be a limited number of people willing and able to get involved.[134] Change in the systems of patient and public involvement was also a reflection of constant revolution within health policy and the ongoing reform of the NHS. At a technocratic level, the organisations tasked with patient representation needed to match up with the reformed NHS, and the changing operation of the health system.

On a more fundamental level, however, the perpetual re-invention of systems for patient involvement spoke to a deeper degree of uncertainty about their function. The new voice mechanisms had multiple, and sometimes conflicting, roles. Government attempts to introduce new methods of accessing patient and public opinion, such as citizens' juries, together with a conscious effort to encourage the engagement of new groups and individuals were part of an endeavour to widen citizen participation in policy and practice. These methods, however, could also be manipulated in order to produce the desired result, casting doubt on their ability to reflect what patients 'really' wanted. Novel organisations like Patient Forums, LINks and Healthwatch combined democratic and consumerist functions, offering opportunities for mutual participation at the same time as improving the lot of the individual. But empirical research on patient and user involvement suggested that there were significant limitations to its ability to effect change due to the superior position of other key actors such as health professionals and managers. Moreover, as the reform of the NHS became directed increasingly towards a market model, emphasis began to shift towards enhancing opportunities for individual voice and individual choice rather than collective empowerment.

The development of such a range of bodies and mechanisms to provide access to and enhance patient voice had other, paradoxical consequences. Although the late 1990s and 2000s saw a rise in the number of disease-specific patient organisations, groups claiming to speak for all patient-consumers, such as the Patients Association, appeared to be being edged out. As government-backed organisations like the PALS, Patient Forums, LINks and Healthwatch took on the responsibility for patient voice, independent organisations struggled to find a role. While groups like the PA continued to exist, they were forced to share a stage with a much bigger cast of characters directed by successive governments that wanted to play a larger role in shaping the figure of the patient-consumer. Meanwhile, the very notion of the generic patient-consumer appeared to be coming under threat. The rise of disease-specific groups and the increased attention placed on individual patients and their voice and choice undermined the idea that any organisation could speak for all patient-consumers irrespective of their condition or population group. Voice, as will be seen in the final chapter, lost out to choice, and with it the idea of the patient-consumer as a collective, rather than just individual, identity.

Notes

1. NHS Management Executive, *Local Voices: The Views of Local People in Purchasing for Health* (London: NHSME, 1992); Liz Cooper, Anna Coote, Anne Davies and Christine Jackson, *Voices Off: Tackling the Democratic Deficit in Health* (London: Institute for Public Policy Research, 1995); Department of Health, *Patient and Public Involvement in the New NHS* (London: Department of Health, 1999); Department of Health, *Involving Patients and the Public in Healthcare: A Discussion Document* (London: Department of Health, 2001); Department of Health, *A Stronger Local Voice: A Framework for Creating a Stronger Local Voice in the Development of Health and Social Care Services – A Document for Information and Comment* (London: Department of Health, 2006); House of Commons, *Patient and Public Involvement in the NHS: Third Report of Session 2006–7* (London: House of Commons, 2007); Department of Health, *Real Involvement: Working with People to Improve Health Services* (London: Department of Health, 2008); National Health Service, *Putting People at the Heart of Care: The Vision for Public and Patient Experience and Engagement in Health and Social Care* (London: NHS, 2009).
2. NHS Management Executive, *Local Voices*.
3. Department of Health, *Involving Patients and the Public in Healthcare*, p. 2.
4. Department of Health, *Strengthening Accountability*, p. iii.
5. Department of Health, *A Stronger Local Voice*, p. 3.
6. Speech by the Rt Hon Alan Milburn MP, Secretary of State, to the Fabian Society, 21 October 2001, www.dh.gov.uk/en/News/Speeches/Speecheslist/DH_4000444, accessed 24 July 2013.
7. NHS, *Putting People at the Heart of Care*, p. 9.
8. Suzanne Wait and Ellen Nolte, 'Public involvement policies in health: exploring their conceptual basis', *Health Economics and Law*, 1 (2006), 149–162, p. 152.
9. Rosemary Rowe and Michael Shepherd, 'Public participation in the new NHS: no closer to citizen control?', *Social Policy and Administration*, 36:3 (2002), 275–290.
10. Wait and Nolte, 'Public involvement policies', p. 152.
11. John Clarke, Janet E. Newman, Nick Smith, Elizabeth Vidler and Louise Westmarland, *Creating Citizen-Consumers: Changing Publics and Changing Public Services* (London: Sage, 2007), pp. 1–7, 27–46. See also Janet Newman and Elizabeth Vidler, 'Discriminating customers, responsible patients, empowered users: consumerism and the modernisation of healthcare', *Journal of Social Policy*, 35:2 (2006), 193–209.
12. Liz Cooper, Anna Coote, Anne Davies and Christine Jackson, *Voices Off: Tackling the Democratic Deficit in Health* (London: Institute for Public Policy Research, 1995), p. i.
13. *Ibid.*, pp. vi–x, 39–46, 68–70.
14. Cm., 4818-I, *The NHS Plan: A Plan for Investment a Plan for Reform* (London: HMSO, 2000), pp. 93, 94.
15. Department of Health, *Patient and Public Involvement in the New NHS*, p. 2.
16. Department of Health, *Involving Patients and the Public in Healthcare*, p. 6.
17. Health and Social Care Act, 2001, Part 1, Section 11.
18. Cm. 5207, *Learning from Bristol: the Report of the Public Inquiry Into Children's Heart Surgery at the Bristol Royal Infirmary 1984–1995* (London: HMSO, 2001), p. 19.

19 Department of Health, *Involving Patients and the Public in Healthcare*, p. 2.
20 Brian Salter, 'Patients and doctors: reformulating the UK health policy community', *Social Science and Medicine*, 57 (2003), 927–936, p. 930.
21 Bruce Wood, *Patient Power? The Politics of Patients' Associations in Britain and America* (Buckingham: Open University Press, 2000), pp. 36–37.
22 Rob Baggott, Judith Allsop and Kathryn Jones, *Speaking for Patients and Carers: Health Consumer Groups and the Policy Process* (Basingstoke: Palgrave Macmillan, 2005), pp. 81, 84.
23 Phil Brown and Stephen Zavestoski, 'Social movements in health: an introduction', *Sociology of Health and Illness*, 26:6 (2004), 679–694, p. 694.
24 *Ibid.*, pp. 685–686.
25 Phil Brown, Stephen Zavestoski, Sabrina McCormick, Brian Mayer, Rachel Morello-Frosch and Rebecca Gasior Altman, 'Embodied health movements: new approaches to social movements in health', *Sociology of Health and Illness*, 26:1 (2004), 50–80, p. 72.
26 Virginia Berridge, 'AIDS and patient support groups', in Roger Cooter and John Pickstone (eds), *Medicine in the Twentieth Century* (Amsterdam: Harwood, 2000), 687–701; Virginia Berridge, 'AIDS and the rise of the patient? Activist organisation and HIV/AIDS in the UK in the 1980s and 1990s', *Medizin Gesellschaft und Geshichte*, 21 (2002), 109–123; Nick Crossley, *Contesting Psychiatry: Social Movements in Mental Health* (London: Routledge, 2005); Alex Mold and Virginia Berridge, *Voluntary Action and Illegal Drugs: Health and Society in Britain since the 1960s* (Basingstoke: Palgrave Macmillan, 2010).
27 For an analysis of the role of health consumer groups in three condition areas, see Baggott, Allsop and Jones, *Speaking for Patients and Carers*. Salter, 'Patients and doctors: reformulating the UK health policy community', p. 934.
28 Author interview with Marianne Rigge.
29 NHS, *Putting People at the Heart of Care*, p. 4.
30 Derek Wanless, *Securing our Future Health: Taking a Long Term View* (London: HM Treasury, 2002).
31 Cm. 6737, *Our Health, Our Care, Our Say: A New Direction for Community Health Services* (London: TSO, 2006).
32 Department of Health, *The Expert Patient: A New Approach to Chronic Disease Management in the 21st Century* (London: Department of Health, 2001), p. 9.
33 Nikolas Rose and Carlos Novas, 'Biological citizenship', in Aiwha Ong and Stephen Collier (eds), *Global Assemblages, Technology, Politics and Ethics as Anthropological Problems* (Malden, MS: Blackwell Publishing, 2005), 439–463.
34 Ian Shaw and Alan Aldridge, 'Consumerism, health and social order', *Social Policy and Society*, 2 (2003), 35–43, p. 40.
35 Stephen Harrison and Maggie Mort, 'Which champions, which people? Public and user involvement in health care as a technology of legitimation', *Social Policy and Administration*, 32:1 (1998), 60–70.
36 Timothy Milewa, Justin Valentine and Michael Calan, 'Managerialism and active citizenship in Britain's reformed health service: power and community in an era of decentralisation' *Social Science and Medicine*, 47:4 (1998), 507–517.
37 Rowe and Shepherd, 'Public participation in the new NHS'.

38 Declan Gaffney, Allyson M. Pollock, David Price and Jean Shaoul, 'NHS expenditure and the private finance initiative – expansion or contraction?', *British Medical Journal*, 319 (3 July 1999), 48–51; David Spilsbury, *Trumpet Voluntary: An Informal History of Central and South Birmingham Community Health Councils 1974–2003* (Birmingham: South Birmingham CHC, 2003), pp. 25–47.

39 BCA MS 2588/7, Birmingham Health Authority, *Consultation on Proposals for the Development of Acute 9 Hospital Services in South Birmingham*, May–August 1999: University Hospital Birmingham NHS Trust: New Hospital Development Project, p. 2.

40 BCA MS 2588/1/26, Minutes of the SBCHC meeting, 19 February 1997; SBCHC, South Birmingham Community Health Council Annual Report, 1997.

41 BCA MS 2588/1/26, Minutes of the SBCHC meeting, 18 June 1997; SBCHC, South Birmingham Community Health Council Annual Report, 1997.

42 BCA MS 2588/1/26, Minutes of the SBCHC meeting, 18 June 1997.

43 Gaffnay, Pollock, Price and Shaoul, 'NHS expenditure and the private finance initiative', p. 48.

44 BCA MS 2588/1/26, SBCHC, South Birmingham Community Health Council Annual Report, 1997, p. 1.

45 BCA MS 2588/7, 'The future of Selly Oak and Queen Elizabeth Hospitals: have your say' CHC survey leaflet, 1997.

46 BCA MS 2588/7, Future of the Queen Elizabeth and Selly Oak Hospitals: comments from the public, n.d. [1997/8].

47 BCA MS 2588/7, Survey of user views on the proposed changes to Selly Oak and Queen Elizabeth Hospitals, n.d. [1998?]

48 BCA MS 2588/7, Shirley McIver and Peter Spurgeon, 'Review of South Birmingham CHC Survey of Users Views' Health Services Management Centre, University of Birmingham, March 1998, p. 3.

49 *Ibid.*, p. 11.

50 *Ibid.*, p. 3.

51 *Ibid.*, p. 16.

52 *Ibid.*, p. 7.

53 *Ibid.*, p. 15.

54 ICM/Guardian Opinion Poll, September 2002. Data from www.guardian.co.uk/society/2002/sep/26/privatefinance.ppp, accessed 9 December 2009.

55 Paul Smith, 'A very private affair', *Health Services Journal*, 29 January 2004, p. 13.

56 Anna Coote and Jo Lenaghan, *Citizens' Juries: Theory Into Practice* (London: IPPR: 1997).

57 Jon Elster (ed.), *Deliberative Democracy* (Cambridge: Cambridge University Press, 1998), Jon Elster, 'Introduction', 1–18, p. 1; Cooper, Coote, Davies and Jackson, *Voices Off.*

58 Susan Pickard, 'Citizenship and consumerism in healthcare: a critique of citizens' juries', *Social Policy and Administration*, 32:3 (1998), 226–244, p. 242.

59 Javier Lezaun, 'A market of opinions: the political epistemology of focus groups', *Sociological Review*, 55(2) (2007), 130–151, p. 131.

60 Javier Lezaun and Linda Soneryd, 'Consulting citizens: technologies of elicitation and the mobility of publics', *Public Understanding of Science*, 16:3 (2007), 279–297.

61 David Price, 'Choices without reasons: citizens' juries and policy evaluation', *Journal of Medical Ethics*, 26 (1998), 272–276, p. 276.
62 Spilsbury, *Trumpet Voluntary*, p. 56.
63 BCA MS 2588/7, Birmingham Health Authority, *Consultation on Proposals for the Development of Acute Hospital Services in South Birmingham*, May–August 1999, 'Attachment 1', p. 35.
64 *Ibid.*, 'Attachment 2', p. 17.
65 BCA MS 2588/7, Birmingham Health Authority (BHA), *Outcome of Consultation on Proposals for the Development of Acute Hospitals in South Birmingham*, September 1999, p. 3.
66 Spilsbury, *Trumpet Voluntary*, p. 60.
67 BCA MS 2588/7, BHA, *Outcome of Consultation on* Proposals, p. 3.
68 *Ibid.*, 'Doctors support hospital plan', *Birmingham Post*, 20 February 1998, p. 10; 'Doctors defend new hospital plan', *Birmingham Evening Mail*, 19 February 1998, p. 5; 'Editorial', *Birmingham Evening Mail*, 8 September 1999, p. 12; Smith, 'A very private affair', p. 13.
69 BCA MS 2588/7, BHA, *Outcome of Consultation on Proposals*; 'A new hospital for a new century', *Birmingham Evening Mail*, 13 May 1999, p. 11.
70 BCA MS 2588/7, Letter from Ursula Pearce (Chair of SBCHC) to Alan Milburn, 22 October 1999.
71 BCA MS 2588/7, Letter from Yvette Cooper to Ursula Pearce, 2 February 2000.
72 Lezaun and Soneryd, 'Consulting citizens', p. 294. For a discussion of how those experienced in patient representation were dismissed as the 'usual suspects', see Christine Hogg, *Citizens, Consumers and the NHS: Capturing Voices* (Basingstoke: Palgrave, 2009), pp. 5, 67.
73 DHSS, *Patients First*, p. 14.
74 Steven Harrison, *National Health Service Management in the 1980s: Policymaking on the Hoof?* (Avebury: Avebury, 1994), pp. 41–42; Fedelma Winkler, 'Consumerism in health care: beyond the supermarket model', *Policy and Politics*, 15:1 (1987), 1–8, pp. 1–8.
75 Graham Moon and Carol Lupton, 'Within acceptable limits: health care provider perspectives on community health councils in the reformed British National Health Service', *Policy and* Politics, 23:4 (1995), 334–346.
76 Mike Gerrard, *A Stifled Voice: Community Health Councils in England 1974–2003* (Brighton: Pen Press, 2006), p. 121.
77 Hogg, *Citizen's Consumers and the NHS*, p. 51.
78 Quoted in Gerrard, *Stifled Voice*, p. 156.
79 Sarah Buckland, Carol Lupton and Graham Moon, *An Evaluation of the Role and Impact of Community Health Councils* (Portsmouth: Social Service Research and Information Unit, 1994), p. iii.
80 ACHCEW, *Performance Evaluation Standards Framework for Community Health Councils* (London: ACHCEW, 1999) (revised edition based on 1996 report), www.achcew.org/uploads/6/6/0/6/6606397/015._performance_evaluation_standards_framework_for_chcs_copy.pdf, accessed 25 July 2013.
81 Hogg, *Citizens, Consumers and the NHS*, p. 110.
82 *Ibid.*, p. 116.

83 Patrick Butler, 'Today, the future of community health councils hangs in the balance', the *Guardian*, 15 July 1998, p. 8.
84 Hogg, *Citizens, Consumers and the NHS*, p. 110.
85 Will Hutton, *New Life for Health: The Commission on the NHS* (London: Vintage, 2000), p. 13.
86 Cm. 4818-I, *The NHS Plan*, pp. 92, 93.
87 Prominent ex-CHC members included Lord Harris (former Chair of ACHCEW); Baroness Pitkeathley, Lord Greaves, Lord Hunt, Tim Loughton and Hazel Blears.
88 Hogg, *Citizens, Consumers and the NHS*, p. 111.
89 *House of Commons Debates*, 26 October 2000, vol. 355, cols 400–410. See also *House of Lords Debates*, 26 October 2000, vol. 618, cols 557–574.
90 'Early day motion on Community Health Councils', 2000–2001, www.achcew.org/uploads/6/6/0/6/6606397/early_day_motion_on_community_health_councils.pdf, accessed 25 July 2013.
91 The Abolition of CHCs – Consultation or Imposition, 17 November 2000, www.achcew.org/uploads/6/6/0/6/6606397/the_abolition_of_chcs.pdf, accessed 25 July 2013.
92 ACHCEW, *Involving Patients and the Public in Healthcare: A Discussion Document Response from the Association of Community Health Councils for England and Wales*, October 2001, www.achcew.org/uploads/6/6/0/6/6606397/003_.involving_patients_and_the_public_in_healthcare_copy.pdf, accessed 25 July 2013.
93 Cm. 4818-I, *The NHS Plan*, pp. 10, 12.
94 *House of Lords Debates*, 26 October 2000, vol. 618, cols 557–574, col. 561.
95 *House of Commons Debates*, 21 November 2000, vol. 357, cols 156–160, col. 159.
96 Angeline Burke, 'The NHS Plan: stifling the patients' voice?', *British Journal of Community Nursing* November 2000, www.achcew.org/uploads/6/6/0/6/6606397/guest_editorial_british_journal_of_community_nursing_november_2000.pdf, accessed 25 July 2013.
97 ACHCEW, 'Watchdog or Lapdog? – the NHS plan and patient empowerment' (n.d., 2000?), www.achcew.org/uploads/6/6/0/6/6606397/watchdog_or_lapdog.pdf, accessed 25 July 2013.
98 *House of Lords Debates*, 26 October 2000, vol. 618, cols 557–574, col. 559.
99 *House of Lords Debates*, 26 October 2000, vol. 618, cols 557–574, col. 571.
100 'Watchdog or Lapdog? – the NHS plan and patient empowerment', ACHCEW.
101 *Ibid.* See also Lord Clement Jones, *House of Lords Debates*, 26 October 2000, vol. 618, col. 568.
102 *House of Lords Debates*, 26 October 2000, vol. 618, col. 570.
103 See *House of Lords Debates*, 26 October 2000, vol. 618, cols 557–574; *House of Commons Debates*, 21 November 2000, vol. 357, cols 156–160; 'Watchdog or Lapdog? – the NHS plan and patient empowerment'; Burke, 'The NHS Plan: stifling the patients' voice; ACHCEW, *Involving Patients and the Public in Healthcare*.
104 E.g. *House of Lords Debates*, 26 October 2000, vol. 618, col. 560.
105 Muzzling the watchdog, Letter from Donna Covey, Chair of ACHCEW to the *Guardian*, 13 September 2000, www.achcew.org/uploads/6/6/0/6/6606397/muzzling_the_watchdog.pdf, accessed 25 July 2013.
106 *House of Lords Debates*, 26 October 2000, vol. 618, col. 560.
107 *House of Commons Debates*, November 2000, vol. 357, cols 156–160, col. 159.

108 Hogg, *Citizen's Consumers and the NHS*, p. 113.
109 *Ibid.*, p. 123.
110 *House of Commons Debates,* 28 November 2000, vol. 357, cols 163–187WH, 185.
111 *Ibid.*, p. 171.
112 *Ibid.*, p. 186.
113 *House of Commons Debates,* 7 December 2000, vol. 359, cols 135–237, col. 153.
114 *House of Lords Debates,* 26 October 2000, vol. 618, col. 572.
115 Department of Health, *Involving Patients and the Public in Healthcare: A Discussion Document,* p. 3.
116 ACHCEW, 'The new patient and public involvement system', 2002, www.achcew.org/uploads/6/6/0/6/6606397/the_new_patient_and_public_involvement_syste1.pdf, accessed 26 July 2013.
117 Rob Baggott, 'A funny thing happened on the way to the forum? Reformulating patient and public involvement in the NHS in England', *Public Administration*, 83:3 (2005), 533–551, p. 542.
118 Department of Health, *A Stronger Local Voice,* p. 17.
119 Hogg, *Citizens, Consumers and the NHS,* pp. 128, 134–135; Baggott, 'A funny thing', p. 540.
120 Hogg, *Citizens, Consumers and the NHS,* p. 131.
121 Baggott, 'A funny thing', p. 542.
122 Expert Panel, *Concluding the Review of Patient and Public Involvement: Recommendations to Ministers from the Expert Panel* (London: Department of Health, 2006), p. 3.
123 House of Commons, *Patient and Public Involvement in the NHS,* pp. 30–31.
124 Commission for Patient and Public Involvement in Health, *Commission for Patient and Public Involvement in Health Report and Accounts* (London: TSO, 2008), p. 3.
125 House of Commons, *Patient and Public Involvement in the NHS,* p. 31.
126 *Ibid.*, p. 33.
127 *Ibid.*, p. 27.
128 Expert Panel, *Concluding the Review of Patient and Public Involvement,* pp. 3–5.
129 Department of Health, *Government Response to A Stronger Local Voice* (London: Department of Health, 2006), pp. 27, 28.
130 Local Government and Public Involvement Act, 2007.
131 House of Commons, *Patient and Public Involvement in the NHS,* pp. 50–54.
132 *Ibid.*, pp. 35, 72.
133 Department of Health, *HealthWatch Transition Plan* (London: Department of Health, 2011) pp. 9, 19.
134 House of Commons, *Patient and Public Involvement in the NHS,* p. 35.

7

Choice

Patient choice has been central to the recent reform of England's National Health Service. Under both the Labour (1997–2010) and coalition governments (2010–), a series of policies were introduced with the intention of giving patients more choice. Initiatives aimed at making it easier for patients to choose their GP, to choose which hospital to go to and to choose between health care providers were put in place. Moreover, choice became the key watchword of health policy, repeated endlessly by health ministers and officials in policy documents and public communications. In 2010, choice was mentioned 84 times in the coalition government's first white paper on health, *Equity and Excellence: Liberating the NHS*.[1] At the time of writing (2014) a visitor to the NHS's website (entitled 'NHS Choices') would find the tag line 'Your health, your choices' on every page.[2] Choice now appears to govern health policy and practice in England to an unprecedented extent.

This chapter will explore how it was that patient choice came to occupy such a central position. It will suggest that although the notion of choice was present in earlier formulations of patient consumerism, the meaning and relative importance ascribed to choice changed in the late 1990s and early 2000s. A crucial shift took place that involved a move away from choice as something that was of importance to patients collectively and towards a focus on choice as an individual matter. Such a focus on the patient rather than patients undermined the position of patient-consumer organisations that aimed to represent patients as a group. Speaking for patients was more difficult when the individual was thought to be best at determining his or her own needs. At the same time, the process that had begun in the late 1980s and early 1990s, where the state took on the lead role in determining the shape of patient consumerism continued, such that by the 2000s patient-consumer groups appeared to have much less of a role in speaking for the patient as consumer than they had in previous decades. The government's adoption of an apparently consumerist agenda had the effect of driving out independent groups with alternative ideas about the meaning and place of consumerism in health. Yet, beneath the surface, traces of older ideas about patient consumption within a collective system remained. Without doubt, choice became a key framing device for health policy, but choice only went so far. The choices offered to patients were quite limited and policies and initiatives that were purported to be about choice often involved other goals, such as reducing waiting lists. Choice was an attractive way to package NHS reform and achieve other political objectives: it was not always about giving the patient more to choose from.

To understand the significance ascribed to choice in recent years, it is necessary to turn back to older approaches to the place of choice in patient consumerism. This chapter will begin with an exploration of ideas about choice in health during the 1960s and 1970s. Choice was of little importance to patient-consumer groups in this period, although it was of interest to health economists like Dennis Lees and social policy theorists like Richard Titmuss. It was during the 1980s and 1990s that choice began to attract more attention, particularly following the introduction of the internal market to the NHS in 1990. Patient-consumer groups were both supportive and critical of such moves: they wanted more choice for the individual patient-consumer but not to the detriment of patient-consumers as a whole. In the second section, this chapter will examine the introduction of policies brought in by the Labour government under the choice rubric. Key initiatives, such as 'choose and book', which allowed patients greater say in when and where they were treated, offered patients more choice than had been available to them in the past. Choice became more common within the NHS in England (and to a much lesser extent in other parts of the UK too) but many limitations remained on the kinds of choices patients could make.[3] The third part of the chapter will go on to consider the reasons why choice came to dominate the agenda from the late 1990s onwards. Politicians and commentators alike suggested that the introduction of choice into health was a response to wider changes in society. Individuals, it was often said, experienced greater choice in other areas of their lives and so expected to find it in health care too.[4] The introduction of more choice was also thought to have other benefits, especially improving the efficiency of health services run on market-like lines. Yet, choice policy was certainly not uncontroversial, and the fourth section of this chapter will consider some of the critiques of choice offered by academics, think tanks and patient-consumer organisations. Chief among these is the suggestion that patients did not actually want more choice; what they wanted was high-quality local services. If such an assertion holds weight, the whole *raison-d'être* of choice policy can then be brought into question. Choice, this chapter will argue, has multiple meanings and implications that stretch beyond the immediately obvious.

Choice before choice policy: the long view of choice and the patient-consumer in the NHS

Historically, the NHS was often assumed to be a system that constrained individual consumer choice in return for comprehensive, universal coverage.[5] The opportunities for patient choice within the early NHS were very restricted. Patients could choose their GP, but these often operated strict catchment areas, thus limiting patient choice. Access to specialist treatment was through the patient's GP: individuals could not select the surgeon or consultant they wished to see. During the 1960s and 1970s, such limitations did not appear to concern patient-consumer groups. As the earlier chapters in this book have demonstrated, patient organisations were more interested in autonomy, representation and complaint than they were in choice. The term 'choice' does not appear in any of the key texts produced by patient-consumer organisations nor in any of their campaigns in the 1960s and 1970s. The absence of choice is perhaps explained by the collective focus of such groups: greater choice for individuals did not appear relevant when the needs of patients rather than the patient were the key goal. Moreover, choice did not feature in health policy at this time. Ian Greener and his colleagues, in an analysis of health policy documents from 1944 to 2000, found that choice did appear in the 1946 White Paper on the establishment of the NHS, but this was in connection with choice of family doctor only. Subsequently, choice, Greener found, disappeared within British health policy documents, only to appear again in 1989 in *Working for Patients*, the white paper that ushered in the internal market.[6]

Choice was, however, of interest to academics throughout this period. An important debate took place in the early 1960s between the economist Dennis Lees and the social policy theorist Richard Titmuss that in many ways typified the different positions on choice in health care that were adopted then and now. In 1961, Lees published a pamphlet entitled *Health Through Choice*. It was published by the right-of-centre think tank, and well-known supporter of the free market, the Institute of Economic Affairs (IEA). Lees was an industrial economist who spent time at the University of Chicago with Milton Friedman. Influenced by Friedman's free-market thinking, Lees argued that health care was like any other consumer good: 'medical care would appear to have no characteristics which differentiate it sharply from other goods in the market'.[7] Within the NHS, however, Lees suggested that 'political decisions replace personal choice. Expenditure on medical care is not considered on its merits but is weighed against other items of public outlay as part of policies to deal with rising prices and expenditure.'[8] Consumer satisfaction would be maximised, Lees contended, if health care were instead supplied through the market.

Richard Titmuss offered a sharp corrective to Lees's pamphlet. Titmuss was the founder of the discipline of social administration (social policy) in Britain, and a key left-wing intellectual and government policy adviser. In 1966, he gave a lecture to the Fabian Society, an important left-of-centre think tank, on choice and the welfare state. The lecture was intended as a counter-argument to Friedman-inspired attacks on the British welfare state, and Lees's *Health Through Choice* in particular. Titmuss argued that medical care was not like any other consumer good, marshalling thirteen different reasons as to why this was so.[9] His central argument against choice revolved around a power and knowledge imbalance between producer (doctor) and consumer (patient), resulting in issues such as the inability of the patient to judge the quality of what he or she was receiving; that patients were unable to return or exchange medical care as they would other goods and services, and so on. Titmuss also made a broader attack on the individualising effects of choice when he compared the market-based system of blood donation found in New York with the collective, voluntary system found in the UK. This was, of course, a theme he was to elaborate on in *The Gift Relationship* some years later.[10] Titmuss used the example of blood donation to make the point that in his view a collective system was superior to one based on individual choice. He asserted that 'I find here no support for the model of choice in the private market; on criteria of efficiency, of efficacy, of quality or of safety.'[11] 'Above all', Titmuss continued, 'it is a system which neglects and punishes the indigent, the coloured, the dispossessed and the deviant.'[12]

Titmuss and Lees put forward two diametrically opposed views on the place of choice in health care. Lees stressed that health care was like any other consumer good, and therefore utility would be maximised when the consumer could choose for him or herself. In contrast, Titmuss argued that health care was unlike other consumer goods, and choice was less important than a good collective service that benefited everyone, not just the individual. Such arguments were repeated often in academic discussions about the place of choice in health, but on a practical level choice played little role in health consumerism until the 1980s.[13] For many patient groups, choice was bound up with other aspirations such as more information and stronger rights, as discussed in Chapter 4 and Chapter 5. Through the trinity of information, rights and choice, patients would become consumers.

But, as patient groups were quick to point out, the capacity for patients to exercise choice within the NHS during the 1980s was very limited. Patients could choose their GP, but, as the NCC remarked, 'It has often been one of the odder mysteries of life in this country that it is very difficult to get simple, factual information about the choice of general practitioners in your area.'[14] To encourage patients actively to choose their GP, Young proposed introducing a voucher system, whereby all NHS patients would be issued with a voucher to give to their preferred GP each year.[15] Moreover, for Young and the CoH choosing a GP was not enough: other kinds of choices for patients were also envisaged. The CoH asserted that 'Active participants in health care must be able to make their own choices'.[16] The kinds of choices discussed by patient groups ranged from small-scale decisions about peripheral services, such as greater choice of food in hospital, to more significant choices about treatment and service provision.[17] Central Birmingham CHC, for example, argued that patients should be able to make informed choices about their own health care and the extent to which they wanted to participate in it: 'We believe that a patient should be able to choose whether to hand over all decision-making to the doctor'.[18] Other kinds of choices were also envisaged: a survey published by *Which?* in 1989 suggested that seven out of ten patients thought it important to be able to choose which hospital to be referred to for specialist treatment.[19]

At the same time as stressing a need for greater capacity for individual choice, some groups also considered the implications of choice for the wider population. The NCC asserted that it made sense for certain services to be provided publicly because 'the mechanisms of individual choice operating in the market place do not lead to the outcome which best serves the interests of all the individuals who constitute society'.[20] For services such as health care, where 'provision should be related to need and not payment', the 'individualistic mechanisms of the market' were not appropriate, but that did not mean that choice could not, or should not, be introduced into the NHS.[21] Instead, the NCC proposed that greater choice be provided by offering variety in services although this would, it conceded, have considerable cost implications. Choice, the Council suggested, should be provided at the collective, not solely individual, level.[22] Similarly, whilst groups like Central Birmingham CHC called for greater individual choice, emphasis was also placed on collective representation. The CHC argued that 'The notion of community participation in health care is an idea whose time has come. It is part of a movement towards a more open, democratic way of planning and organising society.'[23]

Further questions were raised by patient groups about choice and health in relation to publication of the white paper, *Working for Patients* in 1989 and the subsequent introduction of the internal market in 1990. The critique offered by patient groups pursued two ostensibly contradictory lines: on the one hand, choice was portrayed as potentially damaging, and on the other, that the reforms did not go far enough and that more choice should be made available to patients. Julia Neuberger, chair of the PA, pointed out that, under the new arrangements, there would be a perverse incentive for fund-holding GPs not to take on sicker, and therefore more expensive, patients. She argued that

> it will be the case that middle-aged patients will have a greater choice of GP, as will all those categories who use the GP service relatively little. But those who use the service a great deal will be at a disadvantage. They may find it extremely hard to change doctors.[24]

Young also pointed out that not all patients would be able to make choices all of the time. In an emergency, he suggested, patients would rarely have any choice as to where they were admitted, but 'Patients who are frightened, at their most vulnerable and in pain should be able to feel confident about the quality of care they can expect to receive in *any* NHS hospital [original emphasis].'[25] For other groups, it was the nature of choices being offered, and the market-based model in which such choices were to operate, that was problematic. West Essex and District CHC passed a resolution in 1989 expressing concern about what it saw as an 'over emphasis on the market place philosophy' within *Working for Patients*, and the lack of democratic accountability inside the new system.[26]

Such a critique of choice was not necessarily at odds with the stance of the organisations that wanted more choice. Even groups that advocated greater choice did not seem to believe that the choices offered within *Working for Patients* were the right ones: indeed, the advocates and critics of choice (as it was outlined in the White Paper) were often one and the same. The chief criticism was that the reforms did not offer any more choice to patients; indeed, these may have actually limited available choices. Under the new system, so-called 'purchasers' of health care (fund-holding GPs) would be able to control their own budgets and decide on the 'providers' (hospitals) to which their patients should be sent. As a *Which?* report on the reforms noted, the GP, not the patient, would choose which hospital to use, and this decision could be based on budgetary considerations as much as the patient's convenience.[27] For the CoH, 'It is not the patients who will have more choice, but some of the doctors and some of the managers.' As a result 'the White Paper will further enhance not the power of the consumer but the power of the producer and provider'.[28] In similar vein, Neuberger contended that patients 'have little power to make their views felt, and that although the White Paper claims to be about giving patients choice, they in fact get little more choice in GPs than they have before and considerably less choice beyond that stage'.[29] The CoH suggested that, instead of bolstering the power of doctors and managers, the NHS should be more responsive to what patients wanted, through mechanisms such as an improved complaints system, consumer audit and the introduction of standards.[30]

The vision of choice by groups like the College of Health would seem, therefore, to have differed from the government's. Patient groups wanted more real choice for consumers but, on the other hand, were also aware of the potentially negative consequences of giving patients greater choice, especially within a communal system with limited resources. Such a view was underpinned by an understanding of the patient-consumer that was both collective and individualistic: patient organisations were concerned with the choices made available to patient-consumers as a whole, as well as the sole patient-consumer.

Choice and New Labour, 1997–2010

Choice was central to the reform of public services under the Labour government from 1997 to 2010. The introduction of choice was conceived of as a way of simultaneously giving users of public services what they were thought to want (more choice) and improving the services themselves.[31] Choice featured in the Labour government's first major health policy document, the *NHS Plan*, which was published in 2000. The *NHS Plan* promised that 'Patient choice will be strengthened.' This was to be achieved by giving patients more information about GP practices, which would 'make it easier for patients to exercise informed choice'. Patients were also to be afforded more choice over hospital treatment, with a pledge that by 2005 patients would be able to choose the date of their appointments and admissions for specialist treatment.[32]

Patient choice became an increasingly central aspect of health policy following the general election in 2001. Giving patients more choice was a Labour party election manifesto promise, and as a speech by the Secretary of State for Health, Alan Milburn to the Fabian Society in October 2001 made clear, choice was crucial to the government's plan to reform the NHS.[33] Milburn contended that greater investment in the health service would not in and of itself bring about the changes required to meet the demands of modern patients. The NHS, he argued, needed to 'offer not just fairness but choice'.[34] New policies aimed at giving patients greater choice were piloted in specific areas and for particular conditions. In 2002, two separate schemes were trialled. Patients waiting more than six months for treatment for heart surgery were offered a choice of quicker treatment elsewhere within the NHS, with a private health care provider, or even in another country.[35] Another initiative was piloted in London, from 2002 to 2004. Patients waiting for more than six months for specific procedures in selected specialities were offered a choice of being treated more quickly at an alternative hospital.[36]

Following the pilot schemes, a national consultation on patient choice was launched in 2003. Led by Harry Cayton, Director for Patients and the Public at the Department of Health, the consultation involved national expert task groups, local consultations led by Strategic Health Authorities, a national choice consultation survey and engagement with patient and professional groups.[37] It was estimated that 110,000 people were consulted, and the results were overwhelmingly in favour of the introduction of more choice.[38] The government's response to the consultation, *Building on the Best: Choice, Responsiveness and Equity in the NHS*, made it clear that choice was central to the wider expansion and reform of the NHS, and that 'choice has to be real rather than just theoretical'.[39] To achieve this, *Building on the Best* proposed to: give people more say in how they were treated, including to access their own electronic health record; increase choice of access to a wider range of services in primary care; increase choice of where, when and how to get medicines; enable people to book appointments and choose hospitals; widen the choice of treatment and care, starting with maternity services and end of life care; and finally, to ensure that people had the right information at the right time.[40]

Practical policy changes to deliver on such promises focused on elective specialist treatment. From 2004, all patients waiting more than six months for surgery were to be given a choice of treatment elsewhere. The flagship policy in this area was the introduction of the Choose and Book system in December 2005. Under Choose and Book, patients that required a referral for consultation or treatment with a specialist were to be offered a choice of four to five hospitals (or alternative providers) and a choice of date and time for their appointment.[41] In 2008, choice of health care provider was widened still further: under the 'Free Choice' policy patients that required specialist treatment were able to choose from any suitable hospital or clinic, whether this was an NHS trust, foundation trust or independent sector hospital, so long as they could meet NHS prices and standards.[42] In 2009, the *NHS Constitution* stated that patients had the right to choose their GP practice and the 'right to make choices about your NHS care and to information to support these choices'.[43]

Information to allow patients to make choices was provided through the NHS Choices website, introduced in 2007. The NHS Choices website presented information about hospitals, based on assessments made by the Healthcare Commission and other indicators, but it also attempted to communicate health promotion messages, such as advice on diet, exercise and smoking. In this way, the website was advocating an approach put forward in the government's 2004 public health strategy, *Choosing Health*, that healthy living was a choice.⁴⁴ This was a different notion of choice to that based around choice of provider or date and time of appointment, placing emphasis on individual responsibility for health, and for making healthy choices. This was a view further endorsed by *The NHS Constitution* with its assertion that 'You should recognise that you can make a significant contribution to your own, and your family's good health and well-being, and take some responsibility for it.'⁴⁵

By the time of the 2010 election and the end of the Labour government, choice policy thus had three distinct strands. There was a general promise to increase patient choice across the NHS; specific commitments around elective care; and an emphasis on encouraging people to make healthy choices as part of a wider public health strategy. Taken together, these various schemes introduced in the period 2000–10 demonstrated that choice was a key objective across health policy.

Explaining the rise of choice

Explanations for how and why choice came to occupy such a central position tended to fall into two categories. Firstly, the introduction of choice into health was attributed to wider socio-political changes, and in particular the growth of consumerist attitudes and the rise of choice in other spheres of life. Secondly, advocates of choice in health asserted that choice would make health services better: that services would become more equitable, more efficient and of higher quality if more choice was present. The location of patient choice policy within the context of the broader rise of consumer society needs to take into account changes within consumerism itself. As Hilton and others have argued, consumerism meant different things at different times, and it is only since the 1980s that choice came to dominate understandings of consumerism at the domestic and international level.⁴⁶ Choice, according to Clarke and his colleagues, has become a 'master value'.⁴⁷ In the state of 'liquid modernity' described by Zygmunt Bauman life is 'one protracted shopping spree' resulting in 'the ability to treat any life decision as a consumer choice'.⁴⁸

The architects of patient choice policy were keen to locate this policy within such broader socio-political shifts. In his speech to the Labour Party Conference in 2001, Prime Minister Tony Blair said that 'expectations are higher. This is a consumer age. People don't take what they're given. They demand more.'⁴⁹ In his Foreword to a major document setting out plans for the reform of Britain's public services Blair put forward choice as one of the key principles behind reform: the others being national standards, devolution and flexibility. He argued that 'Choice acknowledges that consumers of public services should increasingly be given the kind of options that they take for granted in other walks of life.'[50] Other key New Labour figures, such as the Secretary of State for Health, Alan Milburn, made similar statements. Milburn told the Fabian Society that 'People grow up today in a consumer society. Services – whether they are private or public – succeed [or] fail according to their ability [to] respond [to] modern expectations'.[51] According to Labour politicians radical reform of the health service was needed because the NHS had failed to keep up with the pace of social change, and as a result insufficient attention had been paid to what patients wanted, which was more choice. It was not just Labour politicians, however, that were in favour of more patient choice. Angela Coulter, a social scientist, think-tank director and long-time supporter of a greater role for patients in health care argued that

> Up to now choice has not been a central value of the NHS, but lack of choice now looks like its Achilles heel. We expect to be able to make informed choices in most other aspects of our lives and there are signs of growing frustration with the lack of choice in health care.

It was time, she suggested, 'to redefine the patient's role'.[52]

There was some empirical evidence to indicate that patients did indeed want more choice. A survey carried out as part of the 2003 national consultation exercise found that 76 per cent of those asked wanted more involvement in decisions about their treatment, a finding that was framed as being supportive of greater choice.[53] Another survey also carried out in 2003 by MORI for the Birmingham and Black Country Strategic Health Authority found that 77 per cent of respondents wanted to choose which hospital to be treated in.[54] In 2005, the British Social Attitudes survey reported that 63 per cent of the people interviewed thought that patients should have a choice over which hospital to go to and 65 per cent believed that patients should have a choice regarding the kind of treatment that they received.[55] Other surveys presented similar results. In 2010, a study by the Kings Fund found that 75 per cent of respondents said that choice was either 'important' or 'very important' to them.[56]

Other supporting evidence in favour of choice appeared to come from patient choice pilot schemes. In the London pilot, where patients were offered a choice of faster treatment elsewhere if they had been waiting more than six months, 65 per cent of patients chose to move to another hospital with a shorter wait time and 35 per cent stayed with their local provider.[57] In the coronary heart disease pilot, where patients waiting more than six months for surgery were offered a choice of treatment elsewhere, 57 per cent opted to go to an alternative hospital.[58] Such figures were interpreted as being indicative of widespread support for more patient choice. In the

Foreword to a document outlining developments in choice policy Andy Burnham, Minister for Delivery and Quality, asserted that 'we know that patients want and value choice: evidence from pilots, patient and public surveys and focus groups has shown this'. Giving patients more choice, Burnham continued, would put 'patients in the driving seat' and lead to the creation of 'a health service that provides what is best for patients'.[59]

In addition to being what patients wanted, choice, supporters argued, was being introduced because it would result in a better service. Giving patients more choice was intended to improve the quality and responsiveness of health services. In a document setting out the aims and objectives of the NHS Choices website, Minister for Health Services, Ben Bradshaw contended that

> Information and choice are indispensable if we are to achieve a truly patient-centred NHS in which standards and quality are constantly improved. The public who pay for the health service have a right to know how the performance of their GP or local hospital compares with others and the right to go elsewhere if they wish.[60]

The intention was that by giving patients more choice they would vote with their feet: better services would attract more patients, and good service providers would be rewarded with more income. At the same time, poorer services would be encouraged to improve quality in order to attract more patients. Julian LeGrand, Professor of Social Policy at the London School of Economics, senior adviser to Tony Blair and a leading architect of choice policy, argued that when combined with competition, choice would drive up the standard of services. Choice, he stated, 'provides incentives for providers to offer a higher quality service efficiently and in a responsive fashion'.[61] Moreover, research indicated that the patients that had exercised some form of choice over their provider tended to report higher satisfaction, suggesting that patients' perception of quality was also linked to choice.[62] Following this logic, offering patients more choice would, in and of itself, improve their sense of the quality of service being provided.

Alongside improving the quality and efficiency of services, the other major reason cited for the introduction of more choice to the NHS was that it would improve equity. Choice for all, Blair told the Fabian Society in 2003, would 'boost' equity in three ways. Firstly, choice would give 'poorer people the same choices available only to the middle-classes. It addresses the current inequity where the better off can switch from poor providers.' Secondly, Blair said that 'choice sustains social solidarity by keeping better off patients and parents within the NHS and public services'. Finally, 'choice puts pressure on low quality providers that poorer people currently rely on'. Blair concluded by arguing that 'It is choice with equity we are advancing.

Choice and consumer power as the route to greater social justice not social division.'⁶³ Key ministers, such as Alan Milburn and John Reid, made similar statements on the importance of choice for equity. Reid argued that 'there is no contradiction between the increase in choice and the development of equity in the NHS ... If we make these choices open to everyone, the ability to find their way through the system will belong not just to a few, but to the many.'⁶⁴ To support their statements on equity, ministers and officials turned to the surveys on patients' views on choice. What the research indicated was that people in disadvantaged groups, such as those on lower incomes, were more and not less likely to want to make choices.⁶⁵ This finding, according to Le Grand, made sense, because the middle classes with their 'loud voices and sharp elbows' had long been able to extract what they wanted from public services. By making choice available to everyone, and not just the advantaged, the suggestion was that the NHS would become more equitable.⁶⁶ Choice, then, would improve both the quality and equality of health services.

Critiques of choice

Such claims for choice policy were, however, not accepted universally. Indeed, choice policy and the entire notion of choice within public services came in for considerable criticism by academics, think tanks and patient-consumer organisations. Such condemnation was part of a wider attack on the effects of consumerism in general and choice in particular.⁶⁷ The psychologist Barry Schwartz maintained that 'As the number of choices grows further, the negatives escalate until we become overloaded. At this point, choice no longer liberates, but debilitates. It might even be said to tyrannize.'⁶⁸ Philosopher and sociologist Renata Salecl echoed such concerns, arguing that 'Choice brings a sense of overwhelming responsibility into play, and this is bound up with a fear of failure, feelings of guilt and an anxiety that regret will follow if we make the wrong choice. All this contributes to the tyrannical aspect of choice'.⁶⁹

More specific criticisms were also levelled at the application of choice to health care. The Dutch political philosopher, Annemarie Mol asserted that choice conflicted with care: 'Practices designed to foster "patient choice" erode existing practices that were established to ensure "good care"'.⁷⁰ Other opponents of choice policy took issue with choice as put forward in the reform of British public services. Clarke et al. argued that the concept of choice employed by New Labour had been 'thoroughly colonised by the market model'. They suggested that this was an 'impoverished' and 'indeterminate' notion of choice that ignored alternative understandings of choice and the means through which this might be realised.[71] At the same time, as David Boyle, fellow of the think tank the New Economics Foundation pointed out, government policy documents and pronouncements lacked specificity in their discussions of choice. In his review of choice policy published in 2013, Boyle found that terms such as 'choice', 'competition' and 'co-production' were used interchangeably, when in reality 'As service users know very well, there are times when choice and competition are aligned, but there are times when they cancel each other out'.[72] Some detractors of choice policy also suggested that there were ulterior motives behind its introduction. Forster and Gabe contended that the promotion of choice was a pragmatic decision, designed to win voters to New Labour and deal with public criticism of the health service.[73] Greener claimed that the insertion of more choice was intended to pass responsibility for health onto patients, that 'Health consumerism gives patients the right to demand what they wish from health services, but also requires them to take greater responsibility for their choices'.[74] As Schwartz remarked, 'Responsibility for medical care has landed on the shoulders of patients with a resounding thud'.[75]

Yet, according to Schwartz and others, this was not a responsibility that patients either wanted or were capable of assuming. One of the most frequent attacks on choice policy was the argument that patients did not want more choice; what they wanted was high-quality local services. Research carried out by Which? in 2005 suggested that 'Consumers do not want choice for choice's sake – it is a means to an end. What they do want is better locally-provided services that are more flexible and treat them faster'.[76] Such studies led Clarke et al to suggest that for many consumers, choice might be a compensatory mechanism rather than a first preference.[77] Additional research carried out by Which? in 2011 indicated that for many patients choice of provider undermined the notion that all services met high standards irrespective of their location.[78] Additional questions were raised about the relative emphasis patients placed on choice. Political scientists John Curtice and Oliver Heath examined polling data produced by MORI in 2011 and found that although patients said that they valued choice, this did not necessarily mean that they accorded it high priority. The patients interviewed rated choice of where and when to be treated as the eleventh most important aspect of care out of 16 items, below car parking but above hospital food.[79] Other studies suggested that although patients said that they wanted choice in principle, in practice individuals were less keen to exercise choice. Schwartz cited a study that found that 65 per cent of people interviewed said that if they got cancer they would want to choose their own treatment, but only 12 per cent of people who actually had cancer wanted to do so.[80] As Greener pointed out, there was a difference between patients wanting choices in the abstract, and wanting them when they were actually sick or ill.[81]

Other research indicated that the kinds of choices offered to patients were not necessarily the ones that they wanted. Which? argued that the Choose and Book system represented a 'restricted notion of choice that fails to match many consumers' priorities and preferences'.[82] Boyle found that in addition to choice of hospital, patients wanted a choice over which doctor or health care professional to see. Further kinds of choices that patients wanted but did not always get included the choice to 'exit' the system and seek diagnosis or care elsewhere; the choice to share responsibility; and the choice to contribute.[83] Choice itself was regarded as a choice. Choosing not to choose, according to Which? was an important option: not all patients would want or be able to make choices about their health care.[84]

Indeed, the potential for choice policy to exacerbate existing inequalities within health service provision attracted a good deal of attention. Despite the stated conviction of many policy makers that providing more choice would reduce inequality, critics were concerned that the opposite was true. The King's Fund suggested that introducing a choice of provider might create an incentive for services to improve, but this was not the same as closing inequitable gaps in service provision and quality.[85] Which? feared that 'Choice may also perpetuate or widen existing inequalities because not all consumers have an equal capacity to make and take up choices'.[86] As Clarke and his colleagues noted, the problem was not that disadvantaged groups and individuals lacked the ability to make choices, but rather that they did not have the social and cultural capital to do so.[87] Equality of opportunity to make choices did not necessarily result in greater equity over all. In their reviews of the impact of choice policy, both the King's Fund and Boyle found that individuals in disadvantaged groups, such as ethnic minorities and those on low incomes, wanted choice more than those in advantaged groups but were less able to access this.[88]

One of the reasons for such inequalities lay in the fact that there were many barriers to exercising choice and this was particularly the case for marginalised groups. A key problem surrounded unequal access to information and the ability to use this to make effective choices. The long-standing information imbalance between doctors and patients was exacerbated in a situation where patients were expected to make choices.[89] Which? asserted that patients needed more information in order to arrive at meaningful choices as well as practical support in making these.[90] In the early days of choice policy, according to the King's Fund, there was a lack of good information available on the quality of care and treatment outcomes.[91] Moreover, even when such data did become more readily accessible, patients appeared to make little use of the information provided through official outlets such as the NHS Choices website, preferring instead to rely upon informal sources like recommendations from friends and family.[92] In addition, not all patients had equal access to information: the Boyle review found that people without access to the Internet were at a disadvantage and often came from more marginalised groups.[93]

Such inequalities were also replicated when it came to actually making choices and using health care services. At a practical level, research indicated that there was a difference between choice policy and the extent to which patients were offered choice on the ground. Following the introduction of the Choose and Book scheme in 2006, a study conducted by Judith Green, Zoe McDowall and Henry Potts found that 66 per cent of patients reported not being given a choice of appointment date, 66 per cent reported not being given a choice of appointment time and 86 per cent reported not being given a choice of four hospitals for their appointment. Green and her colleagues concluded that the 'Choose and Book did not deliver choice as portrayed in UK government policy to this patient community.'[94] A few years later, the King's Fund found that although GPs claimed that they always offered patients a choice, just under half of the patients surveyed (49 per cent) recalled being given a choice under the Choose and Book scheme.[95] Moreover, problems with making choices, according to Boyle, began even before patients entered the GP's surgery. In order to access health care, and thus make choices, patients had to negotiate complex systems. Boyle found that some patients, particularly those in disadvantaged groups, had difficulty getting an appointment with their GP, and in certain cases accessing or registering with a practice.[96] Even for those patients who could get to see their GP and were offered choice, there were additional barriers to making use of this. A particular problem for many people in disadvantaged groups concerned access to transport. In order to use an alternative treatment provider, patients often had to travel greater distances and this was difficult for those patients without a car and who had to rely on public transport.[97]

In addition to problems experienced by patients in making and accessing choice, there were difficulties on the system side of the equation. As numerous commentators pointed out, in order for patients to be able to choose between providers there had to be spare capacity elsewhere in the system. Which? argued that 'Without additional capacity, choice can only be extended to some if it is limited for others.'[98] If capacity were to be increased in order to allow space for patient choices, then more resources would be required.[99] Yet, there was a danger that growing capacity could increase costs without improving efficiency.[100] Other difficulties lay in the fact that choice policy was laid on top of an existing system that tended to conspire against those patient-consumers that did wish to make choices. Boyle contended that old bureaucratic structures within the NHS had a negative impact on choice and flexibility. For example, long-term outpatients were expected to travel to see their consultant every six months even if they were well, but were unable to see a specialist at other times when they felt that they needed to.[101]

Professional resistance to choice policy exacerbated such problems. Surveys by both the King's Fund and Boyle found that many GPs believed that their patients did not want choice, even though most patients said that they did.[102] Even the GPs that were enthusiastic about offering choice were reluctant to do so for every patient regardless of their circumstances.[103] Some of the hostility towards choice policy lay in the difficulties practitioners experienced using the Choose and Book system, but Boyle also discovered that certain doctors and patients were reluctant to embrace choice because of what they saw as its wider political implications. Choice, he suggested, 'is sometimes regarded as a confidence trick, a sleight of hand which involves them in what they fear is actually an agenda to privatise services'.[104]

Such distrust about the motivation behind the introduction of choice points to a level of concern about the wider implications of choice policy. As already noted, many commentators were concerned that the introduction of choice would exacerbate existing inequalities. A reduction in equity, critics pointed out, had the potential to undermine key principles of the NHS. There was, Clarke and his colleagues argued, an uncomfortable relationship between choice and equality and choice and need.[105] More advantaged patients were better able to make choices and thus use the system to their benefit, something which challenged the notion that NHS care was provided to all on the basis of need. Choice also brought the collective nature of the NHS into question. Within the existing system, the King's Fund pointed out, 'many health care decisions are collective rather than individual.'[106] Which? cautioned that 'the consequences of individual choice will not necessarily lead to the services that consumers want and need collectively'.[107] Furthermore, giving patients more choice could encourage people to think of themselves as individuals and weaken support for shared goals. Professor of Social Policy, Peter Taylor-Gooby, argued that

> the widespread substitution of market for citizenship-based interactions may tend to promote a different and incompatible framework of values. The risk is that those who participate in individualising institutional frameworks will become less supportive of collective provision and of redistribution to distant and disadvantaged groups.[108]

Choice could thus undermine the very nature of the provision of health care as a public service.

Conclusion

The damage that choice could do to more collective approaches can be seen in the fate of patient-consumer groups. As argued in Chapter 6, by the 2000s, collective voice mechanisms were weak and fragmented. The position of organisations that claimed to speak for patient-consumers as a whole was uncertain in a policy and practice context that placed great emphasis on individual choice. If the patient-consumer was best positioned to make their own choices and satisfy his or her own demands there appeared to be reduced need for collective representation by patient-consumer groups. Although such organisations did not disappear, they were less conspicuous in an increasingly crowded field. An unscientific, but nonetheless interesting marker of the decreasing profile of patient-consumer organisations is offered by their position within the *Health Service Journal*'s list of influential people. Each year the journal publishes a list of important people within British health care. In 2012, Katherine Murphy, Chief Executive of the PA was number 89 out of 100, above entrepreneur Richard Branson, but beneath Andrew Witty, Chief Executive of pharmaceutical giant GlaxoSmithKline.[109] By 2013, Murphy had disappeared from the list, as had any other patient-consumer leaders. The closest the list came to featuring a patient-consumer representative was Dr Kim Holt, founder of the Patients First Campaign, a group that aimed to support whistle-blowers within the NHS.[110] Of course, the *Health Service Journal*'s list was not necessarily an accurate representation of influence, but it does seem to point towards a reduction in the prominence of the patient-consumer organisation.

The apparent demise of the patient-consumer organisation in the age of individual patient choice was rooted in a more fundamental shift around the very meaning of consumerism in health. One of the most strident opponents of the choice agenda was the consumer group Which? Such hostility, according to LeGrand, was 'puzzling', although he suggested that it could be explained by 'the fact that most consumer bodies are resolutely middle class and that both their writers and readers can already obtain what they want from the public sector'.[111] Yet, a more detailed examination of some of Which?'s statements on choice points to a more nuanced interpretation. In their 2003 report the organisation argued that

> It is right for people to have more choices about their healthcare. But we question whether a market-based approach is adequate for achieving the main goal of the NHS – to provide healthcare for everyone on the basis of clinical need not ability to pay.[112]

More recently, in response to the coalition government's white paper, 'Liberating the NHS, Greater Choice and Control', Which? asserted that

Which? embraces choice as one of the fundamental consumer principles. We know that in consumer markets choice can be a mechanism for driving up quality and improving consumer experience. However, we believe that the choice agenda in healthcare must take into account differences between this sector and other markets. We want to see patients enabled to make the choices that are right for them, with adequate and tailored support.[113]

Which? were not opposed to the idea of choice in health per se, but rather to a purely market-based understanding of patient consumerism. This was not surprising, given that Which? and other patient-consumer groups had spent the last fifty years or so building up a notion of patient-consumerism that had little to do with markets. Concerns about autonomy, representation, complaint, rights, information and voice made up an alternative vision of patient consumerism that pre-dated the market- and choice-orientated mode put forward by successive governments since the late 1980s. Although the market 'won', there were signs, as the Conclusion to this book will demonstrate, that the older view of patient consumerism left a legacy. Collective benefit, as well as individual choice, still has a role to play in British health care.

Notes

1. Cm. 7881, *Equity and Excellence: Liberating the NHS*.
2. www.nhs.uk/Pages/HomePage.aspx, accessed 23 July 2014.
3. See Stephen Peckham, Marie Sanderson, Vikki Entwistle and Andrew Thompson, *A Comparative Study of the Construction and Implementation of Patient Choice Policies in the UK* (London: HMSO, 2011) and Stephen Peckham, Nicholas Mays, David Hughes and Marie Sanderson, 'Devolution and patient choice: policy rhetoric versus experience in practice' *Social Policy and Administration*, 46:2 (2012), 199–218. On the more general differences between the NHS in different parts of the UK, and the impact of devolution on health services see, for example, Scott L. Greer, *Four Way Bet: How Devolution has led to Four Different Models for the NHS* (London: UCL Constitution Unit, 2004); Katherine Smith and Mark Hellowell, 'Beyond rhetorical differences: a cohesive account of post-devolution developments in UK health policy', *Social Policy and Administration*, 46:2 (2012), 178–198; Nigel Hawkes, 'How different are NHS systems across the UK since devolution?', *British Medical Journal*, 346 (2013), 18–20.
4. See, for example, Julian Le Grand, *The Other Invisible Hand: Delivering Public Services Through Choice and Competition* (Princeton, NJ: Princeton University Press, 2007); Alan Milburn, Speech by the Rt Hon Alan Milburn MP, Secretary of State, to the Fabian Society, 21 October 2001, http://webarchive.nationalarchives.gov.uk/+/www.dh.gov.uk/en/MediaCentre/Speeches/Speecheslist/DH_4000444, accessed 23 September 2013.
5. See, for example, Angela Coulter, *The Autonomous Patient: Ending Paternalism in Medical Care* (London: TSO/Nuffield Trust, 2002), p. 5; John Appleby, Anthony

Harrison and Nancy Devlin, *What is the Real Cost of More Patient Choice?* (London: King's Fund, 2003), p. 7.
6   Ian Greener, Nick Mills, Martin Powell and Shane Doheny, 'How did consumerism get into the NHS? An empirical examination of choice and responsiveness in NHS policy documents', Cultures of Consumption Working Paper Series, Working Paper no. 29, www.consume.bbk.ac.uk/working_papers/GreenerOctober20061.doc, accessed 30 September 2013; Ian Greener, 'Towards a history of choice in UK health policy', *Sociology of Health and Illness*, 3 (2009), 309–324.
7   D.S. Lees, *Health Through Choice: An Economic Study of the British National Health Service* (London: Institute of Economic Affairs, 1961).
8   Ibid., p. 58.
9   Richard M. Titmuss, 'Choice and the welfare state', in Richard M. Titmuss, *Commitment to Welfare* (London: George Allen, 1968), 138–152, pp. 146–147.
10 Richard M. Titmuss, *The Gift Relationship: From Human Blood to Social Policy* (revised edn, New York: The New Press, 1997).
11 Titmuss, 'Choice and the welfare state', p. 150.
12 Ibid., p. 150.
13 See, for example, Phil Shackley and Mandy Ryan, 'What is the role of the consumer in health care?', *Journal of Social Policy*, 23:4 (1994), 517–541.
14 NCC, *Annual Report and Accounts, 1987* (London: NCC, 1987), p. 8.
15 Michael Young, 'The College of Health's view', in David Green, Julia Neuberger, Lord Young of Dartington and M.L. Burstall, *The NHS Reforms: Whatever Happened to Consumer Choice?* (London: IEA, 1989), 27–46, p. 34.
16 CCC YUNG/6/10/10, Gann and Knight, *College of Health Consumers' Guide to Health Information*, p. 3.
17 Aylesbury Vale CHC, for example, surveyed hospital inpatients and found that patients wanted more choice of food. See ACHCEW CD ROM, *Community Health News*, 47 (October 1989), p. 14.
18 Central Birmingham CHC, *Report*, 1 June 1979–31 May 1980.
19 Anon., 'Doctor, doctor: you and your GP', *Which?*, 32 (October, 1989), pp. 481–485.
20 NCC, *The Consumer and the State: Getting Value for Public Money* (London: NCC, 1979), p. 15.
21 Ibid., p. 62.
22 Ibid., p. 63.
23 Central Birmingham CHC, *Annual report*, 1 June 1979–31 May 1980.
24 Julia Neuberger, 'A Consumer's view', in Green et al., *The NHS Reforms*, 15–25, p. 19.
25 Young, 'The College of Health's view', p. 39.
26 ACHCEW CD Rom, Vol. 2, *Community Health News, supplement on working for patients*, issue 48, November 1989, p. 4.
27 Anon., *Which* (October 1989), 'Doctor, doctor: you and your GP', pp. 481–485.
28 Young, 'The College of Health's View', p. 28.
29 Neuberger, 'The consumers' view', p. 24.
30 Young, 'The College of Health's View', pp. 42–45.
31 John Clarke, Nicholas Smith and Elizabeth Vidler, 'The indeterminacy of choice: political, policy and organisational implications', *Social Policy and Society*, 5:3

(2006), 327–336; John Clarke, Janet Newman, Janet E. Newman, Nick Smith, Elizabeth Vidler, Louise Westmarland, *Creating Citizen-Consumers: Changing Publics and Changing Public Services* (London: Sage, 2007), p. 34.
32 Cm. 4818-I, *The NHS Plan: A Plan for Investment a Plan for Reform* (London: HMSO, 2000), p. 89.
33 Labour Party, *Ambitions for Britain: Labour's Manifesto 2001* (London: Labour Party, 2001), p. 22.
34 Milburn speech, 21 October 2001.
35 Appleby, Harrison and Devlin, *What is the Real Cost of More Patient Choice?*, p. 6.
36 Lorelei Jones and Nicholas Mays, *Systematic Review of the Impact of Patient Choice of Provider in the English NHS* (London: LSHTM, 2009), pp. 14–15, http://hrep.lshtm.ac.uk/publications/Choice%20review%20March%202009.pdf, accessed 30 September 2013; Peter Burge, Nancy Devlin, John Appleby, Charlene Rohr, Jonathan Grant, *London Patient Choice Project Evaluation: A Model of Patients' Choices of Hospital From Stated and Revealed Preference of Choice Data* (Cambridge: RAND Corporation, 2005), www.rand.org/content/dam/rand/pubs/technical_reports/2005/RAND_TR230.pdf, accessed 30 September 2013.
37 National Health Service, *Choice, Responsiveness and Equity in the NHS and Social Care: A National Consultation* (London: National Health Service, 2003).
38 Department of Health, *Building on the Best: Choice, Responsiveness and Equity in the NHS* (London: Department of Health, 2003), p. 7.
39 *Ibid.*, p. 3.
40 *Ibid.*, pp. 7–9.
41 Department of Health, *'Choose and Book': Patient's Choice of Hospital and Booked Appointment: Policy Framework for Choice Booking at the Point of Referral* (London: Department of Health, 2004).
42 Department of Health, *Choice Matters: Putting Patients in Control* (London: Department of Health, 2007), p. 6.
43 National Health Service, *The NHS Constitution for England* (London: National Health Service, 2009), p. 7.
44 Department of Health, *Choosing Health: Making Healthy Choices Easier* (London: Department of Health, 2004).
45 NHS, *The NHS Constitution 2009*, p. 9.
46 Matthew Hilton, *Prosperity for All: Consumer Activism in an Era of Globalization* (Ithaca, NY and London: Cornell University Press, 2009), p. 211.
47 Clarke, Newman, Smith, Vidler and Westmarland, *Creating Citizen-Consumers*, p. 13.
48 Zygmunt Bauman, *Liquid Modernity* (Cambridge: Polity Press, 2000), p. 89.
49 Tony Blair, Speech to Labour Party Conference, 2 October, 2001, www.totalpolitics.com/speeches/labour/labour-party-conference-leaders-speeches/34853/labour-party-conference-2001.thtml, accessed 1 October 2013.
50 Office of Public Services Reform, *Reforming our Public Services: Principles into Practice* (London: Office of Public Services Reform, 2002), p. 3.
51 Milburn speech, 21 October .
52 Coulter, *Autonomous Patient*, pp. 5, 6.

53 Department of Health, *Building on the Best*, p. 38. This figure was cited in support of choice policy in Department of Health, *Choice Matters: Increasing Choice Improves Patients' Experiences* (London: Department of Health, 2006), p. 3.
54 Figures quoted in Le Grand, *The Other Invisible Hand*, p. 49.
55 John Appleby and Arturo Alavarez-Rosete, 'Public responses to NHS Reform', in Alison Park, John Curtice, Katarina Thomson, Catherine Bromley, Miranda Philips, Mark Johnson (eds), *British Social Attitudes: 22nd Report* (London: Sage, 2005), 109–134, p. 120.
56 King's Fund, *Patient Choice: How Patients Choose and How Providers Respond* (London: Kings Fund, 2010). p. xiii.
57 Burge et al., *London Project Patient Choice Evaluation*, p. 13.
58 Figure quoted in Jones and Mays, *Systematic Review of Patient Choice*, p. 14.
59 Department of Health, *Choice Matters: Increasing Choice*, p. 1.
60 Department of Health, *NHS Choices: Delivering for the NHS* (London: Department of Health, 2008), p. 3.
61 LeGrand, *The Other Invisible Hand*, p. 43.
62 Angela Coulter, Naomi Le Maistre and Lorna Henderson, *Patients' Experience of Choosing Where to Undergo Surgical Treatment: Evaluation of London Patient Choice Scheme* (Oxford: Picker Institute, 2005), pp. 66–85.
63 Speech by Tony Blair to the Fabian Society, 17 June 2003, www.theguardian.com/society/2003/jun/17/publicservices.speeches1, accessed 2 October 2013.
64 John Reid in Foreword to Department of Health, *Building on the Best*, p. 5.
65 Appleby and Alavarez-Rosete, 'Public responses to NHS Reform', p. 121.
66 Le Grand, *The Other Invisible Hand*, p. 54.
67 See, for example, Oliver James, *Affluenza* (London: Random House, 2007).
68 Barry Schwartz, *The Paradox of Choice: Why More is Less* (New York: Harper Collins, 2002), p. 2.
69 Renata Salecl, *Choice* (London: Profile Books, 2010), p. 7.
70 Annemarie Mol, *The Logic of Care: Health and the Problem of Patient Choice* (London and New York: Routledge, 2006), p. 1.
71 Clarke et al., *Creating Citizen-Consumers*, p. 41; Clarke, Smith and Vidler, 'The indeterminacy of choice', p. 333.
72 David Boyle, *The Barriers to Choice Review: How are People Using Choice in Public Services?* (London: Cabinet Office, 2013), p. 74.
73 Rudolf Forster and Jonathan Gabe, 'Voice or choice? Patient and public involvement in the National Health Service in England under New Labour', *International Journal of Health Services*, 38:2 (2008), 333–356, p. 353.
74 Greener, 'Towards a history of choice', p. 322.
75 Schwartz, *The Paradox of Choice*, p. 30.
76 Which?, *Which Choice? Health* (London: Which?, 2005), p. 11.
77 Clarke, Smith and Vidler, 'The indeterminacy of choice', p. 333.
78 Which?, 'Consultation response: Liberating the NHS, greater choice and control', *Which?*, 14 January 2011, www.staticwhich.co.uk/documents/pdf/liberating-the-nhs-greater-choice-and-control-which-response-242304.pdf, accessed 6 August 2013.
79 John Curtice and Oliver Heath, 'Does choice deliver? Public satisfaction with the health service', *Political Studies*, 60 (2012), 484–503, p. 486.

80 Schwartz, *The Paradox of Choice*, p. 32.
81 Greener, 'Towards a history of choice', p. 322.
82 Which?, *Which Choice? Health*, p. 89.
83 Boyle, *The Barriers to Choice Review*, pp. 72–73.
84 Which?, 'Consultation response: Liberating the NHS, greater choice and control'.
85 Appleby, Harrison and Devlin, *What is the Real Cost of More Patient Choice?*, p. 33.
86 Which?, *Which Choice? Health*, p. 78.
87 Clarke, Newman, Smith, Vidler and Westmarland, *Creating Citizen-Consumers*, p. 107.
88 King's Fund, *Patient Choice: How Patients Choose and How Providers Respond*, pp. xv, xvi–xix; Boyle, *The Barriers to Choice Review*, p. 21.
89 Deborah Lupton, Cam Donaldson and Peter Lloyd, 'Caveat emptor or blissful ignorance? Patients and the consumerist ethos', *Social Science and Medicine*, 33:5 (1991), 559–568; Ian Greener, 'Who choosing what? The evolution of the use of "choice" in the NHS, and its importance for new Labour', in Catherine Bochel, Nick Ellison and Martin Powell (eds), *Social Policy Review 15: UK and International Perspectives* (Bristol: The Social Policy Press, 2003), 49–68, p. 58.
90 Which?, *Which Choice? Health*, p. 8; Which?, 'Consultation response: Liberating the NHS, greater choice and control'.
91 Appleby, Harrison and Devlin, *What is the Real Cost of More Patient Choice?*, pp. 48–49.
92 King's Fund, *Patient Choice: How Patients Choose and How Providers Respond*, p. xv.
93 Boyle, *The Barriers to Choice Review*, pp. 4–5.
94 Judith Green, Zoe McDowall and Henry Potts, 'Does Choose & Book fail to deliver the expected choice to patients? A survey of patients' experience of outpatient appointment booking', *BMC Medical Informatics and Decision Making*, 8:36 (2008), p. 7.
95 King's Fund, *Patient Choice*, p. 47.
96 Boyle, *The Barriers to Choice Review*, p. 21.
97 *Ibid.*, p. 24; King's Fund, *Patient Choice*, pp. 63–68.
98 Which?, *Which Choice?*, p. 6.
99 Appleby, Harrison and Devlin, *What is the Real Cost of More Patient Choice?*, pp. 23–25.
100 Jones and Mays, *Systematic Review of the Impact of Patient Choice*, p. 10.
101 Boyle, *The Barriers to Choice Review*, p. 31.
102 *Ibid.*, p. 23; King's Fund, *Patient Choice*, p. 34.
103 King's Fund, *Patient Choice*, p. 155.
104 Boyle, *The Barriers to Choice Review*, p. 74.
105 Clarke, Newman, Smith, Vidler and Westmarland, *Creating Citizen-Consumers*, p. 61.
106 Appleby, Harrison and Devlin, *What is the Real Cost of More Patient Choice?*, p. 23.
107 Which?, *Which Choice?*, p. 6.
108 Peter Taylor-Gooby, 'Choice and values: individualised rational action and social goals', *Journal of Social Policy*, 37:2 (2008), 167–185, p. 183.
109 Anon., 'HSJ 100 2012', www.hsj.co.uk/5052606.article, accessed 11 October 2013.

110 Anon., 'HSJ clinical leaders 2013', www.hsj.co.uk/confirmation?rtn=%252f5059698. article, accessed 11 October 2013. On Patients First see www.patientsfirst.org.uk/, accessed 11 October 2013.
111 LeGrand, *The Other Invisible Hand*, p. 167.
112 Which?, *Which Choice?*, p. 88.
113 Which?, 'Consultation response: Liberating the NHS, greater choice and control', p. 1.

Conclusion

In January 2009, Health Secretary Alan Johnson established the *NHS Constitution*. The Constitution set out the principles and values that were to guide the NHS in England (separate constitutions covered Wales, Scotland and Northern Ireland) as well as 24 patient rights, 13 pledges and 9 patient responsibilities. The document also included pledges and responsibilities for NHS staff.[1] The *NHS Constitution*, according to Johnson, was intended to be 'a mixture of poetry and prose – saying how people feel about the NHS as well as providing practical help in as simple and accessible terms as possible'.[2] Covering areas such as access to health services; quality of care; access to drugs and treatment; consent and confidentiality; informed choice; patient involvement; and complaint and redress, the *NHS Constitution* could be seen as the culmination of decades of successful lobbying by patient-consumer organisations. Many of the things that these groups had long campaigned for, such as the right to access health records and the right to complain, and even the very notion of patients' rights itself, now had formal recognition.

Yet, the *Constitution*, like its predecessor the *Patient's Charter*, met with a mixed reaction from patient groups and others. Katherine Murphy, director of the Patients Association remarked that 'We do not expect this document to make any difference to the care patients are receiving.' David Pink, chief executive of the umbrella group National Voices said that 'The NHS constitution could be seen as a gimmick, or as a party political manoeuvre', although he did concede that 'it has huge potential for patients and the public'. Hamish Meldrum, chairman of the BMA, asserted that 'we need more than a "feelgood" document. In its current form, it is unclear how the constitution will change the everyday experiences of patients and staff.'[3] Scepticism about the *NHS Constitution* and its ability to effect change was rooted not just in past experiences with the *Patient's Charter*, but can be traced to more fundamental concerns about the utility of rights language and also who speaks for the patient-consumer. Rights talk held considerable rhetorical power, but as patient-consumer groups found, was essentially empty without a clear sense of the nature of the rights being claimed. Moreover, the publication of the *NHS Constitution* by the Department of Health indicated that it was now the government that commanded the lead role in speaking for the patient-consumer, not patient organisations themselves.

What it meant to be a patient-consumer in the early years of the twenty-first century was in many ways very different to the first, tentative assertions of patient-consumer identity made during the 1960s, although there were important continuities. A brief survey of key recent developments with respect to the central themes of this book around autonomy, representation, complaint, rights, information, voice and choice provides an indication of the distance travelled by the patient-consumer over the last fifty years, but also a sense of déjà-vu as the same issues recur time and again. That is not to say that nothing has changed, but persistent problems, such as whether to address the demands of the individual or the needs of the collective, remain.

Autonomy

The *NHS Constitution* guarantees a number of patient's rights with respect to individual autonomy. The right to refuse treatment, the right to be treated with dignity and respect, the right to consent, the right to information about tests and treatment and the right to privacy are all rights that patient-consumer organisations petitioned for in the past. The right to informed consent, the issue that so incensed Helen Hodgson and prompted her to establish the PA, now has a firm legal basis. In the UK, this right grew up through case law, in contrast to the USA, where a legal right to informed consent was adopted in 1957.[4] In Britain, test cases in the 1950s and 1980s established that medical practitioners could be sued for battery if they performed an examination on a patient without their consent, or they could be sued for negligence if they did not explain sufficiently the risks associated with a procedure.[5] The introduction of the Human Rights Act in 1998 has been seen as establishing a specific right to informed consent to treatment in the UK, as the act prohibits 'inhuman and degrading treatment'.[6]

More broadly, the concept of autonomy has come to play a wider role in British medical policy and practice in concert with the rise of bioethics, especially since the 1980s.[7] The seeking of informed, written consent before surgical procedures and when participating in medical research has become standard procedure. Yet, a number of problems remain with autonomy and consent, both applied and more conceptual. Despite the universalism of declarations regarding informed consent, there are clear limits to this in practice.[8] Studies of consent in real-life situations have demonstrated that patients may not understand fully the information that they have been given. The point of consent procedures, sceptics argue, is not to obtain consent per se, but rather to create a paper trial demonstrating that due process has been followed.[9] This is particularly important for pharmaceutical companies conducting research on their products, and consent practices are often designed with corporate interests, and not solely those of research participants, in mind. The globalisation of medical research may have moved some of the more dangerous experiments away from Britain's shores, but this simply shifts problems with consent to new places.[10] Other critics have questioned the extent to which informed consent involves an active choice, as there may be no meaningful alternative to the treatment being offered.[11] Patients may also participate in experimental treatments in order to utilise care or treatment that they are unable to gain access to elsewhere.[12]

The framing of consent and autonomy as a 'choice' also raises a number of difficulties. Privileging autonomy, according to the sociologist Nikolas Rose, means that subjects are 'not merely "free to choose" but *obliged to be free*, to understand and enact their lives in terms of choice [original emphasis]'.[13] Such an elevation of individual rights and choice, according to the philosopher Onora O'Neill, has damaged the notion of trust and broader, collective objectives within health.[14] As Duncan Wilson and David Reubi point out, the prioritisation of individual autonomy also means that bioethics maps neatly onto neo-liberal concerns for accountability and individual choice.[15] Yet such a focus has not prevented crises from occurring. Indeed, attention to neo-liberal objectives such as targets has been seen as being partly to blame for recent scandals around poor quality care within the NHS.

Representation

In November 2007, Bella Bailey died in Stafford General Hospital. Bella's daughter, Julie Bailey, was appalled by the standard of care her mother had received. She said that 'What we saw after the first few days left us fearing for my Mother's life and too frightened to leave her'.[16] Bailey wrote to a local newsletter detailing her concerns and was met with a flood of replies from other patients and their families also revealing poor care at the hospital.[17] In response to these stories, Bailey formed an organisation – Cure the NHS – to campaign for better standards of care at Stafford Hospital and more widely. The group wrote to the Healthcare Commission outlining Bailey's mother's case and numerous other complaints about treatment at Stafford

Hospital, such as patients not being fed or given sufficient fluids, patients being left in soiled bed-sheets and a lack of adequate pain relief.[18]

The Healthcare Commission were concerned already by reports of an unusually high mortality rate at the Stafford Hospital and in 2008 the Commission conducted an investigation into mortality and care, especially surrounding emergency admissions. The Commission found that not only was the hospital's standardised mortality rate higher than expected, but their investigations also uncovered multiple failings in the care of patients and the management of the hospital and staff. The report concluded that the hospital's 'strategic focus was on financial and business matters at a time when the quality of care of its patients admitted as emergencies was well below acceptable standards'.[19] Following the Healthcare Commission's report, Cure the NHS pressed for a full public enquiry into conditions at the Stafford Hospital. The Labour government rejected their appeal, but did commission two reviews by the Department of Health, and another by Robert Francis, QC.[20] In 2010, the Conservative Health Secretary Andrew Lansley agreed to a public inquiry into conditions at Stafford Hospital, also chaired by Francis. The inquiry, which took 31 months and made 290 recommendations, once again exposed the 'appalling suffering of many patients' but also pointed to flaws in the 'checks and balances which should have prevented serious systemic failure of this sort'. Francis went on to say that 'There were and are a plethora of agencies, scrutiny groups, commissioners, regulators and professional bodies, all of whom might have been expected by patients and the public to detect and do something effective to remedy non-compliance with acceptable standards of care. For years that did not occur'.[21]

The various inquiries into conditions at the Stafford Hospital pointed not only to bad care, but also to failings within the existing mechanisms of patient representation. In her initial letter to the Healthcare Commission, Bailey asserted that the PALS and Patient and Public Involvement systems at the hospital were 'ineffective', a claim later backed up by the Francis Inquiry.[22] Francis concluded that 'The arrangements for public and patient involvement, and for local government scrutiny in Stafford, were a conspicuous failure'. In future, he wrote, 'There must be real involvement of patients and the public in all that is done'.[23]

Although the problems at Stafford should not be seen as the result of inadequate patient representation, the episode does highlight serious difficulties with the present system of patient and public involvement. As discussed in Chapter 6, collective representation has been weakened in recent years despite more attention being paid to individual patient voices. Furthermore, the emergence of a single-issue patient group (at least initially: Cure the NHS now has a broader focus on conditions in all NHS hospitals) suggests that existing, independent patient organisations were not in a position to respond to the problems at Stafford. Groups like the PA did become involved once the scandal gained momentum – they were one of the 'core participants', able to make submissions to the Francis Inquiry and put questions to witnesses – but it was the actions of Cure the NHS that raised awareness about the issues and helped lead to the establishment of a public inquiry into conditions at Stafford Hospital.[24] Significant questions could, therefore, be raised about the effectiveness of patient representation, as well as care and management at Stafford Hospital and more widely.

Complaint

Indeed, the scandal in Staffordshire, and the reaction to it in the media and from politicians and policy makers has many echoes with the reaction to previous NHS scandals. The parallels between Stafford Hospital and past scandals such as those involving Ely Hospital, Farleigh Hospital and Whittingham Hospital during the late 1960s and early 1970s are not exact. These hospitals provided long-term care for the elderly and mentally ill, whereas Stafford was a general hospital, but similarities between these past scandals and more recent events did point to some recurring issues. A key problem surrounded the handling of complaints. The Francis Inquiry, like the inquiries into the earlier scandals, uncovered significant difficulties for patients wishing to make a complaint. Francis reported that during the course of his inquiry numerous former patients or their families wrote to him detailing their complaints, something that, he asserted, 'bore witness to their inability to obtain satisfaction from the complaints and redress systems available to them'. He also found that 'There were inadequate processes for dealing with complaints and serious untoward incidents'.[25] Francis went on to devote a whole chapter in his final report to the issue of complaining, and the report made 14 recommendations with respect to complaints, focusing in particular on practical measures to make it easier for patients to complain.[26]

Following the Francis Inquiry, Prime Minister David Cameron commissioned a review of the NHS complaints system led by Ann Clwyd, Labour MP for Cyon Valley and Professor Tricia Hart, Chief Executive of South Tees Hospitals NHS Foundation Trust. Clwyd had professional experience of the NHS and its systems as a member of the Royal Commission on the NHS from 1977–79 and as a member of the Welsh Hospital Board, 1970–74, but she also had personal experience too. Clwyd saw her husband die in the University Hospital of Wales in December 2012 in conditions she described as being 'like [those of] a battery hen'.[27] Clwyd and Hart's review of the complaints system, published in October 2013, found that patients were often reluctant to complain for fear of implications for their care; patients found the complaints process hard to navigate; patients were concerned about the independence of investigations and they wanted to know that by complaining they would make a difference to future patients. The report made recommendations for change in four areas: enhancing the quality of care; improving the way complaints were handled; ensuring the independence of complaints procedures and whistle-blowing.[28]

The Clwyd and Hart review was the latest in a long line of investigations and reports on complaining in the NHS. There were major reviews of the complaints system published in 1994, 1999, 2001, 2003, 2004, 2005, 2008, 2009 and 2011.[29] The frequency of these reports, and the similarity of their findings and recommendations would suggest strongly that issues surrounding the making and handling of complaints within the NHS were far from resolved. Complaints, almost by definition, were, and are likely to remain, a contentious area as they involve two parties in dispute. In the context of health care the stakes are particularly high, as the matter being contested may involve death, injury or suffering. The persistence of problems with complaints systems, however, also points to wider difficulties. Despite the adoption of rights language with respect to complaining, complaint does not appear to have become substantially easier. The ongoing issues surrounding complaint may be as much to do with problems connected to rights, as they are complaints.

Rights

The introduction of the *NHS Constitution* in 2009 would seem to mark official implementation of the language of rights first put forward by patient-consumer organisations in the 1970s and 1980s. The *Constitution* offered a more comprehensive and considered approach to patients' rights than that found in earlier official documents such as the *Patient's Charter*. The *NHS Constitution* set out the duties and values that underpinned the NHS, was addressed to both patients and staff, and balanced rights with duties.[30] The legal basis of each specific right was also spelled out in a *Handbook to the NHS Constitution*.[31] According to the *Constitution* 'Everyone who uses the NHS should understand what legal rights they have'.[32]

Although the *Constitution* was greeted with some distrust from patient-consumer organisations and others, it did offer the clearest and most far-reaching statement of patients' rights within the NHS ever to have been put forward. The flaws of the *Constitution* were rooted in the drawbacks of rights language as much as with the document itself. When the *NHS Constitution* was introduced in 2009, it was supposed to be renewed every 10 years, and the accompanying handbook every three years. In 2012, Health Secretary Andrew Lansley asked the Future Forum (a group of leading health experts) to assess the effectiveness of the *NHS Constitution*. The Future Forum, led by former chairman of the Royal College of General Practitioners, Professor Steve Field, asserted that the *Constitution* had a 'vital role to play', but its 'effect so far has been patchy, low-key and inconsistent'.[33] Lansley, in his own report on the effectiveness of the *Constitution* (also published in 2012) conceded that 'In general, patients do not use the NHS Constitution as a benchmark for challenge and this suggests that the Constitution is not yet having the effect originally intended'.[34] The Department of Health initiated a consultation on the *Constitution*, which reported in January 2013. In his foreword to the government's response to the Consultation the Health Minister, Norman Lamb, stated that 'The Constitution is an enduring document. The threshold for making changes to it is – rightly – set high. Any changes should be clear and compelling. Politicians, of any party, should not be free to tinker with at will.' But, he argued, 'the Constitution also needs to move with the times – to reflect changes to the law and to ensure that it applies to all those involved in delivering NHS services'.[35] In an appendix, the document set out 21 changes to the patients' rights and pledges listed in the original *Constitution* as well as alterations to the principles, responsibilities and staff duties. Explanatory notes elucidated the reasons for each change, many of which were in direct response to the Future Forum's report and the consultation exercise.[36] Some of the modifications were technical amendments, intended to clarify the rights being set out. Others introduced new rights, such as the right to be informed about how an individual's information was to be used.

The problem with such revisions to the *Constitution* lay not in the changes themselves, but with the fact that they were felt to be necessary at all. A Department of Health civil servant involved in the development and revision of the *Constitution* commented that the document was 'meant to have a degree of permanence and probably we are changing it a bit too much'. The other danger was that by continually adding to the list of rights contained within the *Constitution*, there would be a 'sort of sedimentary building up and then you've got issues about making sure the document doesn't become too big and too unwieldy'. Some of the things added to the *Constitution* could be traced to issues that had attracted interest from the media and campaign groups, such as the pledge to provide all hospital inpatients with single-sex accommodation, or to involve patients in discussions about end of life care. There was, the official remarked, a sense that these commitments had been added to the *Constitution* 'just because at the time there was a debate … So that's a kind of relatively short term political point which makes it into the Constitution to solve a current problem.'³⁷

Indeed, despite Lamb's protestations, the *NHS Constitution* began life as, and continues to be, an intensely political document. One of the original driving forces behind the *NHS Constitution*, the (Labour) Health Minister at the time, Andy Burnham, floated the document as a way to 'test the Conservatives' commitment to a free NHS'.³⁸ There was a sense, a Department of Health civil servant stated, 'that at the time that Labour set up the Constitution, I think they were hoping to set something out that it would be impossible for the Conservative Government to live up to' although he was quick to point out that 'the Coalition Government has honoured the Constitution and everything in it'.³⁹ The *NHS Constitution* then, was as much about attempting to ensure that a particular vision of the NHS persists as it was about guaranteeing patients' rights. Like so many of the charters and rights guides that had preceded it, the *NHS Constitution* was a political document, powerful on the surface, but at the same time lacking in substance at a deeper level. One of the key findings of the Future Forum and the consultation on the Constitution was that 'the Constitution amounts to fine words but no teeth'. Patients did not know where to go to resolve a problem or make a complaint, or how they could use the constitution when they felt that their rights had been compromised. The document, they felt, needed more 'traction'. One of the difficulties was that few patients had heard of the *Constitution*. The Future Forum noted that 'Few people know about it [the Constitution]. Fewer still use it to uphold their expectations of the NHS.'⁴⁰ Like previous declarations of patients' rights, the *NHS Constitution* ran in to a number of political and practical problems that would suggest it was far from being the final statement on patients' rights.

Information

Lack of awareness about the *NHS Constitution* was perhaps more surprising when compared to its predecessor documents, as the *Constitution* was introduced at a time when access to health information was easier and faster than ever before. The development and proliferation of the Internet from the 1990s onwards opened up access to information about health services, conditions and treatment on an unprecedented scale. Information that previously could only be found in reference books in specialist libraries or in hard to locate grey literature was available to anyone with a computer and an Internet connection. David J. Rothman and David Blumenthal argued that 'By democratizing access to information, HIT [Health Information Technology] may reduce or eliminate the asymmetries of information that have justified professional codes of conduct and that have also motivated patients to seek out physicians and reimburse them for their services'.[41] The Internet, and the information patients could find there, it was assumed, would empower patients in their relations with health professionals, rectifying the ancient knowledge–power imbalance between doctor and patient.

Opening up access to information has not, however, resolved such difficulties or many of the other problems surrounding health information pointed to in Chapter 5. To begin with, not all patients or potential patients can access the Internet. In 2013 the Office for National Statistics (ONS) found that 83 per cent of households in the UK had Internet access, but daily computer use (a strong predictor of daily Internet use) was low amongst people aged 65 and over: 37 per cent of individuals in this age group compared to 88 per cent amongst those aged 16–24 and 84 per cent aged 24–34.[42] The ONS did not collect data on socio-economic status or gender, but an earlier study, from 2009, suggested that those in more vulnerable groups, such as families with young children, the physically and socially isolated, those in lower-income groups and disabled people had more difficulty in making use of the Internet.[43] A so-called 'digital divide' existed between those who had access to the Internet and knew how to use it and those who do not.[44]

Even for those patients that were able to gain access to the information that they wanted, questions remained about how this could best be used. As Rothman and Blumenthal argued, greater ability to find relevant health information may empower patients, changing the doctor–patient relationship. In a literature review of patients' use of the Internet to find health information and the impact that this had on their relationships with health professionals, Miriam McMullan asserted that use of the Internet 'can empower them [patients] to make health decisions and to talk to their physician, resulting in a more patient-centred interaction'.[45] Yet, other research found that the concept of 'empowerment' was context dependent: that when ill or in pain patients may value care over empowerment.[46] Fils Henwood, Roma Harris and Philippa Spoel observed that empowerment through access to information was often equated with greater choice, but in practice some patients were resistant to the information-choice imperative, or at least found it hard to realise.[47]

At the same time, new technology has not always delivered the information revolution promised. In 2002, the Department of Health launched the National Programme for IT in the NHS. A key part of this programme was an attempt to create an integrated NHS-wide electronic records system, making up-to-date, accurate patient records available to NHS staff anywhere at any time. The project, however, was a complete failure and was scrapped in 2011 after falling considerably behind schedule and with costs reaching £2.7 billon.[48] Responsibility for delivering electronic records was devolved to NHS Trusts, and in November 2011, Chancellor George Osborne promised that patients would be able to access their own GP records online by 2015.[49] Even if such a promise can be kept, experience from other countries, such as the USA, suggests that electronic records are no panacea.[50] Indeed, new technologies have also raised troubling questions about the confidentiality and ownership of health information. The large datasets and rich personal information that exist within the NHS are attractive to commercial organisations such as private health care firms and pharmaceutical companies. The revised *NHS Constitution* gives patients a right to request that their data would not be used beyond their own care, but the presumption was that unless a patient opted out, their data would be made available to non-NHS parties through the Health and Social Care Information Centre.[51] Meanwhile, a review of health information governance by psychiatrist Dame Fiona Caldicott discovered that individual patients still had difficulties accessing their own records. The review found patients' attempts to see their records were hampered by the charging of fees and refusal to provide access to records in a format that suited them, such as by email.[52] By themselves, technological and legal changes were insufficient to deal with all of the difficulties experienced by patient-consumers connected to health information.

Voice

One way of potentially addressing such issues was through a stronger patient voice. As discussed in Chapter 6, since the mid-2000s patient voice mechanisms within the NHS have undergone constant revolution. The coalition government's major piece of health legislation, the Health and Social Care Act, 2012, shifted responsibility for public health and social care to local authorities and placed the majority of the NHS's budget in the hands of GPs who would then commission services for their patients. Although Clinical Commissioning Groups had a duty to involve patients in the planning of commissioning arrangements; in the development of proposals for change; and in decisions that would affect services; no single model of patient participation was advocated.[53] Across the services provided by the NHS, Local Healthwatch replaced LINks in April 2013, with one for each local authority. It is too early to offer a detailed assessment of these organisations, but some key commentators have articulated scepticism about the ability of Local Healthwatch to provide an effective patient voice mechanism. The Francis report expressed concern that there was no single structure recommended for Local Healthwatch and the funds to support these organisations were not ring-fenced within local authorities' budgets.[54] Without such protection, Francis feared that under significant financial pressure local authorities would reduce the funding of their Local Healthwatch to cut costs but to the significant detriment of patient voice.[55]

At the national level, the Health and Social Care Act also ushered into being Healthwatch England as the 'independent consumer champion for health and social care in England'. Healthwatch England's task is to work with the 152 Local Healthwatches and 'ensure that the voices of consumers and those who use services reach the ears of the decision makers'.[56] Healthwatch England has been explicit in their use of the label 'consumer', although the Chair, Anna Bradley, in her foreword to the organisation's first annual report, recognised that '"Consumer" is an uncomfortable word for some people in health and social care'. Bradley went on to argue that 'we have found that the term consumer helps everyone to think differently; to ask new questions. This is why, we think borrowing from the consumer world will be helpful'.[57] Indeed, the report made explicit use of the UN's *Guidelines for Consumer Protection* in order to develop eight consumer rights for health and social care.[58] These were the right to essential services; the right to access; the right to a safe, dignified and quality service; the right to information and education; the right to choose; the right to be listened to; the right to be involved; and the right to live in a healthy environment.[59]

Healthwatch England's explicit use of consumer rights language suggests two things. Firstly, the organisation appears to view the *NHS Constitution* as inadequate. The report comments 'Our rights [those listed in the report] comfortably encompass the NHS constitution, but they extend beyond it. They are broader, and perhaps most importantly, they apply to all types of health and social care'.[60] Healthwatch England was pressing for a wider and deeper set of rights than those offered by the *NHS Constitution*. Secondly, despite the many problems associated with rights talk, patient-consumer organisations like Healthwatch England were clearly unable to resist its apparent power. The report asserted that 'Rights tell people what to expect from the services they receive. Rights empower people to assert what they need, when they need it'. Rights would help bring about 'a move from grateful patients to empowered citizens and consumers'.[61] Such claims, of course, were not new. The need to move away from gratitude and towards empowerment was at the heart of patient-consumer groups' activities from the 1960s onwards. The overlap between patient, consumer and citizen was present in some of the earliest accounts of patient consumerism, such as RICA's commentary on general practice. What was different, however, was the kind of patient-consumer being envisaged. It is striking that the *NHS Constitution* and Healthwatch England's list of rights both include the right to choose. Choice, which had been almost absent from patient-consumer organisations lists of demands until the 1990s, now forms a central part of patient-consumer identity.

Choice

As discussed in Chapter 7, choice was integral to the reform of the NHS under the Labour government (1997–2010). The position of choice within the coalition government's health policy has shifted somewhat. Although choice is still a central watchword, attention appears to have moved to the supply-side of the equation through the introduction of more competition within health services rather than focusing solely on demand-led patient choice. The Health and Social Care Act opened up the possibility for much greater competition within health services in England by requiring Clinical Commissioning Groups (groups of GPs in a local area) to put all services out to tender.[62] The rationale behind this move was that 'Where there is *competition and choice of hospital* provider it leads to better outcomes, satisfaction for patients and better hospital management [original emphasis]'.[63] Competition and choice were thought to go hand in hand: more competition would deliver more choice for patients. Delivering choice and competition in a time of austerity, however, is likely to be difficult. Although the coalition government did not reduce the NHS budget, rising demand and escalating costs mean that the service is facing an estimated funding gap of £30 billion for the period between 2013/14 and 2020/21.[64] Delivering more choice for individuals is likely to be costly, as choice and competition require spare capacity elsewhere within the system.

The hole in the NHS's finances is just one of the problems facing the service that patient choice cannot resolve and may even exacerbate. In 2013, NHS England issued a 'call to action' detailing the challenges facing the service in the future. In addition to the financial gap, the call identified a series of other problems for the NHS such as an ageing society, increases in long-term conditions and rising health care expectations. Yet, the framing of the document was just as significant as the issues that it raised. The call to action was addressed to 'those who own the NHS, to all who use and depend on the NHS, and to all who work for and with it' and foregrounded the assertion that 'the NHS belongs to the people'. The collective underpinning of the NHS was re-affirmed throughout the document, with statements such as 'The NHS is more than a system; it is an expression of British values of fairness, solidarity and compassion.'[65] Although a cynic may argue that the document was representative of attempts to get the population to share the problems while the individual reaps the benefits in terms of more choice, the call did suggest that collective as well as individual values persist within the NHS.

Such sentiments are more than just words: there are a number of systems in place to attempt to ensure that health care resources are distributed on an equitable basis. The National Institute for Health and Clinical Excellence's (NICE) sets a cost threshold for new drugs to be prescribed by NHS practitioners of £20,000-£30,000 per Quality Adjusted Life Year (QALY). What this means in practice is that individuals do not have unfettered access to any treatment whatever the cost: individual choice may be constrained in order to protect wider goals. NICE assert that 'no publicly funded health care system, including the NHS, can possibly pay for every new medical treatment which becomes available. The enormous costs involved mean that choices have to be made'.[66] The use of the QALY is an attempt to do so fairly. Whatever the policy rhetoric, individual choice has not completely won out within a system that does still work for collective as well as individual benefit.

The distance travelled

How far has the patient-consumer come since its birth in the 1960s? Many of the demands put forward by patient-consumer organisations around issues such as autonomy, representation, complaint, rights and information, appear to have been met. But numerous problems remain. It is difficult to see how patient-consumers can overcome completely the power imbalance with health professionals, and many issues, like complaints, are likely to remain fractious. The tension between individual demands and collective needs also persists, and though more attention is undoubtedly paid to individual desires such as choice, shared aspirations have not fallen away entirely. Rights talk, first employed by patient-consumer organisations in the 1970s, continues to hold groups and individuals in its thrall, despite its many drawbacks. History cannot predict the future, but these long-running issues seem set to continue.

What of the patient-consumer themselves? Made in the 1960s by patient-consumer organisations, further developed by these groups in the 1970s and 1980s, remodelled in the 1990s and 2000s by government, the patient-consumer was, and continues to be, a pliable figure. The patient-consumer is a hybrid, conflicted and even fictional entity: an individual and a group, everyone and no one all at the same time. Such malleability is not a problem for the patient-consumer – far from it – the paradoxical specificity and generality of the patient-consumer is one of the reasons for its persistence. Though it seems likely that the patient-consumer is here to stay, there is always the danger that patient consumerism will come to mean so many things to so many different people that the label 'patient-consumer' ceases to have a useful function. But do not expect to read the patient-consumer's obituary any time soon.

Notes

1. Department of Health, *The NHS Constitution* (London: Department of Health, 2009).
2. John Carvel, 'We didn't want to repeat the mistakes of the Patient's Charter', *Guardian*, 21 January 2009, www.guardian.co.uk/society/2009/jan/20/nhs-constitution-alan-johnson, accessed 8 November 2013.
3. John Carvel, 'NHS Constitution: comment and reaction' *Guardian*, 21 January 2009, www.guardian.co.uk/society/2009/jan/21/nhs-constitution-reaction, accessed 8 November 2013.
4. Ruth R. Faden and Tom L. Beauchamp, *A History and Theory of Informed Consent* (New York: Oxford University Press, 1986).
5. Shelia A.M. McLean, *Autonomy, Consent and the Law* (Abingdon: Routledge-Cavendish, 2010), pp. 70–76.
6. Human Rights Act, 1998. Based on UN Declaration of Human Rights.
7. On the history of bioethics in Britain, see Roger Cooter, 'The resistible rise of medical ethics', *Social History of Medicine*, 8:2 (1995), 257–270; Roger Cooter, 'The ethical body', in Roger Cooter and John Pickstone (eds), *Medicine in the Twentieth Century* (Amsterdam: Harwood Academic Publishers, 2000), 451–468; Duncan Wilson, *Tissue Culture in Science and Society: The Public Life of a Biological Technique* (Basingstoke: Palgrave Macmillan, 2011); David Reubi, 'Re-moralising medicine: the bioethical thought collective and the regulation of the body in British medical research', *Social Theory & Health*, 11 (2013), 215–235.
8. Ingrid Whiteman, 'The fallacy of choice in the common law and NHS policy', *Health Care Analysis*, 21 (2013), 146–170.
9. Oonagh Corrigan, 'Empty ethics: the problem with informed consent', *Sociology of Health and Illness*, 25:3 (2003), 768–792.
10. Adriana Petryna, *When Experiments Travel: Clinical Trials and the Global Search for Human Subjects* (Princeton, NJ: Princeton University Press, 2009).
11. Corrigan, 'Empty ethics'.
12. Petryna, *When Experiments Travel*.
13. Nikolas Rose, *Inventing our Selves: Psychology, Power and Personhood* (Cambridge: Cambridge University Press, 1996), p. 17.
14. Onora O'Neill, *Autonomy and Trust in Bioethics* (Cambridge: Cambridge University Press, 2002).
15. Duncan Wilson, ' Who guards the guardians? Ian Kennedy, bioethics and the "ideology of accountability" in British medicine', *Social History of Medicine*, 25:1 (2012), 193–211; Reubi, 'Ethics governance, modernity and human beings'.
16. www.curethenhs.co.uk/about-cure-the-nhs/, accessed 12 November 2013.
17. www.staffordshirenewsletter.co.uk/Not-In-Use/Letters/NHS-needs-change-and-we-need-your-help-now.htm, accessed 12 November 2013.

18 Letter from Julie Bailey to Mrs Pickersgill, Healthcare Commission, n.d., www.curethenhs.co.uk/wp-content/uploads/2012/10/Letter-HealthCommision.pdf, accessed 12 November 2013.
19 Healthcare Commission, *Investigation Into Mid Staffordshire NHS Foundation Trust* (London: Healthcare Commission, 2009), p. 11.
20 John Carvel, 'Minister rejects calls for public inquiry into hospital scandal', 19 March 2009, www.theguardian.com/politics/2009/mar/19/alan-johnson-nhs-stafford-nhs?guni=Article:in%20body%20link; HC 375-I, *Independent Inquiry into Care Provided by Mid Staffordshire Foundation Trust, January 2005–March 2009* (London: TSO, 2010).
21 HC 947, *Report of the Mid Staffordshire NHS Foundation Trust Public Inquiry: Executive Summary* (London: TSO, 2013), p. 3.
22 Letter from Julie Bailey to Mrs Pickersgill, n.d., www.curethenhs.co.uk/wp-content/uploads/2012/10/Letter-HealthCommision.pdf, accessed 5 December 2013.
23 HC 947, *Report of the Mid Staffordshire NHS Foundation Trust Public Inquiry: Executive Summary*, p. 74.
24 *Ibid.*, p. 12; www.patients-association.com/Default.aspx?tabid=95, accessed 12 November 2013.
25 HC 947, *Report of the Mid Staffordshire NHS Foundation Trust Public Inquiry: Executive Summary*, pp. 16, 44.
26 HC 898-I, *Report of the Mid Staffordshire NHS Foundation Trust Public Inquiry: Volume 1* (London: TSO, 2013), pp. 245–287.
27 Ann Clwyd and Tricia Hart, *A Review of the NHS Hospitals Complaints System: Putting Patients Back in the Picture* (London: TSO, 2013), p. 6.
28 *Ibid.*, pp. 19–23, 31–38.
29 Department of Health, *Being Heard: The Report of a Review Committee on NHS Complaints Procedures* (London: Department of Health, 1994); Henrietta Wallace and Linda Mulcahy, *Cause for Complaint: An Evaluation of the Effectiveness of the NHS Complaints Procedure* (London: Public Law Project, 1999); Department of Health, *NHS Complaints Procedure National Evaluation* (London: Department of Health, 2001); Department of Health, *NHS Complaints Reform: Making Things Right* (London: Department of Health, 2003); Healthcare Commission, *Reforming the NHS Complaints Procedure* (London: Healthcare Commission, 2004); HC 413, *Making Things Better? A Report on the Reform of the NHS Complaints Procedure in England* (London: TSO, 2005); National Audit Office, *Feeding Back? Learning from Complaints Handling in Health and Social Care* (London: TSO, 2008); Healthcare Commission, *Spotlight on Complaints: A Report on Second-Stage Complaints about the NHS in England* (London: Healthcare Commission, 2008); The Local Authority Social Services and National Health Service Complaints (England) Regulations 2009; House of Commons, *Health Committee Sixth Report: Complaints and Litigation* (London: House of Commons, 2011).
30 Department of Health, *The NHS Constitution*.
31 Department of Health, *The Handbook to the NHS Constitution* (London: Department of Health, 2009).
32 Department of Health, *The NHS Constitution*, p. 5.
33 Letter to the Secretary of State for Health from the NHS Future Forum Working Group on the NHS Constitution, 31 October 2012, www.gov.uk/government/

uploads/system/uploads/attachment_data/file/216966/NHS-future-forum-letter.pdf, accessed 13 November 2013.
34 Department of Health, *Report on the Effect of the NHS Constitution* (London: Department of Health, 2012).
35 Department of Health, *Government Report on the Consultation on Strengthening the NHS Constitution* (London: Department of Health, 2013), p. 3.
36 *Ibid.*, Annex 4.
37 Author interview with Department of Health civil servant, March 2013.
38 John Carvel, 'Outspoken off roader', the *Guardian*, 14 February 2007, www.theguardian.com/society/2007/feb/14/guardiansocietysupplement.health?guni=Article:in%20body%20link, accessed 21 November 2013.
39 Author interview with Department of Health civil servant, March 2013.
40 Letter to the Secretary of State for Health from the NHS Future Forum Working Group on the NHS Constitution, 31 October 2012.
41 David J. Rothman and David Blumenthal, 'Introduction', in David J. Rothman and David Blumenthal (eds), *Medical Professionalism in the Information Age* (New Brunswick, NJ: Rutgers University Press, 2010), 1–7, p. 2.
42 Office for National Statistics, *Statistical Bulletin: Internet Access – Households and Individuals, 2013* (London: ONS, 2013), www.ons.gov.uk/ons/dcp171778_322713.pdf, accessed 21 November 2013.
43 Peter Jones, *Internet Access and Use* (Southampton: University of Southampton, 2010), pp. 3–4, www.equalityhumanrights.com/uploaded_files/triennial_review/triennial_review_internet_access.pdf, accessed 21 November 2013.
44 See, for example, Pippa Norris, *Digital Divide: Civic Engagement, Information Poverty and the Internet Worldwide* (Cambridge: Cambridge University Press, 2001); Sally Wyatt, Fils Henwood, Nod Miller and Peter Senker (eds), *Technology and In/Equality: Questioning the Information Society* (London: Routledge: 2000).
45 Miriam McMullan, 'Patients using the Internet to obtain health information: how this affects the patient–health professional relationship', *Patient Education and Counseling*, 63 (2006), 24–28, p. 27.
46 Alicia O'Cathain, Jackie Goode, Donna Luff, Tim Strangleman, Gerard Hanlon, David Greatbatch, 'Does NHS Direct empower patients?', *Social Science and Medicine*, 61 (2005), 1761–1771.
47 Fils Henwood, Roma Harris and Philippa Spoel, 'Informing health? Negotiating the logics of choice and care in everyday practices of "healthy living"', *Social Science and Medicine*, 72 (2011), 2026–2032.
48 HC 1070, *The National Programme for IT in the NHS: An Update on the Delivery of Detailed Care Records Systems* (London: TSO, 2011).
49 Anon., 'Patients to be given full access to GP record by 2015', *Pulse*, 29 November 2011, www.pulsetoday.co.uk/patients-given-access-to-full-gp-record-by-2015/13131402.article#.Uo4uGCjnaYk, accessed 21 November 2013.
50 See Stanley Joel Reiser, *Technological Medicine: The Changing World of Doctors and Patients* (Cambridge: Cambridge University Press, 2009), pp. 94–103.
51 Anon., 'Everyone to be a "research patient" says David Cameron', BBC News, 5 December 2011, www.bbc.co.uk/news/uk-16026827, accessed 21 November 2013; Department of Health, *NHS Constitution* (London: Department of Health, 2013), p. 8; 'Your records', NHS Choices website, www.nhs.uk/NHSEngland/

thenhs/records/healthrecords/Pages/care-data.aspx, accessed 21 November 2013; Paul Dinsdale, 'Fear grows over open access to patient records', *The Observer*, 23 November 2013, www.theguardian.com/society/2013/nov/24/fears-grow-open-access-patient-records?INTCMP=ILCNETTXT3487, accessed 28 November 2013.
52 Department of Health, *Information: To Share or not to Share – The Information Governance Review* (London: Department of Health, 2013), pp. 29–34.
53 Health and Social Care Act 2012, Section 14Z2; Stephanie Varah, *Practices and Patient Engagement: Smart Guides to Engagement* (London: National Association for Patient Participation, n.d.).
54 HC 947, *Report of the Mid Staffordshire NHS Foundation Trust Public Inquiry: Executive Summary*, p. 100.
55 Sarah Calkin and Kaye Wiggins, 'Local Healthwatch at risk of "fractious disputes"', *Health Service Journal*, 13 February 2013, www.hsj.co.uk/home/francis-report/local-healthwatch-at-risk-of-fractious-disputes/5054897.article#.Uo81KSjnaYk, accessed 22 November 2013.
56 www.healthwatch.co.uk/about-us, accessed 22 November 2013.
57 Healthwatch, *Healthwatch England Annual Report, 2012–13* (Newcastle-upon-Tyne: Healthwatch England, 2013), p. 7.
58 *Ibid.*, p. 22; United Nations, *United Nations Guidelines for Consumer Protection* (New York: UN, 1999). Latest version available at www.un.org/esa/sustdev/publications/consumption_en.pdf.
59 Healthwatch, *Healthwatch England Annual Report, 2012–13*, pp. 24–31.
60 *Ibid.*, p. 6.
61 *Ibid.*, p. 21.
62 Health and Social Care Act, 2012, Section 75.
63 Department of Health, 'Choice and competition factsheet', 2012, p. 1, www.gov.uk/government/uploads/system/uploads/attachment_data/file/138269/C4.-Factsheet-Choice-and-competition–270412.pdf, accessed 22 November 2013.
64 NHS England, *The NHS Belongs to the People: A Call to Action* (London: NHS, 2013), p. 15.
65 *Ibid.*, pp. 5, 6.
66 'Measuring effectiveness and cost effectiveness: the QALY', www.nice.org.uk/newsroom/features/measuringeffectivenessandcosteffectivenesstheqaly.jsp, accessed 22 November 2013.

Bibliography

Primary sources

Archives

Birmingham City Archives (hereafter BCA)

BCA MS 1226/15, Maternity and Child Welfare Working Group Papers, 1974–80
BCA MS 1226/16, Maternity and Child Welfare Working Group Papers, 1974–80
BCA MS 2588/1/2, South Birmingham CHC Minutes, 1975
BCA MS 2588/1/3, South Birmingham CHC Minutes, 1976–77
BCA MS 2588/1/4, South Birmingham CHC Minutes, 1978–79
BCA MS 2588/1/26, South Birmingham CHC Minutes, 1993–97
BCA MS 2588/7, The New Hospital Project and its History, 1997–2003

Churchill College Cambridge (hereafter CCC), private papers of Michael Young

CCC YUNG 6/10/1, Correspondence about the College of Health, 1982–83
CCC YUNG 6/10/2, Correspondence about the College of Health, 1984–July 1986
CCC YUNG/6/10/3, Correspondence about the College of Health, August 1986–March 1987
CCC YUNG/6/10/4, College of Health: Background and Aims, n.d. [1987?]
CCC YUNG/6/10/7, Correspondence about the College of Health, 1991
CCC YUNG/6/10/10, Reports and information leaflets published by the College of Health, 1984–86
CCC YUNG/6/10/11, Reports and information leaflets published by the College of Health, 1987–99
CCC YUNG/6/10/12, Guide to Hospital Waiting Lists, 1985–89
CCC YUNG 6/10/13, *Self Health*: the journal of the College of Health. Comprising issues 1–2, 4–12 and 14–10
CCC YUNG 6/27/2, Correspondence about Healthline, 1986–89
CCC YUNG 6/27/3, Correspondence about Healthline, 1986–89
CCC YUNG 6/47/1, Correspondence about the National Consumer Council, 1975–76

Contemporary Medical Archives Centre (hereafter CMAC), Wellcome Library, London

CMAC SA/CME/B/156, Royal Commission on Medical Education: written evidence, the Patients Association, 1965

CMAC PP/MHP/C/1/6-10, Private Papers of Maurice Pappworth, Letters from chairman of The Patients Association concerning founding of the association, newspaper clippings re the association, advice regarding people claiming they were experimented on and the publication of Human Guinea Pigs, 1963–67

CMAC SA/PAT/1/1/1, Minutes of the Meeting of the Committee of the PA, 13 December 1965

CMAC SA/PAT/A/1/2, Patients Association Committee Minutes, January 1968– December 1970

CMAC SA/PAT/A/1/6, Patients Association Committee Minutes, 1981–82

CMAC SA/PAT/C/30, Local Government and Health Rights Project/The Community Rights Project Limited (later called Health Rights), 1983–85

CMAC SA/PAT/D/13/2, Patient Complaints – Family Practitioner Service Procedures, 1975–81

CMAC SA/PAT/D/13/3, Patient Complaints – Family Practitioner Service Procedures, 1981–86

CMAC SA/PAT/D/13/4, Complaints procedures – hospitals, 1973–86

CMAC SA/PAT/D/16/1, Patient Confidentiality, 1973–85

CMAC SA/PAT/D/16/2, Pt 1: Data Protection – Confidential Data Protection, 1976–85

CMAC SA/PAT/D/16/2, Pt 2: Data Protection – Confidential Data Protection, 1976–85

CMAC SA/PAT/D/16/3, 'Access to Medical Records', 1976–86

CMAC SA/PAT/D/39, Patients Rights Handbook (of the National Consumers Council), 1977–84

CMAC SA/PAT/E/1/1, Reports, Circulars, Opinions, etc. on the NHS and patient care, 1960s–1970s

CMAC SA/PAT/E/1/3, Teaching Hospitals and NHS guidance regarding patient consent 1974–79

CMAC SA/PAT/F/1/16, *Patient Voice*, Issues 47–50, 1990

CMAC SA/PAT/F/1/17, *Patient Voice*, Issues 51–54, 1991

CMAC SA/PAT/H/1 Press Cuttings, November 1962–November 1963

CMAC SA/PAT/H/2, Press Cuttings and member circulars, February 1963–June 1964

CMAC SA/PAT/H/3, Press Cuttings, February–September 1965

CMAC SA/PAT/H/4, Letter from Hogdson to the *Guardian*, 24 May 1967

CMAC SA/PAT/K/2/1/11, Medical Records and Access, 1995

CMAC SA/PAT/K/2/1/17, Patients Association Activities and Administration, 1995

Modern Records Centre (hereafter MRC), University of Warwick

MRC MSS.21/1628/1–29, National Association for the Welfare of Children in Hospital: ephemera and papers, 1971–74

MRC MSS.378/APSW/P/10/27/7a, Association of Psychiatric Social Workers: report of the Fourth Annual Congress of the NAWCH

MRC MSS.184 Private Papers of Margaret Stacey, Box 2

The National Archives (hereafter TNA), Kew

TNA ED 129/23, Royal Commission on Medical Education (Todd Commission): Records: The Patients Association, 1965

TNA HO 261/265, The Data Protection Committee: Medical Records – note by the Patients Association, 19 December 1976

TNA LCO 20/840, Lord Chancellor's Department: Royal Commission on Civil Liability and Compensation for Personal Injury: The Patients Association, 1974

TNA MH 150/348, National Association for the Welfare of Children in Hospital: problems of the long-stay child patient; reports, discussion papers and minutes of meetings, 1967–73

TNA MH 159/263, Hospital Complaints Procedure Committee, Correspondence from the public; evidence, papers and memorandums, 1971

TNA MH 159/281, Hospital Complaints Procedure: The Report of the Davies Committee, 1973–74

TNA MH 160/885, Experiments performed on human subjects: Committee on the Supervision of the Ethics of Clinical Investigations in Institutions; reports, papers, correspondence from various bodies and minutes of meetings, 1968–73

MH 160/1185, Co-operation of patients in the clinical teaching of medical students: preparation of guidance following the Todd report recommendations on Teaching on Patients; issue of HM(73)8; drafts, comments and amendments, 1969–73

TNA MH 166/24, Health Service Commissioner, 1967–69

TNA MH 166/25, Health Service Commissioner, 1969

TNA MH 166/27, Health Service Commissioner, 1969

TNA MH 166/28, Health Service Commissioner, 1969–70

TNA MH 166/29, Health Service Commissioner, 1970

TNA MH 166/30, Health Service Commissioner, 1970

TNA MH 166/34, Health Service Commissioner, 1971

TNA MH 166/35, Health Service Commissioner, 1971

TNA MH 166/55, Comments received on the Green Paper 'The NHS: the administrative structure of the medical and related services in England', 1968

TNA MH 166/56, Comments received on the Green Paper 'The NHS: the administrative structure of the medical and related services in England', 1968–69

TNA MH 166/146, Reorganisation of Community Health Councils 1971–72

TNA MH 166/148, Reorganisation of Community Health Councils 1972

TNA MH 166/151, Reorganisation of Community Health Councils 1973

TNA MH 166/157, Reorganisation of Community Health Councils 1974–75

Published primary sources

Anon., 'Patients as consumers: wants and needs', *The Lancet* (29 April 1961), 927–928

Appleby, John and Arturo Alavarez-Rosete, 'Public responses to NHS Reform', in Alison Park, John Curtice, Katarina Thomson, Catherine Bromley, Miranda Philips, Mark Johnson (eds), *British Social Attitudes: 22nd Report* (London: Sage, 2005), 109–134

Appleby, John, Anthony Harrison and Nancy Devlin, *What is the Real Cost of More Patient Choice?* (London: King's Fund, 2003)

Association of Community Health Councils in England and Wales, *Health News Briefing: The Patient's Charter – The Patient's Perspective* (London: ACHCEW, 1994)

Association of Community Health Councils in England and Wales, *Involving Patients and the Public in Healthcare: A Discussion Document Response from the Association of Community Health Councils for England and Wales* (London: ACHCEW, 2001)

Association of Community Health Councils in England and Wales, *Performance Evaluation Standards Framework for Community Health Councils* (London: ACHCEW, 1999)

Association of Community Health Councils in England and Wales, *The Patients' Agenda: What the Patient's Charter Leaves Out – the Rights you don't yet have in the NHS* (London: ACHCEW, 1996)

Audit Commission, *What Seems to be the Matter: Communication Between Hospitals and Patients* (London: Audit Commission, 1993)

Beech, Beverly Lawrence, *Who's Having Your Baby? A Health Rights Handbook for Maternity Care* (London: Camden Press, 1987)

Boyle, David, *The Barriers to Choice Review: How are People Using Choice in Public Services?* (London: Cabinet Office, 2013)

British Medical Association, *Philosophy and Practice of Medical Ethics* (London: BMA, 1988)

Britten, N., J. Bartholomew, R. Morris and L. Zander, 'Consultants' and patients' views about patient access to their general practice records', *Journal of the Royal Society of Medicine*, 84 (May 1991), 284–287

Buckland, Sarah, Carol Lupton and Graham Moon, *An Evaluation of the Role and Impact of Community Health Councils* (Portsmouth: Social Service Research and Information Unit, 1994)

Burge, Peter, Nancy Devlin, John Appleby, Charlene Rohr and Jonathan Grant, *London Patient Choice Project Evaluation: A Model of Patients' Choices of Hospital From Stated and Revealed Preference of Choice Data* (Cambridge: RAND Corporation, 2005)

Carr, Harold, 'The Patients Association: Is it needed?', *Hospital and Health Management* (April 1963), 287–288

Cartwright, Ann, *Human Relations and Hospital Care* (Routledge & Kegan Paul: London, 1964)
Cartwright, Ann, *Patients and Their Doctors: A Study of General Practice* (London: Routledge & Kegan Paul, 1967)
Central Birmingham Community Health Council, *Annual Report*, 1 June 1979–31 May 1980 (Birmingham: CBCHC, 1980)
Central Health Services Council, *The Welfare of Children in Hospital: Report of a Committee of the Central Health Services Council* (London: HMSO, 1959)
Clwyd, Ann and Tricia Hart, *A Review of the NHS Hospitals Complaints System: Putting Patients Back in the Picture* (London: TSO, 2013)
Cm. 555, *Working for Patients* (London: HMSO, 1989)
Cm. 1599, *The Citizen's Charter: Raising the Standard* (London: HMSO, 1991)
Cm. 4818-I, *The NHS Plan: A Plan for Investment a Plan for Reform* (London: HMSO, 2000)
Cm. 5207, *Learning from Bristol: the Report of the Public Inquiry Into Children's Heart Surgery at the Bristol Royal Infirmary 1984–1995* (London: HMSO, 2001)
Cm. 6737, *Our Health, Our Care, Our Say: A New Direction for Community Health Services* (London: TSO, 2006)
Cm. 7881, *Equity and Excellence: Liberating the NHS* (London: TSO, 2010)
Cmnd. 359, *Royal Commission on Medical Education 1965–8: Report* (London: HMSO, 1965)
Cmnd. 3687, *Findings and Recommendations Following Enquires Into Allegations Concerning the Care of Elderly Patients in Certain Hospitals* (London: HMSO, 1968)
Cmnd. 3975, *Report of the Committee on Inquiry Into Allegations of Ill-Treatment of Patients and Other Irregularities at the Ely Hospital Cardiff* (London: HMSO, 1969)
Cmnd. 4557, *Report of the Farleigh Hospital Committee of Inquiry* (London: HMSO, 1971)
Cmnd. 4681, *Report of the Committee of Inquiry Into Whittingham Hospital* (London: HMSO, 1972)
Cmnd. 5012, *Report of the Committee on Privacy* (London: HMSO, 1972)
Cmnd. 5579, *Report of the Committee on the Working of the Abortion Act* (London: HMSO, 1974)
Cmnd. 7341, *Report of the Committee on Data Protection* (London: HMSO, 1978)
Cmnd. 7615, *Royal Commission on the National Health Service* (London: HMSO, 1979)
Cohen, Gerda L., *What's Wrong With Hospitals?* (Harmondsworth: Penguin, 1964)
Cohen, Ruth, *Whose File is it Anyway?* (London: NCCL, 1982)
Commission for Patient and Public Involvement in Health, *Commission for Patient and Public Involvement in Health Report and Accounts* (London: TSO, 2008)
Consumers' Association, *Avoiding Heart Trouble* (London: CA, 1980)
Consumers' Association, *The Which? Guide to Your Rights* (Consumers Association: London, 1980)
Consumers' Association, *Understanding Allergies* (London: CA, 1986)

Consumers' Association, *Understanding Back Trouble* (London: CA, 1991)
Consumers' Association, *Understanding Cancer* (London: CA, 1986)
Consumers' Association, *Understanding Stress* (London: CA, 1988)
Consumers' Association/Patients Association, *A Guide to the National Health Service* (London: Consumers' Association, 1983)
Cooper, Liz, Anna Coote, Anne Davies and Christine Jackson, *Voices Off: Tackling the Democratic Deficit in Health* (London: Institute for Public Policy Research, 1995)
Coulter, Angela, *The Autonomous Patient: Ending Paternalism in Medical Care* (London: TSO/Nuffield Trust, 2002)
Coulter, Angela, Naomi Le Maistre and Lorna Henderson, *Patients' Experience of Choosing Where to Undergo Surgical Treatment: Evaluation of London Patient Choice Scheme* (Oxford: Picker Institute, 2005)
Council of Europe, *Convention for the Protection of Individuals with regard to Automatic Processing of Personal Data, Strasbourg, 1981*, http://conventions.coe.int/Treaty/en/Treaties/Html/108.htms, accessed 26 June 2013
Council on Tribunals, *The Annual Report of the Council on Tribunals 1968* (London: HMSO, 1969)
Department of Health, *A Stronger Local Voice: A Framework for Creating a Stronger Local Voice in the Development of Health and Social Care Services – A Document for Information and Comment* (London: Department of Health, 2006)
Department of Health, *Being Heard: The Report of a Review Committee on NHS Complaints Procedures* (London: Department of Health, 1994)
Department of Health, *Building on the Best: Choice, Responsiveness and Equity in the NHS* (London: Department of Health, 2003)
Department of Health, *Choice Matters: Increasing Choice Improves Patients' Experiences* (London: Department of Health, 2006)
Department of Health, *Choice Matters: Putting Patients in Control* (London: Department of Health, 2007)
Department of Health, 'Choose and Book': *Patient's Choice of Hospital and Booked Appointment: Policy Framework for Choice Booking at the Point of Referral* (London: Department of Health, 2004)
Department of Health, *Choosing Health: Making Healthy Choices Easier* (London: Department of Health, 2004)
Department of Health, *Complaints: Listening, Acting, Improving – Independent Review: A Training and Information Pack for Independent Review Panel Members* (London: HMSO, 1996)
Department of Health, *Government Report on the Consultation on Strengthening the NHS Constitution* (London: Department of Health, 2013)
Department of Health, *Government Response to A Stronger Local Voice* (London: Department of Health, 2006)
Department of Health, *HealthWatch Transition Plan* (London: Department of Health, 2011)
Department of Health, *Information: To Share or not to Share – The Information Governance Review* (London: Department of Health, 2013)

Department of Health, *Involving Patients and the Public in Healthcare: A Discussion Document* (London: Department of Health, 2001)
Department of Health, *NHS Choices: Delivering for the NHS* (London: Department of Health, 2008)
Department of Health, *NHS Complaints Procedure National Evaluation* (London: Department of Health, 2001)
Department of Health, *NHS Complaints Reform: Making Things Right* (London: HMSO, 2003)
Department of Health, *NHS Constitution* (London: Department of Health, 2013)
Department of Health, *Patient and Public Involvement in the new NHS* (London: Department of Health, 1999)
Department of Health, *Patient's Charter* (London: HMSO, 1991)
Department of Health, *Real Involvement: Working with People to Improve Health Services* (London: Department of Health, 2008)
Department of Health, *Reforming the NHS Complaints Procedure – A Listening Document* (London: HMSO, 2001)
Department of Health, *Strengthening Accountability: Involving Patients and the Public – Policy Guidance Section 11 of the Health and Social Care Act, 2001* (London: Department of Health, 2003)
Department of Health, *Report on the Effect of the NHS Constitution* (London: Department of Health, 2012)
Department of Health, *The Expert Patient: A New Approach to Chronic Disease Management in the 21st Century* (London: Department of Health, 2001)
Department of Health, *The Handbook to the NHS Constitution* (London: Department of Health, 2009)
Department of Health, *The NHS Constitution* (London: Department of Health, 2009)
Department of Health and Social Security, *Community Health Councils: HRC(74)4*, January 1974
Department of Health and Social Security, *National Health Service Reorganisation: Consultative Document* (London: DHSS, 1971)
Department of Health and Social Security, *Patients First* (London: HMSO, 1979)
Department of Health and Social Security, *Report of the Committee on Hospital Complaints Procedure* (London: HMSO, 1973)
Department of Health and Social Security, *The Future Structure of the National Health Service* (London: HMSO, 1970)
East Birmingham CHC, *East Birmingham Community Health Council, Second Annual Report, 1976/77* (Birmingham: EBCHC, 1977)
Expert Panel, *Concluding the Review of Patient and Public Involvement: Recommendations to Ministers from the Expert Panel* (London: Department of Health, 2006)
Gann, Bob, 'The Growth of Consumer Health Information in the UK', in Bob Gann and Gill Needham (eds), *Promoting Choice: Consumer Health Information in the 1990s* (Winchester: Consumer Health Information Consortium, 1992)

Gerrard, Mike, *A Stifled Voice: Community Health Councils in England 1974–2003* (Brighton: Pen Press, 2006)

Greater London Council, *Changing the World: A London Charter for Gay and Lesbian Rights* (London: GLC, 1985)

Green, Judith, Zoe McDowall and Henry Potts, 'Does Choose & Book fail to deliver the expected choice to patients? A survey of patients' experience of outpatient appointment booking', *BMC Medical Informatics and Decision Making* 8:36 (2008), 1–8

Greer, Scott L., *Four Way Bet: How Devolution has led to Four Different Models for the NHS* (London: UCL Constitution Unit, 2004)

Hallas, Jack, *CHCs in Action: A Review* (London: Nuffield Hospitals Trust, 1976)

Hallas, Jack and Bernadette Fallon, *Mounting the Health Guard: A Handbook for Community Health Council Members* (Oxford: Nuffield Provincial Hospitals Trust, 1974)

Ham, Chris, 'Power, patients and pluralism' in Keith Barnard and Kenneth Lee (eds), *Conflicts in the National Health Service* (London: Croom Helm, 1977), 99–120

HC 375-I, *Independent Inquiry into Care Provided by Mid Staffordshire Foundation Trust, January 2005–March 2009* (London: TSO, 2010)

HC 413, *Making Things Better? A Report on the Reform of the NHS Complaints Procedure in England* (London: TSO, 2005)

HC 898-I, *Report of the Mid Staffordshire NHS Foundation Trust Public Inquiry: Volume 1* (London: TSO, 2013)

HC 947, *Report of the Mid Staffordshire NHS Foundation Trust Public Inquiry: Executive Summary* (London: TSO, 2013)

HC 1070, *The National Programme for IT in the NHS: An Update on the Delivery of Detailed Care Records Systems* (London: TSO, 2011)

Healthcare Commission, *Investigation Into Mid Staffordshire NHS Foundation Trust* (London: Healthcare Commission, 2009)

Healthcare Commission, *Is Anyone Listening? A Report on Complaints Handling in the NHS* (London: Healthcare Commission, 2007)

Healthcare Commission, *Reforming the NHS Complaints Procedure* (London: Healthcare Commission, 2004)

Healthcare Commission, *Spotlight on Complaints: A Report on Second-Stage Complaints about the NHS in England* (London: Healthcare Commission, 2008)

Healthwatch, *Healthwatch England Annual Report, 2012–13* (Newcastle upon Tyne: Healthwatch England, 2013)

Hewitt, Patricia (ed.), *Computers, Records and the Right to Privacy* (London: NCCL, 1979)

House of Commons, *First Report From the Select Committee on the Parliamentary Commissioner for Administration, 1977–78, Independent Review of Hospital Complaints in the National Health Service* (London: House of Commons, 1978)

House of Commons, *Health Committee Sixth Report: Complaints and Litigation* (London: House of Commons, 2011)

House of Commons, *Patient and Public Involvement in the NHS: Third Report of Session 2006-7* (London: House of Commons, 2007)

House of Commons, *Second Report of the Select Committee on the Parliamentary Commissioner for Administration, 1967-68* (London: HMSO, 1968)

Hutton, Will, *New Life for Health: The Commission on the NHS* (London: Vintage, 2000)

Johnson, Malcolm, 'Patients: receivers or participants?', in Keith Barnard and Kenneth Lee (eds), *Conflicts in the National Health Service* (London: Croom Helm, 1977), 72-98

Jones, Peter, *Internet Access and Use* (Southampton: University of Southampton, 2010)

Kennedy, Ian, *The Unmasking of Medicine* (London: George Allen Unwin, 1981)

King's Fund, *Patient Choice: How Patients Choose and How Providers Respond* (London: King's Fund, 2010)

Klein, Rudolf, 'Control, participation and the British National Health Service', *Milbank Quarterly*, 57:1 (1979), 70-94

Klein, Rudolf and Janet Lewis, *The Politics of Consumer Representation: A Study of Community Health Councils* (London: Centre for Studies in Social Policy, 1976)

Labour Party, *Ambitions for Britain: Labour's Manifesto 2001* (London: Labour Party, 2001)

Lees, D.S., *Health Through Choice: An Economic Study of the British National Health Service* (London: Institute of Economic Affairs, 1961)

Levitt, Ruth, 'Community Health Councils: Evidence for the Royal Commission on the National Health Service', in Christine Farrell and Ruth Levitt, *Consumers, Community Health Councils and the NHS* (London: King's Fund, 1980), 25-41

Levitt, Ruth, *The People's Voice in the NHS* (King Edwards Hospital Fund for London: London, 1980)

Lewis, Jane, *What Price Community Medicine? The Philosophy, Practice and Politics of Public Health Since 1919* (Brighton: Wheatsheaf Books, 1986)

MacKeith, J.S., 'Community participation in health care', *The Hospital and Health Services Review* (December 1974), 425-428

McAlister-Smith, Ed, 'The CHC role in informing and empowering consumers', in Bob Gann and Gill Needham (eds), *Promoting Choice: Consumer Health Information in the 1990s* (Winchester: Consumer Health Information Consortium, 1992), 19-28

Medawar, Charles/Social Audit, *The Wrong Kind of Medicine?* (Consumers' Association: London, 1984)

Metcalfe, David, 'Whose data are they anyway?', *British Medical Journal*, 292 (1 March 1986), 577-578

Ministry of Health, National Health Service: *The Administrative Structure of the Medical and Related Service in England and Wales* (London: HMSO, 1968)

National Audit Office, *Feeding Back? Learning from Complaints Handling in Health and Social Care* (London: TSO, 2008)

National Consumer Council, *Annual Report and Accounts, 1981/82* (London: NCC, 1982)
National Consumer Council, *Annual Report and Accounts, 1983/84* (London: NCC, 1984)
National Consumer Council, *Annual Report and Accounts, 1987* (London: NCC 1987)
National Consumer Council, *Patients' Rights: A Guide for NHS Patients and Doctors* (London: HMSO, 1983)
National Consumer Council, *The Citizens' Charter: Getting it Right for the Consumer* (London: NCC, 1991)
National Consumer Council, *The Consumer and the State: Getting Value for Public Money* (London: NCC, 1979)
National Consumer Council, *The Fourth Right of Citizenship: A Review of Local Advice Services* (NCC: London, 1977)
National Health Service, *Choice, Responsiveness and Equity in the NHS and Social Care: A National Consultation* (London: National Health Service, 2003)
National Health Service, *Putting People at the Heart of Care: The Vision for Public and Patient Experience and Engagement in Health and Social Care* (London: NHS, 2009)
National Health Service Management Executive, *Local Voices: The Views of Local People in Purchasing for Health* (London: NHSME, 1992)
National Health Service, *National Health Service (Community Health Councils) Regulations 1973*. Statutory Instrument No. 2217, 1973
Neuberger, Julia, 'A Consumer's view', in David G. Green, Julia Neuberger, Lord Young of Dartington and M.L. Burstall, *The NHS Reforms: Whatever Happened to Consumer Choice?* (London: IEA, 1989), 15–25
NHS England, *The NHS Belongs to the People: A Call to Action* (London: NHS, 2013)
Office for National Statistics, *Statistical Bulletin: Internet Access – Households and Individuals, 2013* (London: ONS, 2013)
Office of Public Services Reform, *Reforming our Public Services: Principles into Practice* (London: Office of Public Services Reform, 2002)
Pappworth, Maurice, 'Human guinea pigs: a warning', *Twentieth Century*, 171 (1962) 67–75
Pappworth, Maurice, *Human Guinea Pigs: Experimentation on Man* (London: Routledge & Kegan Paul, 1967)
Patients Association, *Can I Insist?* (London: Patients Association, 1974)
Peckham, Stephen, Nicholas Mays, David Hughes and Marie Sanderson, *A Comparative Study of the Construction and Implementation of Patient Choice Policies in the UK* (London: HMSO, 2011)
Pheby, Derek, 'Changing practice on confidentiality: a cause for concern', *Journal of Medical Ethics*, 8 (1982), 12–24
Plaming, Diane and Tony Delamothe, 'The citizen's charter and the NHS: true citizens do more than consume', *British Medical Journal*, 303 (27 July 1991), 203–204

Political and Economic Planning, *Family Needs and the Social Services* (London: PEP, 1961)
Research Institute for Consumer Affairs, *General Practice: A Consumer Commentary* (London: RICA, 1963)
Rigge, Marianne, '"Healthline": a new service from the College of Health', *Health Libraries Review* (1986), 1–10
Rigge, Marianne, 'Involving patients in clinical audit', *Quality in Healthcare*, 3 (1994) supplement, 2–5
Robb, Barbara, *Sans Everything: A Case to Answer* (London: Nelson, 1967)
Ross, Alexander P., 'The case against showing patients their records', *British Medical Journal*, 292 (1 March 1986), 578
Royal Commission on the National Health Service, *Report of the Royal Commission on the National Health Service* (London: HMSO, 1979)
Select Committee on the Parliamentary Commissioner for Administration, *Independent Review of the Hospital Complaints Service* (London: House of Commons, 1977)
Simms, Madeline, 'Abortion law and medical freedom', *British Journal of Criminology*, 14:2 (1974), 118–131
South Birmingham Community Health Council, *South Birmingham CHC First Annual Report, 1975* (Birmingham: SBCHC, 1975)
Spilsbury, David, *Trumpet Voluntary: An Informal History of Central and South Birmingham Community Health Councils 1974–2003* (Birmingham: South Birmingham CHC, 2003)
Stacey, Margaret, 'The health service consumer: a sociological misconception', *The Sociological Review Monograph*, 22 (1978), 194–200
Stocking, Barbara, 'Patient's charter: new rights issue', *British Medical Journal*, 303 (9 November 1991), 1148–1149
Taylor, David, 'A big idea for the nineties? The rise of the citizens' charters', *Critical Social Policy*, 33 (1992), 87–94
The Health Service Ombudsman for England, *Making Things Better? A Report on Reform of the NHS Complaints Procedure in England* (London: House of Commons, 2005)
The Nuremberg Code, 1949. www.hhs.gov/ohrp/archive/nurcode.html.
Titmuss, Richard M., 'Choice and the welfare state', in Richard M. Titmuss, *Commitment to Welfare* (London: George Allen, 1968), 138–152
Titmuss, Richard M., *The Gift Relationship: From Human Blood to Social Policy* (revised edn, New York: The New Press, 1997)
United Nations, *United Nations Guidelines for Consumer Protection* (New York: UN, 1999)
Varah, Stephanie, *Practices and Patient Engagement: Smart Guides to Engagement* (London: National Association for Patient Participation, n.d.)
Wallace, Henrietta and Linda Mulcahy, *Cause for Complaint: An Evaluation of the Effectiveness of the NHS Complaints Procedure* (London: Public Law Project, 1999)

Wanless, Derek, *Securing our Future Health: Taking a Long Term View* (London: HM Treasury, 2002)
West Birmingham Community Health Council, *Annual Report, June 1976–May 1977* (Birmingham: WBCHC, 1977)
West Birmingham Community Health Council, *Annual report of West Birmingham CHC, 1977-78* (Birmingham: WBCHC, 1978)
West Birmingham Community Health Council, *Annual report of West Birmingham CHC, 1979-80* (Birmingham: WBCHC, 1980)
Which?, 'Consultation response: Liberating the NHS, greater choice and control', *Which*, 14 January 2011
Which?, *Which Choice? Health* (London: Which?, 2005)
Winkler, Fedelma, 'Consumerism in health care: beyond the supermarket model', *Policy and Politics* 15:1 (1987), 1–8
World Medical Association Declaration of Helsinki, *Ethical Principles for Research Involving Human Subjects* (Helsinki, 1964), www.wma.net/en/30publications/10policies/b3/17c.pdf, accessed 14 October 2013
Young, Michael, 'The College of Health's view', in David G. Green, Julia Neuberger, Lord Young of Dartington and M.L. Burstall, *The NHS Reforms: Whatever Happened to Consumer Choice?* (London: IEA, 1989), 27–46

Interviews

Interview between Alex Mold and Jean Robinson, 17 March 2009
Interview between Alex Mold and Christine Hogg, 5 February 2009
Interview between Alex Mold and Marianne Rigge, 10 March 2010
NAWCH Roundtable Meeting, Cambridge, 20 June 2009
Interview between Alex Mold and Department of Health civil servant, March 2013

Newspapers, magazines and journals

ACHCEW, *The Golden Age of Patient Involvement in the NHS*, CD ROM, vols 1–3
Birmingham Evening Mail
Birmingham Post
British Medical Journal
Health Services Journal
House of Commons Debates
House of Lords Debates
New Scientist
New Society
Pulse
Secrets: Newspaper of the Campaign for Freedom of Information
Self Health
The Guardian
The Lancet
The Observer
The Times

Time
Which?

Secondary sources

Books

Annas, George and Michael Grodin (eds), *The Nazi Doctors and the Nuremberg Code: Human Rights in Human Experimentation* (New York: Oxford University Press, 1995).
Baggini, Julian, *Complaint: From Minor Moans to Principled Protests* (London: Profile, 2008)
Baggott, Rob, Judith Allsop and Kathryn Jones, *Speaking for Patients and Carers: Health Consumer Groups and the Policy Process* (Basingstoke: Palgrave Macmillan, 2005)
Bauman, Zygmunt, *Liquid Modernity* (Cambridge: Polity Press, 2000)
Beauchamp, Tom L. and James P. Childress, *Principles of Biomedical Ethics*. (5th edn Oxford: Oxford University Press, 2001)
Berridge, Virginia, *AIDS in the UK: The Making of Policy, 1981–1994* (Oxford: Oxford University Press, 1996)
Black, Lawrence, *Redefining British Politics: Culture, Consumerism and Participation, 1954–70* (Basingstoke: Palgrave Macmillan, 2010)
Borsay, Anne, *Disability and Social Policy in Britain Since 1750* (Basingstoke: Palgrave, 2004)
Briggs, Asa, *Michael Young: Social Entrepreneur* (Basingstoke: Palgrave, 2001)
Bulmer, Martin, Kevin Bales and Kathryn Kish Sklar (eds), *The Social Survey in Historical Perspective, 1880–1940* (Cambridge: Cambridge University Press, 1991)
Byrne, Paul, *Social Movements in Britain* (London: Routledge, 1997)
Clarke, John, Janet Newman, Janet E. Newman, Nick Smith, Elizabeth Vidler and Louise Westmarland, *Creating Citizen-Consumers: Changing Publics and Changing Public Services* (London: Sage, 2007)
Coote, Anna and Jo Lenaghan, *Citizens' Juries: Theory Into Practice* (London: IPPR: 1997)
Crossley, Nick, *Contesting Psychiatry: Social Movements in Mental Health* (London: Routledge, 2005)
Crossley, Nick, *Making Sense of Social Movements* (Buckingham: Open University Press, 2002)
Crowson, Nick, Matthew Hilton and James McKay (eds), *NGOs in Contemporary Britain: Non-state Actors in Society and Politics Since 1945* (Basingstoke: Palgrave Macmillan, 2009)
Curtis, Helene and Mimi Sanderson, *The Unsung Sixties: Memoirs of Social Innovation* (London: Whiting and Birch, 2004)
Denham, Andrew and Mark Garnett, *British Think-Tanks and the Climate of Opinion* (London: UCL Press, 1998)

Eley, Geoff, *Forging Democracy: The History of the Left in Europe, 1850–2000* (Oxford: Oxford University Press, 2002)
Elster, Jon (ed.), *Deliberative Democracy* (Cambridge: Cambridge University Press, 1998)
Faden, Ruth R. and Tom L. Beauchamp, *A History and Theory of Informed Consent* (New York: Oxford University Press, 1986)
Fielding, Steven, *The Labour Governments 1964–1970 Volume 1: Labour and Cultural Change* (Manchester: Manchester University Press, 2003)
Finlayson, Geoffrey, *Citizen, State and Social Welfare in Britain 1830–1990* (Oxford: Oxford University Press, 1994)
Foucault, Michel, *Discipline and Punish: The Birth of the Prison* (New York: Vintage, 1979)
Foucault, Michel, *The History of Sexuality, Volume One: An Introduction* (Middlesex: Penguin, 1990)
Fox, Renee C. and Judith P. Swazey, *Observing Bioethics* (New York: Oxford University Press, 2008)
Glendon, M.A., *A World Made New: Eleanor Roosevelt and the Universal Declaration of Human Rights* (New York: Random House, 2001)
Gregory, Roy and Philip Giddings, *The Ombudsman, The Citizen and Parliament: A History of the Office of the Parliamentary Commissioner for Administration and Health Service Commissioners* (London: Politicos, 2002)
Harrison, Steven, *National Health Service Management in the 1980s: Policymaking on the Hoof?* (Avebury: Avebury, 1994)
Hilton, Matthew, *Consumerism in Twentieth Century Britain: The Search for a Historical Movement* (Cambridge: Cambridge University Press, 2003)
Hilton, Matthew, *Prosperity for All: Consumer Activism in an Era of Globalization* (Ithaca, NY and London: Cornell University Press, 2009)
Hoffman, Beatrix, *Health Care for Some: Rights and Rationing in the United States since 1930* (Chicago, IL: University of Chicago Press, 2012)
Hogg, Christine, *Citizens, Consumers and the NHS: Capturing Voices* (Basingstoke: Palgrave, 2009)
Hogg, Christine, *Patients, Power and Politics: From Patients to Citizens* (London: Sage, 1999)
Humphrey, Kim, *Shelf Life: Supermarkets and the Changing Cultures of Consumption* (Cambridge: Cambridge University Press, 1998)
Hunt, Lynn, *Inventing Human Rights: A History* (New York: W.W. Norton & Co., 2007)
Igo, Sarah E., *The Averaged American: Surveys, Citizens and the Making of a Mass Public* (Cambridge, MA: Harvard University Press, 2007)
Illich, Ivan, *Limits to Medicine – Medical Nemesis: The Expropriation of Health* (London: Marion Boyars, 1976)
Ishay, Micheline R., *The History of Human Rights: From Ancient Times to the Globalization Era* (Berkeley, CA: University of California Press, 2004)
James, Oliver, *Affluenza* (London: Random House, 2007)

Jenner, Mark and Patrick Wallis (eds), *Medicine and the Market in England and Its Colonies, c.1450–c.1850* (Basingstoke: Palgrave, 2007)
Keown, John, *Abortion, Doctors and the Law: Some Aspects of the Legal Regulation of Abortion in England, 1803–1982* (Cambridge: Cambridge University Press, 1988)
Klein, Rudolf, *The New Politics of the NHS: From Creation to Reinvention* (Oxford: Radcliffe Publishing, 2006)
Leatherhead, Audrey, *The Fight For Family Planning* (Basingstoke: Macmillan, 1980)
Le Grand, Julian, *The Other Invisible Hand: Delivering Public Services Through Choice and Competition* (Princeton, NJ: Princeton University Press, 2007)
Lowe, Rodney, *The Welfare State in Britain since 1945* (Basingstoke: Palgrave Macmillan, 2005)
McLean, Shelia A.M., *Autonomy, Consent and the Law* (Abingdon: Routledge-Cavendish, 2010)
Marsh, David and Melvyn Read, *Private Members' Bills* (Cambridge: Cambridge University Press, 1988)
Mol, Annemarie, *The Logic of Care: Health and the Problem of Patient Choice* (London and New York: Routledge, 2006)
Mold, Alex and Virginia Berridge, *Voluntary Action and Illegal Drugs: Health and Society in Britain since the 1960s* (Basingstoke: Palgrave Macmillan, 2010)
Moyn, Samuel, *The Last Utopia: Human Rights in History* (Cambridge, MA: Harvard University Press, 2010)
Mulcahy, Linda, *Disputing Doctors: The Socio-Legal Dynamics of Complaints About Medical Care* (Maidenhead: Open University Press, 2003)
Nathoo, Ayesha, *Hearts Exposed: Transplants and the Media in 1960s Britain* (Basingstoke: Palgrave, 2009)
Newman, Janet and John Clarke, *Publics, Politics and Power: Remaking the Public in Public Services* (London: Sage, 2009)
Norris, Pippa, *Digital Divide: Civic Engagement, Information Poverty and the Internet Worldwide* (Cambridge: Cambridge University Press, 2001)
O'Neill, Onora, *Autonomy and Trust in Bioethics* (Cambridge: Cambridge University Press, 2002)
Perkin, Harold, *The Rise of Professional Society: England Since 1880* (London: Routledge, 1990)
Petersen, Alan and Deborah Lupton, *The New Public Health: Health and Self in the Age of Risk* (London: Sage, 1996)
Petryna, Adriana, *When Experiments Travel: Clinical Trials and the Global Search for Human Subjects* (Princeton, NJ: Princeton University Press, 2009)
Pogge, Thomas, *World Poverty and Human Rights* (Cambridge: Polity Press, 2008)
Porter, Dorothy, *Health Civilization and the State: A History of Public Health From Ancient to Modern Times* (London: Routledge, 1999)
Porter, Dorothy and Roy Porter, *Patients Progress: Doctors and Doctoring in Eighteenth Century England* (Stanford, CA: Stanford University Press, 1989)

Reiser, Stanley Joel, *Technological Medicine: The Changing World of Doctors and Patients* (Cambridge: Cambridge University Press, 2009)
Rose, Nikolas, *Inventing our Selves: Psychology, Power and Personhood* (Cambridge: Cambridge University Press, 1996)
Rothman, David J., *Strangers at the Bedside: A History of How Law and Bioethics Transformed Medical Decision Making* (New York: Basic Books, 1991)
Salecl, Renata, *Choice* (London: Profile Books, 2010)
Schmidt, Ulf, *Justice at Nuremberg: Leo Alexander and the Nazi Doctors' Trial* (Basingstoke: Palgrave Macmillan, 2004)
Schwartz, Barry, *The Paradox of Choice: Why More is Less* (New York: Harper Collins, 2002)
Seneviratne, Mary, *Ombudsmen: Public Services and Administrative Justice* (London: Reed Elsvier, 2002)
Sheldon, Sally, *Beyond Control: Medical Power and Abortion Law* (London: Pluto Press, 1997)
Stacey, Margaret, *Regulating British Medicine: The General Medical Council* (Chichester: John Wiley and Sons, 1992)
Vincent, David, *The Culture of Secrecy: Britain 1832–1998* (Oxford: Oxford University Press, 1998)
Williamson, Charlotte, *Towards the Emancipation of Patients: Patients' Experiences and the Patient Movement* (Bristol: The Policy Press, 2010)
Wilson, Duncan, *Tissue Culture in Science and Society: The Public Life of a Biological Technique* (Basingstoke: Palgrave Macmillan, 2011)
Webster, Charles, *The Health Services Since the War, Volume I* (London: HMSO, 1988)
Webster, Charles, *The Health Services Since the War Volume II: Government and Health Care, The National Health Service 1958–1979* (London: The Stationery Office, 1996)
Webster, Charles, *The National Health Service: A Political History* (Oxford: Oxford University Press, 2002)
Weindling, Paul, *Nazi Medicine and the Nuremberg Trials: From Medical War Crimes to Informed Consent* (Basingstoke: Palgrave Macmillan, 2004)
Wolff, Jonathan, *The Human Right to Health* (New York: W.W. Norton & Co., 2012)
Wood, Bruce, *Patient Power? The Politics of Patients' Associations in Britain and America* (Buckingham: Open University Press, 2000)
Wyatt, Sally, Fils Henwood, Nod Miller and Peter Senker (eds), *Technology and In/Equality: Questioning the Information Society* (London: Routledge: 2000)
Young, Alison, *The Politics of Regulation: Privatized Utilities in Britain* (Basingstoke: Palgrave, 2001)

Articles and chapters

Appelbe, Gordon E., 'From arsenic to thalidomide: a brief history of medicine safety', in Stuart Anderson (ed.), *Making Medicines: A History of Pharmacy and Pharmaceuticals* (London: The Pharmaceutical Press, 2005), 243–260

Armstrong, David, 'The patient's view', *Social Science and Medicine*, 18:9 (1984), 737–744
Baggott, Rob, 'A funny thing happened on the way to the forum? Reformulating patient and public involvement in the NHS in England', *Public Administration*, 83:3 (2005), 533–551
Batchelor, C., D.J. Owens, M. Read and M. Bloor, 'Patient satisfaction surveys: methodology, management and consumer evaluation', *International Journal of Health Care and Quality Assistance*, 7 (1994), 22–30
Beaumont, Caitriona, 'Housewives, workers and citizens: voluntary women's organizations and the campaign for women's rights in England and Wales during the post-war period', in Nick Crowson, Matthew Hilton and James McKay (eds), *NGOs in Contemporary Britain: Non State Actors in Society and Politics Since 1945* (Basingstoke: Palgrave Macmillan, 2009), 59–75
Berridge, Virginia, 'AIDS and patient support groups', in Roger Cooter and John Pickstone, *Medicine in the Twentieth Century* (Amsterdam: Harwood, 2000), 687–701
Berridge, Virginia, 'AIDS and the rise of the patient? Activist organisation and HIV/AIDS in the UK in the 1980s and 1990s', *Medizin Gesellschaft und Geshichte*, 21 (2002), 109–123
Black, Lawrence, 'Which?craft in post-war Britain: The Consumers' Association and the politics of affluence', *Albion*, 36:1 (2004), 52–82
Borsay, Anne and Peter Shapely (eds), 'Introduction', in *Medicine, Charity and Mutual Aid: The Consumption of Health and Welfare in Britain c. 1550–1950* (Aldershot: Ashgate, 2007), 1–10
Brown, Phil, Stephen Zavestoski, Sabrina McCormick, Brian Mayer, Rachel Morello-Frosch and Rebecca Gasior Altman, 'Embodied health movements: new approaches to social movements in health', *Sociology of Health and Illness*, 26:1 (2004), 50–80
Brown, Phil and Stephen Zavestoski, 'Social movements in health: an introduction', *Sociology of Health and Illness*, 26:6 (2004), 679–694
Brown, Theodore, Marcos Cueto and Elizabeth Fee, 'The World Health Organization and the transition from "international" to "global" public health', *American Journal of Public Health*, 96: (2006), 62–72
Calnan, Michael and Jonathan Gabe, 'From consumerism to partnership? Britain's National Health Service at the turn of the century', *International Journal of Health Services*, 31:1 (2001), 119–131
Clarke, John, '"It's not like shopping": citizens, consumers and the reform of public services', in Mark Bevir and Frank Trentmann (eds), *Governance, Consumers and Citizens: Agency and Resistance in Contemporary Politics* (Basingstoke: Palgrave, 2007), 97–118
Clarke, John, 'Unsettled connections: citizens, consumers and the reform of public services', *Journal of Consumer Culture*, 7:2 (2007), 159–178
Clarke, John and Janet Newman, 'What's in a name? New Labour's citizen-consumers and the remaking of public services', *Cultural Studies*, 21 (2007), 738–757

Clarke, John, Nicholas Smith and Elizabeth Vidler, 'The indeterminacy of choice: political, policy and organisational implications', *Social Policy and Society*, 5:3 (2006), 327–336

Cohen, Ruth, 'Whose file is it anyway? Discussion paper', *Journal of the Royal Society of Medicine*, 78 (February 1985), 126–128

Condrau, Flurin, 'The patient's view meets the clinical gaze', *Social History of Medicine*, 20 (2007), 525–540

Cooter, Roger, 'The ethical body', in Roger Cooter and John Pickstone (eds), *Medicine in the Twentieth Century* (Amsterdam: Harwood Academic Publishers, 2000)

Cooter, Roger, 'The resistible rise of medical ethics', *Social History of Medicine*, 8:2 (1995), 257–270

Corrigan, Oonagh, 'Empty ethics: the problem with informed consent', *Sociology of Health and Illness*, 25:3 (2003), 768–792

Crawford, Catherine, 'Patients' rights and the law of contract in eighteenth century England', *Social History of Medicine*, 13:3 (2000), 381–410

Crinson, Iain, 'Putting patients first: the continuity of the consumerist discourse in health policy from the radical right to New Labour', *Critical Social Policy*, 18:2 (1998), 227–239

Crossley, Nick, 'Transforming the mental health field: the early history of the National Association for Mental Health', *Sociology of Health and Illness*, 20:4 (1998), 458–488

Crossley, Nick and M. Crossley, 'Patient voices, social movements and habitus: how psychiatric survivors speak out', *Social Science and Medicine*, 52 (2001), 1477–1489

Cueto, Marcos, 'The origins of primary health care and selective primary health care', *American Journal of Public Health*, 94 (2004), 1864–1874

Curtice, John and Oliver Heath, 'Does choice deliver? Public satisfaction with the health service', *Political Studies*, 60 (2012), 484–503

Davis, Gayle, '"A fifth freedom" or "hideous atheistic expediency"? The medical community and abortion law reform in Scotland, c. 1960–1975', *Medical History*, 50 (2006), 29–48

Davis, Gayle and Roger Davidson,'"Big White Chief", "Pontius Pilate" and the "Plumber": the impact of the 1967 Abortion Act on the Scottish Medical Community, c.1967–1980', *Social History of Medicine*, 18:2 (2005), 283–306

Fee, Elizabeth and Manon Parry, 'Jonathan Mann, HIV/AIDS and Human Rights', *Journal of Public Health Policy*, 29: (2008), 54–71

Gaffney, Declan, Allyson M. Pollock, David Price and Jean Shaoul, 'NHS expenditure and the private finance initiative – expansion or contraction?' *British Medical Journal*, 319 (3 July 1999), 48–51

Gorsky, Martin, 'Community involvement in hospital governance in Britain: evidence from before the National Health Service', *International Journal of Health Services*, 38:4 (2008), 751–771

Gorsky, Martin, 'Memorandum submitted to the Health Select Committee inquiry into Public and Patient Involvement in the NHS, January 2007', www.historyandpolicy.org/docs/gorsky_memo.pdf, accessed 2 August 2012

Greener, Ian, 'Towards a history of choice in UK health policy', *Sociology of Health and Illness,* 3 (2009), 309–24

Greener, Ian, 'Who choosing what? The evolution of the use of "choice" in the NHS, and its importance for new Labour', in Catherine Bochel, Nick Ellison and Martin Powell (eds), *Social Policy Review 15: UK and International Perspectives* (Bristol: The Social Policy Press, 2003), 49–68

Greener, Ian, Nick Mills, Martin Powell and Shane Doheny, 'How did consumerism get into the NHS? An empirical examination of choice and responsiveness in NHS policy documents', Cultures of Consumption Working Paper Series, Working Paper no. 29, www.consume.bbk.ac.uk/working_papers/GreenerOctober20061.doc, accessed 30 September 2013

Gregory, Roy and Philip Giddings, 'The ombudsman institution: growth and development', in Roy Gregory and Philip Giddings (eds), *Righting Wrongs: The Ombudsman in Six Continents* (Amsterdam: IOS Press, 2000), 1–20

Gruskin, Sofia, Edward Mills and Daniel Tarantola, 'History, principles and practice of health and human rights', *The Lancet,* 370 (2007), 449–455

Habermas, Jurgen, 'New social movements', *Telos,* 49 (1981), 33–37

Hacking, Ian, 'Making up people', *London Review of Books,* 28 (17 August 2006), 23–26

Ham, Chris, 'Power, patients and pluralism' in Keith Barnard and Kenneth Lee, *Conflicts in the National Health Service* (London: Croom Helm, 1977), 99–120

Hanna, Charles F., 'Complaint as a form of association', *Qualitative Sociology,* 4:4 (1981), 298–311

Harrison, Stephen and Maggie Mort, 'Which champions, which people? Public and user involvement in health care as a technology of legitimation', *Social Policy and Administration,* 32:1 (1998), 60–70

Hawkes, Nigel, 'How different are NHS systems across the UK since devolution?', *British Medical Journal,* 346 (2013), 18–20

Hazelgrove, Jenny, 'The old faith and the new science: the Nuremberg code and human experimentation ethics in Britain, 1946–73', *Social History of Medicine,* 15:1 (2002), 109–135

Hedgecoe, Adam, '"A form of practical machinery": the origins of research ethics committees in the UK, 1967–72', *Medical History,* 53 (2009), 331–350

Hendrik, Harry, 'Children's emotional well-being and mental health in early post-Second World War Britain: the case of unrestricted hospital visiting', in Marijke Gijswit-Hofstra and Hilary Marland (eds), *Cultures of Child Health in Britain and the Netherlands in the Twentieth Century* (Amsterdam & New York: Rodopi, 2003), 213–242

Henwood, Fils, Roma Harris and Philippa Spoel, 'Informing health? Negotiating the logics of choice and care in everyday practices of "healthy living"', *Social Science and Medicine,* 72 (2011), 2026–2032

Hilton, Matthew, 'Michael Young and the consumer movement', *Contemporary British History,* 19:3 (2005), 311–319

Hilton, Matthew, 'The duties of citizens, the rights of consumers', *Consumer Policy Review,* 15:1 (2005), 6–12

Hilton, Matthew, 'The fable of the sheep, or private virtues, public vices: the consumer revolution of the twentieth century', *Past and Present*, 176 (2002), 222–256

Hilton, Matthew and Martin Daunton, 'Material politics: an introduction', in Martin Daunton and Matthew Hilton (eds), *The Politics of Consumption: Material Culture and Citizenship in Europe and America* (Oxford: Berg, 2001), 1–32

Hoffmann, Stefan-Ludwig, 'Introduction: genealogies of human rights', in Stefan-Ludwig Hoffmann (ed.), *Human Rights in the Twentieth Century* (Cambridge: Cambridge University Press, 2011), 1–26

Hogg, Christine, 'Health', in Nicholas Deakin and Anthony Wright (eds), *Consuming Public Services* (London: Routledge, 1990), 155–182

Hugman, Richard, 'Consuming health and welfare', in Russell Keat, Nigel Whiteley and Nicholas Abercrombie (eds), *The Authority of the Consumer* (London: Routledge, 1994), 207–222

Irvine, Rob, 'Fabricating "health consumers" in health care politics', in Sara Henderson and Alan Petersen (eds), *Consuming Health: The Commodification of Health Care* (London: Routledge, 2002), 31–47

Irwin, Alec and E. Scali, 'Action on the social determinants of health: a historical perspective', *Global Public Health*, 2: (2007), 235–256

Johnson, Nigel, 'The changing role of the voluntary sector in Britain from 1945 to the present day', in Stein Kunhle and Per Selle (eds), *Government and Voluntary Organisations* (Aldershot: Ashgate, 1992), 87–107

Jones, Lorelei and Nicholas Mays, *Systematic Review of the Impact of Patient Choice of Provider in the English NHS* (London: LSHTM, 2009)

Kowalski, Robin M., 'Complaints and complaining: functions, antecedents and consequences', *Psychological Bulletin*, 119:2 (1996), 179–196

Lezaun, Javier, 'A market of opinions: the political epistemology of focus groups', *Sociological Review*, 55:2 (2007), 130–151

Lezaun, Javier and Linda Soneryd, 'Consulting citizens: technologies of elicitation and the mobility of publics', *Public Understanding of Science*, 16:3 (2007), 279–297

Lupton, Deborah, Cam Donaldson and Peter Lloyd, 'Caveat emptor or blissful ignorance? Patients and the consumerist ethos', *Social Science and Medicine*, 33:5 (1991), 559–568

McMullan, Miriam, 'Patients using the Internet to obtain health information: how this affects the patient-health professional relationship', *Patient Education and Counseling*, 63 (2006), 24–28

Marshall, T.H., 'Citizenship and Social Class', in T.H. Marshall and Tom Bottomore, *Citizenship and Social Class* (London: Pluto Press, 1992), 3–51

Martensen, Robert, 'The history of bioethics: an essay review', *Journal of the History of Medicine and Allied Sciences*, 56 (2001), 168–175

Mazower, Mark, 'The Strange Triumph of Human Rights, 1933–1950', *The Historical Journal*, 47 (2004), 379–398

Milewa, Timothy 'Local participatory democracy in Britain's health service: innovation of fragmentation of a universal citizenship?', *Social Policy and Administration*, 38:3 (2004), 240–252

Milewa, Timothy, Justin Valentine and Michael Calan, 'Managerialism and active citizenship in Britain's reformed health service: power and community in an era of decentralisation', *Social Science and Medicine*, 47:4 (1998), 507–517

Mold, Alex, 'Patients' rights and the National Health Service in Britain, 1960s–1980s', *American Journal of Public Health*, 102:11 (2012), 2030–2038

Moon, Graham and Carol Lupton, 'Within acceptable limits: health care provider perspectives on community health councils in the reformed British National Health Service', *Policy and Politics*, 23:4 (1995), 334–346

Newman, Janet and Elizabeth Vidler, 'Discriminating customers, responsible patients, empowered users: consumerism and the modernisation of healthcare', *Journal of Social Policy*, 35:2 (2006), 193–209

Nicholson, Malcolm and G.W. Lowis, 'The early history of the Multiple Sclerosis Society of Great Britain and Northern Ireland: a socio-historical study of lay/practitioner interaction in the context of a medical charity', *Medical History*, 46 (2002), 141–174

O'Cathain, Alicia, Jackie Goode, Donna Luff, Tim Strangleman, Gerard Hanlon, David Greatbatch, 'Does NHS Direct empower patients?', *Social Science and Medicine*, 61 (2005), 1761–1771

O'Hara, Glen, 'Parties, people and parliament: Britain's "ombudsman" and the politics of the 1960s', *Journal of British Studies*, 50:3 (2011), 690–714

O'Hara, Glen, 'The complexities of "consumerism": choice, collectivism and participation within Britain's National Health Service, c.1961–1979', *Social History of Medicine*, 26:2 (2013), 288–304

Peckham, Stephen, Nicholas Mays, David Hughes and Marie Sanderson, 'Devolution and patient choice: policy rhetoric versus experience in practice', *Social Policy and Administration*, 46:2 (2012), 199–218

Pfeffer, Naomi, 'Fertility counts: from equity to outcome', in Steve Sturdy (ed.), *Medicine, Health and the Public Sphere in Britain 1600–2000* (London: Routledge, 2002), 260–278

Pickard, Susan, 'Citizenship and consumerism in healthcare: a critique of citizens' juries', *Social Policy and Administration*, 32:3 (1998), 226–244

Pickstone, John, 'Production, community and consumption: the political economy of twentieth-century medicine', in Roger Cooter and John Pickstone (eds), *Medicine in the Twentieth Century* (Amsterdam: Harwood, 2000), 1–19

Porter, Roy, 'The patient's view: doing medical history from below', *Theory and Society*, 14:2 (1985), 175–198

Powell, Martin, Ian Greener, Isabelle Szmigin, Shane Doheny and Nick Mills, 'Broadening the focus of public service consumerism', *Public Management Review*, 12:3 (2010), 324–339

Price, David, 'Choices without reasons: citizens' juries and policy evaluation', *Journal of Medical Ethics*, 26 (1998), 272–276

Reubi, David, 'Re-moralising medicine: The bioethical thought collective and the regulation of the body in British medical research', *Social Theory & Health*, 11 (2013), 215–235

Reubi, David and Alex Mold, 'Introduction – global assemblages of virtue and vitality: genealogies and anthropologies of rights and health', in Alex Mold and David Reubi (eds), *Assembling Health Rights in Global Context: Genealogies and Anthropologies* (London: Routledge, 2013), 1–19

Rogers, Anne and David Pilgrim, 'Pulling down churches: accounting for the British mental health users movement', *Sociology of Health and Illness*, 13:2 (1991), 129–148

Rose, Nikolas and Carlos Novas, 'Biological citizenship', in Aiwha Ong and Stephen Collier (eds), *Global Assemblages, Technology, Politics and Ethics as Anthropological Problems* (Malden, MS: Blackwell Publishing, 2005), 439–463

Rothman, David J., 'The origins and consequences of patient autonomy: a 25-year retrospective', *Health Care Analysis*, 9 (2001), 255–264

Rothman, David J and David Blumenthal, 'Introduction', in David J. Rothman and David Blumenthal (eds), *Medical Professionalism in the Information Age* (New Brunswick, NJ: Rutgers University Press, 2010), 1–7

Rowbotham, Shelia 'Introduction', in Helene Curtis and Mimi Sanderson, *The Unsung Sixties: Memoirs of Social Innovation* (London: Whiting & Birch, 2004), ix–xii

Rowe, Rosemary and Michael Shepherd, 'Public participation in the new NHS: no closer to citizen control?', *Social Policy and Administration*, 36:3 (2002), 275–90

Salter, Brian, 'Patients and doctors: reformulating the UK health policy community', *Social Science and Medicine*, 57 (2003), 927–936

Schmidt, Ulf, 'Cold War at Porton Down: informed consent in Britain's biological and chemical warfare experiments', *Cambridge Quarterly of Healthcare Ethics*, 15 (2006), 366–380

Shackley, Phil and Mandy Ryan, 'What is the role of the consumer in health care?', *Journal of Social Policy*, 23:4 (1994), 517–541

Shapely, Peter, 'Tenants arise! Consumerism, tenants and the challenge to council authority in Manchester, 1968–92', *Social History*, 31 (2006), 60–78

Shaw, Ian and Alan Aldridge, 'Consumerism, health and social order', *Social Policy and Society*, 2 (2003), 35–43

Smith, Graham, 'The rise of the "new consumerism" in health and medicine in Britain, c.1948–1989', in Jennifer Burr and Paula Nicholson (eds), *Researching Health Care Consumers* (Basingstoke: Palgrave Macmillan, 2005), 13–38

Smith, Katherine and Mark Hellowell, 'Beyond rhetorical differences: a cohesive account of post-devolution developments in UK health policy', *Social Policy and Administration*, 46:2 (2012), 178–198

Tarantola, Daniel, 'A perspective on the history of health and human rights: from the Cold War to the Gold War', *Journal of Public Health and Policy*, 29: (2008), 42–53

Taylor-Gooby, Peter, 'Choice and values: individualised rational action and social goals', *Journal of Social Policy*, 37:2 (2008), 167–185

Tomes, Nancy, 'Patients or health-care consumers? Why the history of contested terms matters', in Rosemary A. Stephens, Charles E. Rosenberg and Lawton R. Burns (eds), *History and Health Policy in the United States: Putting the Past Back In* (New Brunswick: Rutgers University Press, 2006), 83–110

Tomes, Nancy, 'The "Information Rx"', in David J Rothman and David Blumenthal (eds), *Medical Professionalism in the Information Age* (New Brunswick, NJ: Rutgers University Press, 2010), 40–65

Trentmann, Frank, 'Citizenship and consumption', *Journal of Consumer Culture*, 7:2 (2007), 147–158

Trentmann, Frank, 'The modern genealogy of the consumer: meanings, identities and political synapses', in Frank Trentmann and John Brewer (eds), *Consuming Cultures, Global Perspectives: Historical Trajectories, Transnational Exchanges* (Oxford: Berg, 2006), 19–69

Trentmann, Frank and Vanessa Taylor, 'From Users to Consumers Water Politics in Nineteenth-Century London', in Frank Trentmann (ed.), *The Making of the Consumer: Knowledge, Power and Identity in the Modern World* (Oxford: Berg, 2005), 53–79

Wait, Suzanne and Ellen Nolte, 'Public involvement policies in health: exploring their conceptual basis', *Health Economics and Law*, 1 (2006), 149–162

Walsh, Kieron, 'Citizens, charters and contracts', in Russell Keat, Nigel Whitely and Nicholas Abercrombie (eds), *The Authority of the Consumer* (London: Routledge, 1994), 189–206

Weindling, Paul, 'The origins of informed consent: the international scientific commission on medical war crimes, and the Nuremberg Code', *Bulletin of the History of Medicine*, 75 (2001), 37–71

Welshman, John, 'Time, money and social science: the British birth cohort surveys of 1946 and 1958', *Social History of Medicine*, 25:1 (2012), 175–192

Whiteman, Ingrid, 'The fallacy of choice in the common law and NHS policy', *Health Care Analysis*, 21 (2013), 146–170

Whong-Barr, Michael, 'Clinical ethics teaching in Britain: a history of the London Medical Group', *New Review of Bioethics*, 1:1 (2003), 73–84

Wilson, Duncan, 'Creating the "ethics industry": Mary Warnock, *in vitro* fertilization and the history of bioethics in Britain', *Biosocieties*, 6:2 (2011), 121–141

Wilson, Duncan, ' Who guards the guardians? Ian Kennedy, bioethics and the "ideology of accountability" in British medicine', *Social History of Medicine*, 25:1 (2012), 193–211

Wivel, Ashley, 'Abortion policy and politics on the Lane Committee of Enquiry, 1971–74', *Social History of Medicine*, 11:1 (1998), 109–135

Theses

David Reubi, 'Ethics governance, modernity and human beings' capacity to reflect and decide: a genealogy of medical research ethics in the UK and Singapore' (PhD diss., London School of Economics & Political Science, 2009)

Other

Gorsky, Martin (ed.), *The Griffiths NHS Management Enquiry: Its Origins, Nature and Impact* (transcript of a witness seminar) (London, 2010)

Index

Abortion Act (1967) 56, 58, 79
abortion services 52, 56–60
Access to Health Records Act (1990) 118, 134, 135, 136
Access to Personal Files Act (1987) 118, 133
accountability 12, 22, 96, 105, 119, 146, 156, 161
   democratic 145, 159, 174
ACHCEW *see* Association of Community Health Councils of England and Wales
AEGIS *see* Aid for the Elderly in Government Institutions
Age Concern 49
AHA *see* Area Health Authority Aid for the Elderly in Government Institutions (AEGIS) 72
AIDS 6, 97, 123, 147
   see also HIV/AIDS
AIMS *see* Association for Improvement in Maternity Services
Aldridge, Ian 148
All Party Parliamentary Group on the CHCs 156
Allsop, Judith 9, 146
Alma-Ata conference (1978) 97
Appleby, Mary 48, 76
area boards 46, 47
Area Health Authority (AHA) 47, 48, 53, 56, 58–61, 74
Armstrong, David 3
Ashley, Jack 86–87
Association of Community Health Councils of England and Wales (ACHCEW) 43, 50, 130, 133, 135, 136, 155–158
   The Patients' Agenda: What the Patient's Charter Leaves out – the Rights you don't yet have in the NHS 108

Patients' Charter: Guidelines for Good Practice 103, 104
Association for Improvement in Maternity Services (AIMS) 104
Association of Trained Patients (ATP) 120
ATP *see* Association of Trained Patients
audit 12
Audit Commission 87
Australian Consumer Council 5
Australian Federation of Consumer Organisations 5

Baggini, Julian 70–71
Baggott, Rob 9, 146, 160
Bailey, Bella 194
Bailey, Julie 194, 195
Bailey, Ron 104
Balsall Heath area, Birmingham 60
Bauman, Zygmunt 177
BBC *see* British Broadcasting Corporation
BCA *see* Birmingham City Archives
Beaumont, Caitriona 27
Beech, Beverly 104
Belson, Margaret (Peg) 27, 28–29, 48
Beveridge, William 44
BHA *see* Birmingham Health Authority
bioethics 10, 19–22, 33, 35, 193
'biological citizenship' 148
biomedicine, dominance of 3
Birmingham and Black Country Strategic Health Authority 178
Birmingham Health Authority (BHA) 152–154
   'Independent Advisory Panel' 152, 153
Birmingham (later British) Pregnancy Advisory Service (BPAS) 57, 59
birth cohort survey 23
Blair, Tony 110, 177–180
Blumenthal, David 199–200

BMA *see* British Medical Association
Bottomley, Peter 156
Bowlby, John 25, 26
Boyle, David 181–184
BPAS *see* Birmingham (later British) Pregnancy Advisory Service
Bradley, Anna 202
Bradshaw, Ben 179
Branson, Richard 185
breast milk substitutes 97
Bristol Royal Infirmary: heart surgery deaths 146
Britain
  and abortion 57
  citizens' rights 98
  development of organised consumerism 22
  emergence of the patient-consumer (1960s) 3
  lack of information given to patients (1960s) 1, 18
  pre-women's liberation activity 27
  rapid growth of pressure groups 44
  rights and health in 96–99
  social science research 23
British Broadcasting Corporation (BBC) 25
British Journal of Community Nursing 157
British Medical Association (BMA) 56, 61, 83, 131, 192
  and Butler's Bill 100
  and confidentiality 127
  and the Davies Committee 77–78
  guide to medical ethics 127, 132
  voluntary code on patient access 133–134
British Medical Journal 85, 109, 128, 133
British Social Attitudes survey (2005) 178
Brook Advisory Centre 57
Brown, Gordon 110
Brown, Phil 146–147
Buckland, Sarah 155
Building on the Best: Choice, Responsiveness and Equity in the NHS 176
Burke, Angeline 157
Burnham, Andy 179, 199

Butler, Joyce 99–100
Butler, Patrick 156

CA *see* Consumers' Association
Cabinet Office 157
Calan, Michael 148–149
Caldicott, Dame Fiona 201
Calnan, Michael 109
Cameron, David 196
Cameron, Dr D.C. 83
Campaign for the Freedom of Information (CFI) 132–135
cardiac catheterisation 21
Carr, Harold 46
Cartwright, Ann 18, 25
  Human Relations and Hospital Care 22, 24
Cayton, Harry 176
CCC *see* Churchill College Cambridge
Central Committee for Hospital Medical Services of the BMA and JCC: Joint Medico-Legal Subcommittee 77
Central Health Services Council 25
CFI *see* Campaign for the Freedom of Information
Charlton, John 151
Charter for a Democratic Health Service 105
CHC News 51, 53, 60, 75
CHCs *see* Community Health Councils
children
  parents' visiting in hospital 10, 20
  treatment of 102
choice 3, 7, 23, 109, 120, 169–186, 203–204
  Blair on 177–178, 179–180
  choice before choice policy 171–175
  choice and New Labour (1997–2010) 175–177
  critiques of choice 180–184
  explaining the rise of choice 177–180
  'Free Choice' policy 176
  informed 108, 117, 118, 121
  prioritisation of individual choice 2, 10, 95
  see also Choose and Book scheme

Choose and Book scheme 13, 176, 182, 183, 184
Choosing Health (2004 public health strategy) 176–177
'citizen-consumer' 4, 7, 144
Citizen's Charter 106, 110
citizenship 4, 7, 109, 110, 111, 144, 148
citizens' juries 13, 110, 142, 145, 152–153, 155, 162
citizens' rights 11, 94, 95, 96, 98, 109
Clapham Omnibus magazine 75, 102
Clarke, John 7, 8, 46, 49, 109–110, 144, 177, 181, 184
Clinical Commissioning Groups 201, 203
Clwyd, Ann 196
CMAC *see* Contemporary Medical Archives Centre
CoH *see* College of Health
Cohen, Gerda 18
Cohen, Ruth 130–131
collective empowerment 119
collective representation 1, 4, 13, 35, 42, 143, 154, 173, 185, 195
collective rights 2, 11, 98, 148
College of Health (CoH) 2, 7, 12, 107, 108, 117, 119–125, 130, 133, 146, 147, 173, 174–175
  Guide to Hospital Waiting Lists 125
Commission for Patient and Public Involvement (CPPIH) 12, 142, 159–161
community, defining 50
Community Health Councils (CHCs) 2, 6, 11, 106, 154, 159, 161
  abolished (2003) 12, 55, 61, 62, 142, 143
  'consumer advocates' 54–55
  demise of 155–159
  'District Health Authority Partners' 55
  effectiveness 53–61
  established (1974) 1, 10, 34, 43
  'independent arbiters' 55
  'independent challengers' 55
  individual CHCs
    Bath 122
    Brent 52, 59, 60, 104

  Central Birmingham 59, 60, 124, 130, 173
  East Birmingham 54
  Greenwich 104
  Hackney and City 8, 61
  Hull 53
  Kensington and Chelsea 51, 52, 60
  North Surrey 52–53
  Oxford 45
  South Gwent 124
  Tameside 124
  West Birmingham 51–52, 60, 74
  West Essex and District 174
  see also South Birmingham Community Health Council (SBCHC)
  members 50, 54
  Mounting the Health Guard 55
  and NAWCH 27
  origins 43–49
  and patients' complaints 73–74, 76
  'patient's friend' 55, 73
  powers 47–48, 49
  proposed (1971) 47–49
  publicity 52–53
  public opinion surveys 51–52
  representativeness 50, 51
  rights and responsibilities 53–54
  role of 42–43, 53, 55, 56, 75
  types of 54–55
community medicine 50–51
community physicians 50
Community Rights Project (CRP; 1983–85) 96, 104–105
comparative testing 124
competition 7, 106, 109, 119, 123, 179, 181, 203
complaints 1, 10, 13, 69–88, 171, 186
  before the NHS 71
  and CHCs 53, 54, 60, 69–70
  Clwyd and Hart's review (2013) 196–197
  complaining about medicine 70–73
  complaints procedures 11, 45, 69, 70, 75–79, 175, 196–197
  defined 70–71

family practitioner services, 1970s
    79–81
Health Service Commissioner
    (Ombudsman) 81–87
    increase in 72
    and patient-consumer organisations
        69–70, 73–75
    patient rights 2, 94, 103
    in PEP survey 24
computerisation 118, 127, 128, 136
consent
    experimental treatment 29
    informed 20, 21, 30, 94, 193, 194
    medical trials 29
    patient right to 2
    and teaching of medical students
        19–20, 30–31, 33, 34, 99–100
Conservative governments 2, 10, 12, 31,
    95, 105, 110, 144, 150, 151, 199
    Patients First consultative paper 61, 62
Conservative–Liberal Democrat coalition
    government (2010–) 161, 169, 199,
    201, 203
Conservative Medical Society 106
constituency-based movements 147
consumer audit 124–125, 175
Consumer Council 43, 47, 82, 84
Consumer Focus 147
Consumer Health Information
    Consortium: 'Promoting choice:
    consumer health information in the
    1990s' conference 122
consumerism
    alien to the early NHS 1
    basic needs/luxuries 111
    as a battle site 4
    changes within 177
    concerns about consumerism in health
        7–8
    development within health care 19
    and information 118
    market 7
    patient 2, 5, 6–7, 9, 10, 61, 110, 117,
        169, 170, 186, 203, 205
    rise of 35
consumer movement 28–29, 98–99, 111,
    118, 124

consumer revolutions 3–4
Consumers' Association (CA; later
    Which?) 2, 23, 69, 74, 118, 119
    comparative testing 124
    Drugs and Therapeutics Bulletin 123
    established (1956) 1, 4, 43, 98–99
    guides to common conditions 122, 123
    led by Michael Young 4, 7
    and patients' access to medical records
        129–130, 134, 135
    and *The Patient's Charter* 107
    role of 4, 43
    Which? Guide to Your Rights 101–102,
        104
Consumers' Councils 43
consumers' rights 11, 94, 95, 96, 98–99,
    109, 111, 121
Cooper, Yvette 154
Cooter, Roger 21
Corrie Bill 57
Coulter, Angela 178
Council of Europe 129
Council of Tribunals 83
    Annual Report (1968) 82
    report (1969) 72
Court, Angela 57
Covey, Donna 158
CPPIH *see* Commission for Patient and
    Public Involvement
Crichel Down affair 81
Crinson, Ian 109
Crossman, Richard 45, 47
CRP *see* Community Rights Project
Cryer, John 156
Cumberlege, Baroness 157
Cure the NHS 194, 195–196
Curtice, John 181

Daily Express 32
Data Protection Act (1984) 118, 129, 131,
    132, 134, 136
Daunton, Martin 4
Davidson, Roger 56
Davies Committee 72, 76–79, 80
Davies, Sir Michael 76
Davis, Gayle 56
Delamothe, Tony 109

Department of Health (from 1988)
  on CHCs (1989) 155
  and CPPIH 159–160
  discussion document (2001) 143, 145, 146
  National Programme for IT in the NHS 200–201
  NHS Constitution (2009) 176, 192–193, 197–199, 201, 202
  Patient and Public Involvement in the New NHS 145
  Patient's Charter 12, 94–95, 106–110, 136
  Putting People at the Heart of Care 144
  Stafford Hospital review 195
Department of Health and Social Security (DHSS; 1968–88) 26–27
  and CHCs 48–49, 50, 52, 53
  and Healthline 123
  and Health Service Commissioner 83–84, 86
  and the PA 46
  and patient complaints 72, 78–83
  patient records 127, 128, 131, 133
  records of social workers' clients 129
  and Rights of Patients Bill 100–101
  teaching hospitals and patient consent circulars 31
'digital divide' 200
disability 6, 52, 72, 86, 104, 109, 147, 200
Disablement Income Group (DIG) 47, 82
disease prevention 54, 105, 121, 123
District Health Authority (DHA) 55, 59, 125
doctor–patient relationship
  changes in 1, 23
  confidentiality 127
  knowledge–power issue 8, 12
  paternalism 5, 18, 22, 69
  and patients' access to medical records 129, 133
doctors
  changing 72
  choosing 182
  patients' complaints 71, 79–81
  regulated by GMC 71
  see also GPs
Dodds, J.R. 83

Doheny, Shane 7
Donaldson, Cam 8
Dorrell, Stephen 106
drugs
  access to pharmaceutical drugs 111
  dumping of pharmaceutical drugs 97
  illegal drug use 6, 44, 147
  safety and efficacy 119, 123–124

East Birmingham Community Health Council (EBCHC) 54
elderly, the
  ageing society 203
  care of 52
  'communities of interest' 50
  mistreatment in NHS hospitals 72
  poorly served by NHS 11, 45
'electronic democracy' 145
Elliot of Harwood, Baroness 82
Ely Hospital, Cardiff 45, 69, 196
Ely report 72–73, 76, 82
embodied health movements 147
ethnic minorities 50, 109
European Community 129, 136
Expert Patient Initiative 148

Fabian Society 144, 172, 175, 178, 179
Fallon, Bernadette 53, 74
family planning services 27
Family Practitioner Committees (FPCs) 52, 79–80, 81, 87, 155
family practitioner services 70, 82
  complaints 79–81
Farleigh Hospital, Somerset, 45, 76, 196
Field, Professor Steve 198
Forster, Rudolf 181
Foucault, Michel 3
Fox, Dr Liam 158
FPC *see* Family Practitioner Committee
France
  Constituent Assembly 96
  National Assembly 96
Francis Inquiry 195, 196, 201–202
Francis, Robert, QC 195, 196
Frankel, Maurice 132, 133–134
Freeman, Roger 134
Friedman, Milton 171, 172
Future Forum 198, 199

Gabe, Jonathan 109, 181
Gann, Robin 126
Gann, Robin and Knight, Sally:
  Consumers' Guide to Health Information 121
General Medical Council (GMC) 71, 80, 86
General Medical Services Committee (GMSC) 61, 80, 83, 133
genetically modified (GM) food 152
Gerrard, Mike 50, 51, 55, 56, 155
'Gift Relationship' 33
GlaxoSmithKline 185
GMC *see* General Medical Council
GMSC *see* General Medical Services Committee
Gorsky, Martin 45, 71
GPs
  appointment systems 52, 183
  choosing 171-173, 174
  Clinical Commissioning Groups 203
  complaints 79-81
  fund-holding 174
  and Health Service Ombudsman 83-87
  and the NHS budget 201
  see also doctors
Graham-Bryce, Dame Isabel 45
Grant, Sharon 160
Greater London Council (GLC) 104, 105
Greener, Ian 7, 171, 181-182
Green, Judith 183
Green Papers
  NHS reorganisation (1968) 46-47, 82
  NHS reorganisation (1970) 47
Griffiths enquiry (1983) 124
Guardian, the (newspaper) 26, 29, 30, 49, 86, 108, 134, 156, 158
Guys Hospital, London 120

Habermas, Jurgen 99
Hallas, Jack 53, 54, 74
Ham, Chris 9, 50, 56
'hameto-social rule' 33
Handbook to the NHS Constitution 197, 198
Harris, Lord 157, 158

Harrison, Stephen 148
Harris, Roma 200
Hart, Professor Tricia 196
Hazelgrove, Jenny 30
Health and Social Care Act (2012) 2, 161, 202, 203
Health and Social Care Information Centre 201
health access movements 147
HealthCall 123
health care
  development of consumerism 19
  equality of access 108
  lack of democracy at local level 145
  patients as partners in own health care 121
  preventative approach 105
Healthcare Commission 176, 194-195
'health consumer movement' 9, 146, 147
Health Consumer Standards Board (proposed) 108
health districts 50
health education 121, 122, 123
health inequalities 43, 60, 105, 145
health information governance 201
Health Information Technology (HIT) 199-200
health insurance 98
Healthline telephone helpline 122-123
health promotion 120, 121, 122, 176
Health Research Group 119
Health Rights Commission (proposed) 108
Health Service Commissioner for England and Wales (Ombudsman) 44, 70, 77, 81-87
Health Services Journal 151, 185
Health Services and Public Health Bill 99
Healthwatch England 101, 142, 161, 162, 202-203
healthy lifestyle choices 120, 125, 148
Heath, Oliver 181
Hedgecoe, Adam 30
Helsinki Declaration (1964) 21
Henderson, Doug 134
Henwood, Fils 200
Hilton, Matthew 4, 43, 110, 118-119

Hirschman, Albert 81
HIV/AIDS 97, 123, 124
Hodgson, Helen 29, 30, 31, 32, 46, 74, 193
Hogg, Christine 5, 51, 54, 55, 60, 80, 106, 158
Holliday, Madeline 104
Holt, Dr Kim 185
homeless people 60, 109
Home Office 134
homosexuality 44
Hoole, Shirley 149–150
Hospital Complaints Procedure Act (1985) 78–79, 87, 136
hospitals
  acute services 52
  capital investment in 149
  choice of 178, 182
  Choose and Book scheme 13
  closures 60
  complaints procedure 11, 70, 72, 75–79
  contributory schemes 98
  food 34, 42, 59, 173
  long-stay 72
  'shoppers' guides 119
  teaching 30–31, 99
  translation 59, 124
  transport services 59
  visiting hours 10, 25–29, 45, 71
  waiting lists 12, 60, 71, 109, 125
House of Commons Health Select Committee 160, 161
House of Commons Select Committee on the Parliamentary Commissioner for Administration
(the Ombudsman) 78, 82, 86
housing 10, 44, 95, 96, 99
Howe, Earl 157, 158
Huckfield, Leslie 45
Hugman, Richard 7
human experimentation 20–21
human rights 11, 94, 95, 96–98
Human Rights Act (1998) 193
Hunt, Lord 159
Hutton, Will 156

ICAS *see* Independent Complaints Advisory Service
ICESCR *see* International Covenant on Economic, Social and Cultural Rights
ICM 109
ICS *see* Institute of Community Studies
IEA *see* Institute for Economic Affairs
Independent Complaints Advisory Service (ICAS) 12–13, 142, 159
information 1, 10, 117–136, 186, 199–201
  access to 94, 111, 117, 118, 122
  access to medical records 128–135
  and choice 108, 117
  confidentiality and medical records 126–128, 131
  freedom of 131, 136
  hospital waiting lists 12
  information, consumerism and the patient-consumer 118–122
  knowledge–power imbalance 8, 12
  patient-consumer groups and information access and generation 122–126
  patients' complaints about its lack 18, 24
information technology 118, 127, 136, 145
Institute for Public Policy Research (IPPR) 144
  Voices Off report (1995) 144–145
Institute of Community Studies (ICS) 22
Institute of Economic Affairs (IEA) 22, 171
internal market 106, 111, 145, 151, 155, 170, 171, 173
International Covenant on Economic, Social and Cultural Rights (ICESCR) 97
International Organisation of Consumer's Unions bill of consumer rights 69
Internet 183, 199, 200
Inter-professional Working Group on Access to Personal Health Information 131
IPPR *see* Institute for Public Policy Research

Irish Development Association 57
Irvine, Rob 5

JCC *see* Joint Consultants Committee
Johnson, Alan 192
Joint Consultants Committee (JCC) 77, 78, 83–86, 100
Jones, Kathryn 9, 146
Joseph, Keith 42, 47, 48, 49, 84, 86

Kennedy, Ian 87, 146
Kennedy report 146, 157
King's College Hospital Medical School, London 121
King's Fund 109, 178, 182, 184
Kirkwood, Archy 132, 134
Klein, Rudolf 43, 44, 45, 49–52, 54, 59
Knight, Sally 121
Kowalski, Robin 71

Labour governments 10, 43, 150, 151, 158, 170, 199
  (1997–2010) 13, 142, 145, 169, 175–177, 195, 203
Labour Party Conference (2001) 177
Lamb, A.M. 49
Lamb, Norman 198, 199
Lammy, David 143
Lamont, Linda 107–108
Lancaster Moor Hospital Management Committee 46
Lancet, The (medical journal) 5, 19, 23, 61, 83, 85
Lane Committee 58, 59
Lansley, Andrew 195, 198
Lees, D.S. 170, 171–172
  Health Through Choice: an Economic Study of the British National Health Service 22, 172
LeGrand, Julian 179, 180, 185
Levitt, Ruth 51, 54, 75
Lewis, Janet 43, 44, 49, 50, 51, 52, 54, 59
Lezaun, Javier 152, 155
Lindrop Committee 128, 129
'listening exercises' 13, 142
Lloyd, Peter 8

Local Government and Health Project 104
Local Health Councils 34
Local Healthwatch 142, 161, 201, 202
Local Involvement Networks (LINks) 142, 161, 162, 201
Lomas, Kenneth 47
London Boroughs Grant Scheme 104
London Electricity Board 119
London School of Economics 179
Long-term Medical Conditions Alliance 9
Lowden, Steve 160
Lupton, Carol 54, 155
Lupton, Deborah 8

MacAlister-Smith, Ed 122
McColl, Ian 120
McDowall, Zoe 183
McIver, Dr Shirley 150, 151
McIvor vs. Southern Health and Social Services Board (Northern Ireland) 129
McLaren, Professor Hugh 56–57, 59
McMullan, Miriam 200
McNair-Wilson, Michael 79–80
Major, John 110
Manchester 56
Mann, Jonathan 97
market models 22, 180
Marre, Sir Alan 85
Marshall, T.H. 98
Maternity and Infant Care Association 82
maternity services 34
Mazower, Mark 96
Medawar, Charles 119, 123
medical charities 19
medical ethics 21, 127
Medical News 46
Medical Officers of Health 50
medical records
  confidentiality 107, 118, 126–128
  National Programme for IT in the NHS 200–201
  and patient complaints 80, 81
  patients' right to access 2, 118, 128–135
Medical Reports Act (1987) 134

Index

medical research
  ethical conduct of 29–30
  globalisation of 194
  human rights in 97
  non-therapeutic 30
  therapeutic 30
medical sociology 21
medical students, patients' participation in their teaching 19–20, 30–31, 33, 99–100
medical technologies 18, 21
medical trials, consent issue 21, 29
Meldrum, Hamish 192
mentally ill patients
  'communities of interest' 50
  in long-stay hospitals 72
  and patient organisations 6, 147
  poorly served by NHS 11, 45
Merrison Commission *see* Royal Commission on the NHS
Metcalfe, Professor David 133
Milburn, Alan 144, 154, 158–159, 175, 178, 180
Milewa, Timothy 7, 148–149
Miller, Maurice 86
Mills, Nick 7
MIND 76
Ministry of Health (1919–68) 25, 26, 27, 31, 75, 82–83
Mol, Annemarie 180
Moon, Graham 54, 155
MORI 109, 178, 181
Mort, Maggie 148
Mother Care for Children in Hospital 26, 27
Mothers' Union 27
Mulcahy, Linda 69, 76, 79
Murphy, Katherine 185, 192

Nader, Ralph 119
NAMH *see* National Association for Mental Health
National Association of Health Authorities 61
National Association of Leagues of Hospital Friends 84

National Association for Mental Health (NAMH) 48, 49, 84
National Association for the Welfare of Children in Hospital (NAWCH) 2, 10, 19, 20, 25–29, 34, 45, 49, 76, 84
National Childbirth Trust 104
National Consumer Council (NCC; now Consumer Focus) 2, 7, 74–75, 99, 109, 119, 121, 147
  and choosing a GP 172–173
  patients' rights 102
  Patients' Rights 102, 104
  and people's access to medical/social service records 129, 130–131
National Council for Civil Liberties (NCCL) 127, 130, 131
National Health Insurance Act (NHI) (1911) 98
National Health Service (NHS)
  access to treatment 94
  auditing of services 12
  choice policy 13
  competition within 7
  'democratic deficit' 144, 152
  democratisation of 104–105
  founded (1948) 18, 32
  general management 105
  health inequalities 43
  Joseph's Consultative Document on NHS reorganisation (1971) 47
  marketisation 12, 13, 110, 118
  Ombudsman 44, 70
  opting out 109
  patient satisfaction surveys 24–25
  poor service to some groups 11
  reform 7, 13, 46–47, 142, 143, 145, 162, 170, 175, 176, 178, 203
  re-organisation (1973) 10, 34, 50
National Health Service Act (1946) 98
National Institute for Health and Clinical Excellence (NICE) 204
National Voices 192
NAWCH *see* National Association for the Welfare of Children in Hospital
Nazi wartime atrocities 96
NCC *see* National Consumer Council

NCCL *see* National Council for Civil Liberties
Neighbourhood Councils (proposed) 48
neo-liberal governments 22
neo-liberalism 22, 33, 194
Neuberger, Julia 174
Newcastle 56
New Economics Foundation 181
New Labour government 143, 144, 146
   and choice 175–177, 180, 181
Newman, Janet E. 7, 8, 46, 49
Newport, Wales 124
New Public Management 149
New Scientist 100
New Society (journal) 80
News of the World 72
NHI *see* National Health Insurance (Act)
NHS *see* National Health Service
NHS Choices website 176, 179, 183
NHS Direct 123
NHS England 203
NHS Executive 143, 156
NHS Plan (2000) 145, 156, 157, 175
NHS Reorganisation Act (1973) 85, 86
NHS Trusts 156, 201
NICE *see* National Institute for Health and Clinical Excellence
Nolte, Ellen 144
North West Thames Region 123
Novas, Carlos 148
Nuffield Provincial Hospital Trust 53
Nuremberg Code (1947) 21
Nuremberg Trials 21, 97

Observer, The (newspaper) 26, 49
Offences Against the Person Act (1861) 56
Office for National Statistics (ONS) 200
O'Hara, Glen 5, 74, 81
O'Malley, Father B.N. 57
O'Neill, Onora 194
Osborne, George 201
OSCs *see* Overview and Scrutiny Committees
Overview and Scrutiny Committees (OSCs) 12, 142, 159

PA *see* Patients Association
PALS *see* Patient Advice and Liaison Service
'Panel of the Public' (Birmingham) 52
Pappworth, Maurice: 'Human Guinea Pigs' 21, 29, 45
Parish Councils 48
Parliamentary Commissioner for Administration (PCA) (the Ombudsman) 44, 81–82, 85
paternalism 5, 18, 22, 69, 130, 131
Patient Advice and Liaison Service (PALS; previously Patient Advocacy and Liaison Service) 12, 142, 156–159, 162, 195
patient autonomy 1, 7, 8, 171, 186, 193–194
   autonomy, bioethics and consumerism 20–23
   demands for enhanced 69
   growing importance 10, 19
   lack of autonomy in 1960s 18
   NAWCH case study 19, 20, 25–29
   patient organisations 9, 13
   Patients Association case study 19–20, 29–34
   privileging autonomy 194
   views of the patient and the patients' views 23–25
patient-consumer organisations
   access to information 111, 117, 122
   and choice 170, 171
   and complaining 69–70, 73–75
   criticism of *The Patient's Charter* 107
   and a health ombudsman 82
   lack of clarity regarding rights agenda 11–12, 94
   and the *Patient's Charter* 12, 94–95
   producing new data 117, 122
   rights guides and charters 11, 94, 95, 101–104, 122
patient-consumers
   changing meaning of the term 1–2
   criticism of the term 8–9
   historical approach to creation of 3–6
   market-style approach 61
   persistence of 204–205

a pliable figure 204
start of consumer perspective 22
patient empowerment 120–121, 122, 135, 156, 200
Patient Forums 12, 142, 156, 158–162
patienthood 3, 20
patient organisations
  campaign for establishment of patients' rights 1–2, 11
  collective vision 111
  construction of the patient-consumer 95
  disease-specific 6, 146, 156, 162
  generic 6
  growth of 9
  health consumerism concept revived in USA (1960s) 4–5
  information 12, 119
  legacy of 13
  and medical paternalism 69
  patient choice 13
patient representation 3, 10, 13, 171, 186
  CHC effectiveness 53–61
  meanings of 49–53
  origins of the CHCs 43–49
  uncertainty about its meaning and purpose 42
patient rights 3, 10, 13, 94–111, 122, 186, 197–199
  collective/individual 11
  Community Rights Project (1983–85) 104–105
  and NAWCH 29
  Patient's Charter (1991–94) 12, 31, 94–95, 96, 106–110, 192
  patients' rights guides and charters, 1970s–1980s 101–104
  rights and health in Britain 96–99
  Rights of Patients Bill, 1972–74 99–101
  right to access medical records 2
  right to complain 2
  right to consent 2, 31–32
patients
  changing political role 18–19
  perceptions of 1
  privacy 32, 95

surveys 51–52, 53, 71–72, 109, 110, 124, 126, 135, 155, 173, 176, 178, 179, 180, 183
  see also doctor–patient relationship
Patients Association (PA) 2, 6, 9, 28, 45, 49, 162, 185, 192, 196
  Can I Insist? 101, 104
  criticises 1968 Green Paper 46–47
  criticises *The Patient's Charter* 107–108
  and decision-making involving patients 33–34
  and doctor–patient relationship 32, 129
  established (1962) 1, 193
  and ethical conduct of medical research 29–30
  lobbies for a patients' bill of rights 11, 95
  and the Ombudsman 70, 82, 84
  and patient autonomy 30, 31–32, 99
  and patient complaints 69–70, 73, 74, 76, 78
  and patients' medical records 127, 128, 131, 133
  patients' participation in teaching of medical students 10, 19–20, 30–31, 33, 99
Patients Association and Consumers' Association: *A Guide to the National Health Service* 102–103, 121
Patient's Charter 12, 31, 94–95, 96, 106–110
Patients First Campaign 185
patient voice 12–13
PCA *see* Parliamentary Commissioner for Administration
Pearce, Ursula 150, 154
PEP *see* Political and Economic Planning
Pfeffer, Naomi 58
PFI *see* Private Finance Initiative
pharmaceutical industry 18, 105, 123, 194, 201
Pheby, Derek 128, 131
Pickard, Susan 152
Pickstone, John 5
Pink, David 192
Plaming, Diane 109

Platt report (1959) 25, 26–27
Platt, Sir Harry 25
Political and Economic Planning (PEP) 5, 22, 71–72
  Family Needs and the Social Services 22
  survey of public services (1957) 23–24, 25
Porter, Dorothy 71
Porter, Roy 3, 71
Potts, Henry 183
Powell, Martin 7
PPI *see* Public and Patient Involvement
PPIfs *see* Public and Patient Involvement Forums
pressure groups 44, 51
Price, David 152–153
primary health care 97, 176
privacy 32, 95, 99–100, 103, 127, 128
Private Finance Initiative (PFI) 150, 151, 154, 158
private health care firms 201
privatisation 95
Pryer, Richard 127
Public Citizen 119
Public Interest Research Centre 119
Public and Patient Involvement Forums (PPIfs) 160, 161
Public and Patient Involvement (PPI) 195
public services
  citizen representation 10
  consumerism in 4
  marketised 110
  PEP's 1957 survey 23–24
  provision in post-industrial society 2
  reform 144, 145, 175, 177, 180

Quality Adjusted Life Year (QALY) 204
Queen Elizabeth Hospital, Birmingham (1933–2010) 59, 149, 150, 152
Queen Elizabeth Hospital, Birmingham (2010–) 149–154

'rational consumer' 4
Red Cross 49
Regional Health Authority (RHA) 61
  abortion issue 58
  CHC members 49, 54
  Wessex 128

Regional Hospital Boards (RHB) 45, 82
  Birmingham 45
  Oxford 45
Reid, John 180
Reith Lectures (1980) 87
representation *see* patient representation
Research Institute for Consumer Affairs (RICA) 5, 22, 44, 102, 119
  General Practice: A Consumer Commentary 22, 202
Reubi, David 33, 194
RHA *see* Regional Health Authority
RHB *see* Regional Hospital Boards
RICA *see* Research Institute for Consumer Affairs
Rigge, Marianne 121, 123
Rights of Patients Bill 95, 99–101
rights talk 11, 88, 94, 95, 103, 193, 202, 204
risk prevention 148
Robb, Barbara and AEGIS: *Sans Everything: A Case to Answer* 72
Robertson, James 25, 26
Robinson, Jean 45, 75, 87–88
Robinson, Kenneth 27, 28, 46, 47
Roosevelt, Eleanor 96
Rose, Nikolas 148, 194
Ross, Alexander P. 133
Rothman, David J. 21, 199–200
Rowbotham, Sheila 99
Rowe, Rosemary 144, 149
Royal Bucks and Stoke Mandeville Hospital 127
Royal College of General Practitioners 198
Royal College of Physicians 100
Royal Commission on Medical Education (Todd Commission) 31, 33
Royal Commission on the NHS (Merrison Commission) 58, 61, 75, 86, 87, 196
Royal Hampshire Hospital, Winchester 133
Ryan, Mandy 8

Salecl, Renata 180
Salter, Brian 146, 147
satisfaction surveys 110, 124

SBCHC *see* South Birmingham Community Health Council
Schwartz, Barry 180, 181
Scott, Doris 30
Scottish Home and Health Department 31
second opinion, right to 11, 94, 101, 103, 108
'self-care' 120
Self Health journal (later *Which? Way to Health*) 120–121, 122, 124
Selly Oak Hospital, Birmingham 149, 150, 152
Serota, Baroness 47–48
Shackley, Phil 8
Shanks, Michael 102, 121
Shaw, Alan 148
Shaw, Dr R.M. 83
Sheffield Regional Hospital Board 28
Shelter 104
Shepherd, Michael 144, 149
Skeffington Report (1969) 44
Smith, Chris 132
Smith, Graham 5
Smith, Nick 7
social administration 172
Social Audit 119, 132
 The Wrong Kind of Medicine 123–124
social citizenship 4, 22
social movements
 health 147
 issues 44
 rights-based 21, 22, 99
social movement theory 9
social rights 32, 33, 96, 98, 111
Soneryd, Linda 152, 155
South Birmingham Community Health Council (SBCHC) 56–59, 74, 149–151, 153, 154
 Maternity and Child Welfare group 58
South Birmingham Health District 56
South Tees Hospitals NHS Foundation Trust 196
Spilsbury, David 152–153
Spoel, Philippa 200
Spurgeon, Professor Peter 150, 151
Stacey, Margaret 8, 9, 32, 76, 78

Stafford General Hospital 194–195, 196
Stanton, Elizabeth 74–75, 102
state, the
 changing nature of 126
 duty to provide universal coverage 95
 positions itself as primary authority on the patient-consumer 2
Stocking, Barbara 109
Stott, Mary 29
Strategic Health Authorities 176
Stroke Association 104
Stuart, Gisela 158
Sunday Express 30
Sunday Telegraph 127
Szmigin, Isabelle 7

Tavistock Clinic, London 25
Taylor-Gooby, Professor Peter 184
thalidomide 21, 29, 69
Thatcher government 111
Thatcherism 110
Thatcher, Margaret (later Baroness) 95, 110
Thomas, George 49
Thomas, Jane 26
Titmuss, Richard 7–8, 33, 171, 172
 The Gift Relationship 172
Todd, Lord Alexander 31
Tomes, Nancy 4–5, 22, 119
town and country planning 44
Town and Country Planning Act (1968) 44
transport 27, 28, 42, 43, 59, 183
Trentmann, Frank 3–4
Truswell, Paul 157
Turner, Jill 80
Two-Year Old Goes to Hospital, A (film) 25–26

UHBT *see* University Hospital Birmingham Trust
UNDHR *see* United Nations Universal Declaration of Human Rights
United Nations (UN): *Guidelines for Consumer Protection* 202
United Nations Universal Declaration of Human Rights (UNDHR) 97

United States
  bioethics 20
  revival of health consumerism concept (1960s) 4–5
universal franchise 96
University of Birmingham 152–153
  Health Service Centre 150
University College Hospital, London 31, 32–33
University Hospital Birmingham Trust (UHBT) 149–151, 153, 154
University Hospital of Wales 196
University of Manchester 133

Valentine, Justin 148–149
Vaughn, Dr Gerard 106
Vidler, Elizabeth 7
Vincent, David 126–127, 128
voice 142–162, 186, 201–203
  'alphabet soup' of short-lived organisations 159–161
  and choice 1, 10, 142, 162, 193
  demise of the CHCs 155–159
  explaining the rise of voice 143–149
  'new voices' 149–155
Voice: The Commission for Patient and Public Involvement *see* Commission for Patient and Public Involvement
voluntary organisations 25, 44, 48, 49, 52, 54, 104, 156

waiting lists 12, 60, 71, 109, 125
Wait, Suzanne 144
Waldegrave, William 106
Walden, Brian 99
Walker, Peter 48
Walsh, Kieron 106
Watson, Irene 53
WBCHC *see* West Birmingham Community Health Council
Webster, Charles 78, 87
welfare state 32, 96, 98, 172
Welsh Hospital Board 196
Welshman, John 23
West Birmingham Community Health Council (WBCHC) 51–52, 60, 74

Westmarland, Louise 7
Which? magazine 118, 122, 124, 130, 133, 173
Which? (previously Consumers' Association) 147, 181, 182, 184, 185–186
Which? Way to Health 122
Whitehorn, Katharine 103, 121
White, James 57
White Papers
  Equity and Excellence: Liberating the NHS 169
  on establishment of NHS (1946) 171
  Liberating the NHS, Greater Choice and Control 185
  Patients First (1979) 2, 155
  Working for Patients (1989) 106, 171, 173, 174
Whittingham Hospital, near Preston, Lancashire 45, 76, 196
WHO *see* World Health Organization
Williamson, Charlotte 5, 9
Williams, Shirley 48
Wilson, Duncan 194
Winkler, Fedelma 8, 61
Winterton, Rosie 143–144
Witty, Andrew 185
women
  child-rearing 27
  groups 69
  rights 22
Women and Medical Practice 104
Women's Institutes (WI) 27
Wood, Brian 146
World Health Organization (WHO) 97, 103
  Global Strategy on AIDS 97

Yellowlees, Sir Henry 77
Young, Baroness 47
Younger Committee 127, 128
Young, Hugo 134
Young, Michael 4, 7, 12, 22, 43, 48, 108, 117, 119–121, 123, 173, 174

Zavestoski, Stephen 146–147